# The Prophets of Israel

# The Prophets
# of Israel

*Leon J. Wood*

Baker Book House
Grand Rapids, Michigan

Copyright 1979
by Baker Book House Company

Library of Congress Catalog Card Number: 79-50172
ISBN: 0-8010-9607-3

*Second printing, March 1981*

*Printed in the United States of America*

# Foreword

It is of great personal satisfaction to me that this book by Dr. Leon J. Wood can be published. Although Dr. Wood has been in the presence of the Lord nearly two years, yet his influence and teaching are still with us through his writing.

Across this country and in many parts of the world men stand to preach and teach the Word of God. They do so with great conviction and power because they believe the Bible to be God's Word to the world. The confidence of some of these men is due in large part to the influence of Leon J. Wood.

In studying the Old Testament many have been confronted with questions and uncertainties that ultimately led to an erosion of their confidence in the Scriptures. I'm certain all of Dr. Wood's students would agree that no such doubts were ever implanted during his teaching ministry. Dr. Wood raised questions, but he also provided answers which built a confidence in the Scriptures, enabling us to face the critics and not be shaken by their arguments. In all of his ministry not once did he imply by statement or question that the Bible, including all of the Old Testament, was anything less than the inspired Word of God. This influence upon us his students has made a difference in our lives, no matter in what area we serve.

We were also taught by word and example to study in order to show ourselves approved unto God, workmen who need not be ashamed of properly handling the word of Truth. Perhaps none of us will ever have the personal discipline exemplified by our teacher. But all who studied with Dr. Wood would testify that his life has had a profound effect upon us, motivating us to do our best for the Lord.

The Lord, in His wisdom, has taken our teacher from us, and we no longer have the joy of studying with him. However, because of his writing ministry during his last years he will continue to teach us, and not only us but generations of Old Testament students who are yet to come. As his students, we say it was a privilege to know him and an even greater privilege to study with him.

*Leon Rowland*

# Contents

# Preface

The prophets of Israel stand in a class by themselves in ancient Near Eastern history. No countries other than Israel had persons who can truly be compared with them. In Israel their significance for the religious condition of the people can hardly be overstated. It is true that there was considerable defection from God's Law in spite of them, but apart from them this waywardness would have been far more extensive.

The best known among this illustrious group were the writing prophets, those whose prophetic books comprise an important part of the Old Testament. It is important to recognize, however, that these were not the only representatives. The earliest prophets who wrote specifically prophetic books date to the ninth century B.C., but long before them were Moses, Samuel, Nathan, Elijah, Elisha, and many others. Sometimes these are almost forgotten in a stress upon the later ones. But God from the first of Israel's history called men to be prophets, and the early representatives were important in their place just as well as those who wrote prophetic books. In the following pages all Israel's prophets, both early and late, come in for discussion.

This book is divided into two parts. The first part takes up matters that are common to the movement of prophecy taken in a general sense. The second part deals with the prophets themselves as persons. Because the prophets fall into three logical divisions, they are so considered in this second part. The first division concerns prophets of the premonarchy period, when the interest centered in keeping people from following the religious ways of

9

the Canaanites. The second concerns prewriting prophets of the monarchy whose interest centered mainly in contacting individuals. And the third concerns the writing prophets, whose ministry was directed more to the nation and against sins of the people generally.

In contrast to many volumes regarding the prophets, the discussion herein is concerned with the prophets themselves as people, rather than with the books they wrote. This has to be true of the early prophets discussed, for there is no record of any prophetic books they wrote. But the same interest is kept in these pages with the later prophets who did record their messages. A study of the men themselves is also most worthwhile, for when one sees them as people, in the day and circumstances in which they lived, he has a distinct advantage for understanding what they wrote.

It is of course necessary in such a study to consider the books to a degree, for often information concerning the writers is found solely in them, but there is considerable difference in how one makes the study, depending on whether he is interested in the books as such or in discovering what sort of a person the author was. It should be added that the books as such do come in for brief notice, too, in the sense that they were major efforts in the lives of the persons concerned.

The scriptural text used in quotations is almost always the better-known King James Version. Only rarely have I seen need for making any change in the interest either of accuracy or clarity.

I wish to add my deep appreciation to my wife, Helen, and daughter, Carol, for their considerable assistance which made this book a possibility.

# Part One

# PROPHETISM

# 1

# Identity

The prophets of Israel hold a unique place in the history of Israel. In fact, it was a unique place in respect to all the Middle East of Old Testament day, and, because of their writing, their influence has been of prime importance in world history. They were great men, courageous men; they were guides for proper religious belief and correct conduct to a people that continually strayed from the Law of their God. Israel Mattuck speaks of "the towering place which these prophets held in the religious history of the Jews,"[1] and R. B. Y. Scott says that "Hebrew prophecy . . . remains incomparable in its spiritual quality and permanent significance for religion."[2]

## A. SPECIAL CALL

One reason for the greatness of the prophets was that they were a specially called people. They did not come to office by inheritance, having been born into a prophetic tribe or family; nor was a son of a former prophet automatically made a prophet because he was the son of such a person. Each prophet was selected by God and called to a work God had for him to do.

In this, prophets differed markedly from priests in Israel. Priests did receive their office by inheritance. If a person was a descendant of Jacob's son Levi, he was constituted a Levite; and if in addition he descended from Aaron

[1] Israel Mattuck, *The Thought of the Prophets*, p. 11.
[2] R. B. Y. Scott, *The Relevance of the Prophets*, p. 1.

13

he was a priest. He did not have to choose to be a Levite or a priest, nor did he have to be called to either office; he became one or both by birth. Prophets, however, were chosen men, picked from among others. This made it a distinct honor to be a prophet. One had to be specially called by God. The call properly designated a prophet as such and gave him an authority for his work. False prophets were false simply because they were not called. God said to Jeremiah concerning false prophets, "The prophets prophesy lies in my name; I sent them not, neither have I commanded them" (14:14). And to the false prophet Hananiah, Jeremiah declared, "The LORD hath not sent thee but thou makest this people to trust in a lie" (28:15).

Concerning Jeremiah's own call, Jeremiah quoted God as saying to him: "Before I formed thee in the belly I knew thee; and before thou camest forth out of the womb I sanctified thee, and I ordained thee a prophet unto the nations" (1:5). The prophet Amos referred to his call in these words: "I was no prophet neither was I a prophet's son; but I was an herdman, and a gatherer of sycamore fruit: and the LORD picked me as I followed the flock, and the LORD said unto me, Go, prophesy unto my people Israel" (7:14, 15). The great man Moses was called through the miraculous incident of the burning bush (Exod. 3:4); Isaiah was called through a vision he saw of Almighty God in His holiness, high and lifted up in the temple (Isa. 6); Ezekiel was called as he dwelt by the river Chebar in Babylonia (Ezek. 1:1; 2:2, 3).

It is noteworthy that the prophetic call was often given in connection with an outstanding experience that helped the prophet realize its authenticity. Moses was called as he saw a bush miraculously burning. He would long remember the vivid picture; it reinforced the reality of the call. Isaiah had a vision of God high and lifted up in the temple when he received his call. Again he would long remember the dramatic scene and be reminded of the call. Ezekiel was commanded to eat a scroll at the time he was summoned; we are told that he did eat it and that it was in his mouth "as honey for sweetness" (Ezek. 3:3). Such occasions gave body and substance to the reality of the call and increased its effectiveness as a foundation for the prophet's work.

The prophetic call frequently involved some aspect of preparation for the work in view. Moses was equipped with miraculous credentials (Exod. 4:1–9), and was assigned his brother Aaron to be a spokesman for him. Isaiah's lips were purified by a burning coal placed upon them, fresh from the temple altar. And Ezekiel, having eaten the scroll, was symbolically filled with God's word for effective proclamation.

## B. RECOGNITION (BUT NOT PRESCRIPTION) IN THE LAW

God gave His Law to Israel at Mount Sinai. It constituted the foundation for all religious activity and social relationships of the people. It was in fact a sort of constitution for the nation of Israel. In the Law were lengthy prescriptions concerning Israel's priests. Their identity was set forth, as well as their customs, their duties, their clothing, and considerable information regarding the ceremonial activity they were to supervise. The same was not true, however, regarding the prophets. Neither their role nor their duties were described and even their existence was not really established, though it was recognized.

This recognition of the prophets is found in Deuteronomy 18:9–22, which should be noticed. The first eight verses of the chapter give further indication as to the Levitic office, but with verse 9 comes a change which tells of the prophetic recognition. Moses says that the people upon entering Canaan should not try to communicate with God by any form of divination[3] after the pattern of other nations—for such was an abomination to the Lord— but instead God would give a divine communication through a prophet. The word *prophet* is used in the singular and carries a first reference to Christ, but it is commonly agreed that it has a secondary reference to prophets generally. In this passage, then, God was saying that His people should look to prophets for their divine revelations and not to forms of divination as did the peoples of the world around them. This gave a definite place for prophets, though the passage does not set forth a legal prescription as to who they should be or the nature of their functions.[4]

## C. COURAGEOUS INDIVIDUALS

One reason why an inheritance relationship was not suitable for the prophets was that each had to be a special kind of person. Not just anyone would do. The priestly office did not find this nearly so true. A weak son could still carry on rather well, for the work was quite routine. And one may expect that there were some mediocre priests, who functioned simply because they had become priests by inheritance.

The prophet, however, did not act by pattern. He had often to chart a new course that might be different from any before. Even when God gave him instructions as to his work and the course he was to take, that course often carried with it a great challenge. The prophet might anoint a king to office; later he might bring this very king a severe reprimand. He might bring cheer, or he might impart cause for sorrow. His assignment might lead to great danger or to high honor. He had to be prepared for suffering and

[3]Various forms of divination are here listed; see Edward J. Young, *My Servants the Prophets*, pp. 21–22, for a discussion of each form of divination as well as of the entire passage.
    [4]See Young, *My Servants the Prophets*, pp. 29–35; G. F. Oehler, *Theology of the Old Testament*, pp. 362–363.

injustice as well as ease and plaudits. He had always to be an individualist in courage and ingenuity. There was no room for mediocrity.[5]

The first act of Samuel as God's newly called prophet was to tell no one less than the high priest, Eli, that his house had been rejected by the Lord (I Sam. 3:4–18). This was certainly a challenging task for Samuel, when he probably was not more than ten years old. Later Samuel was to anoint Israel's first king Saul (I Sam. 9:15–21; 10:1–8) and after this to inform him that he, too, had been rejected (I Sam. 13:11–14). And later still he was to anoint Israel's second king, the great David (I Sam. 16:1–13). Nathan was instructed in due time to rebuke David for his sin with Bathsheba (II Sam. 12:1–12). It was certainly a challenge to give this form of a message to the greatest king of the day, but Nathan did so. Then a few years later the prophet Gad was sent to give David a choice of three punishments for his sin in taking a census (II Sam. 24:10–17). The prophet Ahijah had first to promise the new nation of Israel to Jeroboam (I Kings 11:29–39) and then to tell him that it would be taken away (I Kings 14:6–16). "A man of God" was sent to reprimand Jeroboam for his false altar at Bethel (I Kings 13:1–10). Elijah warned of a famine and effected a remarkable contest on Mount Carmel (I Kings 17:1; 18:25–38). Elisha announced to Hazael that he would be king over Syria and wept while doing so because of the havoc he knew this man would bring on Israel (II Kings 8:7–13). Jonah was sent even to the foreign and feared city of Nineveh to preach repentance (Jonah 1:2; 3:1, 2).

All this means that a person had to be an outstanding individual to qualify as a prophet. Prophets had to be people of outstanding character, great minds, and courageous souls. They had to be this by nature and then, being dedicated to God, they became still greater because of the tasks and special provisions assigned them. Thus they became the towering giants of Israel, the formers of public opinion, the leaders through days of darkness, people distinguished from all those about them either in Israel or other nations of the day.

## D.  TERMS OF DESIGNATION AND TASK

There are three terms which are especially important for designating prophets. The most important is *nabhi'*, regularly translated "prophet." It is used nearly three hundred times in the Old Testament in its noun form alone. The other two are used much less. They are both translated "seer." The one is *ro'eh*, from the verb *ra'ah*, "to see," and the other *hozeh*, from the root *hazah*, "to see." The meaning of the term *nabhi'* will be discussed at a

---

[5] Says George Gray (*Sacrifice in the Old Testament*, p. 224), "The great personalities are to be sought among the prophets; the living force in times of crises is theirs but the maintenance of a permanent, ethical and religious condition . . . was the task of the priest."

later time. Its etymology and meaning are not established as easily as the other two terms. Mention should be made also of still a fourth term, though it is used the least of any. It is the phrase "man of God" (*'ish elohim*). Its significance is quite obvious; it simply refers to the prophet as one who had been chosen and sent by God.[6]

The task of the people designated by these terms is presented in the Old Testament as basically of two parts. The one is that of receiving a message from God through revelation and the other of speaking forth that message to people. Not all of the prophets are depicted as occupied with the first but all are with the second. Very likely some, if not many of the prophets, conveyed a message which they learned from other prophets or composed from the need of the day as they were inspired by God. A number of the prophets, however, did hear directly from God by supernatural revelation.

It is of interest to note that priests also had a twofold task, though of a slightly different nature. Their first responsibility was to offer sacrifices on behalf of the people, and their second was also to give God's message to the people. Their approach to giving this message, however, differed from that of the prophets. The priests taught the people, and their subject matter was the Law that God had given on Mount Sinai; they taught this by a precept-upon-precept, line-upon-line method (Isa. 28:13). The prophets, on the other hand, exhorted the people to obey the Law. The priests addressed basically the minds of the people, informing them what they should know, while the prophets addressed the emotions and wills, urging the people to do what they had already learned.[7]

There was also a parallel in respect to revelation. It was noted that prophets had as their first responsibility the reception of a message from God. The priests also had a way of receiving information from God. This did not apply to all priests, but to the one priest, the high priest. He was given the device called Urim and Thummim. Very little is known as to how the Urim and Thummim worked, but it was related somehow to the ephod which the high priest wore as a part of his apparel; and by this means he was able to initiate and receive a revelation from God. The prophet, on the other hand, did not have a way of initiating revelation. It was for him only to wait for God's moment of imparting information. But when the information came it was in propositional form and more extensive than that which the high priest received through the Urim and Thummim.

It is worthy to note, further, that high respect was accorded to prophets even from very early days. Evidence of this may be taken from the time of Saul after he had just visited Samuel (I Sam. 9:1—10:16). Saul and a servant had gone to Samuel to enquire of him regarding lost animals from his father's

[6]For discussion of all these terms, see chap. 4, pp. 57–62.
[7]For an enlargement on these thoughts, see chap. 8, pp. 116–117.

herd. He learned from Samuel not only that the animals had been located but, far more important, that he, Saul, was to be Israel's first king. On returning home, Saul spoke to his uncle who apparently was waiting for him. He did not tell the uncle concerning the announcement of kingship, but he did indicate that he had just spoken to Samuel. As soon as the uncle learned this he quickly urged, "Tell me, I pray thee, what Samuel said unto you" (I Sam. 10:15). Since Saul had not indicated anything regarding the kingship announcement, the interest of the uncle could not have been prompted for that reason; his interest could have been only because of whom Saul had just seen, namely, Samuel. The form of expression which the uncle used showed urgency on his part, too, as he made the request. He employed the emphatic imperative verb, "Tell me," and he used the enclitic particle for stress, "I pray thee" (*na'*). If the uncle of Saul was this interested in what Samuel said, it is likely that other people were also, and, if Samuel was this important in the minds of people, it is probable that other prophets carried a place of distinction as well.

## E. QUESTION AS TO WHETHER THE PROPHETS WERE PROFESSIONALS

### 1. Two respects in which they were

The term *professional* needs definition when it is used, for it can be employed in a number of ways. For instance, the pastor of a church may be called a professional in the sense that the pastorate is his occupation or profession. Again the term may be used in the sense that a man is capable in his work. He is not an amateur in the way he does it, but he is professional, doing it in a proper and commendable manner. Both of these meanings have a good connotation. On the other hand, the term may be used in the sense that the pastor is not truly interested in his work. He does it as a routine function. His heart is not in it. He is merely professional in his manner, going through the actions that he was hired to do. When used in this sense the word does not have a good connotation.

Most of the true prophets were professionals in the first two senses just noted. The majority were professionals in the sense of their occupation. It is true that there were a few who were only part-time prophets and had other work for their occupation. Amos, for instance, says that he was a farmer, a keeper of sheep, and one who tended sycamore trees, and from this work God called him to be a prophet for a time. Also, most prophets were professionals in the sense of ability. It has been noted that they were courageous, capable, ingenious people. They were not amateurs in their tasks. They were truly professionals. The true prophets, on the other hand, were not professionals in the sense of being merely functionaries, routinely doing their jobs. They were called men, they were assigned important tasks, and they did them with a full heart and true interest. They did not merely go through the motions.

## 2. Another respect in which they were not

There is still another sense in which true prophets were not professionals. This sense is related to the one just mentioned, but it concerns factors of a wider scope that call for some elaboration.

These factors involve an erroneous view of the early prophets (those from Samuel to the writing prophets) set forth by various scholars. This view holds that early prophets lived in bands or guilds and moved about in groups. It is observed that Samuel had such groups under him (I Sam. 10:5, 10) and later Elijah and Elisha had similar groups under them (II Kings 2:3, 5, 7, 15). And Ahab is depicted as having had four hundred prophets on whom he could call (I Kings 22:6).

Since Elijah wore a sheepskin or goatskin garment and a leather loincloth (II Kings 1:8), it is suggested that these bands of prophets had a distinctive dress. It is further believed that they probably wore a mark of identification on their foreheads. One day a prophet covered his forehead to disguise himself from King Ahab, and it is thought that, in doing this, he covered this mark of identification (I Kings 20:35f.). Because jeering boys one day told Elisha, "Go up, you baldhead; go up, you baldhead" (II Kings 2:23), it is held further that these prophets likely shaved their heads wholly or in part. The bands are thought to have lived together in a common dwelling house, from which they traveled through the land, playing music and raving in ecstasy. In so doing they delivered oracles in response to people's questions.[8]

It is believed that these groups of prophets were energetic in their ecstatic activity in the early years of Israel's history, but then came to lose this original spontaneity and took on a regulated and standardized manner. Thus they fell into a routine professionalism. In time this professionalism became normal prophetism, as these groups of men came to pursue ways which they felt would please people most and especially the king in case he should call on them. As T. J. Meek says, "Thus did prophecy become commercialised and

[8]For elaboration of these ideas see J. Lindblom, *Prophecy in Ancient Israel*, pp. 65–70.

professionalised. It went the way of the priesthood and for that matter of all institutions. It lost its spontaneous, inspired character and became in time as professional as the priesthood against which it was originally a protest."[9]

The view then holds that occasionally a reactionary prophet would arise who would be against the professional group. A pioneer in this reaction is thought to have been Micaiah, who withstood the four hundred prophets of Ahab (I Kings 22:13–28).[10] Such a person was considered at the time a reactionary to the normal professional prophets, and, therefore, an "outsider" to the main group.[11]

There is truth in this view in the sense that there were two types of prophets in Israel and Judah. There was the kind who were king-pleasers, and in that sense professionals. There were also those like Micaiah. The viewpoint is false, however, in believing that the so-called professional prophets were the historic, traditional prophets. A careful study of Old Testament passages shows that actually the type of prophet characterized by Micaiah was the traditional prophet and that the king-pleasers were those who came in as extras later on. Before Micaiah, there were people like Samuel, Nathan, Gad, Jehu, Hanani, Shemaiah, Ahijah, Elijah, and Elisha. These men were not king-pleasers, they were not professionals in the sense described. They were fearless men, those who were willing to stand for the word they believed God had given them, and these were the traditional prophets. One cannot think of them as persons who had lost their interest in what they believed was true.

Another way in which this view is erroneous is in thinking of the early prophets as groups of rather wild, ecstatic people who moved about in bands. Groups of prophets did live in the day of Samuel and later in the time of Elijah and Elisha, but they were not wild men.[12] Rather they were probably training groups, men getting ready to become prophets as their lifework. Samuel in his day and Elijah and Elisha in their day seem to have been their teachers. It is probable that, when their days of preparation were over, the members of these groups became true fearless prophets like their teachers.

Among prophets of the day—whether so trained or not—there were indeed those who forsook their basic commitments and became king-pleasers. That is, they became professionals in the sense that has been mentioned. These, however, were few in number in earlier years, though they did

---

[9]*Hebrew Origins*, p. 174.

[10]Theodore H. Robinson (*Prophecy and the Prophets in Ancient Israel*, pp. 39–40) writes, "The first person of whom this independence is recorded is Micaiah."

[11]Part of this thinking is often that it was from such reactionary prophets that the later writing prophets developed and that they came to think of the older professional type as "false" prophets; see chap. 7 for discussion.

[12]There is no scriptural evidence that supports the idea of their being wild, ecstatic people. See chaps. 2 and 3 for consideration of passages alleged to give such evidence.

become more numerous in later years. They were the ones Jeremiah, for instance, spoke of as false prophets (23:9–40); and they were in the majority by his day. They were not, however, the main stream of prophets. They were defectors who became weak in their commitment and desire to please God.

In summary, true prophets were not professionals in the sense of king-pleasers. They were committed men, men who were ready to do what God wanted them to do no matter the task and no matter the danger. Only those who defected from this group came to be professionals in the sense of king-pleasers.

# 2

# Contemporary "Prophets"

It should be realized that Israel was not an island in its day, set apart from influences of peoples round about. Israelites existed as a people among other peoples and they experienced pressures from their neighbors to follow customs that were not in keeping with God's Law. There is disagreement among scholars as to the degree Israel was influenced. Some believe the influence was extensive, while others see it as minimal. The Bible itself indicates there was at least some. For instance, many Israelites are depicted as having come to worship Baal, the god of the Canaanites (Judg. 2:13, 14; 3:7, 8; 6:25–30).

Because prophetism was so important in Israel, and because a type of prophetism existed in the world of the day outside Israel, it is necessary to consider the question of whether or not Israel borrowed from others in respect to prophecy. Viewpoints vary on the question. Gustav Holscher, for instance, believes that almost all aspects of Israel's prophecy were borrowed from Canaan.[1] J. Lindblom, on the other hand, does not believe Israel borrowed from Canaan, but, rather, observed the phenomenon of prophecy simply because all the world did.[2] The Israelites were like other peoples and did as others in their religious activities. Abraham Heschel, following more closely the presentation of Scripture itself, sees Israel's prophets as a unique people and their writings as in a class by themselves.[3]

[1] *Die Propheten*, pp. 140f.
[2] *Prophecy in Ancient Israel*, pp. 98f.
[3] Abraham Heschel, *The Prophets*, pp. 472–473.

Since views are varied, and since the Bible itself indicates that Israelites were influenced in some measure religiously, it is necessary to investigate the matter and make evaluations as a beginning aspect of our study. To do so, we will consider the principal nations with whom Israel had contact.

## A.  A SURVEY OF MIDDLE EAST "PROPHECY"

### 1. Mesopotamia

It is well to begin the survey with the general region of Mesopotamia which held a place of unique importance throughout the Middle East during the Old Testament time. Though Israel came in contact directly with Canaanites rather than Mesopotamians, Canaanites in turn were significantly influenced by the Mesopotamian region. This was true in considerable part because of two major migrations from Mesopotamia to Canaan in the early years of the second millennium B.C. The first was of Amorites, the second (shortly after) of Hurrians. Both groups greatly influenced Canaanite thinking.[4]

Speaking first generally, religion was of paramount importance to the Mesopotamians. People did little or decided few matters apart from an interest in religion and a concern for the will of the gods. For this reason they had an extensive priesthood which served their temples. There were actually four classes of priests: first, the *Ashipu*, who were exorcists, believed to be able to relieve persons of demons; second, the *Kallu*, who had responsibility for temple music; third, the *Qadishtu*, priestesses whose main function seems to have been religious prostitution; and, fourth, a group of four priests, the *Baru*, the *Sha'ilu*, the *Shabru*, and the *Mahhu*, who had the common function of divination and were really the most important of all. People came to them with questions, and they returned what were thought to be divine answers by employing a variety of techniques. Among these four the *Baru* priests were considered the most significant.

The means of divination practiced may be divided into two classes: unarranged forms and arranged forms. As to the unarranged, these concerned any omen-type events that might occur in the natural course of a day. The Mesopotamians had a lengthy list of such omens and their meanings.[5] Usually

---

[4]See for discussion S. H. Hooke, *Babylonian and Assyrian Religion*, p. vii.

[5]A. Guillaume (*Prophecy and Divination Among the Hebrews and Other Semites*, pp. 35–37) says divination "was systematized to a meticulous degree unknown in any other part of the world." As to the amount of literature on the subject, Morris Jastrow (*The Religion of Babylonia and Assyria*, p. 355) says, "Fully one fourth of the portion of Ashurbanipal's library that has been discovered consists of omens."

when something happened on the right of a person it was a good omen, and when something happened on the left it was bad. Included in the unarranged types of omens were those pertaining to nature, heavenly bodies, the flight of birds, dreams, and weather conditions.

Of the arranged types two were most important. The first was hydromancy in which oil was poured upon water or vice versa. Since oil and water do not mix, the action of these when put together was observed and that which happened was thought to be significant as an omen. The other means was hepatoscopy which was the most important of all. This was the reading of a sheep's liver though sometimes the kidneys of an animal might be observed. This organ apparently was thought of as the seat of life of the animal and therefore significant for revelation.

The procedure for reading the liver was as follows: First the sheep was killed, usually to the accompaniment of chanting and music. The priest then inspected the organs and entrails as they lay in the opened stomach of the sheep. After this, according to prescribed rules, he lifted the entrails of the stomach up for closer examination and then drew them out to expose completely the organs lying beneath them. At this point it was possible to distinguish the favorable and the unfavorable aspects of the liver itself. S. H. Hooke says that "no less than one hundred and fourteen different signs"[6] were thought to be registered in connection with depressions of the liver thus laid bare.[7]

The answer that was found in such divination activity was limited to either a "yes" or a "no." However, by asking many questions considerable information could be received. For example, the Assyrian emperor, Esarhaddon, wanted to know whether the one seeking his daughter in marriage, Bartatua, king of Ishkuza, should be allowed to do so. His questions were worded as follows: "Is he to be trusted, will he fulfill his promises, will he observe the decrees of Esarhaddon, the king of Assyria, and execute them in good faith?" Also, in respect to his son, Esarhaddon asked, "Is the entrance of Siniddinabal, the son of Esarhaddon, the king of Assyria, whose name is written on this tablet, into the government in accord with the command of thy great divinity? Is it to come to pass?"[8]

The importance of divination in the life of Mesopotamians can hardly be overstated. Kings, with all their power, seldom made a decision or attempted an action without consulting these priests. For instance, in the Book of Daniel one finds Nebuchadnezzar calling in his wise men to interpret his dreams (Dan. 2, 4) and later Belshazzar did the same for reading and inter-

---

[6] *Babylonian and Assyrian Religion*, pp. 89–90.
[7] For detail regarding this function of hepatoscopy, See H. Dillon, *Assyro-Babylonian Liver Divination*.
[8] Jastrow, *Religion of Babylonia and Assyria*, p. 329.

preting the handwriting that appeared miraculously on his banquet hall (Dan. 5). The wise men involved in these occasions were simply these types of priests, supposedly expert in handling all such matters. Since dream interpretation was one of their specialities, the fact that Nebuchadnezzar asked the priests to interpret his dreams was not unusual. And though the reading of miraculous writing would have been unique for them still they were the logical ones for Belshazzar to call. Belshazzar would have believed that if they could not read it then no one could.

Because some scholars believe Israel's religious personnel used similar forms of divination, it has been appropriate to notice these of Mesopotamia, but more scholars find parallels in what are called prophetic-type texts of the region, and attention must now be given to them. They are texts which read somewhat like the way the prophets of Israel wrote. Among these texts are the "Oracles of Arbela," which date from the time of Esarhaddon. In these oracles priestesses use the first person in speaking on behalf of the goddess Ishtar. Occasionally they use the expression, "Fear not," which Hebrew prophets also use, and they give promise of help to the king from the goddess. Guillaume gives a few lines from one of these oracles:

> O, Esarhaddon, king of lands, fear not!
> Thy foes shall flee from before thy feet
> Like marsh hogs in the month of Siwan.
> I am the great Beltis.
> I am Ishtar of Arbela who destroyed thy foes before thy feet.
> Thy foes, like Ukai, I will deliver into thy power.
> I am Ishtar of Arbela.
> I will go before thee and behind thee. Fear not. . . .[9]

Another illustration of a prophetic-type text is the "Myth of Irra." Here the plague-god, Irra, is depicted as devastating the world in wrath. Hugo Gressman gives a portion of this text:

> Then shall the sea-country relentlessly slay the sea-country,
> Subartu shall slay Subartu,
> The Assyrian shall slay the Assyrian,
> The Elamite shall slay the Elamite,
> The Kassite shall slay the Kassite . . .
> Then shall Akkad arise and shall fell them all,
> Shall fling them all down together.[10]

A text which some believe carries the nearest Mesopotamian parallels to Hebrew prophecy comes from the kingdom of Mari on the Middle Eu-

[9] *Prophecy and Divination*, p. 43.
[10] *Altorientalische Texte und Bilder zum Alten Testament*, p. 228.

phrates.[11] The text was written by a person who knew of an oracle delivered by an *apilum* (meaning "respondent," the designation for "prophet" here) from the god Hadad. Since the oracle was really directed to the king (probably Zimrilim), the writer felt obliged to send it on to him, though the *apilum* himself apparently would not necessarily have seen to it that it was so delivered. The oracle, which was given in the words of the god himself, is as follows: The king is to be reminded that he had been raised on Hadad's knees and been placed by Hadad on the throne. He should also realize that, as Hadad had instated him there, so the god could now take Alahtum (apparently an area situated in the region of Aleppo) out of his hand, if the king did not bring animals for a libation. Indeed, Hadad would take all he had given to the king—the throne, the territory, and the city. However, if, on the contrary, the king would fulfill Hadad's desires, then the king would be given "thrones on thrones, houses on houses, territories on territories, cities on cities, and the country from the east to the west."

Three parallels to Hebrew prophecy can be seen: first, the very words of the deity are used; second, there is a reminder to the king of his dependence on the god; and third, there is promise of blessing if he does what the god wants and warning of trouble if he does not. There are also some distinct differences: first, the *apilum* does not deliver the message himself and so does not appear as a spokesman for the god as did the Hebrew prophet; second, the god Hadad is presented merely as Lord of Kallasu, which means he was thought of as localized to this particular place rather than universalized over all the world; and third, that which the king is expected to do to please Hadad is offer a cultic libation, whereas Israel's kings were regularly enjoined to observe moral obedience before God. A fair appraisal finds these differences far outweighing the parallels.

## 2. Egypt

Another principal area of the world bringing strong influence on Canaan was Egypt to the south. Just as in Mesopotamia, religion played an important role here. It had its own distinctive character, however, for though some factors were similar to Mesopotamia many others were different. From the early days of Egypt priests carried a strong place of influence in the land. By the time of the eighteenth dynasty (sixteenth to fourteenth centuries) the priesthood had become extremely wealthy, and in the days of Rameses III (c. 1200 B.C.) priests owned approximately one-tenth of the country.

Three grades of priests were recognized.[12] The *Uab* was the first. This

[11]A. Lods, "Une tablette inédite de Mari, intéressante pour l'histoire ancienne du prophetisme Sémitique," *Studies in Old Testament Prophecy*, ed. H. H. Rowley, pp. 103–110.
[12]Flinders Petrie, *Religious Life in Ancient Egypt*, p. 48.

person examined animals for sacrifice and performed routine tasks around the temple. The *Kherheb* was next. He was a learned man who could recite all the liturgy with proper effect and give direction to the ceremonial activities. He is sometimes called the "magician." The *Hemu neter* was third and the most important. He was roughly equivalent to the *Baru* priest in Mesopotamia. He was in charge of oracular activity.

Several types of divination were used in Egypt. The first and perhaps foremost was the dream. Dream interpretation may have been stressed even more in Egypt than in Mesopotamia. Long lists indicating the significance of dream omens have been found in Egypt just as in Mesopotamia. John Wilson gives a few illustrations: If in a dream a man sees himself looking at a large cat, a large harvest will come; if he sees himself plunging into a river, he will be cleansed from all evils; if, however, he sees someone catching birds, it is a bad omen for his property will be taken away.[13]

A second type of divination concerned the observation of phenomena in nature and especially the stars. Many parallels existed here between Egypt and Mesopotamia.

A third type concerned the movement of sacred animals. For instance, the sacred bull Apis was watched to see which of two chambers he might choose to enter. Also, utterances of children who were near the bull were often considered significant, and the same was true regarding dreams experienced by those associated with this animal. Sacred bulls were highly honored; and when one would die, another would be chosen to replace him, according to specific criteria.

Still another type of divination concerned movable parts of statues. A statue of the falcon god, Horus, located in the Oriental Museum, University of Chicago, has two holes running the length of its body, leading to its head and beak. Apparently a priest would pull strings leading to the head and the beak to make the god give answer to questions posed by enquirers.

Then from Egypt also have come a few texts which have been compared with Hebrew prophetic writings. There is first the "Memphite Drama" dating from the beginning of the dynastic period. It discloses the earliest-known written recognition of approved and disapproved conduct.[14]

Second are the pyramid texts.[15] These consist of thousands of lines of hieroglyphic writing on the galleries and passages of the pyramids. The intention of these texts was to insure the eternal felicity of the king. It is said that they contain the earliest written reflections on the thought of death.

From the fifty dynasty come the maxims of Ptah-hotep, which give the earliest formulation of right conduct ever found. Included, for instance, is the

---

[13] *Ancient Near Eastern Texts*, ed. James B. Pritchard, p. 495.
[14] J. H. Breasted, *The Dawn of Conscience*, p. 41.
[15] For two extracts, see *Ancient Near Eastern Texts*, pp. 32–33.

observation that Ptah-hotep had obtained 110 years of life because of "doing right" for the king "even until the grave."[16]

From the so-called feudal age of 2000 B.C., there are some compositions on social justice which are said to make their authors the first social "prophets." The best-known were written by Ipu-wer. His writings have been called the closest to Israelite prophecy found in Egypt. He fearlessly denounces the king of his day for the social disorder then existent. He notes the difference between how the king rules and the manner in which an ideal king would rule. He says, for instance, "Royal command, knowledge, and righteousness are with thee," but "it is strife which thou puttest in the land, together with the sound of tumult." Further, he says, "The laws of the judgment hall are cast forth, men walk upon them in the public places, the poor break them open in the midst of the streets." And still again, "The man of virtue walks in mourning by reason of what has happened in the land."[17]

The one feature here which carries a parallel to Hebrew prophecy is that Ipu-wer is critical of the king and of social conditions of his time, even reminding the king of his responsibility to make them better. Over against this, however, are several contrasts which should be noted. The first is that the concern of Ipu-wer is with the chaos and confusion of the land rather than with any collapse of moral and spiritual values of the people. The Hebrew prophets, in contrast, are regularly concerned with the people and their oppression and not with chaotic conditions in the land. Second, Ipu-wer does not lay blame for this situation on any moral or spiritual deficiency of the people but finds it in the gods, especially the god Ra. The Hebrew prophets never lay blame upon God for anything; it always belongs to man. And third, Ipu-wer does not speak for or as any god, but only for himself as a social critic of the day, and this also is quite at variance with the Hebrew prophets.

The best-known social "prophet" is Nefer-rohu. Though the text concerning this man was written about the time of the beginning of the twelfth dynasty (2000 B.C.), it concerns the much earlier day of the fourth dynasty when a man named Snefru ruled. This king is presented as desiring entertainment one evening and as calling for Nefer-rohu, a priest of Bastet, to provide it. When Nefer-rohu arrives, the king tells him that he wishes to know about the future. Nefer-rohu pauses for a time and then begins to speak. He first says the land is in a miserable condition and that no one is concerned about it. Then he gives the unexpected statement, "I shall speak of what is before my face: I cannot foretell what has not [yet] come."[18] However, he proceeds to do this very thing. He speaks of a time when the son of a Nubian woman born in Upper Egypt will come into the land and restore

---

[16]Ibid., p. 414.
[17]Breasted, *Dawn of Conscience*, p. 199.
[18]*Ancient Near Eastern Texts*, p. 445.

justice. The name used in the text for this person is Ameni, which is clearly a reference to the first king of the twelfth dynasty—Amen-em-hep I. Nefer-rohu then proceeds to show some of the fine and splendid actions this king would undertake.

The main "prophetic" feature of this text is its so-called messianic character. That is, Nefer-rohu points to a coming king who will be a savior for the land of Egypt. It should be realized, however, that the text actually was written when this savior, Amen-em-hep I, had already begun to reign. There really is no prophecy in the text, then. It should be observed also that the whole context of the writing is one of lighthearted entertainment. King Snefru simply wants someone to come in and say things regarding the future. Further, Nefer-rohu himself does not make a pretense of being a prophet, even stating that he cannot tell the future.

### 3. Canaan

Canaan, of course, must be considered as well, for whether its culture was borrowed or native, it was the culture that brought direct influence on Israel. Not nearly as much is known regarding Canaan as is known regarding Mesopotamia and Egypt, though discoveries at Ras Shamra have helped substantially. Actual Canaanite temples have been found at several places, including Bethshan, Megiddo, Lachish, Shechem, and Hazor in Palestine. Animals were sacrificed at these temples and also holy women served as sacred prostitutes. The head god was El, but the god whom the people considered the most important was Baal. Baal could be thought of in the singular as the god of all the land or in the plural as localized manifestations of the national deity. For this reason one finds such names as Baal-peor (Num. 25:3), Baal-meon (Num. 32:38), and Baal-hermon (Judg. 3:3).

Evidence of divination in Canaan is comparatively meager, but a few texts can be cited which at least show its existence. There is first an indication of bird-watching; a text from Ugarit reads:

> Over the house of her father eagles are hovering,
> A flock of vultures are soaring.
> Pgt weeps in her heart,
> She sheds tears in her liver.[19]

And an Amarna text says: "Send to me an asker [sa'ili] of eagles." A well-known text regarding Idrimi, a young ruler exiled from Alalakh, reads:

[19]Alfred Haldar, *Associations of Cult Prophets Among the Ancient Semites*, p. 80.

And I dwelt in the midst of the *'Apiru people* for seven years. I interpreted [the flight of] birds, I inspected [the intestines of] lambs, while seven years of [?] the storm god turned over [?] my head.[20]

There is indication also that dream interpretation was observed. Another text from Ras Shamra reads as follows:

And when he falls asleep at his crying,
the humming of the sleep fatigues him,
and he lies there [in the] sighing and
[overflowing with tears—or the like]
[then] in his dream 'll descends,
In his vision the father of man.[21]

A few texts of a more "prophetic type" also exist. In one the king of Hamath, Zakir, at the time of being attacked by Ben-hadad of Syria says that the god, Ba'alsemin, spoke to him through "seers" and "prophets" as follows: "Fear not, for I have made thee [king] and I will stand at thy side and I will save thee from all these [kings]. . . ."[22]

The well-known story of Wenamon contains another account which is said to be prophetic in character. Wenamon was an Egyptian official of the eleventh century who was sent from Egypt to Byblos on the Phoenician coast to procure lumber. His situation became desperate when he was embroiled in an argument over money with the Byblos officials. For a month he was told to leave the harbor without his lumber, but then a young man of Byblos, apparently in a possessed state of ecstatic frenzy, gave an oracle. The oracle was taken as a divine indication that Wenamon should be treated kindly, and he was.[23]

## B. EVALUATION

With these illustrations of Middle East "prophecy" in view, it is appropriate to make an evaluation as to what degree Israel was influenced by it. Some scholars believe this influence was extensive. One argument to this end is based on the assumption that since Israel was a nation in the world of that day, its people of course did as neighboring countries. This "comparative

---

[20]William F. Albright, "Some Important Recent Discoveries: Alphabetic Origins and the Idrimi Statue," *Bulletin of the American Schools of Oriental Research*, 118 (1950):11–20.

[21]Ivan Engnell, I Krt, lines 31b–37a, *Studies in Divine Kingship in the Ancient Near East*, p. 151.

[22]Haldar, *Cult Prophets*, p. 75.

[23]Heschel, *The Prophets*, p. 460. For text and discussion, see John Wilson's treatment in *Ancient Near Eastern Texts*, p. 26.

religions" type of argument comes in for notice at various places in the discussion following, but a passing word is appropriate here. This assumption simply is not valid. The Old Testament continually presents Israel as a unique people in the world, different from other nations especially in its religious belief and practice. This means that to prove Israel was like other countries in respect to prophecy, objective evidence is necessary.

### 1. Consideration of alleged divination passages in Scripture

Objective evidence is sought in a few Scripture passages which are believed to show that divination was practiced in Israel.[24] One passage which probably is referred to more than any other is Genesis 44:5, 15. Here Joseph has had his silver cup put into the sack of Benjamin prior to sending his brothers back to their father, Jacob. In verse 5 the messenger, whom Joseph sends after the brothers to accuse them of stealing the cup, is told to say, "Is not this it in which my lord drinketh and whereby indeed he divineth?" Then in verse 15 Joseph indicates to the brothers, who by this time have returned to him, that he knew of what they had done because he could "certainly divine." It is alleged that these statements show that Joseph used the cup for divining the will of God.

In response four observations may be made. First, even if what is alleged could be proven true, this would show only that a person who had long been away from home, under the direct influence of the pagan religious system of Egypt, had come to accept one of the religious practices of this country. It would not indicate that the family of Jacob—and certainly not the later nation of Israel—had come to the same manner of thinking. Second, the overall story of Joseph argues strongly that, in spite of this Egyptian influence, Joseph was not brought to the place of accepting divination. Never is this devout person found at any other time seeking the will of God by any such instrument of divination. He prays to God directly and hears from God without employment of anyone or anything. Third, when Joseph speaks of this cup in a direct descriptive phrase, he calls it "the silver cup," not "the divining cup" (44:2). This suggests the real nature of his own thinking regarding the cup. Fourth, the verb used in the two crucial verses here, 5 and 15, is not *qasam*, the regular word for "divine," but *nahash*, which means "to whisper, to mumble formulations, to prophesy." In the light of this choice of verb, and particularly in view of the two prior observations, it may well be

---

[24]For instance, Lindblom, *Prophecy in Ancient Israel*, pp. 88f., while admitting that the Old Testament forbids divination, still says, "However, Israelite tradition knows also of divination which was not opposed to the Yahweh religion," and then proceeds to cite such passages as noted in the text above.

that Joseph's intention in speaking to his brothers was merely to let them know that his cup was special in importance (v. 5) and that he in his high position had access to information not available to ordinary people (v. 15).

A second passage concerns Saul's visit to the woman of Endor in I Samuel 28. Because there is an evident appearance of Samuel at this time, it is alleged that the passage gives indication of spiritism being practiced in Old Testament time. It is true that there were people who attempted to practice spiritism, but this passage surely does not indicate it to have been approved by God. For one thing, the woman when Samuel appears is extremely frightened, showing that her manipulations have not brought about the appearance. Apparently God has done so supernaturally. Then there is the fact that Samuel's message given to Saul at the time is anything but a message that either the woman or Saul would have wanted given. It is a message that God Himself would have wanted Saul to hear, for it foretells the catastrophe of Saul's defeat by the Philistines to occur on the following day.

Another passage pointed to is II Samuel 5:24. Here David is fighting the Philistines. He has already won a first battle and now a second is ready to be joined. God tells him to change the direction of his attack and to do this when he hears the "sound of a going in the tops of the mulberry trees." It is alleged that this is a reference to a form of divination employing the rustling of leaves. Again, however, one must see this passage in the light of David's overall manner of contact with God. Like Joseph his contacts are always direct; either God reveals to him or he prays to God, both without intermediate help. Never is he seen employing any form of divination. Here the plain indication is that God Himself miraculously stirred the leaves of the designated trees.

A further passage is Isaiah 8:19, which reads as follows: "And when they shall say unto you, Seek unto them that have familiar spirits and unto wizards that peep, and that mutter: should not a people seek unto their God? for the living to the dead?" When one reads this passage in its context, however, he finds that actually this seeking unto familiar spirits and wizards is something condemned. Rather than doing this, the people were directed to go "to the law and to the testimony" (8:20). The verse can in no way be used to show that God approved wizards or those who resorted to familiar spirits.

Reference is also made to Ezekiel 21:21, where the king of Babylon is presented as standing at the fork of a road and using divination apparently to know which way to go. Ezekiel says, "He made his arrows bright, he consulted with images, he looked in the liver." Three significant words appear in the passage: *qesem*, "divination"; *sha'al*, "enquire, consult"; and *ra'ah*, "see, inspect." It is asserted that Ezekiel not only shows his knowledge of Mesopotamian divination here but that he may well have been sympathetic to it himself. It is true that Ezekiel certainly knew about Mesopotamian divination, for he lived in Babylonia during the captivity period. That he was sympathetic to it, however, is something else. Never is he shown to use any form of divination himself, but rather his contact with God, like that of the others who have been noted, is always direct.

## 2. Refutation

The view of the Old Testament regarding divination is made clear in Deuteronomy 18:10f., which reads: "There shall not be found among you anyone that maketh his son or his daughter to pass through the fire, or that useth divination, or an observer of times, or an enchanter, or a witch, or a charmer, or a consulter with familiar spirits, or a wizard, or a necromancer. For all that do these things are an abomination unto the LORD" (cf. Lev. 19:26, 31; 20:6, 27). Following this passage, Moses, the human penman, tells the people that, instead of seeking a word from God by such means, they are to go to the prophet whom God would raise up for this purpose. By this, Moses sets the prophets of Israel in direct contrast to these forms of divination employed by countries round about.

These considerations show that all forms of divination were disapproved by the Law of God given to the Israelites. Then, in respect to the so-called parallel prophetic-type texts, we should notice several general contrasts (in addition to those already pointed out) between these texts from other lands and the texts of the Hebrew prophets.

First, as to date, the texts from both Mari and Egypt which evidence the nearest parallels long antedate any of the prophets of Israel. Many centuries lapsed between the time of the "prophecies" represented by them and the prophetic messages of Israel's great prophets.[25] And there have been no similar texts found from these countries that are contemporary with the representatives from Israel. Second, prophecy in Israel has been of lasting benefit for mankind since, but "prophetic" writings of other countries were known only in their own day. They left little or no impact on posterity. Heschel says the reason is that "prophecy in Israel was not an episode in the life of an individual, but an illumination in the history of the people."[26] Third, Israelite prophecy finds no parallel in terms of continuous duration. The prophets of Israel stretched over centuries of time, as Heschel says, "From Abraham to Moses, from Samuel to Nathan, from Elijah to Amos, from Hosea to Isaiah, from Jeremiah to Malachi." He concludes, "This is a

[25]Egypt's "prophecies" precede 2000 B.C. and the "prophet" of Mari dates to the eighteenth century B.C. In contrast, the first of Israel's writing prophets fall in the ninth century B.C.

[26]The Prophets, p. 472.

phenomenon for which there is no analogy."[27] Fourth, the Hebrew prophets were a committed people, full of vitality and ready even to die for the message they proclaimed. To them, as Scott indicates, "the prophetic tradition was a living thing, which had become part of themselves through their own commission at Yahweh's hand."[28] A similar attitude is not indicated or implied in texts from other countries.

Fifth, though Hebrew prophets speak of social decay in something of the way that Egyptian samples show,[29] they find the reason for this decay in the sin of the people. This is never the case in texts from other countries. Sixth, Hebrew prophecy shows "an intimacy between God and prophet" which is almost "entirely lacking" in adjacent regions.[30] Seventh, in contrast to the exalted aspects of prophecy in Israel, the prophetic-type people of other countries "never succeeded in disengaging themselves from the meshes of sorcery, witchcraft, magic, and necromancy."[31] And eighth, Franz Bohl rightly indicates a contrast as to degree of punishment foreseen. He says it was "the typically Israelite idea that God can and will destroy his own chosen people as punishment for their sins," which is a thought adjacent prophets never came close to mentioning. He adds the reason—this would have meant the end of their own power as well.[32]

In conclusion, one may properly say that, though there are some general similarities between the prophecy of neighboring countries and that of Israel, these are not of sufficient detail or number to give evidence of borrowing on Israel's part. And as Irving Wood states, "it is likeness of detail" which is necessary to prove dependency.[33] Israel's prophecy, then, was a unique phenomenon, different from any other in the world, or, as Heschel says, "The Biblical prophet is a type *sui generis*."[34]

It is true that in the discussion thus far the matter of ecstasy among the prophets has not been considered, and many scholars find a parallel on this basis, if not on any other. The following chapter, however, will take up the matter of ecstacy and will find again that there is a marked difference between what was existent in countries around Israel and Israel itself.

---

[27]Ibid.; cf. R. B. Y. Scott, *The Relevance of the Prophets*, p. 57.

[28]Ibid., p. 58.

[29]A. B. Mace, "The Influence of Egypt on Hebrew Literature," *Annals of Archaeology and Anthropology*, 9 (1922):23.

[30]Guillaume, *Prophecy and Divination*, p. 59.

[31]J. M. P. Smith, "Semitic Prophecy," reprint from *The Biblical World*, 35 (1910):226.

[32]"Some Notes on Israel in the Light of Babylonian Discoveries," *Journal of Biblical Literature*, 53 (1934):142.

[33]"Borrowing Between Religions," *Journal of Biblical Literature*, 46 (1927):98.

[34]*The Prophets*, p. 473.

# 3

# Israel's Prophets Were
# Not Ecstatics

Many scholars believe that Israel's prophets were ecstatics, especially the early prophets. Some believe in fact that an ability to become ecstatically frenzied was an essential characteristic if people of the day were to accept the prophets as authentic. A comment by E. O. James is only typical: "It was this type of shamanistic behavior . . . that constituted the principal role of the professional ecstatics described in Israel as *nebi'ism*."[1] Other writers speak of an ability for ecstaticism as actually a badge of authority for the prophets, without which people would not have accepted them as true prophets.[2]

It is held that Canaan was the source of this phenomenon for Israel.[3] Many believe that this was one of the principal ways in which Israel was dependent upon Canaan for its development of prophecy. A still earlier influence, however, came on Canaan from Asia Minor. Theophile J. Meek says the movement swept through Asia Minor "toward the end of the second millennium into Greece on one side and into Syria and Palestine on the other."[4] W. O. E. Oesterley and Theodore H. Robinson add that "these

---

[1] *Prophecy and Prophets*, p. 79.
[2] See N. W. Porteous, "Prophecy," *Record and Revelation*, ed. H. Wheeler Robinson, pp. 216–249, for references.
[3] J. Lindblom (*Prophecy in Ancient Israel*, pp. 66, 97f.), however, disagrees though he is in the minority. He believes that ecstaticism existed commonly all over the world and so in Israel as in other nations.
[4] *Hebrew Origins*, p. 55.

37

phenomena at a later time were spread over the whole Mediterranean world,"
though without reaching Egypt until the fifth century B.C.[5] Gradually this
phenomenon spread further in the world and finally to all parts. E. O. James
gives a list of the principal areas and says that probably the oracle of Delphi
was the most famous of ancient ecstatic centers.[6] He describes the action
there as follows:

> It would appear the inspired prophetess, when an oracle was demanded, arrayed
> herself in long robes, a golden headdress, and a wreath of laurel leaves, and
> drank of the sacred spring Kassotis. She then, it is said, seated herself on a tripod
> over a vaporous cleft in a chasm of the cave below, unless she actually entered
> the cave to encounter the vapor, in order to obtain a state of enthusiasm. In this
> condition she gave counsel as the mouthpiece of Apollo.[7]

Certain forms of ecstasy were carried out only as a ritualistic exercise for
some festal celebration, but the type to which prophecy is compared was
motivated by a desire for revelation. The spirit world was sought, and to that
end a release from contact with reality was desired. To achieve this ecstatic
state, various means were employed, including a vaporous gas, a sacred
dance, rhythmic music, or even narcotics. Reason needed to be set aside and
the mind made open for the reception of the divine word. Accompanying this
rapport with the spirit realm was normally a physical seizure, which T. H.
Robinson describes as follows:

> It consists of a fitful attack which affected the whole body. Sometimes the limbs
> were stimulated to violent action and wild leaping and contortions resulted.
> These might be more or less rhythmical and the phenomenon would present the
> appearance of a wild and frantic dance. At other times there was more or less
> complete constriction of the muscles, and the condition became almost catalep-
> tic. The vocal cords were sometimes involved, noises and sounds were poured
> out which might be unrecognizable as human speech.[8]

This type of prophecy is what is believed to have been shared by the
Israelite prophets. The earliest of them—assigned to the day of Samuel
usually—are thought to have assembled as bands and to have moved through
the countryside, offering their services to all who were interested. People
would make enquiry of them regarding the divine will, and they would seek
the answer by this form of ecstatic frenzy. Various methods could be used to
loose the earth-bound state of reason to find a rapport with the deity. Because

---

[5] *Hebrew Religion: Its Origin and Development*, pp. 185–186.
[6] *The Nature and Function of Priesthood*, pp. 30–31.
[7] Ibid., p. 40.
[8] *Prophecy and the Prophets in Ancient Israel*, p. 31.

of their ecstatic displays, often involving music and vigorous dancing, they came to be called "madmen" (*meshugga'*).

A main argument for this view that Israelite prophets engaged in ecstatic frenzy is based upon a study of comparative religions. As with prophetism in general, it is asserted that one should naturally expect Israelites observed the practice, since other people did. The conservative scholar, however, who believes that Israel was unique in its world, having been especially called to existence by God and given its Law and instruction supernaturally, places little reliance on this manner of argument. No doubt Israel borrowed some aspects of its culture from the Canaanites, but, as seen in the prior chapter, this was not in basic matters. As individuals, many of the people did defect to Baal worship as practiced in Canaan, but officially Israel's religious belief had been given by God through Moses already at Mount Sinai prior to the conquest of the land.

There are a few biblical passages, however, to which adherents of the ecstatic view appeal, and these call for discussion. Such questions as the following should be considered: Did the individuals concerned in these passages engage in ecstaticism? If not, how should the occasions described be understood, some of which truly are surprising in nature? And what is the correct explanation of the actions portrayed by the persons involved? It is well, first, to look at the passages in their contexts and later to consider the argumentation taken from them. There are three passages that are used principally and then a few others which are used in a supporting role.

## A. PASSAGES USED AS EVIDENCE FOR THE VIEW

### 1. Main passages[9]

#### a. NUMBERS 11:25–29

The first passage, Numbers 11:25–29, concerns the occasion when God appointed seventy elders to aid Moses in administering the affairs of Israel while in the wilderness. Moses had become overburdened in his immense task, and God told him to select this group of seventy to be his assistants. He told Moses further that He would take of the "Spirit" already on Moses and place it upon them. This He did and then all the group began immediately to "prophesy" (*yithnabbe'u*). Most of the group ceased in this activity after a

[9]For a similar treatment of these passages see my work, *The Holy Spirit in the Old Testament*, chap. 9, pp. 92–100.

short time, but two did not. Eldad and Medad continued to prophesy as they ran through the Israelite camp, and Joshua seeing them complained to Moses and urged that they be stopped. Moses mildly rebuked Joshua by saying that he wished all the "people were prophets and that the LORD would put his spirit upon them." No message is indicated as having been spoken either by the whole group of seventy or by Eldad and Medad.

### b. I SAMUEL 10:1–13

The second passage, I Samuel 10:1–13, involves the anointing of Saul by Samuel as Israel's first king and a resulting occasion of prophesying by Saul. Saul, while still a young man, along with his servant had come to Samuel to ask concerning lost donkeys. Samuel answered their question but, more important, anointed Saul as Israel's new ruler. Because of the importance of the act, and no doubt the apparent astonishment of Saul, Samuel further told the young man of three events that would befall him as he returned home. He implied that these occasions would provide assurance to Saul that the anointing had been authentic.

One of these events concerned Saul's encounter with "a company of prophets coming down from the high place with a psaltery, and a tabret, and a pipe, and a harp before them," who would be in the act of "prophesying" (*mithnabbe'im*, a participle, indicating continued action) at the time (10:5). Samuel further stated that the Spirit of the Lord would come upon Saul with the result that he also would "prophesy" (*hithnabbi'tha*) and "be turned into another man" (10:6). All three events did occur just as Samuel had predicted. Saul met the company of prophets, experienced the Spirit's coming upon him, and then did prophesy along with those he met (10:10). In doing this he exhibited a manner that was sufficiently different from what was normal for him that people looking on asked, "What is this that has come on the son of Kish? Is Saul also among the prophets?" (10:11).

### c. I SAMUEL 19:18–24

The third passage, I Samuel 19:18–24, also involves an occasion when Saul prophesied. By the time concerned he had served as king for most of his forty-year reign (Acts 13:21) and was engaged in efforts to kill David, whom he recognized as a rival to the throne. He learned that David had recently fled to Samuel at Ramah,[10] and he sent three different groups of messengers to apprehend and return David to him. None were successful because all three, on coming to David, found Samuel and a company of prophets engaged in

[10]Ramah is best identified with Er-Ram, five miles north of Jerusalem in Benjamin.

prophesying, and they successively experienced "the Spirit of God" coming on them and all joined in prophesying as well. Finally Saul himself went, in apparent disgust and anger, but on the way the "Spirit of God" came on him also and he began to "prophesy" (*yithnabbe'*) even before arriving at Ramah. Later he "stripped off his clothes" and "lay down naked all that day and all that night" (19:24).

## 2. Supporting passages

Besides these three main passages, a few others are appealed to as giving supporting evidence. It is believed that these show the word *prophesy* (*naba'*) carried a wider meaning than merely "to speak for God," and one which carried a significant relationship to the idea of ecstatic frenzy. Three passages are believed to manifest the meaning of *raving* and three the meaning of *madness*.

### a. THE RAVING PASSAGES

*1) I Samuel 18:10.* The first passage, I Samuel 18:10, again concerns Saul during the time when he made numerous attempts to kill David. In extreme anger one day, as the "evil spirit from God came upon" him, "he prophesied" (*yithnabbe'*) in the midst of his house as David played his instrument before him. The result was that Saul threw a javelin at the young man to take his life. Because of the situation and because no message from God was spoken by Saul, the implication is that this "prophesying" was an outburst of angry, raving emotion.

*2) I Kings 18:29.* The second passage, I Kings 18:29, concerns the frenzied activity of the prophets of Baal on Mount Carmel. Elijah had arranged a contest with them to prove that the God of Israel, rather than Baal, was the one true God. The issue concerned which God could send fire miraculously to set a sacrifice ablaze. In attempting to procure fire from Baal, these prophets "cried aloud, and cut themselves after their manner with knives and lancets," and "leaped upon the altar" (18:28, 26) but all without avail. In carrying on this activity, they are said to have "prophesied" (*mithnabbe'im*, participle). Since no message from Baal was spoken by them, the implication is quite clear again that this *raving* activity constituted the act of prophesying in reference.

*3) I Kings 22:10–12.* The third passage, I Kings 22:10–12, does not show the *raving* idea as clearly, but still it is often cited by adherents of the view. It concerns the occasion when four hundred prophets of Ahab are said to have "prophesied" before King Ahab and his guest, King Jehoshaphat of Judah. These prophets had been asked to discover God's will regarding a projected battle with the Aramaeans of Damascus at Ramoth-gilead. They replied, "Go up, go up; for the LORD shall deliver it into the hand of the king" (22:6). To give force to the message, one of the prophets, Zedekiah, "made him horns of iron: and he said, Thus saith the LORD, with these shalt thou push the Syrians until thou have consumed them" (22:11). At this, "all the prophets prophesied [*mithnabbe'im*, participle], Go up, go up to Ramoth-gilead and prosper: for the LORD shall deliver it unto the king's hand" (22:12).

The reason why this passage does not show the *raving* idea as clearly as the others is that a message was delivered this time. Though the action of one of these prophets, Zedekiah, in making iron horns, exhibited some emotional excess, it fell short of what Saul did before David or what the prophets demonstrated on Carmel. And no message was communicated either of those times. In this instance of Ahab's four hundred, the prophesying may have consisted in a united presentation of what was believed to be God's word to the two kings.[11] If so, there is no connotation of *raving* in the use of the word *prophesy* for this passage.

b. THE MADNESS PASSAGES

Three passages are cited which are believed to show that people considered prophets to be "madmen" (*meshugga'*). This is believed to support the idea of ecstaticism in that if prophets did not put on ecstatic displays as claimed, this would have made it natural for people to apply the idea of "madmen" to them. It is not nearly so clear in these passages, however, that the point intended is valid, for the passages all seem to indicate that only a few particularly characterized people considered prophets to be "madmen." This will be pointed out as we consider the passages.

*1) II Kings 9:1–12.*   The first passage, II Kings 9:1–12, concerns a young prophet in training that Elisha sent to anoint Jehu to be king of Israel. Jehoram was king of the land at the time, and Jehu was a captain in his army. Jehoram had just lost a battle with the Aramaeans of Damascus and he had returned wounded to Jezreel in Israel. Jehu was still with Israel's defeated army at Ramoth-gilead, where the battle had taken place. It was there that the young prophet found Jehu. He made his announcement to the captain and then quickly departed. Following this, one of Jehu's men asked Jehu, "Is

[11] Though the whole story reveals the message of these prophets was false, still they may have believed it to be true and presented it in this way.

all well?" and then added the significant words, "Wherefore came this mad fellow [*meshugga'*] to thee?" (9:11). Since the actions of the young prophet had been quite proper when he had been there, the characterization of him by this soldier as "mad fellow" must have resulted from the soldier's customary manner of thinking regarding prophets.

The weakness of the evidence here is that the person who called the young prophet a "mad fellow" was a soldier of the army. It is not uncommon for men of an army to have a distorted opinion of religious people, and therefore this man's opinion did not necessarily represent the thinking of people generally.

*2) Jeremiah 29:26.* The second passage, Jeremiah 29:26, concerns a letter written by one of the captives of Judah in Babylon, Shemaiah, which he sent to people in Jerusalem. Though the letter was sent to oppose Jeremiah's work there, Jeremiah evidently had seen a copy of it, and he speaks of its contents. Included in the contents, he says, was the derisive remark, "Every man that is mad [*meshugga'*] and maketh himself a prophet." This remark showed that the thinking of Shemaiah concerning prophets was that they were "madmen."

Once again a weakness in the evidence exists in that the letter showed only one man's opinion of prophets, and this man clearly was not a friend of prophets. His letter had been written to oppose Jeremiah, the leading prophet of the day and the one concerning whom the designation was primarily intended. Again, then, that a person like Shemaiah thought of Jeremiah and other prophets as "madmen" is insufficient to show that this thinking was general among the people.

*3) Hosea 9:7.* The third passage, Hosea 9:7, occurs in a context where Hosea is describing the wrong thinking of Israelites in his day. He speaks of the people as being unfaithful to their God (Hos. 9:1), and as he characterizes their thinking, he uses the statement, "The prophet is a fool, the spiritual man [*'ish ha-ruah*, 'man of the spirit'] is mad [*meshugga'*]." The parallelism employed in the statement has the force of saying that prophets, being men of the Spirit, were "madmen."

Though a much larger group of people is characterized this time as having such thinking regarding prophets, still the point in issue remains unproven. Hosea was intending to characterize the thinking of Israelites who were opposed to God and therefore opposed to those who represented God in their speaking. One cannot say, then, that because these people thought ill of prophets, therefore prophets were ecstatics who put on mad, emotionally charged demonstrations.

## B.  ARGUMENTS FOR ECSTATICISM

Adherents of the ecstatic view take their arguments mainly from the first three passages cited. These arguments may be grouped under seven heads.

### 1.  A comparison of religions

One argument is based simply on a comparison of Israel's religion with what was common in the world of the day, using these passages as a general basis. Israel had come to live among Canaanites, and Canaanites included ecstatic frenzy in their religious system. Because it is normal for a migrating people to be influenced by customs of people among whom they come to settle, it is thought to be logical that Israel would have experienced such an influence in this case. One should expect, therefore, that they came to accept ecstatic frenzy as a part of their religious system. In this line of thinking the two variant meanings noted for "to prophesy" are thought to be of special significance. It is believed that the idea of *raving* and the alleged idea of *madmen* are close to the thought of ecstatic frenzy and therefore make this additional meaning likely.

### 2.  Involvement of a Canaanite-type high place

A second argument concerns the involvement of a Canaanite-type high place in one of the three passages. The company of prophets Saul met on his return home after being anointed by Samuel was coming down from "the high place" (I Sam. 10:5). Such a high place (*bamah*) was Canaanite in background, and so it is logical to conclude that these prophets were influenced by Canaanite practice themselves, being associated with a Canaanite-type institution.

### 3.  Musical instruments

A third argument concerns the involvement of music in this same instance. It is stated that the company of prophets came down from the high place "with a psaltery, and a tabret, and a pipe, and a harp before them" (I Sam. 10:5). Music is known to have been employed in other countries as a way of inducing the ecstatic state, and so it was likely being used for the same purpose here.

An instance recorded in II Kings 3 is often noted in support of this contention. In the incident Elisha tells three kings, Jehoshaphat of Judah, Jehoram of Israel, and the king of Edom, that he will see if God will reveal to him how they may obtain water in their great need for it at the time. The point in issue is that he then asked that a minstrel be brought in before him. The assertion is made that the minstrel was to play music so that an ecstatic state might be engendered in Elisha, whereby he could receive the communication from God (II Kings 3:15).

## 4. Saul's being "turned into another man"

A fourth argument rests on Samuel's statement that Saul would "be turned into another man" (I Sam. 10:6) and on the later indication that, when Saul did meet the prophets and prophesied, he was changed so that onlookers were surprised at his conduct and asked if Saul was not "among the prophets" (I Sam. 10:11). Such a change, it is alleged, can be accounted for only if Saul became ecstatically frenzied. As R. B. Y. Scott says, the phrase "God gave him another heart" means "he became delirious."[12] It is believed that only such a delirious, ecstatic condition could have caused those who looked on to react in the way indicated.

## 5. Saul's lying in an apparent stupor many hours

A fifth argument is taken from Saul's later encounter with Samuel's prophets when David had fled to Ramah, as recorded in I Samuel 19. In that instance Saul not only prophesied but then removed at least a part of his clothing and lay in an apparent stupor all that day and all that night (19:24). Such an action, with this resulting state of stupor, is said to be in the pattern of other ecstatics of the time and is best explained, therefore, as a demonstration of ecstatic frenzy. Since the indication is given that Saul "prophesied" in connection with this action and that people again wondered regarding him following the incident, the "prophesying" must have once more been a display of ecstatic frenzy.

## 6. The prophesying of the seventy

A sixth argument is really a response to a possible objection to the viewpoint that Numbers 11 records an incident of ecstaticism. That incident,

---

[12] *The Relevance of the Prophets*, p. 47.

which involved the prophesying of the seventy elders in the wilderness, occurred long before Israel entered the land of Canaan and came under Canaanite influence. The objection in view is that if this prophesying occurred before the Canaanite influence had been experienced, the prophesying involved could not have been due to it. The response given by adherents of the view is that the story is couched in the language and concept of a much later day, when Canaanite influence had long been felt. Those who hold to the viewpoint that Israelite prophets were ecstatics are principally of the liberal, critical school who do not accept the idea of a Mosaic authorship of the Pentateuch. They believe that it was written by numerous authors from a comparatively late date in Israelite history, when Israel had been in the land of Canaan for many years. On this basis, it is alleged that the use of the term *prophesy* should be attributed to the concepts of these later writers rather than regarded as an indication of what really happened, though the writers probably thought that what they wrote did happen.

### 7. The involvement of the Spirit of God

A seventh argument is based upon the fact that the "Spirit of God" is mentioned in each of the main passages. The Spirit of God came upon the seventy in the wilderness and upon Saul in both I Samuel 10 and I Samuel 19. The argument is that this term *Spirit of God* referred to the power, attributed to the Deity, that brought on the state of ecstatic frenzy. In other words, the very fact that "Spirit of God" is found in these passages is in itself an indication that the ecstatic state was experienced by each of those involved.

### C. REFUTATION OF THE ARGUMENTS

Now that we have seen the principal arguments taken from these passages, it is appropriate to give response to them. The idea of ecstaticism among Israel's prophets is rejected by most conservative scholars. Accepting the position that the Old Testament is the product of supernatural revelation, they believe that prophets were especially called of God and given their messages by direct supernatural communication. They believe that the occasions when "a company of prophets" is mentioned do not reflect the idea of bands of ecstatic mad fellows, but, rather, groups of prophets in training looking forward to the prophetic ministry. These men when trained no doubt became individual proclaimers of God's message, even as other matured prophets. It is believed that prophets maintained their reason at all times in their work and were especially enabled for their task by the Spirit of God.

Admittedly, the passages noted present an unusual meaning for the word *prophesy* and call for careful consideration. Each passage, however, is subject to quite a different interpretation than what the adherents of the ecstatic view make of it. To show this to be true, it will be well first to give a refutation of the seven arguments noted and then to present a few counter-arguments in favor of the conservative position. The seven arguments will be taken up in the same order in which they were presented earlier.

## 1. A comparison of religions

The first argument depends for its validity on the extent to which Israel followed the religious customs of peoples of the day. It was observed in the preceding chapter that this was only in the broadest factors and not in detail. In respect to fundamentals of religion, Israelites who remained true to official Israelite religious practice did not borrow at all. They could not have done so because their official religion had been given to them even before they entered the land of Canaan. Moses, who died before Canaan was entered (Deut. 34:5–8), was the human instrument through whom God revealed His regulations on Mount Sinai. God did this so that the people would not later borrow the ideas of their Canaanite neighbors. Accordingly, the people were duly warned not to be influenced by them and even commanded to drive the Canaanites out of the land so this might be avoided. It is true that individual Israelites defected in some glaring ways from these fundamental regulations after entering the land, and in this respect some influence was exerted by the Canaanites. One must distinguish, however, between what was done by individual defecting Israelites, and what was official Israelite practice.

Actually the three main passages noted, when taken at face value (without restructuring their records to accord with liberal presuppositions), are in keeping with this viewpoint. This will appear as we proceed in our refutations. Regarding the fact that no messages from God are spoken in these passages when the word *prophesy* is used in them, one must say that the word does here carry a different meaning from what is normal for it. But that this variant meaning is "ecstaticism" does not necessarily follow. It could be something else and a suggestion as to what it is will be made shortly. Regarding the meanings *raving* and *madness*, the latter has already been shown to have little or no argumentative value for the position, and the former is not the same thing as ecstaticism. The relation the word as used in these passages carries to the basic meaning of "to prophesy" will be shown in a later chapter, when the meaning of this verb will be examined at greater length.

## 2. Involvement of a Canaanite-type high place

A Canaanite-type high place was involved at the time of Saul's first meeting with the company of prophets, and it is true that these centers of worship did come into Israel as a result of Canaanite influence. Accordingly, they are regularly disapproved in the Old Testament with the exception of one period of time. That was the period following the loss of the sanctuary at Shiloh[13] until the building of the Jerusalem temple by Solomon, during which time there was no official place of worship (I Kings 3:2). It was during this time when the incident here concerned occurred. Consequently, that prophets were coming down from such a high place at this time does not necessarily imply that they were Canaanite in type. Samuel, as is generally agreed, was not a Canaanite-type prophet, and during this period he even offered sacrifices at such high places (I Sam. 9:19).

## 3. Musical instruments

The prophets that Saul met coming down from this high place were playing musical instruments, and it is true that music was used in other countries to induce ecstasy. These prophets, however, need not be thought to have been using their instruments for this purpose. There may have been numerous other purposes for the music, and one will be suggested shortly which is in keeping with a nonecstatic type of explanation. In fact, the manner in which these musical instruments are mentioned suggests that they were not being used for an ecstatic purpose. The instruments are spoken of in connection with the prophets "coming down" from the high place as though they were being played as the prophets walked down from this location. Music that produces ecstasy, however, is not played while one walks along; it is a very particular type of music, with designed rhythm and beat, that is played while a person dances in long, repeated movements. Martin Buber recognizes the inconsistency in this argument as he speaks of this very passage:

> [Ecstasy] is not stirred up in a people of early culture by such acts as these, but by an enthusiastic singing of monotonous songs. Truly such singing is ecstatic, but it is also bound up with a strict rhythm and is accompanied by rhythmic movements of all its members.[14]

---

[13]The tabernacle was moved from Shiloh to Nob (I Sam. 21:1), apparently shortly after the ark had been taken from the tabernacle to the battle at Aphek, when it was lost to the Philistines (I Sam. 4:1–11).

[14]*The Prophetic Faith*, p. 63.

A similar observation may be made regarding the instance of Elisha in II Kings 3. There he asks for a minstrel to be brought in before him as he seeks out the mind of God. One minstrel (the word[15] refers to a person who plays a stringed instrument) could hardly stir up a type of music to induce an ecstatic state. If that had been Elisha's thinking, he would have asked for a number of musicians. Rather, the thought is that Elisha wanted the minstrel to play soothing music so that his mind might be cleared and his heart laid open to a possible revelation from God. Apparently, the visit of the three kings had been disturbing and had given him a mental attitude which was not conducive to contact from God. It is a recognized psychological fact that the state of ecstatic frenzy can be achieved only when a participant is sympathetic to the idea of becoming so engaged. The person has to want to be an ecstatic and even to work diligently to achieve the state. It is really not easy to do this, and many people cannot do it at all. Needless to say, neither Saul, as he met this company of prophets, nor Elisha, as he listened to the soothing music of a single minstrel, give any indication of putting forth effort to becoming ecstatically frenzied.

### 4. Saul's being "turned into another man"

When Samuel foretold Saul's encounter with the prophets, he said that Saul would then be "turned into another man." Two factors, however, stand opposed to the idea that this was a prediction of ecstaticism on Saul's part.

First, Samuel was the one who gave the prediction, and in doing so, he implied approval. But this would be directly at variance with the anti-Canaanite attitude of Samuel. His ministry was characterized all through life by urging Israelites to forsake Canaanite Baal worship and return to a true faith in Israel's God (e.g., I Sam. 7:3, 4). One finds it difficult to think of Samuel favorably predicting that Saul would become ecstatically frenzied to the point of becoming "another man." He must have had some other thought in mind, and the nature of that thought constitutes the basis of the second factor.

This second factor is that it is logical to connect Samuel's prediction regarding Saul with a similar notice in I Samuel 10:9 that "God gave him another heart." This notice, however, does not suggest a loss of self-control in ecstaticism. Rather, "another heart" speaks of a new attitude, a new emotional outlook on life. And this thought fits well into the story as a whole. Saul had expressed hesitation about going to see Samuel (I Sam. 9:5–10),

---

[15] It is *nagan*, used fourteen times in the Old Testament with twelve definitely referring to a player of stringed instruments, and the other two possibly (Ps. 68:25; Ezek. 33:32).

which suggests a lack of self-confidence on his part (cf. I Sam. 10:22). But now Samuel had just anointed the young man to be Israel's first king and this called for marked confidence. No doubt, a first objection that came to Saul's mind concerned the fact of his timidity, and Samuel realized it. Accordingly, there was need for Saul to experience a change in this regard, and this was the change he underwent when he received "another heart." The change apparently was so pronounced that when onlookers saw the young man—whom they otherwise knew to be timid—actually engaging in the activity of prophesying with the company of prophets, they were amazed and wondered if Saul was also among the prophets.

This change quite clearly was effected by the Spirit of God coming on Saul (I Sam. 10:10), a matter to be studied in chapter 6. Apparently the change was only temporary at this time, however—anticipatory in force, then, to when he would actually become king—because the same timidity was shown later when Saul was selected by God in the presence of Israel's elders. He was found hidden "among the stuff" (I Sam. 10:21, 22). The change did not yet need to be permanent at this early time, for Saul would not become actual king for several months. The Spirit apparently came on him in a permanent way just before the Jabesh-gilead battle (I Sam. 11:6), following which he did become Israel's king (I Sam. 11:15).

### 5. Saul's lying in a stupor many hours

In Saul's second encounter with a prophetic group, he not only prophesied but then partially disrobed[16] and lay in an apparent stupor many hours. One must say that such conduct indicates an aspect of lack in self-control. A normal person does not act in this way. But two factors again show that this abnormal action was not the result of self-induced ecstasy.

The first is that Saul alone, of all who prophesied at the time, experienced this response. Many others also prophesied. This included the prophetic group in attendance and the three groups of messengers that Saul had earlier sent to apprehend David (I Sam. 19:20, 21). At least some of these partially disrobed as well, for the word *also* (*gam*) is used of Saul's action at this time (I Sam. 19:24), but it is quite clear that none of the others lay in a stupor. The comment of astonishment by onlookers also concerned Saul alone. If Saul's response of stupor was a result of ecstatic display, the ques-

---

[16]This disrobing probably did not involve complete nudity. In such prophesying activity, ease of movement was likely desirable. This could have been achieved by removing the cumbersome outer robe. The word *naked* (*'arom*) can mean merely partially clothed; see Job 22:6; 24:7, 10; Isa. 58:7.

tion is quite pertinent why others who prophesied and partially disrobed did not act in the same way. One is thus left to look for another reason for Saul's individual action, a reason that had to do with him alone.

The second factor is that Saul was a most unlikely prospect for an experience of ecstatic frenzy at this time. It has already been noted that the state of ecstasy is not easily achieved, and one must not only be sympathetic to the idea but actually work at becoming thus frenzied to achieve the state. In this instance, however, Saul not only did not work at becoming an ecstatic but he was not in the least sympathetic to the idea. He came actually in a state of anger and frustration that three messenger groups had not been able to apprehend David. As he came, then, he was thinking only of taking the young man and of dealing with him most harshly; he was not thinking about becoming an ecstatic. Another reason, therefore, must exist both for his prophesying at all and for the resulting stupor. There is one, and it will be presented later, in chapter 6.

### 6. The prophesying of the seventy

Nothing in addition to matters noted when argument (6) was presented above needs to be added here. In order to account for the idea of ecstasy being involved in a story this early in Israel's history, adherents of the view have to deny Mosaic authorship of the Pentateuch.[17] No conservative scholar, however, will admit to this denial of biblical, supernatural inspiration.

### 7. The involvement of the Spirit of God

The Spirit of God is said to have come upon participants in each of the three passages concerned, and it is believed this is further evidence that each involved ecstaticism. However, this thought follows only if one interprets the phrase "Spirit of God" as adherents of the view do. They believe it means the divine power to make a person ecstatic. But this view is not the presentation of the Bible. The Spirit of God is the Third Person of the Godhead, who in these instances supernaturally enabled the participants to do things they could not, or would not, have done of themselves. When this viewpoint is accepted, no evidence for ecstaticism remains in the argument.

[17]For a typical presentation, see Lindblom, *Prophecy in Ancient Israel*, pp. 100–102.

## D. COUNTERARGUMENTS

It is now appropriate to move on from refuting arguments to presenting positive evidence in favor of a viewpoint in keeping with the biblical presentation.

### 1. The basic meaning of "to prophesy"

Adherents of the ecstatic viewpoint base their thinking on the belief that "to prophesy" could mean—if it did not commonly mean—to become ecstatically frenzied. Therefore, whenever the term is found in a passage where any hint of a possibility of such activity is present at all, the conclusion is made that ecstatic frenzy is the thought involved. When the term is studied in its numerous scriptural contexts, however, the evidence is very clear that its basic meaning is something quite at variance with the idea of ecstasy. This will be investigated in some detail in chapter 4. For now it is sufficient merely to say that to presume the meaning of ecstatic frenzy, on the basis that this was a common if not a fundamental meaning of the term, is not at all warranted.

### 2. Israel's resistance to Canaanite influence

Though liberal scholars of a past generation were ready to say that Israel was greatly influenced by Canaanite culture, this is not the most accepted view of recent time. For instance, in 1910, J. M. P. Smith wrote, "It is now generally recognized that not a single institution of Israel's life was exclusively Hebraic."[18] Or W. C. Graham as late as 1931 stated, "Little by little, in the long process of settlement, they [the Israelites] became in all but name Canaanites."[19] In contrast, William F. Albright writing in 1938 said, "Every fresh publication of Canaanite mythological texts makes the gulf between the religion of Canaan and Israel increasingly clear."[20] A main reason for this change in viewpoint is that archaeological research has not borne out the older ideas. Layers of excavated tells, dating to Israelite times, do not show the kind of dependence on Canaan that liberals formerly assumed.

That Israel was not influenced more by Canaanite ways means that

---

[18]"Semitic Prophecy," reprint from *The Biblical World*, 35 (1910):233.

[19]"The Religion of the Hebrews," *Journal of Religion*, 11 (1931):244.

[20]"Recent Progress in North Canaanite Research," *Bulletin of the American Schools of Oriental Research*, 70 (1938):24; see also G. Ernest Wright, *The Old Testament Against Its Environment*, p. 74.

strong factors of resistance had to exist among the people against such influence; for it is common knowledge that a migrating people, like Israel under Moses, is normally influenced in a major way by the culture of the people among which it settles. This is even more true if the native populace is substantially advanced in material culture over the migrators, and excavation has shown that this was the case in respect to the Canaanites and Israel. Canaanites were highly advanced in their day, showing strong cities, fine tools, and excellent pottery. Israel, on the other hand, was fresh from a life in the wilderness, where the people did not have to build cities or grow crops. This latter was true because they had been fed manna during the wilderness days, miraculously at the hand of God. Furthermore, a new generation now lived who had not known even the former ways learned in Egypt. During the forty years of wandering, the older generation had died as a punishment from God for rebellion shown at Kadesh-barnea (Num. 14:23). This new generation, then, was far less knowledgeable of technical skills than were the Canaanites among whom they came to settle.

The Israelite tribes had only a minimum of civil government to provide resistance.[21] They did, however, have a well-developed religious system. The most probable resistance factor to account for the comparatively little influence experienced, then, would have been religious in kind. The priests certainly played a major role, being scattered in forty-eight cities conveniently located near the people for grass-roots contact. Another religious office was that of the prophet, and it is unthinkable that God would have permitted him a message different from that of the priests. Prophets, then, must also have provided resistance to Canaanite influence and therefore were not Canaanite in either their origin or practice.[22]

## 3. "To praise" as a meaning of the term *prophesy*

The main question in issue concerns the meaning of "to prophesy" as used in the three main passages concerned. It is true that in none of the three is a message spoken for God, and the basic meaning of "to speak for God" cannot apply. The question then is: What was the meaning, if it was not ecstatic frenzy?

The answer is well illustrated in I Chronicles 25:1–3. Here the meaning "to praise" is ascribed to the term. In this passage, David is depicted as selecting certain people to lead in praising activity at the house of God. In

[21]They had no king, nor even a head of each tribe, but only elders serving in local communities and certain judicial officials (Num. 11:16, 17; Deut. 16:18; 17:8f.; 19:12).

[22]See Walter Eichrodt, *Theology of the Old Testament*, pp. 328–329, where he voices the same idea.

verse 1 of the passage, the sons of Asaph, Heman, and Jeduthun are selected, men "who should prophesy [*nebbe'im*] with harps, with psalteries, and with cymbals." Then in verse 2, other men are indicated as selected, and they too are said to be those "which prophesied [*nibba'*] according to the order of the king." And in verse 3, still other men are selected and of them the significant indication is given, "who prophesied [*nibba'*] with a harp, to give thanks and to praise the LORD." The prophesying activity of these men, then—all of whom were classified as Levitic singers—consisted in rendering praise to God as they employed harps, psalteries, and cymbals for accompaniment to their singing.

Associating this meaning with the three passages concerned, one finds it fitting very well. In the instance of the seventy who were selected to help Moses in the wilderness, the thought would be that they began to render praise to God when the Spirit was placed upon them. Such praise would have had no direct relationship to their intended task of aiding Moses, but it would have been a natural response in view of being freshly empowered by God's Spirit. This praise was probably in the form of one or more songs sung, as the songs came to their minds and seemed fitting in view of the gracious blessing of God in selecting them for the important work. That two of the number, Eldad and Medad, continued to render praise, when the others had ceased, is not strange. They probably enjoyed singing and perhaps were given to more exuberance in their joy than were the others.

In the first of the two instances regarding Saul (I Sam. 10), the thought would be that the company of prophets, coming down from the high place with musical instruments, were again engaged in praising God. Edward J. Young suggests that they may have "been to Gibeah upon pilgrimage."[23] This is possible, but they may also have just been dismissed from a class session at the high place, for these were prophets in training and they could have been using the high place as a location for meeting. This would account for Samuel's knowing ahead of time that they would be so engaged when Saul met them. In any event, they apparently had the custom of singing as they walked along to their place of residence. Then when Saul did come upon them, the thought would be that he joined in praiseful singing with them. The change manifested in his doing this would have been a sharp contrast to his otherwise timid nature, for he did not ordinarily engage in this form of outgoing activity.

In the second of the two instances regarding Saul (I Sam. 19), the thought would be similar. Here, however, the first to become involved in rendering praise would have been the three groups of messengers sent by Saul to apprehend David. Coming to where the young prophets were en-

[23]*My Servants the Prophets*, p. 85.

gaged in a song fest and experiencing the influence of the Spirit of God coming upon them, each group in turn joined in singing with the prophets. The total group would have made a substantial choir by the time Saul arrived. That Saul himself, being in a disgruntled state of mind, should have joined in singing praise is admittedly difficult to understand. It is not as difficult as accounting for his becoming ecstatically frenzied, however. The scriptural text accounts for his joining in praise on the basis of the Spirit of God coming upon him. The significance of this, as well as an explanation for his lying down in a type of stupor for many hours following, will be discussed in chapter 6.

Attention should still be called to two other passages that are cited by some adherents of the ecstatic view, though neither passage mentions the idea of prophesying. One is I Kings 18:46, where Elijah is described as running before Ahab's chariot all the way from Mount Carmel to Jezreel. The occasion followed directly after Elijah's contest with the 450 prophets of Baal on Mount Carmel. The other passage is II Kings 8:7-13, which gives the account of Elisha predicting Hazael's reign over Syria. At the time, the prophet wept for he said he knew "the evil" that Hazael would do unto the children of Israel. Lindblom, who distinguishes between what he calls "orgiastic" ecstasy and "passive" ecstasy believes the first occasion was an instance of the former and the second of the latter.[24] By orgiastic ecstasy he means the type of ecstatic frenzy that has already been described. By passive ecstasy he means an abnormal state of concentration in which one becomes intensely absorbed in an idea or feeling so that "the normal stream of cyclical life is more or less arrested" and a trancelike state is achieved.[25] Lindblom believes that most of the early prophets experienced orgiastic ecstasy and most of the latter passive ecstasy.

Lindblom thinks that Elijah, running before Ahab's chariot, presents a case of the former, for it is said that "the hand of the LORD" was upon him. Lindblom sees this phrase as "an expression of an ecstatic fit."[26] He believes that the phrases "hand of the LORD" and "Spirit of the LORD" are quite synonymous in meaning.[27] Lindblom thinks the case of Elisha with Hazael is of the latter type, because neither of these expressions is there used nor is the term *prophesy*. Elisha simply predicted that Hazael would be the next king, and Lindblom believes this came as a result of an intense concentration upon the subject so that, through a trancelike inspiration, he was able to produce the prediction.

A response to this theory is not difficult, when one takes the text at face

[24]*Prophecy in Ancient Israel*, pp. 4-5, 48, 106.
[25]Ibid., p. 4.
[26]Ibid., p. 48.
[27]Ibid., p. 174.

value. That the "hand of the LORD" came upon Elijah in no way has to mean that he became ecstatically frenzied. The phrase "hand of the LORD" means simply that God supernaturally empowered Elijah to make the strenuous run. Elijah had experienced an exhausting day and needed special strength in order to accomplish the feat, and God gave it. As to Elisha, the fact that he was able to predict Hazael's reign was again due to a supernatural provision by God. God informed him that Hazael would be Syria's next king, and Elisha passed this information on to Hazael. There is no reason to think in terms of ecstasy, whether conceived of as orgiastic or passive. The problem is really whether or not a person will accept the idea of supernatural intervention by God. If he does, he has no problem in taking these passages at face value without inserting some idea of ecstatic frenzy.

# 4

# The Meaning of "To Prophesy"

The discussion of the prior two chapters has sought to show the uniqueness of Israel's prophets in their day. Countries round about Israel did have prophets of a kind, but their work really did not parallel those of Israel nor were they nearly as many in number. Their functions, including that of ecstatic frenzy, simply were not those of Israel's prophets. The great proclaimers from Israel stand out in marked uniqueness from all others of their time.

It is now appropriate to move on to direct consideration of the work these individuals performed. A first matter concerns the meaning of the term *prophesy*. It has been observed that it did not mean to become ecstatically frenzied. This leaves the question of what it did mean. It is well to begin with a study of the terms used in the Old Testament to designate prophets. There are several of these with one being employed much more than the others. We will begin with those used less frequently and then come to the principal one.

## A. MINOR DESIGNATIONS FOR THE PROPHETS

### 1. *Ro'eh* and *hozeh*

The first two terms to notice are *ro'eh* and *hozeh*. The first is used only twelve times in the Old Testament and the second eighteen. This is far less than the number in which the principal term *nabhi'* is employed. Still the two terms carry a particular importance and call for study.

Both terms are participles and come from verbs which are practically synonymous. The first comes from *ra'ah* and the second from *hazah*, both of which mean "to see." The participles mean "one who sees" or, as translated commonly in the Old Testament, "seer." For instance, Saul and his servant used this term for Samuel; approaching the city of the great prophet, they asked a maiden, "Is the seer here?" (I Sam. 9:11).

Since both terms mean the same thing, the question arises as to why both were used. Morris Jastrow suggests that the *ro'eh* may have been a "seer" for anyone, while the *hozeh* was "more specifically the official diviner of the court."[1] There may be some truth to this, but a more basic distinction is likely found in respect to the time when each of these terms was commonly used. Both did have their respective periods of popularity: *ro'eh* in the time of Samuel with eight of the twelve occurrences coming then,[2] and *hozeh* in the day of David, with four of the seven persons so designated living in his time.[3] Further support for the thought that a name change occurred with the passage of time is found in I Samuel 9:9, which reads, "Beforetime in Israel, when a man went to enquire of God, thus he spake, Come, and let us go to the seer: for he that is now called a Prophet was beforetime called a Seer." This verse says specifically that the term *seer* (*ro'eh*) did change in popular usage to become *nabhi'*. It is true that the term *hozeh* does not appear here, but if there was a change from *ro'eh* to *nabhi'*, there could well have been a change also from *ro'eh* to *hozeh*.

A word is also in order as to an alleged relationship between this *ro'eh-hozeh* person and the Babylonian *Baru*. The *Baru* was referred to in chapter 2 as a priest of divination in Mesopotamia. The term *Baru* also means "seer." Accordingly, Jastrow believes that the Israelite *ro'eh-hozeh* was basically the same in function as the *Baru*, which he believes was inspecting "something with a view to obtaining an answer to a given question."[4] In other words, he believes that the *ro'eh-hozeh* was basically a diviner like the *Baru*. There is, however, no evidence in the Old Testament to this effect. On the contrary, in the instance of Saul and his servant coming to ask Samuel regarding lost donkeys, Samuel not only did not consult any physical instrument of divination, but he received his information regarding Saul directly from God (I Sam. 9:15, 17). Samuel, it should be realized, is thought to have been a typical seer of the time. If then he did not use divination, it is in no way likely that others did, and it may be added that no others to whom the term is

---

[1]Morris Jastrow, "*Ro'eh* and *Hozeh* in the Old Testament," *Journal of Biblical Literature*, 28 (1909):52.

[2]All eight are applied to Samuel himself. After him Zadok is once so called (II Sam. 15:27), Hanani twice (II Chron. 16:7, 10), and once the term is used generally (Isa. 30:10).

[3]The four are: Gad (II Sam. 24:11), Heman (I Chron. 25:5), Asaph (II Chron. 29:30), and Jeduthun (II Chron. 35:15). Later individuals called by the term are: Iddo (II Chron. 12:15), Hanani (II Chron. 19:2), and Amos (Amos 7:12).

[4]"*Ro'eh* and *Hozeh*," pp. 46-47.

applied ever consulted any instruments. The term when applied to them simply means that they were considered discerners of the will of God, who could relay that information to people.

From the point of view of the Old Testament, it is more important to observe the relationship between this *ro'eh-hozeh* person and the high priest in his use of the Urim and Thummim. The Urim and Thummim was a device which God gave to the high priest for making enquiry concerning God's will in respect to specific questions (Exod. 28:30; Num. 27:21). Thus in a sense the high priest in using this device was also a "seer," that is, he was able to discern the will of God.

However, at least three distinctions between the activities of the high priest and the *ro'eh-hozeh* person may be pointed out. The first is that the Urim and Thummim constituted a physical device by which enquiry could be made. This is indicated by the fact that it was kept in the "breastplate" of the ephod of the high priest (Exod. 28:30). The *ro'eh-hozeh* person is never described as having any such device. Second, because of having this device, the high priest could initiate a time of revelation, though indeed God might not answer, as was the case with Saul on one occasion (I Sam. 28:6). On the other hand, the *ro'eh-hozeh* is never depicted as initiating a time of revelation. Third, the questions posed by the high priest were always in connection with official business in Israel (see Num. 27:21; Josh. 7:16–18; 9:14; I Sam. 14:18, 19). The *ro'eh-hozeh*, however, would ask questions regarding almost any important topic, as for instance the matter of Saul's lost animals.

## 2. Man of God

A third designation is simply "man of God" (*'ish elohim*). It is used, for instance, of the man who came to denounce the false altar of Bethel, and was later detained by the old prophet of Bethel (I Kings 13). Its significance is merely to point the man out as one who knew God and was sent by God on a particular mission. The term is also used of prophets who are otherwise well known by name (for instance, Moses, Deut. 33:1; Samuel, I Sam. 9:6; Elisha, II Kings 4:9).

## B.  *NABHI'*

### 1. Etymology

It has been observed that the principal word for prophet is *nabhi'*. It is used in its noun form alone nearly three hundred times and it is related closely to the verb *nabha'*, which is used approximately three hundred more times. It is found throughout the Old Testament. Our first consideration concerns the meaning of the word. A determination of the meaning of the earlier terms was not found difficult, but the same is not true regarding this one.

Many suggestions have been made as to the etymology of *nabha'*. Gesenius finds it in *nabha'*, meaning to "bubble up."[5] He sees this concept in keeping with ecstatic behavior on the part of the prophets in which their emotional fervor bubbled up within them. Theophile Meek says the verb should be linked to the Akkadian *nabu*, meaning in its active voice "to speak," thus giving the idea, "speaker."[6] He is followed in this by Aubrey Johnson[7] and by R. B. Y. Scott.[8] William F. Albright also favors an Akkadian root but says that, since *nabu* is commonly used in the passive voice, this is the sense that should be taken for the etymology of *nabhi'*. This gives the meaning of "one spoken to" or "called," thus stressing the person's call to service.[9] He is followed in this by H. H. Rowley.[10] Others have seen a relationship to the Arabic *naba'a*, meaning "to announce," or to the Assyrian god Nebo, who is then thought of as "speaker," or even the Hebrew root *bo'*, meaning "to come" or "to enter in."[11] It thus becomes apparent that etymology alone is not conclusive. What is more important, therefore, is the meaning ascribed to the term in the Old Testament.

## 2. Usage in the Old Testament

Because *nabhi'* is used so frequently in the Old Testament, one might appeal to a large number of places to show its basic meaning. There are a few passages, however, which are particularly helpful and our discussion will be confined to them.

One of the most significant is Exodus 7:1. To see its significance one must consider it in the light of Exodus 4:10-16. Here Moses objects to God's call for him to return to Egypt, claiming among other things incapability of speech. To this God first responds by reminding Moses that He has made man's mouth and so can enable Moses in his speaking. When Moses still objects, God says that He will instruct Aaron, Moses' brother, to speak for

[5] *Hebrew and Chaldee Lexicon* (translator, Tregelles), p. 525.
[6] *Hebrew Origins*, p. 147.
[7] *The Cultic Prophet in Ancient Israel*, p. 213.
[8] *The Relevance of the Prophets*, p. 45.
[9] *From the Stone Age to Christianity*, p. 231.
[10] *Prophecy and Religion in Ancient China and Israel*, p. 4.
[11] Cf. Rowley, *The Servant of the Lord and Other Essays on the Old Testament*, p. 97; also Geerhardus Vos, *Biblical Theology*, pp. 209-210.

him. He emphasizes this by adding, "He shall be thy spokesman unto the people; and he shall be, even he shall be to thee instead of a mouth, and thou shalt be to him instead of God" (4:16). So, then, there would be a relation between Moses and Aaron like that between God and a spokesman for Him, with this spokesman being characterized as a "mouth."[12] And then in 7:1 God speaks of Aaron, in this relationship to Moses, as Moses' *nabhi'*, saying, "And Aaron thy brother shall be thy prophet [*nabhi'*]." Thus a *nabhi'* was one who spoke in the place of another. Norman Gottwald, after commenting on this verse, concludes, "The pith of Hebrew prophecy is not prediction or social reform but the declaration of divine will."[13]

We have already referred to another key passage—Deuteronomy 18:15–22. Here Moses promises that God would raise up a prophet like unto himself for the people. It would be to this person that people should look for information rather than to the various forms of divination listed in earlier verses. Then, in verse 18, the words of God Himself are given, "I will raise them up a Prophet from among their brethren like unto thee [Moses], and will put my words in his mouth; and he shall speak unto them all that I shall command him." Again, the task of the prophets is indicated as speaking the words of God.

A third classic text is Amos 7:12–16. Here Amos is at Bethel in Israel, speaking against the false altar which Jeroboam had erected. Amaziah, the Bethel priest, encounters the prophet and says, "Oh thou seer, go, flee thee away into the land of Judah and there eat bread and prophesy there: but prophesy not again any more at Bethel; for it is the king's sanctuary and it is the king's court." To this Amos replies, "I was no prophet, neither was I a prophet's son; but I was an herdman, and a gatherer of sycamore fruit: and the LORD took me as I followed the people, and the LORD said unto me, Go, prophesy unto my people Israel." The point concerns the significant usage of the verb *prophesy*. Amaziah urges Amos not to "prophesy" any more at Bethel, and Amos in turn says that God had sent him to Israel in order to "prophesy." Thus what he had been doing at Bethel, and motivated Amaziah's rebuke, was "prophesying." And what this had been of course was speaking God's message.[14]

A fourth indication may be taken from the nature of the assignment given to prophets at the time of their call. Isaiah was instructed: "Go, and tell

---

[12]The idea of "mouth" as applied to God is mentioned by the later prophets. For instance, Jeremiah says that the false prophets of his day are those who do not speak out of the "mouth of the LORD" (23:16). And Ezekiel speaks of himself as "a watchman unto the house of Israel," to whom the Lord says, "Hear the word at my mouth" (3:17).

[13]*A Light to the Nations*, p. 277.

[14]It is recognized that a broad difference of opinion exists relative to Amos' statement that he was "no prophet," but this does not bear upon the point in issue here. The matter will be taken up when Amos as a person is discussed in Part Two of this book.

this people" (Isa. 6:9). God told Jeremiah: "Go to all that I shall send thee, and whatsoever I command thee thou shalt speak" (Jer. 1:7). And to Ezekiel the command was: "I send thee unto the children of Israel . . . and thou shalt say unto them" (Ezek. 2:3, 4). The same type of command was given again and again to prophets when summoned to service.

And fifth, it is of significance that whenever prophets are depicted as either being given assignments or carrying them out, the thought is always centered in speaking God's message.

The basic idea of the word, therefore, is established beyond question: it is "speaker for God." It may well be, then, that this meaning came etymologically from the Akkadian word *nabu* ("to speak") when taken in its active sense. At least the basic meaning in the Old Testament is beyond question, and it should be realized that this meaning is observed in the vast majority of instances. As indicated in prior chapters, the few exceptions that exist are the passages to which adherents of ecstatic frenzy appeal. It is hardly proper, however, to base a viewpoint on these few occurrences when the preponderance of passages indicate the meaning very clearly.

## C. THE SIGNIFICANCE OF THE MINOR MEANINGS

Since these few passages do exist, however, in which the minor meanings noted in prior chapters are set forth, it is appropriate to relate these meanings to the principal meaning. If the word could be used in the sense of these other meanings at all, they must give some color to the basic meaning; for, if the basic meaning as such was all that the word could mean, even the few occurrences could not exist. The question then is: What do these few variant meanings indicate by way of an additional idea to the basic thought, "to speak for God"?

Two variant meanings were established in the prior discussion: *raving* and *praising*. A third, *madness*, was found doubtful. Thus, more specifically, the question concerns what these two meanings have in common with the main meaning that will give a full-orbed idea to the concept *to prophesy*.

The answer is not difficult. The two variant meanings—or even the third one if a person should insist upon it—have a common denominator in the idea of emotional fervor. When Saul *raved* in his palace and threw the spear at David, he was emotionally disturbed. The thought, no doubt, is that he became intensely angry and shouted in a violent way. The idea *praising* is also an emotional concept. When one praises he does so with a heart that is stirred. In the occasions noted, each of the participants who were praising God were doing so with fervent emotional involvement. Even the idea of *madness* suggests one who is emotionally distraught. Thus, the idea of emotional involvement must be added to the principal idea of speaking for God, and the two go together very well. A prophet was one who should speak for God with strong emotional involvement, and indeed the prophets did so. They were not merely to give recitations; they were to bring vital messages that would change lives. This called for speaking fervently. Thus the conclusion seems well established that "to prophesy" in its fullest significance meant "to speak fervently for God."

## D. RELATION OF THE *RO'EH-HOZEH* TO THE *NABHI'*

It is appropriate now to make a comparison between the *ro'eh-hozeh* person and the *nabhi'*. In terms of basic idea, a distinction does exist. Since both words, *ro'eh* and *hozeh*, mean "to see," the fundamental thought signified by them concerns insight regarding God's will. In other words, these terms refer to the revelational aspect of the prophets' work, when they heard from God and discerned His will. On the other hand, *nabhi'*, as just indicated, refers to the speaking of the prophets, when they would give forth the information that God had previously given at the time of revelation. The terms *ro'eh-hozeh*, then, refer to the reception of the message, and the term *nabhi* to the giving forth of the message.

No distinction need be made as to the office held by those designated by these terms, however. The designations simply referred to the same person from two different points of view. The same person might be called by any of the three terms.

Some scholars have attempted to point out a difference in office, however. Such distinctions as the following have been noted: first, that the *ro'eh-hozeh* was a nonecstatic diviner while the *nabhi'* was a frenzied ecstatic; second, the former worked alone while the latter worked in groups; third, the former waited for people to consult him, while the latter spoke readily wherever opportunity presented itself.[15] H. H. Rowley, speaking of these distinctions, states that "all these neat divisions break down" when the passages themselves are studied.[16] One way he shows this is by noting that a few persons are actually called by both terms, *nabhi'* and *hozeh*, including the important representatives Gad, Iddo, and especially Amos.[17]

Moreover, these distinctions are based on insufficient evidence. Regard-

[15]For instance, Theodore H. Robinson, *Prophecy and the Prophets in Ancient Israel*, pp. 28–29; also Jastrow, *"Ro'eh* and *Hozeh,"* p. 56.
[16]*The Rediscovery of the Old Testament*, p. 137.
[17]Gad in I Sam. 22:5; II Sam. 24:11; I Chron. 21:9; II Chron. 29:25; Iddo in II Chron. 9:29; 12:15; 13:22; Amos, one of the great writing prophets, in Amos 7:12.

ing the *ro'eh-hozeh* using divination, evidence has already been found lacking. Never is anyone who is called by either term depicted as using divination in any form. Regarding the second distinction (the *ro'eh-hozeh* works alone and the *nabhi'* in groups) the argument rests mainly on the contrast between the groups of prophets of Samuel's day and Samuel himself, who was alone when he was consulted by Saul. It is clearly stated, however, that Samuel was the head of these very groups (I Sam. 19:20) and, accordingly, identified with them; indeed, he is himself called a *nabhi'* (I Sam. 3:20). And regarding the third distinction (the *ro'eh-hozeh* waits for consultation, while the *nabhi'* does not), this thought is taken again from Samuel's being consulted by Saul. But elsewhere it is stated that Samuel also moved about in his work—for instance, he led in the Mizpeh revival (I Sam. 7:1–14); he made a regular circuit (I Sam. 7:16, 17); he anointed and later rebuked Saul (I Sam. 10:1–25; 13:10f.; 15:1f.); and he anointed David (I Sam. 16:1–13). It appears that these distinctions are based more on theoretical conjecture than on solid evidence from Scripture.

It is appropriate also to notice again I Samuel 9:9, where it is directly stated, "He that is now called a Prophet was beforetime called a Seer." The thought is that the person who was called a "seer" (*ro'eh*) in the time of Samuel came later to be called "prophet" (*nabhi'*) in the time when I Samuel was written. Thus this verse identifies the two terms and indicates that only a change in name had occurred.

A word of caution is necessary in respect to this change in terminology, however. The name *nabhi'* did not begin to be used only after Samuel's day, for Samuel himself is called a *nabhi'* (I Sam. 3:20), and he used the term in speaking to Saul (I Sam. 10:5). Indeed, Moses already in his day used the term in respect to himself (Deut. 18:15). The thought is that the term in popular usage changed.[18] It was more customary for people to say *ro'eh* in Samuel's day, though *nabhi'* might be used, and *nabhi'* in the later day of the author of I Samuel.

Further evidence that no distinction need be made as to office between the *ro'eh-hozeh* person and the *nabhi'* is found in Isaiah 30:9,10. The passage reads: "That this is a rebellious people, lying children, children that will not hear the law of the LORD: which say to the seers, See not; and to the prophets, Prophesy not unto us right things, speak unto us smooth things, prophesy deceits." Here the sinful people of Judah are depicted as bidding the prophets not to speak unto them "right things" but "smooth things" and "deceits." In other words, the people wanted the prophets to speak in a way which pleased them rather than in a way which brought sin to remembrance. The point to notice is that the activity in mind is "speaking," whether it concerned right

[18]See Edward J. Young, *My Servants the Prophets*, pp. 63–64.

things or wrong things, and that the term employed for the prophets is not *nabhi'*. In fact it is both of the other terms, *ro'eh* and *hozeh*, the term *ro'eh* being translated "seer" and the term *hozeh* "prophet." So then the *ro'eh-hozeh* could be thought of as one who spoke for God just as well as one who received messages from God. In other words he could be thought of as doing the very same thing as the *nabhi'*.

# 5

# The Function of the Prophet

Our interest now turns to the function or work of the prophet in Israel. The prior chapter has indicated that it consisted basically of two parts: to receive revelation from God and to speak forth the message God had given.[1] Both parts of this activity need to be enlarged upon. This chapter concentrates on speaking the message; the following chapter is concerned with receiving it.

## A. METHOD

### 1. Preaching

The manner of speaking by the prophet may be best characterized as *preaching*. Here the idea of preaching is used as over against the idea of teaching. In teaching one addresses primarily the mind of the hearer, while in preaching he addresses the emotion and will. The interest of teaching is to

[1]Cf. J. Lindblom, *Prophecy in Ancient Israel*, p. 148.

impart information, the interest of preaching is to stir reaction and response. The work of Israel's priests was to do the former; that of the prophets was to do the latter.

Accordingly, one reads of Hosea declaring, "Hear the word of the LORD, ye children of Israel" (4:1), and again, "Hear ye this, O priests; and hearken, ye house of Israel; and give ye ear, O house of the king" (5:1). In both instances the prophet brings his message in a way to inspire the people to turn from their sin and live truly for God. Amos tells Amaziah, priest of Bethel, that the Lord had taken him from following the flock to "prophesy unto my people Israel" (7:15), and what Amos was doing was encouraging the people of Israel similarly to turn from sin and follow the Lord. Neither man was instructing the people what the Law said. Rather both were encouraging the people to do what they already knew the Law commanded. Jeremiah was told by God, "Go and cry in the ears of Jerusalem" (2:2). At one time he was to do this while standing "in the gate of the LORD's house" (7:2); at another "in the gate of the children of the people," meaning the city gate (17:19); and at still another in the valley of Hinnom, which was by the "entry of the east gate" (19:2). All of these were public places, so that the proclamation in view was to be given to people as they passed through these entry points, either into the temple or the city of Jerusalem.

In this connection, it is well to relate the ideas of preaching and prediction. It is true that prophets did predict, and it is important to make this point clear in answer to those scholars who deny genuine prediction on the part of the prophets. For instance, A. B. Davidson writes, "The Prophet is always a man of his own time, and it is always to the people of his own time that he speaks, not to a generation long after nor to us."[2] By this, Davidson means, among other things, that prophets did not predict in a supernatural manner what was to happen in days far in the future. This, however, is not the teaching of Scripture. Isaiah, who preceded Cyrus by a century and a half, predicted the rule of Cyrus and even referred to him by name (Isa. 44:28; 45:1). Daniel in vision saw the four great empire periods stretching before him—the Babylonian, the Medo-Persian, the Grecian, and the Roman— which were to run for more than nine hundred years into the future (Dan. 7).

On the other hand, people err when they think that the main task of prophets was to predict the future. Sometimes the term *prophecy* is taken to be synonymous with prediction, so that when one speaks of prophecy he speaks of prediction. This is equally incorrect. Though the prophets did predict at times, as God gave them this kind of information, the greater part of their declarative ministry was in preaching to the people of their own time. They were really much like preachers of today, urging people to live in a manner

[2]"Prophecy and Prophets," *Hastings Dictionary of the Bible*, VI, p. 118b.

pleasing to God. They used prediction in their preaching only on occasion, whenever it was necessary to impart a message God wanted given.

## 2. Key individuals

The moral and religious condition of any country depends in large part on the leadership of those in authority. If leaders conduct themselves properly, people will more than likely do the same. Hence, another aspect in the prophetic method was to contact key individuals of Israel and urge them to conform to God's will. Kings were especially sought out.[3] Isaiah, for instance, went to King Ahaz of Judah and encouraged him to ask "a sign of the LORD" (Isa. 7:11); and when Ahaz piously said he would not thus "tempt the LORD" (7:12), Isaiah gave him a sign anyway (7:14), and then told him of the danger of an Assyrian invasion.

Sometimes a king would actually ask a prophet to come and give him information from God. This was done by Zedekiah, Judah's king in the day of the siege pressed by Nebuchadnezzar. He sent two men to Jeremiah with the words, "Inquire, I pray thee, of the LORD for us," desiring to know whether God would come to the help of His people in their dire circumstances (Jer. 21:2). Jeremiah's answer at the time was anything but what Zedekiah wished to hear: he said, "Thus saith the LORD God of Israel ... I myself will fight against you with an outstretched hand and with a strong arm, even in anger, and in fury, and in great wrath" (21:4, 5).

A list of prophets who contacted kings directly reads as follows: to Saul came Samuel; to David, Nathan and Gad; to Rehoboam, Shemaiah; to Jeroboam, Ahijah and the "man of God"; to Ahab, Elijah and Micaiah; to Jehoram and Jehu, Elisha; to Asa, Azariah and Hanani; to Jehoshaphat, Jehu; to Joash, Zechariah; to Amaziah, "the prophet"; to Uzziah, Zechariah; to Ahaz and Hezekiah, Isaiah; and to Jehoiakim and Zedekiah, Jeremiah.

These contacts with key individuals, of course, were individual contacts rather than preaching occasions. Earlier prophets gave primary attention to such contacts, while later prophets gave them a lesser place. As has been noted, later prophets were concerned more with the larger audience. They did make individual contacts, however, when they were especially needed, much as did their earlier counterparts.

## 3. Symbolic actions

In the work of declaring God's word, prophets employed various measures for stressing points they wished to make. One of these was the symbolic

---

[3]Cf. Johannes Pedersen, *Israel: Its Life and Culture*, I-II, p. 109.

action. That is, they would perform certain actions, or instruct others to do them, actions which they would explain to be symbolic of truths they wished to convey.

For instance, Elisha one day told King Jehoash of Israel to shoot an arrow through an open window. The king did and Elisha gave the symbolic indication: "The arrow of the LORD's deliverance and the arrow of deliverance from Syria: for thou shalt smite the Syrians in Aphek till thou have consumed them" (II Kings 13:17). Then he told the king to take arrows and smite upon the ground. The king did so and struck the ground three times. This angered the prophet, and he told the king that because he had struck the ground only three times he would smite the Syrians only three times (13:18, 19). In other words the striking of the arrows on the ground was symbolic of the number of times Jehoash would defeat his enemy, the king of Syria.

At a time when the Assyrians were campaigning against Ashdod, on the Mediterranean seaboard, God told Isaiah to remove the sackcloth from his body and the sandals from his feet. The symbolism was that the Assyrians one day would "lead away the Egyptians prisoners and the Ethiopians captive, young and old, naked and barefoot, even with their buttocks uncovered, to the shame of Egypt" (Isa. 20:4). The thought that prompted this symbolism was that God wanted Israel to be warned against any alliance with Egypt as over against Assyria.

Jeremiah on an occasion procured an earthen bottle from a potter and took it with him to the valley of Hinnom. There, as people looked on, he proclaimed God's word against the sins being committed and then dramatically broke the bottle in the sight of all as he declared, "Thus saith the LORD of hosts; even so will I break this people and this city, as one breaketh a potter's vessel, that cannot be made whole again: and they shall bury them in Tophet till there be no place to bury" (Jer. 19:11). The vivid picture of the flying pieces of this smashed vessel would have made a very forceful impression on the people's minds.

On another occasion, Jeremiah employed Rechabites to provide an effective symbolism. One of the ancestral customs of the Rechabites was to refrain from drinking wine. Jeremiah brought a group of Rechabites into the temple and set jars of wine before them and exhorted them to drink it. These men, however, refused, being faithful to their ancestral principle. Jeremiah then used this fine demonstration of obedience to symbolize to those who watched that they too should be faithful to the instructions God had given them (Jer. 35:1–17).

Ezekiel too used symbolic actions to impress his points. One day at God's command he drew a picture of the siege of Jerusalem on the face of a building brick, symbolizing that this siege would indeed take place (Ezek. 4:1–3). At another time he shaved off the hair from his head and the beard from his face and then, according to God's direction, burnt some of it, cut some of it, and scattered some of it in the wind (5:1, 2). The symbolism was that the people of Israel would similarly be burned, smitten, and scattered in the coming captivity.

Perhaps the best-known example of symbolism involved Hosea's marriage to his wife, Gomer. One day God told Hosea to marry this woman, indicating to him that she would become unfaithful and be a "woman of whoredoms" (Hos. 1:2).[4] Hosea married Gomer, and children were born even as God had also predicted. The names of the children were symbolic in meaning. The first was named Jezreel, and the symbolism was that God would "avenge the blood of Jezreel upon the house of Jehu" and so would cause "the kingdom of the house of Israel" to cease (1:4). The second child was named Lo-ruhamah, meaning "not pitied." The symbolism was that God would "no more have mercy upon the house of Israel" (1:6). The third child was named Lo-ammi, meaning "not my people." The symbolism was that Israel, because of her sin, would no longer be considered the people of God (1:9).

Gomer then left Hosea due to her unfaithfulness, apparently returning to her father's house. After a time God told Hosea to go and love her once again (3:1–3). This would have been very difficult for the prophet in view of his previous experience, but he still obeyed. When Gomer now came to him, he warned her strongly against continuing the type of life she had pursued when he had taken her the first time.

The symbolism of this marriage—in addition to the symbolism of the names we have noticed—is that, as Hosea took Gomer and she became unfaithful to him, so God had taken Israel to Himself and the people had become unfaithful to Him. Then, as Gomer left Hosea and went after her several lovers, so Israel had forsaken God and sought after the false gods of nations round about. And, further, as Hosea took Gomer back to himself again, in spite of her unfaithfulness, so God had frequently taken Israel back to Himself in spite of her waywardness.

## 4. Object lessons

Another literary device employed by prophets was the object lesson. Some item or action which the prophet saw illustrated a truth to his mind. He would use the item or action symbolically to express that truth in a forceful way. Probably Jeremiah used this device as much as any.

For instance, one day Jeremiah noticed "a rod [twig] of an almond tree" (Jer. 1:11, 12). God immediately spoke to him, saying, "Thou hast well seen: for I will hasten my word to perform it." The Hebrew name for the almond

[4]Though viewpoints are varied concerning this marriage, the proleptic view here espoused has the most in its favor.

tree (*shaqedh*) means "the wakeful, the vigilant." Jeremiah was inspired to see in this young shoot of the almond branch a symbol of God's vigilance to keep His word of warning to His people. God would be watchful to fulfill all the warnings of punishment He had said would come upon the people.

Shortly after, Jeremiah saw a pot of food boiling on the fire, with its face or front pointed toward the north (1:13, 14). Again God indicated a divine symbolism: "Out of the north an evil shall break forth upon all the inhabitants of the land." The boiling pot represented trouble and difficulty. The fact that it was facing north indicated that this difficulty would come from the north. The significance of the northerly direction was that Babylonia, the country that God would use in bringing judgment upon Israel, would come upon Jerusalem from the north. Though Babylonia lay to the east of Palestine, the course to be followed was up along the Euphrates River, over the Fertile Crescent, and thus down into Palestine and to Jerusalem from the north.

At another time Jeremiah used an object lesson involving a linen girdle (13:1-11). God told Jeremiah to purchase the girdle, to wear it for a time, not to wash it, and then to carry it all the way to the Euphrates River and hide it "in a hole of the rock" (13:4). Jeremiah did this and later God told him to return to the Euphrates, find the girdle, and bring it back to the land of Palestine. The girdle by this time had become marred, and God indicated to Jeremiah, "After this manner will I mar the pride of Judah and the great pride of Jerusalem" (13:9). The symbolism concerned the portended punishment of captivity for wicked Judah in the land of Babylon. The girdle, being worn by Jeremiah for several days and becoming soiled, represented that the people of Judah had been God's people for a time and become soiled with sin. As Jeremiah took his girdle to the Euphrates, so God would in time take the people to the Euphrates, and even beyond to Babylon in captivity. There they would be as it were buried, and would thus become marred through punishment. And as Jeremiah later went back to the Euphrates and retrieved the girdle, so God in due course would go to the people in Babylon and bring them back to their land again.

It has been objected by some expositors that the Euphrates River was too far away for Jeremiah to go there twice, simply to bury and later recover a linen girdle.[5] It is true that the distance was long—at least 250 miles to the nearest point of contact with the river—but the fact of going there twice was important to the symbolism intended. The people would indeed be taken this far away for a time of punishment because of their soiled condition of sin.

Jeremiah found another object lesson when he visited the house of the potter (18:1-10). In visiting the potter he found that the craftsman had made a vessel which was marred. He then saw the potter destroy the vessel and

[5]E.g., Lindblom, *Prophecy in Ancient Israel*, pp. 131-132.

from the clay make a new vessel, which this time was beautiful and fine. The principal lesson God pointed out to Jeremiah was that, as the potter had power over the clay to make the marred vessel into a good vessel, so God had power over the Israelites to make them into a new people, changing them from a nation marred by sin into one pleasing to Himself. A secondary lesson was implied concerning the coming captivity. Israel at the time was a marred vessel in the sight of God—marred because of sin. God would in time crush this marred vessel through the suffering of captivity, so that it might be remolded in a new and better fashion.

A last instance to notice concerns a time when Jeremiah saw two baskets of figs before the temple of the Lord (24:1–10). The one basket had "very good figs, even like the figs that are first ripe," and the other had very bad figs, "which could not be eaten, they were so bad" (24:2). The good figs are described as those that were "first ripe"; figs that were the first harvested (at the end of June) were a prized fruit. The symbolism God pointed out to Jeremiah concerned the captivity again, but this time in a different sense. The difference concerned the precise time when Jeremiah saw the figs. The time was just after Jehoiachin had been taken captive (597 B.C.). At that time, Zedekiah was placed on Judah's throne.

God said the good basket of figs represented those who had just been taken away. God would set His eyes on these for good in their captivity and bring them again to their own land in due time. He would build them and not pull them down; He would plant them and not pluck them up (24:6). The result would be that they would come to know God and be given a new heart. God said the bad figs represented the people left in the land under the leadership of Zedekiah. In contrast to those taken away, they would suffer hardship as they remained there and would become a reproach and a proverb, a taunt and a curse, in all places where God would drive them (24:9). In other words, there was greater blessing in store for those who had been taken captive than for those who had been left in the land.

## B. MISSION

We now come to consider the mission of the prophets. Of concern here is the purpose behind the methodology which has just been examined. What were the goals and tasks the prophets were assigned?

### 1. Reformation, not innovation of new teaching

A generation ago it was common for scholars to see Israel's writing prophets as basically innovators of new teaching. It was believed that these men introduced new ideas relative to monotheism and ethical requirements; they were the first to think of God as the only God and to see Him as requiring proper ethical conduct on the part of His worshipers.[6] Of late, however, many are calling these prophets reformers rather than innovators, saying that their message was not new but had been implicit in the teachings of Israel for some years past.[7]

This more recent position is much more in keeping with the presentation of Scripture. The writing prophets were not innovators of an ethical monotheism. From earliest days Israel had believed that God was the one true God and also that God required ethical living. No divergence on this point should be made between prophets who were earlier in Israel's history and the later writing prophets.[8]

The main task of the prophets, then, was reformation. They wanted the people to turn from what they were doing in their sinful practices back to the teachings of the Law. The writing prophets worked at this task mainly by speaking to larger audiences and then recording their messages; the earlier prophets did it mainly by contacting single individuals. The prophets could not have been innovators of new thought, because what the people were to believe had already been revealed prior to entrance into the land. The Law of God had been given to Moses on Mount Sinai and this Law had been taught from the first by priests.

## 2. The urging of conformity to the Law

This idea of reformation calls for closer examination. Several related matters need to be made clear.

### a. NO TEACHING OF THE LAW AS SUCH

The prophets did not teach the Law as such. This was the task of the priests, as has been indicated. The priests taught the people, precept upon precept, line upon line. This kind of teaching required a classroom type of

---

[6]For instance, W. O. E. Oesterley and Theodore H. Robinson, *Hebrew Religion: Its Origin and Development*, pp. 234f., 299, writing in 1937; Robert Pfeiffer, *Introduction to the Old Testament*, p. 580, writing in 1941; and R. B. Y. Scott, *The Relevance of the Prophets*, pp. 106f., writing as late as 1953.

[7]A comment by John Bright (*A History of Israel*, p. 246) is typical: "The classical prophets ... were certainly not the spiritual pioneers, specifically the discoverers of ethical monotheism, that they have so repeatedly been made out to be." Then he adds that they were "not innovators, but reformers who stood in the main stream of Israel's tradition." Cf. A. C. Welch, *Prophet and Priest in Old Israel*, p. 35.

[8]Walter Eichrodt (*Theology of the Old Testament*, pp. 339f., 345f.) states clearly that no fundamental change transpired but only a change to a greater understanding of the reality of God's presence and that this gave the writing prophets greater urgency for their task and an increased concern for the portending judgment of the people.

situation, continuous contact with students, and permanence of residence. These requirements were met by priests in their designated cities, but ordinarily not by prophets who moved from place to place. Furthermore, what was taught by the prophets is revealed in their books, and, though they speak about the Law, they never state its precepts in a line-upon-line form.[9]

### b. THE URGING OF REFORM IN VIEW OF THE LAW

As has been stated, what the prophets did do was urge the people to conform their lives to the Law. And they did so on both a social and religious level. The writing prophets have much to say on both counts. Regarding the social, Amos cries, "Hear this word, ye kine of Bashan, that are in the mountain of Samaria, which oppress the poor, which crush the needy, which say to their masters, Bring and let us drink" (4:1). And Isaiah proclaims, "Woe unto them that decree unrighteous decrees . . . to turn aside the needy from judgment, and to take away the right from the poor of my people, that widows may be their prey, and they may rob the fatherless" (10:1, 2). Regarding the religious level, the prophets called the people back to God. Norman Gottwald rightly says, "Everything in their outlook was grounded in Israel's relation to Yahweh, in the persistent preaching of religious meaning into every facet of life."[10] Hosea, for instance, urges, "Come, and let us return to the LORD: for he hath torn, and he will heal us; he hath smitten, and he will bind us up" (6:1). And Micah pleads, "Hear ye now what the LORD saith" (6:1).

The view that the earlier prophets were just as much reformers as were the writing prophets is easily substantiated. Samuel's inauguration into the role of reformer came early in life, when he was called upon to tell Eli of God's judgment upon his wayward household (I Sam. 3:1–18). His persistent reforming efforts with the people were crowned with success in a clear decision for God on their part at Mizpeh (I Sam. 7:1–14). The "man of God" urged reform on Jereboam (I Kings 13:1–10). Hanani did the same with Asa (II Chron. 16:7–9). And Elijah's effort on Mount Carmel, in respect to the regime of Ahab and Jezebel, is well known (I Kings 18). In fact, the reason for mentioning most of these earlier prophets in the Scriptures is some occasion in which they urged reform on one or more individuals.

### c. INFREQUENT MENTION OF THE LAW

In preaching this message of reform, the prophets do not often refer to the Law by name. This is surprising, for one would expect they would in

---

[9]Cf. the viewpoint of Walter G. Williams, *The Prophets, Pioneers to Christianity*, p. 39, who says, "Traditionally, the priests had been the educator . . . as a teacher, the priest knew how to work painstakingly with people, leading them step by step."
[10]*A Light to the Nations*, p. 276.

that they were so interested in having the people conform their lives to the Law. A question, therefore, arises as to the reason for this infrequency. Eichrodt investigates the matter and suggests an answer which is probably correct. He believes that the mention of the name *Law* (*torah*) was kept to a minimum to lessen the danger of "dead externalism in religious practice and mechanical routine in religious thought."[11] That is, the people tended to think of the ceremonies of the Law as effective in themselves, and came to identify the Law with those ceremonies. The prophets, realizing that this erroneous viewpoint had already led the people into a dead externalism, desired to do nothing which would foster this thinking, such as an undue use of the name *Law*. Accordingly, they proclaimed the message contained in the Law without often employing the name. In keeping with this explanation is the fact that the prophets do speak repeatedly against such dead externalism in sanctuary service (see, e.g., Isa. 1:11–14; Amos 5:21–24).

### d. Lack of Prescription in the Law

It has been observed that though prophets are recognized in the Law, they are not legally prescribed as are the priests. The reason may be found in the point here made, that prophets were reformers rather than innovators of new thought. Reformers, after all, are needed because of an abnormal situation. People have wandered away from a proper course and they need to be brought back to it again. They need to be reformed to what they once were or at least to what they should have been. The Law was laid down for the ideal state of the people. And in that ideal state the people could be expected to follow the teachings of the Law when it was set forth by the priests. If the people had done this, there would not have been a need for reformers. So then, prophets filled an emergency role, and this type of activity did not call for any legal prescription in the "ideal-state" Law. It is in keeping with this fact that the recognition given prophets in Deuteronomy 18 does not refer to them in this role of reformers, but only as recipients of divine revelation to answer the questions of the people.

### 3. Testing, service as watchmen, and intercession

The mission of prophets also called for them to function in three capacities besides reformation. The three together would have occupied but a small part of their time, but nonetheless they are distinguished in the Old Testament and call for mention.

The first is testing the people in terms of what was good and what was

[11] *Theology of the Old Testament*, p. 304.

bad in their activity and conduct. God told Jeremiah, for instance, "I have set thee for a tower and a fortress among my people that thou mayest know and try their way" (6:27). Jeremiah was to be as strong as a tower and a fortress as he moved among the people and evaluated them, testing their works and making a judgment whether they were pleasing to God or not. The criterion he would have followed, of course, would again have been the Law. No doubt people looked to him frequently to determine whether or not they were acting in a way that was pleasing to God.

Another capacity was to serve as watchmen among the people; prophets were to point out wrong conduct and warn of judgment and punishment that would come in view of it. Ezekiel writes plainly on this point, giving God's word as follows: "Son of man, I have made thee a watchman unto the house of Israel: therefore hear the word at my mouth and give them warning from me" (3:17). God then said that if the prophet would give such warning he would not be responsible for the people if they should die in their sins, but if he did not, he would indeed be responsible and their blood would be on his hands. A similar thought is expressed in Ezekiel 33:7f. This task of the prophet was vitally important in God's sight, therefore. He was a person to give warning in the face of danger; if he gave the warning and people still plunged on to their death, his own hands at least were free from guilt, but, if he did not, God held him responsible for not being the watchman he should have been.

The third capacity was to serve as intercessor. Priests, of course, were prime intercessors, as they presented sacrifices on behalf of the people. Prophets, however, also served in an intercessory way, apart from ceremonial activity. There are several examples of prophets interceding for people before God.

Among early prophets, one may point to "the man of God" sent from Judah to prophesy against the altar at Bethel. There King Jeroboam attempted to stop the prophet, but in doing so he found his hand had withered. Immediately he urged the prophet, "Entreat now the face of the LORD thy God and pray for me, that my hand may be restored me again" (I Kings 13:6). The man of God did as Jeroboam asked, thus serving as an intercessor, and the king's hand was restored. Elijah one day interceded on behalf of the dead son of the widow in Zarephath to the end that his life might be returned. God heard his intercession and brought the boy back to life, much to the joy of the mother (I Kings 17:17–24). In a somewhat similar fashion, Elisha, a few years later, interceded on behalf of the little son of the Shunammite woman. The boy had died and his mother had come quickly to Elisha for help. He went to the house of the mother and there interceded for the child and saw him restored to life, again much to the joy of the mother (II Kings 4:18–37).

The writing prophets also presented intercession for the people at various times. Amos, for instance, as he saw the land devoured by locusts, cried to God, "O LORD God, forgive, I beseech thee: by whom shall Jacob arise? for he is small" (Amos 7:2). The text then indicates that, as a result, "The LORD repented for this" and said to Amos, "It shall not be." In other words, a devastation similar to what Amos had seen brought by the locusts would not be brought by the Lord on the people as a result of the prophet's intercession. Probably Jeremiah gives more indications of intercessory work than do any of the other prophets. For instance, he cries out, "Let mine eyes run down with tears night and day, and let them not cease: for the virgin daughter of my people is broken with a great breach, with a very grievous blow" (14:17). Again, he says, "We acknowledge, O LORD, our wickedness, and the iniquity of our fathers, for we have sinned against thee. Do not abhor us; for thy name's sake, do not disgrace the throne of thy glory; remember, break not thy covenant with us" (14:20, 21). At times, God even bids Jeremiah not to intercede in behalf of the people. For instance, in Jeremiah 7:16 God says, "Pray not thou for this people, neither lift up cry nor prayer for them, neither make intercession to me: for I will not hear thee" (cf. 11:14).

## C. NOT ANOTHER ORDER OF PRIESTS

A viewpoint identified especially with Scandinavian scholars holds that the prophets functioned as another order of priests, closely associated with cultic service. It is believed that priests engaged in sacrificial activity at the altar, while prophets gave divine oracles in response to questions of the people.[12] Sigmund Mowinckel is credited with innovating this line of thinking in his *Psalmenstudien III; Kultprophetie und Prophetische Psalmen*, which he wrote in 1923. One of the sources of evidence to which he points concerns several psalms that depict God speaking in the first person.[13] Mowinckel believes these occasions have reference to prophets as they spoke for God in giving reply to questions of enquirers. Alfred Haldar followed this thinking of Mowinckel and carried it further as he sought to compare Israel's priests and prophets with Babylonia's two priestly groups, *Baru* and *Mahhu*.[14] Haldar believed there were significant parallels between the priests and prophets of Israel on one hand, and the *Baru* and *Mahhu* of Babylonia on the other. Since the *Baru* and *Mahhu* were both priestly groups, he concluded that Israel's priests and prophets must both have been priestly groups.

[12]Otto Eissfeldt, "The Prophetic Literature," *The Old Testament and Modern Study*, ed. H. H. Rowley, pp. 113-161, gives an excellent survey of viewpoints.

[13]E.g., Psalm 60, 75, 82, 110.

[14]*Associations of Cult Prophets Among the Ancient Semites*. For numerous references to literature on this subject, see H. H. Rowley in *Journal of Semitic Studies*, 1 (1956):338f.

Another exponent is Aubrey Johnson,[15] who takes a position somewhat mediating between Mowinckel and Haldar. To show that early prophets were cultic personnel, he points to the following evidence: (1) the seventy elders, when they prophesied in the presence of Moses, were stationed near the tabernacle; (2) Samuel the prophet was reared at the tabernacle in Shiloh; (3) Saul in I Samuel 10 found the company of prophets coming down from a high place; (4) David was consulted by the prophet Nathan in reference to building the temple (II Sam. 7:4–17); (5) Nathan the prophet and Zadok the priest cooperated in making Solomon king of Israel (I Kings 1:32–40); (6) Elijah the prophet sacrificed on an altar he made on Mount Carmel (I Kings 18:25–40); (7) Elisha resorted to Mount Carmel (II Kings 4:25), where, according to the Elijah episode, there was an altar; and (8) Jehu called both prophets and priests of Baal to their temple at the time he ordered their slaughter, showing that both were cultic officials for the Canaanites, a possible parallel to what was true in Israel (II Kings 10:19).[16] It should be added that Johnson also cites parallel argumentation from the writing prophets, but since it is so similar in kind to this, a rehearsal of it would be superfluous.

To give a refutation, it is unnecessary to treat each of these arguments separately for they are almost all of the same type. They assume that, because a prophet was either near or somehow related to an altar, a priest, or the temple at some time, therefore he functioned as a priest. This, however, does not follow. The mere fact that seventy elders were near the tabernacle, when they prophesied as the result of the Holy Spirit's being placed upon them, does not indicate that they were members of the priesthood serving at the tabernacle. The tabernacle simply was a likely place for them to be assembled for this empowerment by the Holy Spirit. Similar observations may be made regarding the other evidence. Prophets, being people of God, were of course interested in religious matters and certainly visited the place where offerings were being presented on numerous occasions. But this did not mean they were members of the priesthood doing the work there. Then, the last argument, pertaining to a possible parallel with Canaanite personnel, is also based only on inference. The probability is, however, that these Canaanite officials were similar to the religious personnel of Babylonia, rather than to that of Israel.[17] There is simply no evidence that they were parallel to Israel's priests and prophets. To substantiate the general position it would be necessary to find a clear case of one or more prophets giving oracular utterances out of the central sanctuary, but this is not found.

In contrast, what is found is an attitude on the part of the prophets which is sometimes actually critical of current cultic practices. Isaiah, for instance,

---

[15] *The Cultic Prophet in Ancient Israel.*
[16] Ibid., pp. 26f.
[17] The Babylonian personnel were priestly; see chap. 2, p. 24.

quotes God as saying, "To what purpose is the multitude of your sacrifices unto me? . . . I am full of the burnt-offerings of rams, and the fat of fed beasts; and I delight not in the blood of bullocks, or of lambs, or of he-goats. . . . Bring no more vain oblations; incense is an abomination unto me" (1:11–13). Jeremiah (6:20; 7:21–23), Hosea (6:6), Amos (5:21–25), and Micah (6:6–8) all speak similarly. A few years ago many scholars thought these prophets displayed even a definite anticultic attitude. This viewpoint is also wrong, just as wrong as it is for scholars now to swing to an opposite extreme and see these same prophets as themselves playing a prominent role in cultic service.

Another argument against the position may be taken from the fact that the Law of Moses neither prescribes nor recognizes any such activity on the part of prophets. Great detail is given regarding sanctuary regulations, but prophets are not once named in connection with them. Therefore, given the lack of both legal prescription and historical example for believing Israel's prophets were cultic personnel, the conclusion is warranted that Israel did not include prophets in her sanctuary service. They were not another order of priests.

## D. THE ISSUE OF WHETHER THE PROPHETS WROTE THEIR BOOKS

A question that has stirred considerable discussion concerns the recording of the books of prophecy. The question involves whether the prophets, whose names these books bear, wrote the books or whether someone who knew of their teachings wrote them. If the prophets penned them, then this writing constitutes another aspect of their work. A discussion of the matter therefore is called for in this chapter.

### 1. The view that others wrote them

#### a. THE VIEW PRESENTED

The view of Lindblom may be taken as typical of what is held by many others.[18] He believes that all of the major prophets had numerous followers who learned from them and were quite willing to help both in the oral ministry and later in recording this information. He believes that such groups were probably descendants of those from the early days of prophecy which he calls guilds. He sees these men as responsible for listening well to the

---

[18]*Prophecy in Ancient Israel*, pp. 159f.; cf. Scott, *The Relevance of the Prophets*, pp. 81–83.

prophets as they spoke, for fixing their messages firmly in mind even to the point of learning them by heart through diligent repetition, and for preserving them for future generations. He believes that part of this preservation was probably only in oral form at first and that all was put in writing by later hands.

## b. EVIDENCE FOR THE VIEWPOINT

Evidence for the viewpoint consists mainly of three arguments.

One is the scriptural indication that the task of prophets was speaking the Word of God; there is no mention that it included writing. The assumption that other people would have done the recording is thought plausible. But the mere fact that prophets were primarily speakers in no way precluded them from being writers as well. After all, their books are not so long that a great amount of time would have been required to write them, and prophets were the most familiar with their own information to record it accurately.

A second is that two of the great prophets, Isaiah and Jeremiah, speak of disciples who followed them. Isaiah does this in 8:16, where he says, "Bind up the testimony, seal the law among my disciples." The word for "disciples" is *limmubbim*, meaning "learners." R. B. Y. Scott, speaking of this verse, says, "In Isaiah 8:16 the prophet commits his message to his disciples."[19] The verse, however, does not say this. It simply indicates that Isaiah wanted the testimony bound up and the Law sealed among his disciples as they moved among the wayward people of the day. The testimony and Law in view very likely were not the information Isaiah had been proclaiming, but the basic Law that had been taught by the priests and reinforced by the prophets down through the years. And the disciples in mind probably were not merely those who were Isaiah's own followers; in fact it is more likely that he had reference to any righteous people of the day who were seeking to maintain the way of God, those who had been learning from him as he had been preaching.

Jeremiah is referred to because he had Baruch as his friend and secretary. In fact, the indication is that Jeremiah dictated his material to Baruch, who wrote it down; Jeremiah 36:4 reads, "Then Jeremiah called Baruch the son of Neriah: and Baruch wrote from the mouth of Jeremiah all the words of the LORD . . . upon a roll of a book." When King Jehoiakim maliciously burned this book, Jeremiah wrote it again at God's direction and once more by dictation to Baruch (Jer. 36:32). One must say, however, that one man hardly makes a group of disciples. Moreover, it is directly stated that Jeremiah wrote his own book, using Baruch only as a secretary. Note that the general thinking of this school of thought is that well after the time of the prophet's own

[19] *The Relevance of the Prophets*, p. 82.

preaching, and possibly after his death, the disciples wrote down what they had learned at his lips.

A third argument, as indicated by Lindblom, is that this manner of recording the prophetic revelations would account for what he calls the "many obscure passages, many discrepancies, many doublets, many gaps, and many additions" in the prophetic books.[20] Lindblom believes such factors exist in the prophetic writings and sees this explanation of authorship as the best way to account for them. Conservative scholars, however, view these alleged problems in quite a different light. They will agree that there are some obscure passages, that is, passages which are difficult to understand. But these occur in many places of the Bible, and often where there is no question as to authorship. Moreover, Lindblom does not cite any specific discrepancies, and it is difficult to refute the assertion when this is not done. One may just as well say that there are no discrepancies, and conservative scholars believe this is the case. Admittedly there are passages which present problems, but these are normally subject to more than one explanation, each of which is in keeping with the inspiration of Scripture. Regarding doublets, again none are indicated, and one may answer that whatever portions Lindblom may have in mind are subject to one of two explanations: either they are doublets for the sake of emphasis or they are not really doublets at all but merely passages which show similarities.

As to gaps, one may say that there are places in the prophetic writings where one could wish additional information was given, but this is characteristic of Scripture. Only those materials are recorded that are considered religiously significant, and therefore information that one would like to know is sometimes omitted, but this in no way is contrary to the idea of the author's being the prophet himself. And concerning many additions, one has to wonder just what Lindblom has in mind. Apparently he believes that the disciples of the prophets made additions to what the prophet himself said, but this would be extremely hard to prove. Presumably, he has in mind certain claims of supernaturalism which he believes the prophet himself, being more rational than his zealous followers, would not have made. Conservative scholars, however, have no problem with passages which give evidence of supernatural activity.

### 2. The view that the prophets themselves wrote their books

The view that the prophets wrote their own books has much more to commend it. It is true that God could have inspired this information just as

[20] *Prophecy in Ancient Israel*, p. 164.

well through one or more followers, but the prophet himself was the one who was inspired for his preaching in his lifetime, he knew the information best, and therefore it is likely that he would have been the one inspired to give the written record. If he used a secretary on occasion, as Jeremiah used Baruch, this would still be a matter of the prophet himself serving as author. Baruch wrote only what Jeremiah told him.

It has been alleged that there is a remarkable silence in the prophetic books regarding authorship, and this is true to a point. However, one may note several indications in the books that make the idea of authorship by the prophets themselves altogether plausible. Isaiah, for instance, was told to take a great scroll and to write upon it with the pen of a man (8:1). This was not an indication to write his own book, but it does show that he knew how to write and that he did write upon such scrolls. A similar observation may be made relative to a time when Isaiah was told to go and write in the presence of the Egyptians in a book "that it may be for the time to come forever and ever" (30:8). Ezekiel was commanded to record in writing the law of the temple and its ordinances (43:11, 12). Likewise, Habukkuk was directed to write down his vision and make it sufficiently plain on tables so that one who was running could read it (2:2). Then, regarding Jeremiah, the indication is direct that he dictated the information God had given him to his secretary, Baruch. And at the close of his prophecy, it is stated, "So Jeremiah wrote in a book all the evil that should come upon Babylon, even all these words that are written against Babylon" (51:60).

It is true that none of the books of the writing prophets declare as such that they were written by the prophets. In fact, each one begins with a third-person reference to the prophet. For instance, the Book of Isaiah begins, "The vision of Isaiah, the son of Amoz (1:1); and the Book of Ezekiel, "The word of the LORD came expressly unto Ezekiel the priest, the son of Buzi, in the land of the Chaldeans by the river Chebar" (1:3). Judging on the basis of only these third-person references, one could conclude that persons other than the prophets wrote them.

However, after beginning in the third person, many of the books revert to the use of the first person now and again, and this is much in keeping with the idea of the prophets themselves being the writers. For instance, when Isaiah presents the occasion of his call, at the time he saw God high and lifted up, the first person is employed: "In the year that King Uzziah died, I saw also the LORD sitting upon a throne, high and lifted up, and his train filled the temple." Later he says, "Then said I, woe is me for I am undone, because I am a man of unclean lips," and still later, "Then said I, here am I; send me" (Isa. 6:1–8). Again, in Jeremiah, following the third-person introduction in 1:1, the first person is used in 1:4, "Then the word of the LORD came unto me, saying." There follows the occasion of Jeremiah's call as having been from the womb of his mother. A little later in chapter 1, we read, "Moreover the word of the LORD came unto me, saying" (1:11); and other references in the first person continue to occur. Ezekiel actually begins his book with a first-person reference, for the third-person reference mentioned above does not occur until verse 3; verse 1 reads, "Now it came to pass in the thirtieth year, in the fourth month, in the fifth day of the month, as I was among the captives by the river of Chebar, that the heavens were opened and I saw visions of God." Then in 1:4 one reads, "And I looked, and, behold, a whirlwind came out of the north," and again, in 2:1, "And he said unto me, Son of man, stand upon thy feet and I will speak unto thee." Not all of the prophets have similar first-person references, but several do, including Hosea, Amos, Micah, Habakkuk, and Zechariah.

In considering this evidence, one must say that the third-person reference is easier to account for in terms of the prophet himself being the author than is the first-person reference in terms of someone else being the author. The reason is that a third-person form is common throughout the Bible where there is no question that the one speaking in the third person is himself the author. On the other hand, it is difficult to find any place where in a first-person reference (other than for God Himself) the one in view is not the person doing the writing. Any such occasions are clearly indicated as to who is in mind, and that is not true in these instances from the prophets.

Taken together these evidences lead to the conclusion that the prophets were the writers of their own books. It is one thing to assert that, just because they were speakers, therefore they were not writers, and it is another to give evidence to that end. The evidence presented for the view is in no way conclusive. Matters in favor of the prophets being the authors are much more convincing. Therefore, it is appropriate to say that one more function of the writing prophets was the recording of the information contained in their books. Likely most of the information had been preached by them earlier, though not necessarily all. What was recorded was what God wanted permanently written down, so that future generations might profit as well as the generation then living.

# 6

# The Holy Spirit and Prophecy

Our discussion has now arrived at a point where we may logically consider the basic question of the relation of the Holy Spirit to the work of the prophets. Each of the three preceding chapters has anticipated this subject. In chapter 3, the matter of ecstasy and the prophets was considered, and it was noted that each of the three main passages employed by adherents of the ecstatic view includes a reference to the Holy Spirit. It was observed that the meaning of this reference would be taken up later. In chapter 4, the discussion concerned the meaning of "to prophesy." The meaning of this term was explored with some care, but it was noted that the meaning in its complete form could not be set forth until a discussion regarding the Holy Spirit was pursued. And in the immediately preceding chapter, the matter of the function of the prophet was considered. In order for the prophet to carry on his function of both receiving and declaring God's word, there was again an important relationship to the work of the Holy Spirit. It is in order, then, that we now come to discuss this fundamental subject and provide answers to questions left open in these prior chapters.[1]

## A. IDENTITY

Scholars of a liberal persuasion believe that mentions of the Holy Spirit in the Old Testament are merely references to the power of God or the

[1]For a full discussion of this subject see my *The Holy Spirit in the Old Testament*. A substantial part of the information in this present chapter is based upon that book.

influence of God in the world. When these references are used with respect to prophets in particular, liberal scholars regard them as denoting a power coming upon the prophets to make them ecstatically frenzied. As noted in chapter 3, this viewpoint is flatly denied by conservative scholars, for they believe the Holy Spirit is one of the three persons of the Godhead, along with the Father and the Son.

It is the thinking of some conservative scholars that, though the Holy Spirit was truly a person of the Godhead, people of Old Testament day did not yet realize His existence in this capacity. It is believed that thinking simply had not developed this far yet and people thought of the Spirit as merely a power or influence which God exerted in the world.

There seems reason to believe, however, that informed Old Testament people conceived of the Holy Spirit in a more advanced way than this. No doubt they would not have been able to make a theological formulation regarding the Trinity, but still they seem to have made a distinction between the Spirit of God and God Himself and this in a way to characterize the Spirit as having qualities of personality. For instance, the psalmist writes, "Thou sendest forth thy spirit, they are created: and thou renewest the face of the earth" (Ps. 104:30). The verb *sendest forth* is hardly applicable to merely a power or influence of God. On that basis, one would simply expect an expression such as, "Thou didst create and renew the face of the earth by thy power." A spirit which could be sent forth must be distinct from the being by whom it is sent forth, and if that spirit in turn could create and renew, then an aspect of personality is implied.

Again, one day Elisha asked that a "double portion" of Elijah's "spirit" (II Kings 2:9) be given to him. In the same context, fifty young "sons of the prophets" (prophets in training) referred to the "Spirit of the LORD." The implication is that this "Spirit of the LORD" was the same as the "spirit" Elisha asked from Elijah. If so, the Spirit here in view was distinguished from God Himself, and, since the context indicates Elisha was greatly empowered when this Spirit came upon him, the aspect of personality is again implied.

Later still, Ezekiel, who speaks so frequently regarding the Spirit, refers to the Spirit's doing something to or for him in most significant ways. For instance, in 3:12 he says, "Then the spirit took me up" for the purpose of transporting him to the city of Tel-abib. In 11:1, he states, "Moreover the spirit lifted me up and brought me unto the east gate of the LORD's house." Such language once more shows that the prophet distinguishes between the Spirit of God and God Himself, and, since the Spirit thus does these things either to him or for him, personality for the Spirit is implied.

It is also important to recognize that the matter of the identity of the Holy Spirit in the Old Testament is not so much a question of what people thought regarding this member of the Godhead as it is what the intention of God Himself was, who inspired the writers. His intention is indicated in numerous passages. For instance, in Genesis 1:2, where the Spirit of God is said to have moved or brooded upon the face of the waters following the initial creation, certainly the meaning is that the Third Person of the Godhead so moved or brooded. Or years later, when God told Zechariah that his work was done "not by might nor by power but by my Spirit" (Zech. 4:6), the reference surely was to the Third Person of the Trinity as the One responsible for God's work being accomplished. Our question here, then, is basically what the relation was, as God saw it, between the work of this Third Person and prophets in the work of prophesying.

## B. EMPOWERMENT BY THE HOLY SPIRIT

The Holy Spirit is frequently indicated to have come upon people in Old Testament time and sometimes also to have left them (e.g., I Sam. 16:14). It can be demonstrated that none of these occasions concern the salvation of the person (or the loss of his salvation) but the empowerment of the person for an assigned task. Space does not permit extensive illustration, but a few examples may be noted.

Four of the judges, for instance, had the Spirit come upon them. One was Othniel (Judg. 3:10), of whom it is said, "The Spirit of the LORD came upon him and he judged Israel and went out to war." The purpose is clear in respect to this coming of the Spirit: it was to enable Othniel to go out to war. Another judge who is said to have been empowered was Gideon; Judges 6:34 reads, "But the Spirit of the LORD came upon Gideon, and he blew a trumpet; and Abi-ezer was gathered after him." This coming of the Spirit was to enable Gideon to gather a group together that he might fight invading Midianites. A third was Jephthah; Judges 11:29 states, "Then the Spirit of the LORD came upon Jephthah, and he passed over Gilead." The purpose of this coming of the Spirit was to enable Jephthah for the looming battle with the Ammonites. A fourth was Samson, who four times is said to have had the "Spirit of the LORD" come upon him (Judg. 13:25; 14:6, 19; 15:14). Each of these times the Spirit came on Samson just before he had a great feat of strength to perform, and the implication is that the Spirit of God enabled him for the occasion.[2]

## C. THE EMPOWERMENT OF PROPHETS

When one considers prophets being filled in this way by the Holy Spirit, he finds a distinction being made. First, there were prophets who

[2]Other instances will come in for mention later in this chapter. Still others, that will not be mentioned, include Bezaleel (Exod. 31:3; cf. 35:31), Balaam (Num. 24:2), Joshua (Num. 27:18; cf. Deut. 34:9), Amasai (I Chron. 12:18), and Zechariah (II Chron. 24:20). All involve empowerment for a task.

were filled in a way parallel to what has just been seen regarding the judges; that is, they were filled for a temporary occasion of responsibility that faced them. For instance, it is said of Azariah, before he spoke to King Asa of Judah who was returning home from a conquest, "The Spirit of God came upon Azariah the son of Oded." After this Azariah delivered a message from God (II Chron. 15:1-7). The implication is that the Spirit of God came upon him to equip him for speaking the message. Another occasion concerns Jahaziel, of the reign of Asa's successor Jehoshaphat, when news had just come of an invasion of the land by three strong enemy powers. Jehoshaphat prayed to God for help, and in response, "upon Jahaziel... came the Spirit of the LORD in the midst of the congregation" (II Chron. 20:14). The result was that he spoke a divine message of encouragement and instruction to the people.[3]

The other group consists of prophets who were continuously empowered. Seldom do members of this group—and these include all the great writing prophets—make any mention of being personally filled or empowered by the Holy Spirit. In fact, only two (Micah and Ezekiel) out of the sixteen writing prophets give such an indication. Since one might think, therefore, that these prophets were not empowered, it is appropriate to give evidence that they were. The discussion will show at the same time that this empowerment was continuous.

One source of evidence is found in two significant postexilic references to preexilic prophets. Nehemiah 9:30, which speaks of Israel's sin of prior days, says regarding God, "Yet many years didst thou forbear them and testifiedst against them by thy Spirit in thy prophets." The reference must be to preexilic prophets and, since no particular prophets are designated, the implication is that all such prophets were enabled by the Holy Spirit as they testified to the people. The other passage is Zechariah 7:12, where the prophet speaks in similar fashion regarding the sin of preexilic Israel and particularly regarding the people's unwillingness to hear "the words which the LORD of hosts hath sent in his Spirit by the former prophets." The same observation is in order regarding this passage, and both passages imply that the empowerment in view was continuous.

A second source of evidence may be taken from those prophets that do speak of themselves as empowered by the Holy Spirit and this in a continuous sense. The first two to consider are Elijah and Elisha. The occasion in view is that noted above, when Elisha asked Elijah for a double portion of his spirit. In that Elisha made this request, it is evident that Elijah had been so empowered (continuously) before that time, and certainly Elisha's interest was that he might be similarly empowered from that time on. A third prophet is

[3]Cf. I Chron. 12:18; II Chron. 24:20.

Micah, one of the two writing prophets who do speak of their own empowerment, and he uses words that connote again continuous filling: "But truly I
am full of power by the Spirit of the LORD" (Mic. 3:8). It should be noticed
that Micah does not merely say, "I am being filled," or that "The Spirit of the
LORD came on me." He uses the perfect form of the verb to indicate that the
filling had occurred some time in the past, and the context shows that he recognized this filling was still true of him at the time of writing.

The fourth prophet is Ezekiel. Ezekiel gives many indications regarding
his consciousness of being dependent on the Spirit. For instance, in 2:2 he
says, "The spirit entered into me," with the result that he was given a
message to speak. In 3:12 he says, "Then the spirit took me up," and in 3:14,
"So the spirit lifted me up and took me away." In fact, no less than eleven
times he states either that the Spirit entered into him for some purpose[4] or
that He transported him to some distant locality. Such a consciousness of the
ministry of the Spirit proves that Ezekiel was continuously empowered by
the Spirit, and was unusually aware of it.

A third source of evidence may be taken by analogy from other people
who were important to Israel's life and who give evidence of continuous
empowerment by the Spirit. Those especially in point were administrators of
the land.

A first to notice is Moses. Though there is no record of an occasion when
the Spirit first came upon Moses, there is in the account of the seventy elders
being empowered in the wilderness clear evidence that he was continuously
Spirit-filled. As noted in chapter 3, these seventy were set aside to help
Moses, and God indicated to His servant that He would "take of the Spirit"
that was on him and share it with them (Num. 11:17). The implication is
clear that, from this time on, the seventy were continuously empowered for
their new work, and it is equally clear that Moses had been so empowered
before that time and continued to be.

A second to notice is Israel's first king, Saul. As indicated also in chapter
3, the Spirit of God came upon him temporarily in I Samuel 10, but then
continuously in I Samuel 11:6 just before the Jabesh-gilead battle. This latter
occasion must have been a continuous infilling, because in I Samuel 16:14 the
Spirit of God is said to have left him, and there is no time in between when it
is said that the Spirit came upon him.

A last to notice is Israel's second king, the great David. In I Samuel
16:13, the verse preceding that which tells of the Spirit's departing from
Saul, the indication is given, "And the Spirit of the LORD came upon David
from that day forward." The last phrase is especially significant—"from that

---

[4]The use of different verbs in these instances when the Spirit filled Ezekiel, as well as other
considerations, gives evidence that he was not filled merely temporarily as the first group of
prophets were.

day forward." The occasion in view was the anointing of David by Samuel as the future king of Israel. Also, David's well-known words of Psalm 51:11 are noteworthy: "Take not thy Holy Spirit from me." In this request to God, David implied his own recognition of continuous Spirit-empowerment. He knew that he possessed the Spirit at the time, and he did not want this to change. He had seen a change with Saul that brought sad consequences, and he did not want the same to happen with him.

The matter in point is that if these important people were continuously Spirit-filled, it is altogether likely that the prophets, being similarly important, were also Spirit-filled on a continuous basis.

That a few prophets were only temporarily filled, while the majority were continuously, was due, no doubt, to a lesser importance held by them for God's work. That is, men like Azariah or Jahaziel were men that God used for only one occasion to bring a prophetic message. Never again are they mentioned in the Scriptures. The great writing prophets, however, or men like Elijah and Elisha, were prophets on a regular basis. Their occupation was being a prophet, and God used them continuously in His service. Therefore, it was important that they be continuously empowered.

## D. THE THREE PASSAGES CONSIDERED AGAIN

It is appropriate now to look again at the three important passages noted in chapter 3: Numbers 11:25–29; I Samuel 10:1–13; and I Samuel 19:18–24. These are the three principal texts that adherents of the ecstatic view draw upon for scriptural evidence. We have observed that serious problems arise when one attempts to find in them evidence for ecstaticism. A much better explanation was found in the idea of "praising," a meaning substantiated in I Chronicles 25:1–3. It was also observed that on each of the occasions the Holy Spirit is said to have come upon the people involved. Because the coming of the Holy Spirit on any occasion in the Old Testament concerned the empowerment of one or more individuals, it may be expected that empowerment was involved in all three of these instances.

### 1. Numbers 11:16–30

The first passage concerns the seventy elders at the time they were equipped by God for sharing in Moses' work of administration. God told Moses that He would take of the Spirit that was upon him and put it also upon the seventy. This was done and all seventy began to "prophesy." When they ceased, two of them, Eldad and Medad, continued this activity as they ran through the camp. The point in issue concerns what this coming of the Holy Spirit on the seventy had to do with their action in prophesying.

One can hardly say that the purpose was to prompt these men to prophesy in this way, for this prophesying was not the goal in view. The goal was the equipping of the men to be assistants to Moses in administration. Therefore, it follows that this coming of the Holy Spirit was to make the men capable assistants. After all, the work of administration and judging people was a very important work. Prophesying must have been merely an accompanying activity that went along with the coming of the Holy Spirit.

Actually, such an accompanying activity is not surprising. These men, before this time, had not been thus empowered. Now suddenly the Holy Spirit had come upon them, and they were empowered. Just how they knew they were is not indicated, but somehow they did know, and the result of this knowledge gave them real joy of heart. Such joy could well have led to a praising activity in song together. It may well be that several songs were sung.

Then regarding Eldad and Medad, apparently they liked to sing more than did the others, and perhaps they were more emotionally exuberant by nature. They wanted all the camp to know of the blessing bestowed on them and of their reason for joy. Therefore, they moved through the camp, singing out in praise to God. This distressed some of the people and caused them to complain to Joshua, and he conveyed their complaint to Moses. That these men were simply giving praise to God makes Moses' semi-rebuke of Joshua understandable. He wished that all the people were prophets and would give praise to God in the way Eldad and Medad were.

## 2. I Samuel 10:1–13

In the passage concerning Saul's first contact with the prophets, the indication is given, "The Spirit of God came upon him, and he prophesied among them" (10:10). Again the coming of the Spirit of God is closely related to an act of prophesying. What is the relation this time?

The answer once more must be that the prophesying was only a by-product of the main purpose for the Spirit's empowerment. As seen earlier, the purpose this time was to change Saul in personality. He had been timid and needed to be given a new sense of confidence if he was to serve as Israel's king. It was not that he would become king immediately, but that he needed a preview of what the Spirit could and would do for him when he did. The purpose, then, was not to make him prophesy. That he did, however, when the Spirit of God enabled him with a new aggressive attitude, is not surprising. Like the seventy in the wilderness, he burst forth in song, giving praise to God. The company of prophets were already singing, and Saul, with his new heart, simply joined with them. He had much to praise God for, having been told he would be king and now having received a foretaste of the new personality God would give him for the position.


### 3. I Samuel 19:18–24

In the passage regarding Saul's second contact with the prophets, the indication is given, "The Spirit of God was upon him also, and he went on and prophesied" as he continued his walk to Ramah where David was in the company of Samuel (19:23). Prior to this, the Spirit of God had come also upon the messengers of Saul, with the result that they had prophesied (19:20). So then with both these messengers and Saul, the act of prophesying for the third time is related closely to a coming of the Spirit of God. What was the relation in this instance?

The answer is different this time. No aspect of empowerment was called for other than the prophesying itself. The messengers were not enabled for any special assignment, and Saul had already lost his special empowerment for rule some years before (I Sam. 16:14). Also, a clear reason for empowerment in respect to the prophesying itself is apparent this time. It involved the sparing of David's life.

The three groups of messengers needed to be turned from their assigned intention to bring David back to Saul, and Saul himself needed to be restrained so that he would not apprehend the young man. Saul wanted to kill David. He had tried to do this more than once already, but David had always escaped. He wanted to be sure of taking him in this instance, and what he would have done had he been successful is all too clearly indicated by what he did do to the eighty-five priests at Nob not long after. He killed all of them along with their wives and children, and destroyed their possessions (I Sam. 22:18, 19). But it was not in God's permissive will that such a thing happen to David.

Therefore, the Spirit of God was sent to effect an action on the part of both the messengers and Saul to keep this from occurring. All were instilled with a desire to render praise to God. Neither the messengers nor Saul would have done this of themselves. The messengers were probably military people, accustomed to the toughened life of soldiers and not given to singing songs of praise. And Saul was an even more unlikely candidate at this time, being angry at David and now also at three apparently inept groups of messengers. Such an attitude is surely not conducive to singing, especially singing in praise to God. To prompt both the messengers and Saul to be so changed therefore required a special intervention by the Spirit of God. The three groups of messengers experienced this change only when they came to where the young prophets already were singing, and Saul experienced it before he arrived. For some reason, God saw a need for his heart to be altered even before he came where the others were. It is most significant that, having been thus affected, he did not give any order for David to be apprehended, even though he had come in such anger and desired to have this very thing happen.

The question of Saul's resulting stupor must still be accounted for. Though the messengers had also stripped off their outer robes, Saul alone lay in a stupor for a period of several hours. It should be noticed also that the text does not relate the coming of the Spirit on Saul to this action. The Spirit came on him before he reached Ramah. At that time he began to prophesy. It was only after his arrival at the scene where the others were praising that he lay down in the stupor. It is logical to ask why he lay down in this way when none of the others did.

The answer is that Saul was suddenly taken with a sense of melancholy and despair. The general story shows that he was given to emotional moods of this kind. At this time, he had been highly disturbed relative to David and the young man's popularity with the people. He had twice been unsuccessful in trying to kill David with a spear (I Sam. 18:11; 19:9, 10). Then he had experienced what he thought to be treason on the part of his own daughter Michal, when she had let David down from an outside window so that he might escape her father's soldiers (I Sam. 19:11–17). And now he had sent three groups of messengers who had failed to apprehend his talented rival. Finally he had come himself to the scene where he saw these very messengers singing in praise to God, along with Samuel's prophets, and especially he observed David in the protective favor of the great Samuel. The story is clear that Saul had always kept a high regard for Samuel. That David now enjoyed Samuel's favor spelled out unmistakably the end of Saul's hopes for a continuing rule for his family. As a result, Saul was overcome with a sense of despair. Emotional excesses are subject to pendulumlike changes, and Saul now moved from one extreme to the other. Thus drained of all emotional and physical strength, he lay down in a stupified condition for the rest of that day and all the following night.

## E. THE PROPHETIC FUNCTION CONSIDERED
## AGAIN

In chapters 4 and 5, it was observed that the function of the prophet consisted basically of two responsibilities: to receive revelations from God and to declare God's message to the people. The declaration of the message was considered at some length in both chapters, but little was said in reference to the reception of revelations. It is necessary now to relate the work of the Holy Spirit especially to the reception of revelations, though a brief word is still necessary in respect to the declaration of God's message.


## 1. The declaration of the message

It was observed that the basic meaning of *nabhi'* was "to speak for God." It was observed further that when the minor meanings of "raving" and "praising" were related to this, the fuller meaning was "to speak fervently for God." It was also seen that this fervent speaking was basically a preaching activity in which various techniques were used for making the declaration more emphatic. Among these techniques were the employment of symbolic actions, object lessons, and speaking to key individuals.

The relationship of the empowerment by the Holy Spirit to this activity is easy to see. It was simply that, in carrying out this work of declaring God's word, the prophets needed special empowerment. As the word was preached, whether using symbolic actions, object lessons, or speaking to key individuals, the prophets needed power from heaven so that the word might carry the greatest weight and effectiveness. This would have applied to accuracy of memory in recalling exactly what God had said on occasions of revelation, and it would have involved the collection, classification, and selection of information to be used when other than revelatory materials were employed.

Since the subject of writing the prophetic books was also treated in chapter 5, it is appropriate to mention that the Holy Spirit would have especially empowered the prophets for this task. In fact, since these books were to become a part of the Sacred Scriptures, the degree of empowerment involved with their inscripturation was no doubt more than with oral proclamation. The Scriptures claim for themselves to have been supernaturally inspired to the point of infallibility, even in the words, and it is doubtful that this was true of oral messages. The prophets were empowered for the giving of oral messages to insure that they were accurate and authoritative, but to say that every spoken word was infallibly inspired is more than the Scriptures claim. The written Word, however, was a product fully without error.


## 2. The reception of the message

It was seen in chapter 4 that the aspect of the prophet's work which was especially connoted by the names *ro'eh* and *hozeh* was the reception of revelation. It was observed also that this was the aspect delineated for the prophets in the Law, especially in Deuteronomy 18. The prophets were to be recipients of revelation on behalf of the people so that the people would not resort to some form of divination. In a real sense, therefore, this aspect of the prophet's work was primary, because the people would need to hear from God whether or not they had fallen into sin. In other words, even in the ideal state—for which the Law was written—prophets would be necessary in this respect. The work of reformation—which involved mainly message-declaration—came in time to occupy the major attention of prophets, but the aspect of message-reception still continued and had been primary from the first.

### a. INVOLVEMENT OF AN *ab extra* FACTOR

The discussion of chapter 4 gave evidence showing that the revelational experience of prophets did not involve ecstatic frenzy. This leaves the question open as to what it did involve. Lindblom compares the experience to that of writers and prophets of any day.[5] This is another extreme, however, which must be avoided, for, though the prophets did not have an ecstatic experience in receiving revelation, they did have one which surpassed normal, natural functions. The natural mind somehow learned what it had not known before. In other words, an *ab extra* factor was involved, whereby a divine contact was made from without, and an event of supernatural revelation occurred. It is logical to try to discover the nature of this factor by considering the occasions of the revelations. When one does several matters become evident.

*1) No indication of self-stimulation.* The first matter is that no times of revelation show any form of self-stimulation having been employed. This fact gives further evidence against the idea of ecstatic frenzy. The music of the band of prophets in I Samuel 10 was found to be explained in a better way. David's so-called "sacred dance" of II Samuel 6 has received mention by scholars in this connection, and at that time David did lead others in a sacred procession involving leaping and dancing before the ark. No revelation, however, was involved; David's activity had nothing to do with seeking a message from God. Moreover, David's rational faculties were well under control. He proceeded to have sacrifices offered and later blessed the people and gave them all bread and wine before bringing the occasion to a close. Then Elisha's call for a minstrel to play before him, that "the hand of the LORD" might come upon him (II Kings 3:15), was cited earlier and explained to be other than an

---

[5]J. Lindblom, *Prophecy in Ancient Israel*, pp. 2f.

ecstatic experience. It is true that revelation was involved and that music was played, but nothing else from the occasion fits the idea of self-stimulation to achieve an ecstatic state. There are simply no passages which indicate any form of self-stimulation, when these passages are allowed to stand as they are found in the text.

*2) No indication of initiating the revelational experience.* A second matter is that no times of revelation give any indication of a prophet's initiating the revelational experience.[6] God did the initiating; the prophets simply awaited His word. As noted in chapter 4, this was in contrast to the high priest's use of the Urim and Thummim, for the high priest did initiate revelational contact with God by this means. The pattern of the prophets, however, is illustrated graphically with Samuel. While Samuel was still a lad (I Sam. 3:4–14), God spoke to him in the night and Samuel thought it was Eli speaking, the high priest of the day and teacher of Samuel. Three times God called, and on the third time Eli realized that it was God who was speaking and counseled the boy accordingly. On the fourth time, Samuel indicated his readiness to hear what God had to say, and God revealed the message intended. God initiated the occasion in every respect; Samuel did nothing to bring it about. It is true that prophets could and did pray for times of revelation. In I Samuel 8, Samuel asked God for counsel relative to the people's request for a king, and it was given. God, however, still controlled the revelation. Samuel could only wait after having given the request.[7]

*3) No indication of a loss in rational power.* A third statement is that no times of revelation indicate any loss of rational power on the part of prophets at the moment of revelation. Adherents of the ecstatic idea believe that a loss in rational consciousness was not only experienced but was diligently sought. No case of this can be found. Instead, one finds Moses being able to think very quickly of reasons why he could not respond to God's call to return to Egypt, when he was spoken to out of the burning bush (Exod. 3:4). The lad Samuel, just mentioned, the following morning after his revelation could yet relate to the high priest all that God had told him. Or Isaiah, after his memorable vision in the temple, was able to think of his own unworthiness and volunteer himself to be God's emissary to the Israelite people (Isa. 6:1–8).[8]

---

[6]Walter Eichrodt (*Theology of the Old Testament*, p. 318) states, "Israel knows nothing of the prophet's being able thus to gain mastery over God and to force his way into the divine world."
[7]Cf. other instances: Exod. 5:22—6:1; 15:25; II Chron. 20:5–7.
[8]Stanley Cook (*The Old Testament, a Reinterpretation*, pp. 188–189) writes, "It was the sanity of the prophets and not their manticism which made them such tremendous factors in human history."

*4) But involvement of more than human reason.* A fourth matter is that the prophet's experience of revelation was more than an exercise of rational abilities. Though the prophet did not experience ecstatic frenzy, he did experience an *ab extra* factor in the form of an influence from the outside. Reason was transcended, while it still retained its natural power. There was contact with the divine, without any negation of the human. The human mind was enabled to transcend its own finite limitations and come away from the moment knowing more than it had before.

The center of this experience was always "the word of God." A message was communicated and the prophet was convinced that God had spoken it. Afterwards, he would go forth and assert without hesitation, "Thus saith the LORD." And he was prepared to suffer and even die for the word thus given. Micaiah was willing to endure confinement in prison (I Kings 22:26–28). Zechariah was prepared to die by stoning (II Chron. 24:20, 21). Jeremiah was ready to be cast into a cistern-type dungeon, intended to bring about his death (Jer. 38:4–6).[9]

### b. THIS *ab extra* FACTOR A WORK OF THE SPIRIT OF GOD

It was this *ab extra* factor which was produced by the Spirit of God. The Spirit brought the occasion of revelation about and effected the transfer of information conveyed. The following argumentation may be cited in support.

First, the occasion had to be brought about by a supernatural agency since more than a natural result was achieved. The recipient came to know information he had not known before nor could have gained by any natural activity of his own. For instance, a "man of God" was informed that a descendant of David named Josiah would one day offer the priests of the high places of Israel upon the altar of Bethel (I Kings 13:1, 2), and this indeed came true approximately three hundred years later (II Kings 23:16).[10] Again Isaiah predicted the rule of Cyrus, king of Persia, by name about 150 years before this man lived (Isa. 44:28; 45:1).[11]

Second, that this supernatural agency was the Holy Spirit, the Third

---

[9]Even liberal critics are compelled to take notice of this fact. H. Wheeler Robinson, for instance ("The Philosophy of Religion," *Record and Revelation*, p. 314), says, "When we would trace the most essential part of the Old Testament religion back to its most essential elements, we find a man standing in the presence of God, and so wrought upon by Him that he comes away from that presence ready to declare in the teeth of all opinion and all persecution, 'Thus saith Yahweh.'"

[10]The revelation was given to the "man of God" in the day of Jeroboam I shortly after 931 B.C.; Josiah began to rule in 640 B.C. and probably carried out this prediction around 620 B.C.

[11]Isaiah's revelation would have been some time before 700 B.C. and Cyrus came to power approximately 550 B.C., capturing Babylon in 539 B.C.

Person of the Godhead, is indicated by two factors. One is that the Spirit of God was closely associated with the revelational experience whenever it was given (e.g., Num. 24:2f.; I Chron. 12:18; II Chron. 15:1f.; 20:14f.; 24:20; Ezek. 2:2f.; 3:24f.; 11:5f.). The other is that it was the particular work of the Holy Spirit to make such contact with man in man's God-related experiences. The Spirit has always brought to completion the work of grace made possible by the Father through the Son, and any revelation of heaven-sent information is a part of that work. This last is made clear by II Peter 1:21: "For the prophecy came not in old time by the will of man: but holy men of God spake as they were moved by the Holy Spirit." The word *moved* is from the Greek root *pherō*, meaning "to move along by carrying." The last part of the verse might be translated, "as they were borne along by the Holy Spirit." So, then, prophecy came through the prophets as they were thus "borne along."

The term *borne along* appears to be a key indication in reference to the Holy Spirit's work in revelation. It is appropriate, then, to make enquiry as to what the term means. This should help to indicate the nature of the occasion when the Holy Spirit gave revelation. A study of the many times of revelation shows that at least three factors were involved:

The first is that the occasion was made appropriate for revelation by a proper attitude on the part of the prophet. The revelational contact by the Spirit was not given at just any time. The prophet had to be a proper recipient, with a mind and heart made ready for such a grand and significant occasion. As noticed earlier, Elisha asked that a minstrel play soothing music—perhaps something from the temple services—that would help bring him to this kind of an attitude. Apparently he recognized his recent contact with the three kings—the heathen king of Edom, the Baal-worshiping Jehoram, and the backslidden Jehoshaphat, who otherwise was a true follower of God (II Kings 3:9–12)—had made him an unfit recipient so that the atmosphere had to be changed if the Spirit was to reveal information. Daniel had been fasting and praying for three weeks when a grand heavenly messenger brought God's information to him (Dan. 10:2–6). And the apostle John years later states that he was "in the Spirit on the Lord's day" when he received his great revelation of the glory of the Son of God (Rev. 1:10–16). Most occasions do not give this type of specific information, but all that do point in this direction and none suggest that the prophet was in any attitude inappropriate to the occasion.

The second is that these occasions were times when the prophet's natural and mental ability was heightened so that he could understand and remember in an unusually capable way. This factor is evidenced by simple force of logic. Revelational information was extremely important, being sent from heaven. As it came from God, it was fully accurate and in the form desired by God. It was true, sufficient, and suitable to the occasion. But God would have wanted it conveyed in this same form to the people for whom it was ultimately intended. Therefore, the human instrument was vitally important as the conveyor, and he needed to be equipped to do his work properly. This means that, rather than losing rational powers, the prophet needed to have them made the sharpest possible. He needed to be inspired so that his mental faculties were raised to the highest point of efficiency and his understanding and memory heightened to their finest quality.

The third is that the occasion involved an actual transfer of heaven-sent information into the intellect of the human instrument. With the prophet in a suitable attitude of mind and heart, and with his mental faculties thus sharpened, the Spirit found the situation appropriate for adding information to what the prophet already knew. This addition seems to have been effected at times by an audible voice, something which clearly occurred with Moses at the burning bush (Exod. 3:4f.). More often, it probably came by a simple inaudible insertion into the human mind. The prophet, in the state of heightened mental powers, would suddenly recognize that he knew information he had not known before. And not only would he know this information, but he would be certain that it had come from God, for he then was ready to go forth and declare, "Thus saith the LORD," in spite of any danger or opposition.

### c. Dreams, visions, and theophanies

Besides this direct form of revelation, God also used the means of dreams, visions, and theophanies to communicate with human instruments. These means were not used as often as the direct method of contact just described, and especially not with prophets. But since they were at times employed, and to some extent with prophets, they call for consideration. The following observations are in order:

First, certain basic distinctions between these means call for notice. A revelation by a dream found the recipient in a passive, nonconscious state, with the reality of what was dreamed found only in noncorporeal mental images. At the other extreme, revelation by theophany (especially the Angel of the Lord) found the recipient in an active, conscious state, with the One revealing possessing an objective, corporeal body. And, between the two, a revelation by a vision found the recipient in an active, conscious state (like the theophany) but with the reality of what was visualized found only in noncorporeal mental images (like the dream).

Second, because of these distinctions, the three forms of revelation were appropriate for use in different situations. The dream was more suitable to people of little or no spiritual discernment. Pharaoh of Egypt, Abimelech of

Gerar, Nebuchadnezzar of Babylon, all of whom were pagans, were given dreams. Never did such a person receive either a vision or an appearance by theophany. In a dream the recipient was neutralized in his personality. He was only an inert instrument to whom information could be imparted, unable to respond in a paganistic, improper manner.[12] Jacob dreamed at Bethel (Gen. 28:12-15) and Joseph while still a lad (Gen. 37:5-10), but both may well have been quite immature in spiritual stature at the time.

On the other hand, an appearance by theophany was normally reserved only for persons of high spiritual maturity. It was an Abraham, a Joshua, a Gideon, a Manoah, or later Daniel's three friends in the fiery furnace (Dan. 3:25), or Daniel himself (Dan. 6:22) to whom such an appearance was given.[13] They had spiritual understanding that made them suitable respondents to this manner of personal, face-to-face contact.

God also employed visions with spiritually mature people. Abraham had a vision (Gen. 15:1), also Nathan (I Chron. 17:15), Ezekiel (Ezek. 1:1; 8:3), and Daniel (Dan. 8:1). Visions continued to occur also in New Testament time: for instance, with Ananias (Acts 9:10), Peter (Acts 10:3, 17, 19), and Paul (Acts 16:9). Visions seem to have been employed more often than either dreams or theophanies.

Third, though none of the three forms are ever said to have been particularly the work of the Spirit of God, this is likely. As has been seen, revelational activity fits into the general type of work assigned to the Third Person of the Godhead. He did effect the direct manner of revelational contact, and it is logical to believe He did the same with these more indirect methods. That is, He sent the dream and the vision and superintended in the coming of the Second Person in an appearance by theophany.

---

[12]Geerhardus Vos, *Biblical Theology*, pp. 83-85.

[13]An exception seems to be found with Hagar (Gen. 16:7-13; 21:17-19) and Balaam (Num. 22:22-35), though the very fact that the Angel of the Lord appeared to both may indicate a spiritual relationship to God on their part otherwise not disclosed.

# 7

# False Prophecy in Israel

Another much discussed question regarding Old Testament prophetism concerns the false prophet. Thus far our discussions have involved almost solely the true prophet in Israel. There was, however, the false prophet as well. He is mentioned numerous times and in various ways. For instance, he is in mind in Deuteronomy 18:20: "But the prophet, which shall presume to speak a word in my name, which I have not commanded him to speak, or that shall speak in the name of other gods, even that prophet shall die."

The true prophets themselves refer to these false prophets frequently. Hosea says, "The prophet is a fool . . . a snare of a fowler in all his ways," and such "have deeply corrupted themselves" (9:7–9). Isaiah writes, "The priest and the prophet have erred through strong drink . . . they err in vision, they stumble in judgment" (28:7). Micah accuses them of making "my people err" as they "divine for money" (3:5, 11). Zephaniah calls them "light and treacherous persons" (3:4).

Jeremiah speaks of them the most strongly, stating at one time, "From the prophet even unto the priest everyone dealeth falsely" (6:13), and later, devoting most of a chapter to the subject, "Both prophet and priest are profane. . . . They prophesied in Baal, and caused my people Israel to err. . . . They commit adultery and walk in lies; they strengthen also the hands of evil-doers" (23:11f.). He also depicts God as saying of them, "I have not sent these prophets, yet they ran; I have not spoken to them, yet they prophesied. . . . I have heard what the prophets said, that prophesy lies in my name.... Therefore, behold, I am against the prophets... that steal my words every one from his neighbor" (23:21f.). Ezekiel too speaks forcefully against these people, as he says, "Woe unto the foolish prophets, that follow their own spirit, and have seen nothing!... They have seen vanity and lying divination" (13:3–6). He also refers to God as declaring, "Mine hand shall be upon the prophets that see vanity and that divine lies.... They have seduced my people, saying, Peace; and there was no peace" (13:9, 10).

The question in point concerns the identity of these people. Who was the person the true prophets called false? Why was he called false, and what marks so identified him? Even more important, how could the average person discern between a prophet who was true and one who was false? What tests could be applied?

## A.  TWO ERRONEOUS VIEWPOINTS

### 1.  Cultic versus noncultic prophets

A viewpoint which is not as popular today as a few years ago concerns an alleged conflict between cultic and noncultic prophets. H. H. Rowley describes this viewpoint as a "division between cultic prophets and true prophets, that would identify the cultic prophets with the opponents of the true prophets."[1] The viewpoint is based on a belief that true prophets came to repudiate the sacrificial system of the central sanctuary and therefore to consider any prophets false who were associated with the system. This belief is founded on passages like Amos 5:21, 22: "I hate, I despise your feast days, and I will not smell in your solemn assemblies. Though you offer me burnt-offerings and your meat-offerings, I will not accept them." Similar in intent is Hosea 6:6: "For I desired mercy, and not sacrifice; and the knowledge of God more than burnt-offerings."[2]

Connected with this viewpoint is the thought that the ceremonial system of Israel had been borrowed in large degree from the Canaanites, and therefore true prophets repudiated it because they were opposed to anything Canaanite. Great immorality was connected with Canaanite practices and the prophets wished to avoid this for the Israelite people. As W. Robertson Smith says, "When the prophets positively condemn the worship of their contemporaries, they do so because it is associated with immorality."[3]

[1]H. H. Rowley, *The Unity of the Bible*, p. 37.
[2]See also Isa. 1:11–14; Jer. 6:20; 7:21–23; Mic. 6:6–8.
[3]*The Old Testament in the Jewish Church*, p. 288. Cf. Johannes Pedersen, *Israel: Its Life and Culture*, III–IV, p. 299.

This view is in error, however, and few scholars hold to it today.[4] As indicated in chapter 5, a view completely contrary came to be espoused by the Scandinavian school, in which it was believed that cultic prophets were not only approved in Israel, but were considered the regular prophets. It was shown that this viewpoint is also in error, since Israel's prophets were not prophets of the cultus at all. A viewpoint that is halfway between these two extremes is commonly set forth today, and it is much nearer the biblical presentation. It sees the criticisms which the prophets made concerning sacrifices as pertaining to a wrong attitude on the part of the people in presenting them, rather than a negation of the sacrifices as such. In the words of Rowley, "The prophets were really saying that obedience was more important than sacrifice, and that for lack of obedience sacrifice was invalidated."[5]

## 2. Ecstatic versus nonecstatic prophets

A viewpoint held more widely concerns ecstatic behavior. It was observed in chapter 3 that many scholars believe Israel's prophets, especially the early ones, moved about in groups and observed the practice of ecstasy. This viewpoint holds that gradually prophets emerged, either out of such groups or in protest to them, who disdained the use of ecstaticism and came to call those who continued to use it false, as over against themselves as true. The first of this new type of prophet is thought to have been Micaiah of the day of Ahab (I Kings 22:7–28). Because of Micaiah's comparatively late date in Israel's history, many adherents have come to make a sharp distinction between early and late prophets. The later prophets are believed to have continued in the line of Micaiah, and among these are the writing prophets.

Of scholars who have made this distinction, none is more important than Sigmund Mowinckel. He maintains a sharp distinction between those he calls "spirit" prophets and "word" prophets.[6] The "spirit" prophets were the early ecstatic prophets, and the "word" prophets mainly the later writing prophets. He says, "The idea of Yahweh's spirit in the older *nabhi'ism's* practice of ecstaticism refers almost exclusively to the ecstatic behavior and activities of the *nabhi*. His possession by the Spirit was what made him ecstatic."[7] So then for Mowinckel almost all the early prophets were ecstatic prophets while the later prophets were prophets of the "word." By the "word" he means the rational message these prophets believed came from God and which they

[4]Cf. Rowley, *The Unity of the Bible*, p. 33.
[5]Ibid., p. 39; cf. H. Wheeler Robinson, *Redemption and Revelation*, p. 250.
[6]"The 'Spirit' and the 'Word' in the Pre-exilic Reforming Prophets," *Journal of Biblical Literature*, 53 (1934):199–227.
[7]Ibid., p. 199.

then proclaimed. He points out that instead of saying, "The Spirit of Yahweh came upon me," the writing prophets used the expression, "Yahweh showed me," or "The word of Yahweh came to me."[8] He describes this word in the following way, "It is a real active force, a potency which Yahweh can 'send forth' and which can 'descend upon' a people with devastating effect. . . . The prophet feels it within himself 'like a fire in his bones,' and must needs give utterance to it (Jer. 20:9)."[9]

In evaluation of this view, one may say that Mowinckel is right in much of what he says regarding the writing prophets. He believes that they knew nothing of the trance, the hypnotic state, the wild frenzy of those who observed ecstaticism, but does accept the idea that they felt an elevation of spirit, a drive to give out the word. He is right also in speaking of their "prophetic call" and in regarding that this was "not merely felt to be a certainty," but was "in them as a *compelling force* from which they" could not escape.[10]

He is in error, however, in making a sharp distinction between "spirit" and "word," and in seeing the early prophets as ecstatics. Discussion of ecstaticism in chapter 3 showed that the early prophets did not observe this phenomenon and that all the prophets were equally sane people who received their messages by revelation from God. The Scriptures when taken at face value do not make a sharp distinction between early and later prophets.


## B.  IDENTITY OF THE FALSE PROPHETS

Having seen that these viewpoints do not reflect the teaching of Scripture, we must now make investigation of what the true biblical position is. Who was the false prophet and how could people know that he was false?


### 1.  Preliminary questions

Before considering the basic question, it is necessary to give attention to certain preliminary matters. The first concerns the origin of the idea *false*. Some scholars have suggested that when people of the Bible spoke of certain prophets as false, they did so unfairly.[11] The idea is that this other group of prophets might just as well have thought those opposed to them were false and they themselves were true. And one must agree that there was a real

[8]Ibid., p. 210.
[9]Ibid., pp. 212-213.
[10]Ibid., p. 211.
[11]For discussion, see A. B. Davidson, *Old Testament Prophecy*, p. 307.

antagonism between the two groups, as is made clear by Jeremiah. In chapter 26 Jeremiah tells how these opposing prophets, along with priests and others, declared that, because of his denunciations regarding Jerusalem, he should die. They did not like Jeremiah, and Jeremiah spoke strongly against them.

But whether or not the group called false is properly so designated by the biblical writers is decided by a person's viewpoint of the Scriptures. If the Scriptures are taken as authoritative, then of course they are correct in referring to the one group as false and the other as true. As has been evident from prior discussion, my viewpoint is that the Bible is altogether trustworthy and accurate, and therefore one need not hesitate in speaking of these prophets as indeed false.

Another question concerns which of the two types of prophets came first, the false or the true. Many scholars believe that the false were first. The viewpoint of these scholars has been noted in other contexts. The thought is that the false prophets were the ecstatic prophets and that it was out from among these, or else in protest to them, that those who later came to be called true arose. This, however, has already been shown to be incorrect.[12] The biblical presentation is that the true prophets were the first prophets and that out of this group emerged those who were false. In other words, false prophecy was a deterioration and perversion of true prophecy.

This leads to a third question concerning the motivation for this rise of false prophets. Why did they come to exist? Why did they move out from the ranks of the true prophets?[13] One suggestion is that, though most prophets did not become involved in ecstatic frenzy, some did due to the pressure of Canaanite influence. Coming thus to observe the foreign practice, they came to be considered by others as false. Another suggestion is that, though certain prophets did not receive a true word from God, they thought they did due to some unusual experience. Others, however, knowing that they had not received a true word called them false. And still a third suggestion is that certain prophets, under the impulse for position, reputation, or monetary considerations, allowed themselves to become caterers to the whims of people and especially of kings. Thus they came to lose their dedication to the true word of God and to speak out of their own minds what they knew the king or other influential person wanted to hear.

There may be some truth to these suggestions. Though the typical Israelite prophet surely was not an ecstatic, it may be that a few who purported to be prophets were influenced by Canaanite ways and gave themselves to the practice of ecstasy. If they did, certainly true prophets would

---

[12]Cf. chap. 3.
[13]Cf. Heinrich Ewald, *Commentary on the Prophets of the Old Testament*, I, pp. 15–25.

have considered them false. It is also true that some of the prophets may have been confused in their own thinking as to what was truly a word from God. They would have known that true prophets did experience divine revelations and, through some emotional stimulation, they could have believed that they too had received such a heavenly word. True prophets, knowing about them and the manner of their lives, would of course have considered them false. And it is also correct that out from among the true prophets there could have been those who defected in a desire to be king-pleasers and to enjoy the ease of a court rather than the rigors of a true prophet's life.

As Edward J. Young declares, however, "The real reason for the existence of false prophecy . . . is to be found, not in such external circumstances, but rather in the corruption of the human heart."[14] Any one of the three suggestions we have made may have been involved in a secondary sense, but the basic cause of false prophecy was sin and rebellion in the lives of those involved. History since has always known those who purported to be true proclaimers of God's word, but were not. They were false; they did not have the truth but only claimed to have it. This is true today in preachers who declare another gospel, as it was true also in the day of Paul who spoke of those who "would pervert the gospel of Christ," and stated that they should be accursed (Gal. 1:6–9).

## 2. Micaiah and the false prophets of Ahab

Micaiah, the son of Imlah, has often been called the first prophet who set himself off as a true prophet over against false prophets. The false prophets involved in this case were the four hundred prophets that Ahab had and on whom he regularly called for advice. Since this instance is recorded in detail, and since Micaiah did hold an important place in the history of true and false prophecy, it is appropriate to study the occasion to see what light may be drawn from it for our basic question.

The setting of the story is found in a desire on the part of Ahab, king of Israel, to have Jehoshaphat, king of Judah, go with him to battle against the Aramaeans of Damascus (I Kings 22). Before Jehoshaphat would consent, however, he asked that enquiry be made of God, and Ahab then called for his regular group of four hundred prophets to fill this request. They purported to do so and told the king to indeed go forth to battle for God would give him victory. They thus showed themselves to be in the pattern of false prophets, giving a word to the king that he desired. Jehoshaphat, however, was not

---

[14] *My Servants the Prophets*, p. 151.

satisfied with this, apparently recognizing the four hundred to be the kind of prophets they were, and he asked whether or not there was a true "prophet of the LORD besides," that they might enquire of him (22:7). Ahab responded that there was such a man, namely Micaiah, but said regarding him, "I hate him; for he doth not prophesy good concerning me but evil" (22:8). Still Micaiah was called to please the king of Judah.

The messenger that was sent to bring Micaiah urged him to speak that which the king desired, but Micaiah responded, "As the LORD liveth, what the LORD saith unto me, that will I speak" (22:14). On coming to the two kings, his words were, "I saw all Israel scattered upon the hills, as sheep that have not a shepherd" (22:17). He further indicated that the reason why the four hundred had predicted as they had was that God had sent a lying spirit into their mouths to deceive the king. At these words, Ahab, instead of responding properly, became angry and ordered Micaiah put in prison until Israel's forces would come again safely from the battle. In response Micaiah said, "If thou return at all in peace, the LORD hath not spoken by me" (22:28). So then Ahab was determined to go to battle in spite of Micaiah's warning, and Micaiah was willing to go to prison rather than change the word he knew God had given him to speak.

Several matters are illustrated in this occasion. One is that false prophets did exist and in considerable number, at least in Israel. It should be remembered that Israel was in rebellion against God's truths as represented in the temple in Jerusalem, and so false prophets were no doubt more numerous in Israel than in Judah. Another matter is that these prophets catered to the desire of the king. They knew that King Ahab wanted to go to Ramoth-gilead to fight and they encouraged him to do so, promising victory. And a third matter is that these prophets were deceived by an outside source prompting their false prophecy. The indication is that God permitted a "lying spirit" to go forth and delude them. Apparently, supernatural powers sometimes were involved in the false prophecies of such people.[15] Usually, however, false prophets are said to have spoken out of their own heart and mind (see, e.g., Isa. 9:14f.; Ezek. 13:7, 9).

The occasion reveals also a few matters regarding true prophets. One is that true prophets were very scarce in Israel at the time of Ahab. Though he had four hundred false prophets, he could think of only one true prophet who was close at hand. Another is that the true prophet was willing to stand alone against the majority. Micaiah, though a single prophet and opposed by four hundred, gave the word of God as he knew it in spite of this strong opposition. And a third is that he was willing to do this even if it meant suffering as

[15]This "lying spirit" most certainly was a demon that God permitted to bring the deception.

a result. Following the giving of his word to Ahab, Ahab assigned him to prison and Micaiah was willing to go rather than change the prophecy he had related.

## 3. Identity considered

### a. Two classifications

False prophets may be classified under two general heads: those not properly called prophets of God, nor claiming to be, and those who did make that claim.[16] The first group is in mind in Deuteronomy 13:1–3, which says, "If there arise among you a prophet... saying, Let us go after other gods which thou hast not known, and let us serve them; thou shalt not hearken unto the words of that prophet." Of these, also, Jeremiah writes: "They prophesied in Baal and caused my people Israel to err" (23:13). Against such prophets Elijah contested on Mount Carmel (I Kings 18), and they were prophets of Baal whom Jehu slew in the house of their deity (II Kings 10).

It is not with this first group, however, that we need to be concerned. That they were prophets of deities other than Israel's own God is clear to us today and surely was to the people to whom they sought to minister. The case is different with the second group, for they claimed to serve the one and only God, even as the true prophets. It is against these, primarily, that the invectives of the true prophets were directed. They evidently caused confusion in the minds of people. It may have been quite difficult for some people to determine exactly who were true and who false. It is on these false prophets that our interest centers. What was it that marked them as false?

### b. The basic answer

The basic answer is of two parts. The first is that true prophets were those who received their messages from God, while false prophets did not. The false were those who would say, "Thus saith the LORD God, when the LORD had not spoken" (Ezek. 22:28). To accept this distinction one must believe in the existence of one supreme God, as over against other so-called deities, and must acknowledge that this God could and did reveal to men in Bible days. The issue is not whether a prophet only thought he heard from God, or what features may have prompted him so to think, but whether he really did have a communication from heaven. True prophets had such communication and therefore had a message of divine origin and authentic-

[16]Cf. Davidson, *Old Testament Prophecy*, p. 298.

ity; false prophets did not have this. They may have thought they did and claimed to have it, but actually they did not. They were those who "followed their own spirit" and had seen "nothing" (Ezek. 13:3).

The second part is that true prophets were especially called of God to their ministry, while false prophets were not. The subject of the call of true prophets was discussed in chapter 1. It was observed that they had to be special and courageous individuals because of the challenging task they had to carry out. Therefore they were a called group, as over against the priests who inherited their office. Jeremiah asserts that he was ordained and called of God already at the time of his birth (1:5). In contrast he speaks of God as saying regarding false prophets, "I sent them not, neither have I commanded them" (14:14; cf. 29:8, 9).

c. DISTINGUISHING MARKS

Though these two features were basic in distinguishing true and false prophets, neither of them was subject to examination by the people; and both true and false prophets claimed to represent the true God and both asserted that they had been called. Thus, it was up to the people to discern which one was true in his claims and which was not. This means that people needed objective signs by which to make an identification. It is important, then, to consider the signs that existed. Among these signs the following probably were the most helpful.

*1) Divination not employed.* One clear sign was whether or not a prophet employed divination. If he did, he was thereby indicated to be false; if he did not, there was a chance that he was true. Deuteronomy 18:9-14 sets forth in detail the many areas of divination practiced by heathen nations, and Moses states that Israelites were not to resort to any of them. Rather, God would raise up prophets to whom He would reveal and give accurate information. One would think that, in view of this clear warning, no prophets would have wanted to employ divination, but they did. Jeremiah, speaking of such prophets, says, "They prophesy unto you a false vision and divination" (14:14); and Micah states, "Then shall the seers be ashamed, and the diviners confounded" (Mic. 3:7; cf. v. 11 and Ezek. 12:24). There is no way to know how many false prophets employed divination, but at least those who did could be thereby distinguished as false. The true prophets received their information solely by direct revelation from God.

*2) Character of the message.* A second mark, which would have applied to all prophets, concerned the character of the message proclaimed. False prophets spoke messages that catered to the delights and whims of people.

This was seen in the four hundred that gave the message to Ahab regarding the battle at Ramoth-gilead. They told him what he wanted to hear. Micaiah, on the other hand, told him what he did not want to hear. This in itself was a mark that Micaiah was true.

Jeremiah spoke of the message brought by false prophets as one that declared, "Peace, peace; when there is no peace" (8:11; cf. Ezek. 13:10). They were saying that everything was all right and that the people had nothing to fear, when this was not the case. At another time Jeremiah put the thought from a different point of view when he said to the false prophets, "The prophets that have been before me and before thee of old, prophesied both against many countries, and against great kingdoms, of war, and of evil, and of pestilence" (Jer. 28:8). Jeremiah's point is that, whereas false prophets of his day were speaking of peaceful times, the former prophets—and by this he means true prophets—had spoken regarding war and evil and pestilence. Thus a mark of a false prophet was that he never spoke of judgment, but only of peace and good times.

3) *Character of the prophet.*    Not only was the type of message significant, but also the character of the prophet himself. This again would have been an objective mark that applied to all. In the opening paragraphs of this chapter, several charges brought by true prophets against false were listed, and they pertain primarily to this area. The false prophets were accused of deceiving, lying, drunkenness, pretending to be what they were not, and speaking for God when God had not sent them. Micah speaks specifically of moral deficiency in divining "for money" (3:11). At another place he refers to the same idea by saying that false prophets would predict peace for people who provided food for them but quite the opposite for those who would not (3:5). In other words, false prophets would indicate things that were pleasant for those who paid, but not for those who did not pay. False prophets may have tried to hide their true character, but their success at this would have been only temporary; people would eventually have found out.

4) *Willingness for self-effacement.*    A fourth mark is related to the one just discussed, being a special aspect of it. It was the willingness of the prophet to suffer self-effacement for the sake of his message. By this he demonstrated his sincerity and degree of commitment. False prophets were not willing to do this, for they desired an easy life, a life which would come from catering to the desires of a king. But true prophets were willing to endure considerable loss and even suffering. One classic example has been noted: Micaiah, in the day of Ahab. Even though great opposition faced him on the part of four hundred false prophets, he stated God's word clearly and without equivocation. And even when Ahab told him that he would be assigned to prison

"with bread of affliction and with water of affliction" until Ahab came home in peace, Micaiah boldly replied, "If thou return at all in peace, the LORD hath not spoken by me" (I Kings 22:27, 28).

Another great example is Jeremiah. Jeremiah lived and prophesied in the time when the city of Jerusalem was under siege by the Babylonians. Other people of Judah were urging everyone to be courageous and withstand the enemy, but God's word to Jeremiah was that the people should capitulate. Such a message, of course, was unpopular, and Jeremiah was accused of being disloyal. It must not have been easy to continue giving this message, but Jeremiah did so in spite of popular opinion and the opposition of false prophets. He was put in prison so that he would be silenced, but when he was released he spoke in the same way, saying, "This city shall surely be given into the hand of the king of Babylon's army, which shall take it" (Jer. 38:3). As a result, further efforts were put forth to imprison him, and, when Zedekiah gave permission, Jeremiah was cast into a cisternlike dungeon where he was expected to die in a short time. God did not leave him there, however, but prompted Ebed-melech to draw Jeremiah out (Jer. 38:4–13). Jeremiah was willing to suffer the most extreme self-effacement for the word of God. Though this mark no doubt may not appear so dramatically in regard to all true prophets, a general tone in keeping with the attitude is apparent in their manner and work.

*5) Harmony of the message.* A fifth mark is that the message of the true prophet harmonized with the Law of God and with the messages which other true prophets were giving. The Law had been in existence from the time of Moses, and priests had been teaching it with varying degrees of faithfulness down through the years. Therefore, the people would have known what it said, at least in general terms. Certainly, also, a body of information had been building in people's minds from the messages of true prophets. Such information would have served as a criterion of whether or not further messages were true. If they were consistent with what had been taught before, they could be expected to be true; if they were not, they would certainly be shown to be false.

An interesting case in point concerns again Jeremiah. In Jeremiah 26, the prophet predicts clearly the fall of Jerusalem. The leaders of the people are depicted as crying out to the king that Jeremiah should die for such speaking. In the midst of this situation there

> rose up certain of the elders of the land, and spake to all the assembly of the people, saying, Micah the Morasthite prophesied in the days of Hezekiah, king of Judah, and spake to all the people of Judah, saying, Thus saith the LORD of hosts; Zion shall be plowed like a field, and Jerusalem shall become heaps, and

the mountain of the house the high places of a forest. Did Hezekiah king of Judah and all Judah put him at all to death? did he not fear the LORD, and besought the LORD, and the LORD repented him of the evil which he had pronounced against them? Thus might we procure great evil against our souls (vv. 17–19).

These words indicate that elders of the land recognized that what Jeremiah was saying was in harmony with what Micah had said many years before, and that, therefore, no harm should be done to Jeremiah. Interestingly, at this time, nothing was done to the prophet. Because his message was consistent with what had been proclaimed earlier, he was spared.

6) *Fulfillment of predictive prophecy.*    A sixth mark would have been applicable only in certain instances, depending upon whether a prophet predicted future events and whether these events could be and were fulfilled in the time when the contemporary generation lived. That this was a true mark, and one important in the sight of God, is indicated by a reference to it in the significant passage, Deuteronomy 18:21, 22: "And if thou say in thine heart, How shall we know the word which the LORD hath not spoken? When a prophet speaketh in the name of the LORD, if the thing follow not, nor come to pass, that is the thing which the LORD hath not spoken, but the prophet hath spoken it presumptuously: thou shalt not be afraid of him."

Only a comparatively small portion of all that the prophets spoke concerned prediction, but, when it did, an important mark existed as to the trueness of the prophet by whether or not the prediction came to pass. Micaiah, noted above, predicted that Israel would be as sheep without a shepherd if Ahab went to battle against the Aramaeans. That prediction came true, for Ahab was killed as he fought in the battle and Israel was left without a king until a new one was crowned. In the day of Jeremiah, the false prophet Hananiah predicted that the people taken captive would return within two years (Jer. 28:2–4). This prediction was made in direct opposition to Jeremiah's earlier indication that the captivity would last seventy years (Jer. 25:11, 12). Therefore, Jeremiah rebuked Hananiah and foretold his death, with the result that Hananiah did die the same year in the seventh month (Jer. 28:15–17). Thus Jeremiah was proven before the people as a true prophet and Hananiah false.

7) *Authentication by miracle.*    A seventh mark would also have been limited in its application, but still was evidential on occasion. This was the mark of a performance of miracle. A study of miracles in Scripture shows them to have occurred in groups and for specific occasions. These occasions were normally times of additional revelation from God or times of unusual significance in the divine program. The day of Moses, when Israel was

becoming a nation, was such a day, and many miracles were performed by Moses in authentication of himself as God's prophet and leader to the people. God gave him two miraculous signs to demonstrate before Pharaoh: the ability to change a rod into a snake and then back into a rod, and also to make his hand first leprous and then whole again by simply inserting it into his garment. Later came the ten great plagues, and later still the crossing of the Red Sea and the miracles that occurred through the wilderness journey. Joshua[17] was authenticated as leader and prophet by the division of the waters of the Jordan, by the falling of the walls of Jericho, by the prolonging of a day so that he might defeat an enemy and by the pelting of that enemy by great stones (probably hailstones) from heaven.[18] Samuel called for thunder and rain in the midst of the dry season to demonstrate the validity of his words to Israel (I Sam. 12:16f.). And the miracles performed by Elijah and Elisha in their day are well known.

The sign of the miracle, however, was not a conclusive evidence of prophetic authenticity; false prophets at times could also produce signs that were beyond human ability. Their source of power would have been Satan himself. Regarding the last days, it is said, "False Christs and false prophets shall rise and shall show signs and wonders, to seduce, if it were possible, even the elect" (Mark 13:22). And it is stated that the antichrist and his false prophet will be able to perform "with all power and signs and lying wonders" by the "working of Satan" (II Thess. 2:9). In keeping with this, Moses early warned the people:

> If there arise among you a prophet, or a dreamer of dreams, and giveth thee a sign or wonder, and the sign or the wonder come to pass, whereof he spake unto thee, saying, Let us go after other gods, which thou hast not known and let us serve them; thou shalt not hearken unto the words of that prophet, or that dreamer of dreams (Deut. 13:1–3).

The people could know, then, that any prophet who tried to get them to follow another god was false, even if he was able to perform a sign or wonder. They would know that the sign or wonder had not been worked as the result of the power of God.

*8) Spiritual discernment.* The last mark to be mentioned is of a different kind than the others. The others have all pertained to the kind of person the prophet was or what he did as people observed him. This one concerns the

---

[17]Though Joshua is never called a prophet, he served in the capacity of a prophet by both receiving messages and giving them to the people.

[18]Of course, these miracles had a wider purpose than merely authenticating Moses or Joshua.

person who did the observing and the condition of his heart. It is to the effect that persons who were spiritual, knowing God and loving the truth, would be better able by this fact to discern between a true prophet and one who was false. When Jesus was on earth, He spoke of His followers as those who knew His voice and would not follow strangers, but would flee from strangers, since they knew not the voice of strangers (John 10:4, 5). And Paul later wrote, "But the natural man receiveth not the things of the Spirit of God: for they are foolishness unto him; neither can he know them, because they are spiritually discerned" (I Cor. 2:14). If this was true in New Testament time, it must have been true also in Old Testament days. People of that time needed to be able to discern, just as well as people in the present age. It was no doubt mainly the person who was himself far from God who had difficulty in distinguishing between true and false prophets. The person who was truly following the Lord would usually have recognized quickly when a person was false in his teaching.

In conclusion one may say that the list of marks of a true prophet, as against a false prophet, is surprisingly long. Not all of the marks would have been applicable in every case, and yet some were. All the marks would have applied in some cases. For persons who really wanted to know and were true followers of God themselves, there would have been little, if any, question as to who was a true prophet and who was false.

# 8

# A General Overview

Before coming to Part Two of our study, in which the various prophets will be considered in their respective personal characters and life situations, it will be helpful to look in a general sense at the history of which they were a part. A few basic matters call for notice, and then the history will be surveyed.

## A. GENERAL MATTERS

### 1. An increase in the numbers of prophets

The number of Israel's prophets, living at any one time, increased as the years of history passed. During the early period of the judges, there were comparatively few. Some scholars believe there were almost none, but this is incorrect as will be seen later. There were not as many, however, as later on. Between the time of Samuel and the days of the writing prophets, there were more, and names of a number of these are listed. It was during the period of the writing prophets that the prophets became the most numerous and the most influential.

The reason for this increase is best found in the enlargement of the task prophets were called to perform. As has been seen, prophets at first were to

115

serve only as recipients of revelation from God, so that people might go to them rather than to diviners (Deut. 18:9–22). If no additional responsibility for prophets had arisen, their numbers probably would never have become very large. A few would have been able to serve in this limited capacity. As has been seen, however, prophetic responsibility did increase. It became necessary for them to serve as reformers. It had been the task of the priests to teach the people, and, ideally, the people should have obeyed what was taught without special urging by reformers, but the people had not done so, and therefore prophets were needed. God evidently saw that prophets were the type of religious persons best suited to carry out this task. As the people grew in number and the degree and seriousness of sin increased as well, there was need for more prophets to do this work.

It should be realized that at any period in Israel's history more prophets were living than are mentioned in the Scriptures. There is no place where the Scriptures give a complete list of prophets or have any reason for giving such a list. Rather, those prophets are mentioned who were involved in a story being told or a truth being related. Those not so involved are not included. Lindblom is no doubt right when he says, "The prophets whose revelations have been transmitted to us in the prophetic books were only a small minority of the prophets who were active in Israel."[1]

## 2. Relation to the priests

There is need to clarify the relation of prophets to priests. An understanding of this relationship is necessary if one is to see prophets in their true light as religious functionaries. Rather than being closely related in the cultus of the day, as the Scandinavian school holds,[2] priests and prophets carried on distinct ministries. They both had the same interest of encouraging people to obey God, but they had different aspects of work in carrying out that interest. The priests did so in a twofold manner.

First and best known, they supervised the ceremonial activity at the central sanctuary, presenting sacrifices in behalf of the people. This was a work principally intercessory in kind, as they sought to make the people acceptable in the sight of God on the basis of slain sacrifices. The second task, equally important, was teaching the people the Law of God (Lev. 10:11; Deut. 33:10). God had revealed the Law, but, unless the people knew it, it could be of little benefit to them. God required obedience but obedience could not be rendered if the Law remained unknown. The teaching of its

[1]J. Lindblom, *Prophecy in Ancient Israel*, p. 202.
[2]See chap. 5, pp. 78–80.

content was the particular task of the priests. They were assigned forty-eight levitic cities (Josh. 21:41), scattered evenly among the tribes, so that they would be near the people and have opportunity for close contacts. In other countries of the day, the normal thing was for priests to live near the central sanctuary. God, however, wanted His priests and Levites to live among the people. It is significant that God also gave priests and Levites ample time for this teaching ministry. David was led to divide them into twenty-four courses, with each course to serve at the central sanctuary one week in turn. This meant that only two weeks a year was normally spent at the temple, thus giving some fifty weeks in which to be home for the teaching ministry.

Prophets, on the other hand, did not live in assigned cities. They often lived in the cities of their birth, and moved out from there to discharge their assignments. They are never seen in a local class-type instructional situation, but are depicted as moving among the people, urging conformance to God's requirements. This means that the prophets' work as reformers presupposed the work of the priests as instructors. The priests addressed the minds of the people, informing them what the Law said; the prophets built on this instruction and addressed the hearts of the people, urging obedience to what had been taught. It is true that there were some areas of information which the Law did not cover but which the prophets did speak about. In these areas, there was an aspect of initial instruction, though still this was not given in a classroom-type situation. These areas included especially predictive matters which might concern warning of punishment to come or of grand times of exaltation and honor in the far future. These at times involved messianic predictions, speaking of the coming of Christ either in His first or second advent.

There was also a difference in the numbers of priests in contrast to prophets. It has been observed that prophets were numerous, but priests were much more so. Priests after all were descendants of Levi. Everyone who descended from this fourth son of Jacob became automatically a Levite and if he also descended from Aaron in that line, he was a priest. This meant that the members of one whole tribe of Israel became either priests or Levites, thus providing a very large number. In passing, it may be observed that the rationale for having such a large number is not found in the ceremonial activity of the priests. They even had to be divided into twenty-four courses so that there would not be too many to serve at one time. It is found rather in their teaching ministry. God wanted the people to know the Law and He wanted ample teachers available to impart it to them. On the other hand, prophets never approached this number. There probably were several score prophets living in many periods of Israel's history, but this would have fallen far short of the large number of priests who were active.

3. Relation of the earlier prophets
   to the later writing prophets

A view held more commonly a few years ago than today is that a major change came in Israelite prophecy when the writing prophets began their work.[3] The thought is that the earlier prophets were ecstatic in kind, as described in chapter 3,[4] while the later prophets were thinking men who became leaders in rational thought pertaining to moral and religious concepts. Moses Buttenwieser, for instance, wrote in 1914, "The inspiration of the great literary prophets has nothing in common with the ecstasy of the prophets of the older type."[5] Earlier discussions herein have shown this viewpoint to be in error. Actually the movement of prophetism in Israel was a single movement with basic similarities continuing all the way through the history. Similarity is found in a common desire to reform the prople and bring them to a place of obeying the Law of Moses as taught by the priests.[6]

Though the basic message and purpose did not change, variation did come in methods that were followed. One variation pertained to the manner of reference to sin. Earlier prophets spoke of the sins of individual people, as for instance Nathan's rebuking David for the sin with Bathsheba and Uriah, or later Gad's reprimanding David for taking a census of the nation (II Sam. 12:1–14; 24:10–25), whereas later prophets spoke of the sins of the people generally. These did not speak of individual sins but of the sins of the nation. In keeping with this distinction, the earlier prophets mainly contacted individual people, as in the case of Nathan with David, Elijah with Ahab (I Kings 21:17–24), or Hanani with Asa (II Chron. 16:7–10).[7] Later prophets, however, spoke to audiences of many people. A third distinction is that earlier prophets gave messages only orally, while many of the later prophets wrote and their books still remain.[8]

---

[3]Though for a comparatively recent statement see Isaac Mattuck, *The Thought of the Prophets*, pp. 19, 21, 31–33.

[4]Cf. also Mowinckel's view, chap. 7, pp. 103–104.

[5]*The Prophets of Israel from the Eighth to the Fifth Century*, p. 138. John Skinner in 1922 (*Prophecy and Religion*, p. 5) spoke of "the older *nabi'ism* of the period from Samuel to Elisha" and "the new type inaugurated by Amos," and C. Sauerbrei in 1947 ("The Holy Man in Israel: A Study in the Development of Prophecy," *Journal of Near Eastern Studies*, 6 [1947]:209) wrote that the distinction was so great that the later prophets must even have developed separately from the early "ecstatics." On the other hand, John Bright, in his more recent *History of Israel*, p. 247, says that the similarities between the prophets should be stressed since "the entire prophetic attack is rooted and grounded in the tradition of the Mosaic period."

[6]Theodore H. Robinson in 1923 (*Prophecy and the Prophets in Ancient Israel*, pp. 36–46) also maintained a fundamental similarity in the prophets, but did so on the basis that all were ecstatics. This view has been more recently espoused by Lindblom, *Prophecy in Ancient Israel*, pp. 105–106. It must be rejected just as well as the view that there was a sharp distinction.

[7]For a list of kings contacted, see chap. 5, p. 69.

[8]For evidence that prophets wrote their own books, see chap. 5, pp. 82–84.

The reason for these changes is best found in the growth of the population, an increase in sin by the people, and the nearness of impending punishment for this sin. In other words the need for prophetic contact with people became greater, and, therefore, not only did the number of prophets increase but their methods had to be redesigned to reach more people at one time. Writing fitted into this need for it served to reinforce the oral proclamation so that people could later read what had earlier been preached.

Sometimes the observation has been made that the later writing prophets were greater and more capable men than earlier prophets. A judgment of this kind, however, is difficult to make. It may be true that on the whole the writing prophets were more capable than earlier prophets, but when one begins to compare individuals, this is not necessarily true. For instance, Samuel was one of the very early prophets and yet he would measure up with any who came later on.

It is also sometimes asserted that, among the writing prophets, the minor prophets were men of less stature than the major prophets. This does not necessarily follow either. Certainly Isaiah, Jeremiah, and Ezekiel were outstanding individuals and were used mightily by God, but this was true also of Amos, Hosea, Micah, and others of the minor prophets. The distinction between major and minor should not be thought of so much in terms of individual capability as in the length of the books written. For some reason, God inspired the major prophets to write books of greater length than those of the minor prophets. This, however, does not mean that what the minor prophets wrote was any less important or significant, or that they as people were any less effective in their ministry.

## B. SURVEY OF THE HISTORY

We come now to a brief survey of the history of prophets in Israel. The history divides itself into clearly defined periods of time. These periods need to be recognized and then each prophet needs to be located in his respective period in order to understand him and his message.

### 1. Premonarchy prophets

The first period closed with the establishment of the monarchy under Saul. Until that time political conditions had been entirely different for the tribes and, accordingly, a particular type of prophetic message had been needed. Some scholars believe that Samuel was the first that could really be called a prophet. For instance, Lindblom says that Abraham, Moses,

Miriam, and Deborah can be called prophets only in "a loose sense, referring to a supernatural endowment."[9] He gives no evidence for this, however; the assertion seems to be built on the mere fact that the idea of these people being prophets does not fit into Israelite history as he sees it. But the Bible calls these people prophets, using the same term *nabhi'* as used regarding Samuel and later men who are accorded this designation by Lindblom and others. There is no reason for denying the term to the earlier representatives.

Regarding Abraham, however, who is called a prophet in Genesis 20:7, a distinction does need to be made. He was a prophet, true enough, in that he received revelations from God and communicated information that he had heard to others, but he lived before Israel became a nation. He was the father of the nation, but the nation was not realized until the time of Moses. If we speak, then, of prophets of the nation of Israel, we can hardly include Abraham as one of them.

The first person of the nation who is so called is Moses. He identified himself as a prophet in the classic text, Deuteronomy 18:15, when he said, "The LORD thy God will raise up unto thee a Prophet . . . like unto me." And at the time of Moses' death the statement is made, "And there arose not a prophet since in Israel like unto Moses, whom the LORD knew face to face" (Deut. 34:10). Moses, then, was a prophet, the first in Israel's history and an example for all other prophets. Miriam, Moses' sister, is called a prophetess (the feminine form, *nebhi'ah*). Just why she qualified for the classification is not clear, but evidently she spoke for God somewhat after the pattern of her brother and perhaps occasionally even received information from God, though no indication of this is given. It would seem that Joshua also should be included because, though the term *nabhi'* is not used for him, he served in the capacity of a prophet. He received divine communications and he declared these to the people. This was the role of the prophet. Probably the reason why the term is not used of him is that no particular instance called for it. Balaam, son of Beor, is sometimes included in the list, because he is so called in II Peter 2:15, 16. He was not a member of the Israelite nation, however, but called by King Balak of Moab from faraway Mesopotamia to come and curse the Israelite people. Accordingly he can hardly be included as an Israelite prophet.

The next on the list is Deborah, one of the judges, who is called a prophetess (*nebhi'ah*) in Judges 4:4. She may well have received and communicated information from God even before she became a judge; the latter office indeed may have arisen for her because of her earlier work as a prophetess. In Gideon's day, a prophet is mentioned, though not by name, as having come to warn the people concerning their sin of following Baal wor-

[9]*Prophecy in Ancient Israel*, p. 96, n. 71; cf. pp. 99–100.

ship (Judg. 6:8–10). Samuel, of course, is the prophet best known from this period, and he was recognized as a prophet even early in life by "all from Dan to Beersheba" (I Sam. 3:20). Then he in turn superintended a group of young prophets, evidently stationed for a time at Naioth near Ramah, where Samuel maintained his headquarters (I Sam. 10:5–10; 19:18–20). They appear to have been members of a training school which probably Samuel himself started.

These are all the people that are definitely called prophets from this period. There are a few clues, however, that suggest there were others. First, Moses' own prediction that prophets like himself would arise, to whom the people should go for divine communication, is hardly fulfilled by these few alone.[10] Second, the manner in which Deborah is mentioned as a prophetess implies that others were living. Her identification as a prophetess is uncalled for in terms of the story related, for it depicts her only in the capacity of a judge. The thought must be, then, that she was simply another prophetess like others the people would know. Third, the prophet mentioned from Gideon's time is also brought in very casually. The manner implies that prophets simply were not unusual for the time and that one of them was sent in order to bring the message indicated. Fourth, there is the well-known verse from Samuel's time which implies that the prophet, or seer, was thought of as quite a common person. The verse reads, "Beforetime in Israel, when a man went to enquire of God, thus he spake, Come, and let us go to the seer: for he that is now called a Prophet was beforetime called a Seer" (I Sam. 9:9). As indicated in an earlier connection, this verse shows a change in nomenclature for men of this vocation. Such a change means that prophets were spoken of quite frequently, and, therefore, many must have been living. And, fifth, there is no reason why all should have been mentioned. There is no listing of all the prophets in any other period either, but only of those involved in the history related.

On the basis of this evidence, it seems safe to say that there were prophets living at any given time during the period of the judges and they were probably several in number, in order to serve the purpose God had designated through Moses in Deuteronomy 18. People needed to have a person to whom they could go with their questions so that they would not have to resort to techniques of divination.

One central theme dominated the messages proclaimed by these prophets. It is indicated both by the need of the day and by the words given by two of the representatives. The need of the day was resistance to Canaanite influence and especially the Baal worship observed by native inhabitants

---

[10]On the basis of the early date of the exodus, the time involved lasted over three hundred years.

of the land. There were attractions for Israel to go after the ways of Canaan because of the cultural advantage held by Canaanites, since the Israelites had just come in from the desert region. Especially did they need to know how to farm, and, in order to farm properly, the Canaanites believed one needed to worship Baal, since he was the god of storm and rain. Israelites would have been susceptible to this thinking, therefore, and so there was need that prophets, as well as priests, combat the influence that would have resulted.

The two prophets that show this message actually being proclaimed were Samuel and the anonymous figure of Gideon's time.[11] The message of each shows this same stress. Samuel urged the people, "If ye do return unto the LORD with all your hearts, then put away the strange gods and Ashtaroth from among you, and prepare your hearts unto the LORD, and serve him only: and he will deliver you out of the hands of the Philistines" (I Sam. 7:3). And the prophet of Gideon's day first reminded the people of God's past deliverances, then of God's command that they "fear not the gods of the Amorites," and finally reprimanded them for not obeying. The "gods" to which he referred were the same Baal and Ashtaroth mentioned by Samuel.

### 2. Monarchy prophets who preceded the writing prophets

Following the time of Samuel, when the kingdom came into existence, prophets became more numerous and also occupied a more influential place among the people.

### a. IDENTIFICATION

A list of those designated as prophets from this second period is measurably longer than for the period of judges. In listing the names it will be well to note in whose reign they served.

In the time of David, Nathan (II Sam. 7:2; 12:25) and Gad (II Sam. 24:11), with Zadok the priest being called a "seer" upon one occasion (II Sam. 15:27), and the Levite Heman being similarly referred to (I Chron. 25:5);[12] in the time of Jeroboam, Ahijah (I Kings 11:29; 14:2-18), a "man of God" who spoke against Jeroboam's altar (I Kings 13:1-10), and an "old prophet in Bethel" who tricked the "man of God" (I Kings 13:11-32); in Rehoboam's reign, Shemaiah (II Chron. 11:2-4; 12:5-15), and Iddo (II Chron. 9:29;

---

[11]The messages of these two are the only ones recorded.

[12]Samuel was also both a Levite (I Chron. 6:27, 28, 33, 34) and a prophet. There was nothing to prohibit one serving in a priestly office from serving also as a prophet.

13:22);[13] in Asa's reign, Azariah (II Chron. 15:1-8), and Hanani (II Chron. 16:7); in Baasha's reign, Jehu, son of Hanani (I Kings 16:1-12); in Jehoshaphat's reign, Jahaziel (II Chron. 20:14) and Eliezer (II Chron. 20:37); in Ahab's reign, Elijah (I Kings 17-19), Elisha (I Kings 19:19-21),[14] one simply called "the prophet" (I Kings 20:13-28), and Micaiah (I Kings 22:8-28); in the reign of Joash of Judah, Zechariah (II Chron. 24:20); and in the reign of Amaziah, "a prophet" (II Chron. 25:15).[15]

Twenty different prophets are here designated. The length of time involved runs from the establishment of the kingdom until the reign of Jeroboam II, or approximately two-and-a-half centuries.[16] In this span of time, were there more prophets than this? It is certain that there were. Indeed, the fact is directly stated in that groups of prophets, likely in training, lived in Bethel, Jericho, and Gilgal. These groups appear to have been under the supervision, if not the instruction, of Elijah and later Elisha. It may be that Elijah continued the training-school idea that Samuel years before had started. It is said that some fifty of these young prophets watched as Elijah and Elisha made their way across the Jordan, just before the home-going of Elijah (II Kings 2:7), and there is a later implication that one hundred lived at Gilgal (II Kings 4:43). The groups seem to have grown in number so that new quarters for housing were needed (II Kings 6:1, 2).[17]

Then there are again a few incidental clues that show additional prophets lived. For instance, if there happened to live an "old prophet" in Bethel at the time the "man of God" denounced the altar there, it is likely that other cities housed the same (I Kings 13:11-32). Also, in the reign of Joash, following the death of the high priest Jehoiada, it is stated that "prophets" (plural) were sent to reprimand the faithless princes of the day (II Chron. 24:19). However, only one prophet is named for the time, Zechariah. And further, the same observation is in order that one should not expect all representatives to have been reported.

b. MESSAGE

More information is given from this period as to what the prophets said. Interestingly, their messages were quite different from those of the period of

---

[13]Iddo was also active already in Solomon's reign.

[14]Elisha's ministry continued into the reigns of Ahaziah, Jehoram, Jehu, Jehoahaz, and Jehoash (II Kings 2-13).

[15]The next prophet to be mentioned in the Old Testament is Jonah, one of the writing prophets, in Jeroboam II's reign (II Kings 14:25). Both Obadiah and Joel, however, probably preceded Jonah; see chap. 16, pp. 262-264, 266-268.

[16]Latter half of the eleventh century to the first half of the eighth.

[17]For discussion see G. F. Oehler, *Theology of the Old Testament*, pp. 392-393.

the judges, when the concern involved Canaanite influence. This Canaanite problem, however, had been well solved when the monarchy had come to existence, especially by David, and the interest now lay in a different direction. Four main subject areas were involved.

*1) Social reform.*   The first was the general area of social reform, something which the later prophets took up in greater detail. Two occasions of prophetic announcements of this kind came from David's time and involved David himself. Nathan brought the first when he rebuked the king for sinning with Bathsheba and later ordering the murder of her husband Uriah (II Sam. 12:1-14). Gad brought the second when he reprimanded the king for taking a census (II Sam. 24:10-14). A third was brought by Elijah to Ahab for his injustice with Naboth in seizing his vineyard (I Kings 21:17-26).[18] And a fourth was brought by Eliezer in reprimanding Jehoshaphat for joining himself with Ahaziah, king of Israel, in a maritime venture (II Chron. 20:37).

*2) Unfaithfulness to God.*   There were four occasions in which general rebuke was administered for disobedience to the requirements of God. Shemaiah brought rebuke to Rehoboam, warning that, because of his disobedience, God had "left" him in the hand of Shishak, king of Egypt, who was then invading the land. Rehoboam and his princes showed a repentant spirit as a result, and it is stated that God granted him some reduction in the extent of destruction Shishak would bring (II Chron. 12:1-8). Azariah brought reprimand to Asa and found a repentant heart also with him, as the king "put away the abominations out of all the land" and "renewed the altar of the LORD" (II Chron. 15:1-8). Hanani was less successful at a later time with the same king, however, for Asa then responded by imprisoning the prophet. The rebuke had concerned Asa's trusting in his own abilities rather than in the delivering hand of God (II Chron. 16:7-10). And then Zechariah suffered even worse in the time of Joash when he rebuked the people for transgressing the "commandments of the LORD," for they "conspired against him, and stoned him with stones at the command of the king" (II Chron. 24:17-21).

All four instances show the desire of these prophets that the kings conduct their office in a manner pleasing to God. The kings involved, being all of Judah, where the true Law continued in effect, should have known how to rule properly. These prophets believed that God's blessing depended upon this being done and accordingly brought the reprimands. Two of them suffered greatly for their efforts.

---

[18]Though Jezebel directed the actual injustice with Naboth, still Ahab was in charge of his kingdom and therefore responsible for the action.

*3) False worship at Dan and Bethel.*   The third subject area concerned the false religious centers at Dan and Bethel in the northern nation of Israel. Here Jeroboam had instituted this substitute worship of God because he did not want his people to return to the temple in Jerusalem. The first reprimand for this defection came from a prophet called simply "a man of God" sent north from Judah.[19] Jeroboam was personally addressed as the prophet predicted that a future king, Josiah, would one day offer upon the Bethel altar the bones of the priests there officiating.[20] Jeroboam, stretching forth his hand in rebuke, found it suddenly withered and then besought the prophet to pray for its restoration (I Kings 13:1-6). The second reprimand also concerned Jeroboam. This came from Ahijah, who had earlier foretold to Jeroboam that he would rule (I Kings 11:9-38). This time, however, he told him through his wife that God had now rejected his family: they would no longer hold the throne. The reason was that Jeroboam had "done evil above all that were before" him, particularly in respect to the substitute worship (I Kings 14:5-16). This prediction was fulfilled when Jeroboam's son Nadab was killed in office. Then Baasha, the assassin and successor of Nadab, received the third rebuke. Jehu brought it, warning of a similar end for Baasha's dynasty since he was continuing to walk "in the way of Jeroboam" (I Kings 16:1-12). And the fourth rebuke is the well-known word of Micaiah to Ahab. He did not speak directly of the substitute worship, but he implied it in his withstanding the four hundred prophets associated with it (I Kings 22:8-28).

*4) Worship of false gods.*   The fourth area concerns not only the forsaking of God, but the giving of allegiance to false deities. Both Judah and Israel were involved.

The first rebuke was given in reference to Solomon. Ahijah brought it at the time he foretold to Jeroboam that he would rule over ten of the tribes. Ahijah cited as a reason the fact that Solomon had forsaken God and "worshiped Ashtoreth the goddess of the Sidonians, Chemosh the god of the Moabites, and Milcom the god of the children of Ammon" (I Kings 11:29-38). A second rebuke in Judah came a century and a half later when "a prophet" reprimanded Amaziah on a similar count. Amaziah had recently returned from a victory over the Edomites and brought back with him some of their "gods" and set them up as his own. The prophet asked the penetrating question, "Why hast thou sought after the gods of the people, which could not deliver their own people out of thine hand?" (II Chron. 25:15).

In Israel the occasions of these reprimands concerned Baal worship,

[19]It is noteworthy that a prophet had to be sent from Judah. True prophets clearly were very few in Israel at this time.
[20]See chap. 6, p. 97, n. 10.

introduced by Jezebel. The instance with Elijah on Mount Carmel is well known, when he solicited and received the assent of the people that Israel's God, rather than Baal, was true. Elisha, following, did not have as much to say of Baal worship, but in at least two instances his implications regarding it are clear enough. One occurred in southern Moab as three kings resorted to his counsel in their dire need for water. Jehoram, son of Ahab, was one, and to him Elisha significantly stated, "Get thee to the prophets of thy father, and to the prophets of thy mother." In other words, since Jehoram had been holding these Baal prophets in high regard before, why did he not resort to them now (II Kings 3:9–14)?[21] The other occurred in the anointing of Jehu as successor to Jehoram. One of Jehu's actions in his blood purge of Ahab's house was the slaughter of the Baal prophets. Since Elisha had directed his anointing, instructing him to destroy "the house of Ahab," it is likely he included an order for this destruction of the Baal prophets as well (II Kings 9:1–10; 10:19–28).

### 3. The writing prophets

The interest now turns to the writing prophets, who are the best known. Their preaching and writings stand in a class by themselves for the world of that day. These men were great spirits, with remarkable minds and hearts. The glory of their message was rivaled only by the courage with which they gave it. As to identification this time, there is little point in listing those involved, for they are known so well from the books they wrote. What is important, however, is to see them classified as to the time when they wrote, for they came in groups, not being evenly spaced. And to understand them in their true relationship to each other, it is imperative to see them in their relation to those of their own groups. As to their messages, it will not be appropriate now to consider these. They are too expansive, covering whole books which the prophets wrote, and will come in for consideration in Part Two of this writing as they give evidence of the kinds of persons the writers were.

Before taking up these group classifications, it is in order again to note that many more prophets lived during the period than are named. Our interest can be only with the writing prophets themselves, for they are the only ones that we know about, but there are again numerous clues that other prophets lived.

In respect to the reign of Manasseh, it is said that God "spoke by his servants the prophets" (II Kings 21:10), and only Nahum is otherwise known

---

[21]Jehoram may have had some of these prophets with him. If so, Elisha was referring to them. If not, he was chiding him for not having brought them for just such an emergency.

as possibly having begun to prophesy late in Manasseh's time. Jeremiah
mentions Urijah for his day (Jer. 26:20-23), but he did not write. Jeremiah
also speaks of God as having sent his servants, the prophets, early and late
from the time of Israel's exodus from Egypt even to that day (7:25; 11:7), and
the language suggests many more prophets than are actually named. Huldah
is listed as a prophetess in Josiah's time (II Kings 22:14), and Isaiah refers to
his wife by the same designation (8:3).

### a. NINTH-CENTURY PROPHETS: OBADIAH AND JOEL

Though Amos of the eighth century has frequently been called the first
of the writing prophets,[22] there is reason to believe that at least two prophets,
Obadiah and Joel, ministered already in the ninth century. Argumentation to
this end will be presented in Part Two when each prophet is discussed.
Obadiah likely was the first and lived in the time of Jehoram, son of
Jehoshaphat, who had married his son to wicked Athaliah of Israel (I Kings
22:44; II Chron. 18:1; 21:6; 22:3, 4, 10). It was probably as the result of
Athaliah's influence that Jehoram killed all of his brothers in an effort to
safeguard his throne (II Chron. 21:4). Athaliah herself actually killed all her
grandchildren in order to seize the throne at a later time (II Chron. 22:10).
Obadiah's ministry, then, came in a very turbulent time. It is of interest that
God, in spite of this, did not prompt him to write of his own country but
rather of Edom to the south. He predicted the fall of Edom, due to her
haughty actions towards the people of God (Obad. 11-14).

Joel is best placed in the reign of Joash who had been anointed at the age
of seven years. Following the rule of Jehoram, his son Ahaziah had reigned
one year, and when he was killed, Athaliah had declared herself ruler. She
ruled for six years and then under the direction of the godly high priest,
Jehoiada, young Joash was brought to the throne and Athaliah was killed.
For many years, while Joash was growing to an age to govern for himself,
Jehoiada was the leading spirit in the nation. It is likely that Joel's ministry is
to be placed during the time when Jehoiada was thus directing things in a
way pleasing to God.

### b. EIGHTH-CENTURY PROPHETS: AMOS,
HOSEA, ISAIAH, MICAH, AND JONAH

Four of the eighth-century prophets date themselves so that no question
is left as to when they served. Amos speaks of himself as prophesying during

---

[22]So Lindblom, *Prophecy in Ancient Israel*, p. 105; R. B. Y. Scott, *The Relevance of the
Prophets*, p. 72.

the reign of Jeroboam II in Israel and Uzziah in Judah (1:1), which means sometime between 767 B.C. (the year when Uzziah began his sole reign) and 753 B.C. (the year of Jeroboam's death).

Hosea states that his ministry occurred during the reigns of Uzziah, Jotham, Ahaz, and Hezekiah of Judah and Jeroboam II of Israel. Hence, the beginning of his ministry was again sometime between 767 B.C. and 753 B.C., with the time continuing at least until 715 B.C., when Hezekiah assumed sole rule of Judah.

Isaiah lists Uzziah, Jotham, Ahaz, and Hezekiah as kings who ruled during his time of prophecy, without mentioning any kings from Israel. The reason for not mentioning the latter is that Isaiah was a prophet to Judah and not to Israel, in contrast to both Amos and Hosea. He speaks of himself as having been called in the year King Uzziah died, which was 740 B.C. He refers also to the death of the Assyrian emperor Sennacherib (37:38), which did not come until 681 B.C., and so apparently he ministered for the long intervening period of approximately sixty years. This probably was the longest period of service of any of the prophets. Micah also dates his prophecy only to reigns of kings of Judah since he too was a prophet of Judah. He lists Jotham, Ahaz, and Hezekiah. He apparently began to serve sometime after Isaiah and likely finished before. Since Jotham ceased ruling in 731 B.C. and Hezekiah began his sole rule in 715 B.C., at least the years between these two dates saw him active.

The fifth prophet, Jonah, does not date his book in this manner. One reason, no doubt, is that his writing concerned Nineveh and not Israel or Judah. As will be observed in Part Two, there are mainly two dates suggested by scholars at which to locate Jonah. The one preferred herein is the approximate time of the ministry of Amos, about 760 B.C. In II Kings 14:25 it is stated that Jonah prophesied to Jeroboam II, which locates him in the first half of the eighth century. The same passage indicates that he served as prophet to Israel—as well as to Nineveh—for it is stated that he foretold the restoration by Jeroboam of Israel's boundary to Hamath and south to the Dead Sea.

Though Jonah may have ministered primarily in the first half of the eighth century, the other four of these prophets all ministered at least after 760, and three, Hosea, Isaiah, and Micah, after 740. Thus there is a collection here of four prophets, two to Israel and two to Judah, that are grouped together in the middle and latter part of the eighth century.

c. Seventh-century prophets: Nahum,
   Jeremiah, Zephaniah, and Habakkuk

Nahum does not date his ministry specifically, but it had to occur sometime between the destruction of Thebes in Egypt (663 B.C.; No equals

Thebes), as indicated in 3:8, and of Nineveh (612 B.C.), whose destruction is the theme of the book. Because this is the theme, it is likely that Nahum's prophecy regarding the destruction did not precede that occasion by many years, so Nahum began his work probably about 630 B.C.

Jeremiah dates his work specifically as beginning in the thirteenth year of Josiah. This was 627 B.C., for Josiah began to rule in 640 B.C. Since Jeremiah continued to serve until after the time when Judah was taken captive, he prophesied during the reigns of Josiah, Jehoahaz, Jehoiakim, Jehoiachin, and Zedekiah, and then until the occasion when he was taken down into Egypt by people who remained in Jerusalem following the fall of the city (Jer. 43:1–7). He preached also to these people in Egypt (Jer. 43:8—44:30), but no indication is given of how long this lasted until he died. Since Jerusalem did not fall to the Babylonians until 586 B.C., however, he probably lived at least until 580. This means he prophesied from 627 until approximately 580 or about forty-seven years.

Zephaniah also dates his book to the time of Josiah (1:1). Josiah ruled for thirty-one years, but probably Zephaniah served in the earlier part of that time, at least before 621 B.C., for he mentions foreign cults as still existing (1:4), and Josiah put these away at that time. It may well be that Zephaniah, along with Nahum and Jeremiah, brought influence on Josiah to institute such reforms.

Habakkuk also does not date his prophecy precisely. It is clear from his first chapter (vv. 5, 6), however, that the Babylonian invasion had not yet occurred, for it is predicted there. This means that he prophesied at least before 605 B.C., when Nebuchadnezzar first came against Jerusalem. Perhaps the most likely time for his ministry was at the close of Josiah's rule, about 609 B.C., and on into the reign of Jehoiakim following.

It will appear that again we have a definite group of prophets. None of these date to the first half of the seventh century but all to the second half, in fact to the latter part of the second half. They come just before the Babylonian captivity and it will be observed in Part Two that a reason for their coming as a group together at this time is likely found in this fact.

## d. EXILIC PROPHETS: DANIEL AND EZEKIEL

Though Daniel was not a prophet by vocation, being an administrator in the palace of Babylon, he is properly included among the prophets because of the predictive visions God gave him.[23] Daniel's time is known precisely. He was taken captive along with his three friends, Hananiah, Mishael, and Azariah, to Babylon in the summer of 605 B.C.—the third year of Jehoiakim

---

[23]It should be realized, however, that the Hebrew Bible places his book among the Writings (*Kethubhim*), rather than the Prophets.

(1:1), which ended October, 605 B.C. He continued until after Cyrus captured Babylon in 539 B.C. and at least until the third year of Cyrus after that
(10:1). His life in Babylon thus lasted nearly seventy years.

Ezekiel was taken captive in 597 B.C. (see 33:21; 40:1; cf. II Kings
24:11-16), which was the time when King Jehoiachin was taken to Babylon.
He continued at least until the twenty-seventh year of the captivity (29:17),
which means 571 B.C., while Nebuchadnezzar still ruled. He may have lived
longer but no doubt much less than the aged Daniel. While Daniel served in
the palace, Ezekiel ministered as a prophet among the captive people of
Judah.

### e. Postexilic prophets: Haggai, Zechariah, and Malachi

Haggai and Zechariah may be noted together because they both indicate
their time of prophecy as coming in the second year of Darius (520 B.C.; see
1:1 of their books). All of Haggai's prophecy pertains to that year, while
Zechariah had revelations from God at that time and also later. The primary
theme of both is the need for the temple of Jerusalem to be rebuilt. The
people had started to rebuild the temple when they had first returned from
captivity in 538/537 B.C. They had become discouraged at that time and
ceased building, however, and for some sixteen or seventeen years the building had lain as merely a useless foundation, much to the dishonor of God in
the eyes of people about. Haggai and Zechariah finally were instructed in 520
B.C. to encourage the people to begin again and their ministry was effective.
The people did begin and in the year 515 B.C. the building was completed.

Malachi is more difficult to date but he clearly followed the time of
Haggai and Zechariah. He shows for instance that a Persian governor was in
authority during his time in Jerusalem (1:8). He speaks of religious ceremonies being carried on at the temple (1:7-10; 3:8), meaning that the temple
had been reconstructed by his time. He also brings reprimands for sins being
practiced and those named are similar to sins indicated by both Ezra and
Nehemiah in their time. These matters suggest a date for him around the
time of Ezra and Nehemiah. Since he is not mentioned in either of these
books, it is likely that he followed the time when they were written by a few
years. Thus he was active in the latter part of the fifth century.

Looking back over all of these writing prophets, we note that the general
order of listing of the minor prophets gives an indication as to the time when
they ministered. The first of the minor prophets were all from either the
ninth or eighth century—Hosea, Joel, Amos, Obadiah, Jonah, and Micah.
Isaiah is not included among them for he was a major prophet. Then the next
three are seventh-century prophets—Nahum, Habakkuk, and Zephaniah.

Jeremiah is not included because he was a major prophet. Then the last three—Haggai, Zechariah, and Malachi—are postexilic prophets. The two prophets of the exile, Daniel and Ezekiel, are not included because they were major prophets. Thus, remembering the order in which the minor prophets appear in the Bible helps us to keep their respective periods in mind.

# Part Two

# THE PROPHETS

# Section One

# THE PRE-MONARCHY PROPHETS

# HISTORY CHART I

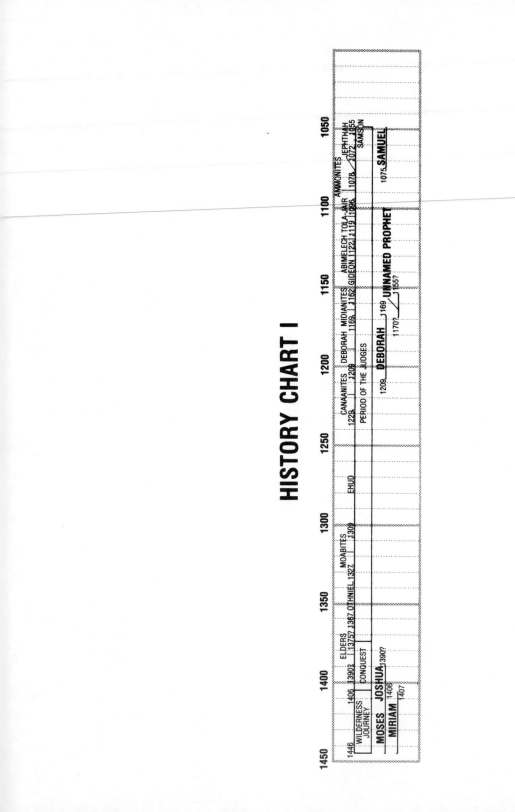

| | 1450 | 1400 | 1350 | 1300 | 1250 | 1200 | 1150 | 1100 | 1050 |
|---|---|---|---|---|---|---|---|---|---|

ELDERS
1375? 1367 OTHNIEL 1327

MOABITES
1309

CANAANITES
1229

DEBORAH
1209

MIDIANITES
1169

ABIMELECH TOLA-JAIR
1126 GIDEON 1122 1119 1096

AMMONITES

JEPHTHAH
1078 1072 1055
SAMSON

EHUD

WILDERNESS
JOURNEY
1446 1406 390?

CONQUEST

PERIOD OF THE JUDGES

**MOSES**

**JOSHUA** 1406 390?

**MIRIAM** 1406
1407

1209 **DEBORAH** 1169 **UNNAMED PROPHET**
1170? 155?

1075 **SAMUEL**

# 9

# Three Early Prophets

We come now to consider the prophets themselves. Thus far the interest has been with the movement called prophetism. The prophets, however, were the people that constituted the movement and were involved with the activities and functions that have thus far been studied. It is with them in their personalities, abilities, goals, and aspirations that we now concern ourselves.

It should be realized that this concern is with all the prophets of Israel and not merely the writing prophets. A major place will be given to the writing prophets, for they were certainly great servants of God and call for close attention. Other prophets preceded them, however, and God also used them in most significant ways. Information regarding the earlier nonwriting prophets is found primarily in the historical books of the Old Testament. Information regarding the writing prophets appears almost entirely in the books they wrote.

Prophets listed in chapter 8 for the premonarchy time included the following: Moses, Miriam, Joshua, Deborah, an unnamed prophet from the time of Gideon, Samuel, and a company of prophets taught by Samuel. Of this group the present chapter deals with three, Miriam, Deborah, and the unnamed prophet. Moses and Joshua are not treated at all because both men were primarily administrators rather than prophets. They were successively Israel's two great leaders in moving from Egypt to Canaan and making conquest of the Promised Land. As a result, their lives are comparatively well known and hardly call for treatment herein. Samuel and the group of prophets he taught will be treated in the following chapter.

To provide a background for the study of Miriam, Deborah, and the unnamed prophet, it is appropriate first to note the history in which they played a part. The history begins with the birth of Moses in Egypt. Because of a royal edict calling for the death of all Israelite male babies, Moses at the age of three months was placed on the Nile River in an "ark of bullrushes." His sister—no doubt the Miriam of our interest—was placed nearby to observe developments. Soon the baby was found by the daughter of Pharaoh who came to the river to bathe, and Moses' sister arranged with her for a nurse to care for the child until it should be weaned. The nurse the sister had in mind was the mother of the baby herself. Moses then was returned to his home, but in time had to be taken to the palace to be with the daughter of Pharaoh who adopted him as her own. Moses remained at the palace until the age of forty, and then he became a fugitive from the royal family until the age of eighty. At this time, God called him to lead the bondaged Israelites out of Egypt to their Promised Land.

When the Israelites left Egypt in due time, Miriam was one of the number. Though she is not mentioned often in the story of the wilderness wanderings that followed, the references that do exist indicate she played a rather important role as an assistant to her younger brother Moses. She occupied this role from the first of the journey, for she was active already when the people crossed the Red Sea (Exod. 15:20, 21). Her death came at the beginning of the fortieth year of Israel's wanderings, at a time when the people were at Kadesh-barnea (Num. 20:1).

The other two prophets of our concern, Deborah and the unnamed prophet, lived many years later, in the time commonly called the period of the judges. Following Miriam's death, the Israelites made progress toward entering the Promised Land by going around the eastern side of the Dead Sea and moving into the land by crossing the Jordan River. Just before crossing, God made a change of leadership, calling Moses home to be with Himself and installing Joshua in his place. Joshua served in conquering the land and also in allotting the land to the various tribes. Following Joshua's death the period of the judges began.

The period of the judges has sometimes been regarded as of minimal importance in Israel's history, but actually it was a most significant time in God's program for His people. It carried a marked potential for blessing. God had promised the land of Canaan already to Abraham as the place his posterity should live, and one may believe that the intervening centuries had seen God preparing both people and land for the time when the people would be ready to enter the region as their own. The reason why God had made a people for Himself was that there was no other people in all the world who were worshiping Him. God had made the world and brought the nations to existence, but no nations were following Him. He wanted one that would and so He made a new one from Abraham's descendants.

It follows that a great potential for blessing indeed lay before the twelve tribes as they entered their land. Even if direct indications did not exist, one could guess that God would have wanted this people to be prosperous. If they were to be a proper advertisement for Him in the world, they should be a people that others would admire. Their economy should be strong and their armies victorious. One need not merely guess, however, for God did give direct indications. He told them that He would set them "on high above all nations of the earth" (Deut. 28:1). He further told them, "The LORD shall open unto thee his good treasure, the heaven to give the rain unto thy land in its season and to bless all the work of thy hand . . . And the LORD shall make thee the head, and not the tail; and thou shalt be above only, and thou shalt not be beneath" (28:12, 13). God's only condition for such blessing was that the people obey His regulations.

One factor in Israel's potential for blessing was that God gave the tribes a true theocratic government. Never before had such a form of rule been instituted, though a theocracy is actually the highest form of government possible. God Himself was sole king, and the people were to give allegiance directly to Him without the mediation of earthly rulers. God had given His Law to Moses so that the people had regulations to follow, and He had instituted a priesthood to give instruction in this Law so that the people had no excuse for not knowing it. Had the people followed what God wanted them to do, this theocratic form of rule would not only have worked to the glory of God but would have served the highest benefit of the people. One benefit, for instance, would have been relief from high taxes, since there was no civil government to support.

The day of Joshua, which was characterized by great blessings and outstanding miracles as the Canaanites were soundly defeated, provided an excellent backdrop for the beginning of this period. When Joshua died, the people of Israel held a high reputation in the land. The Canaanites had learned to fear them, and people even at some distance must have been impressed with the ease with which Israel had conquered this strong people. It was a fine and promising way to begin the great day of blessing God had in store for the period of the judges.[1]

Yet as the period actually got under way, this fine potential never came to reality. Israel's high reputation gained during the time of Joshua did not continue. Israel did not develop as a prosperous people. Instead, Israel came

---

[1]For an enlarged discussion of these ideas, see my *Distressing Days of the Judges*, especially chaps. 3 and 6.

to be thought of as a state easy to conquer and a people easy to pillage. Mesopotamians, Moabites, Canaanites, Midianites, Ammonites, and Philistines all in turn campaigned against the tribes and imposed servitude. The reason for this distressing development was that the people did not follow the one requirement God laid down. They did not observe His regulations. They obeyed rather well as long as Joshua and the elders of his time lived, but as soon as they were dead the people "did evil in the sight of the LORD and served Baalim: and they forsook the LORD God of their fathers, which brought them out of the land of Egypt, and followed other gods" (Judg. 2:11, 12).

One measure God employed to counter this downgrade into sin was the establishment of judges to serve as temporary intermediaries between Himself and the people. It is because of these leaders that the time is called the period of the judges. Another measure was the employment of prophets (Deut. 18:15–22). Moses had indicated that the task of these people would be to receive revelation from God, which they might pass on to the people in answer to questions, and this certainly was a function the prophets carried out. In view of the tragic development of sin, however, one may believe that their work soon became enlarged to preaching reform. This became a major part of the work of later prophets, and it may well have involved a considerable amount of time also of these who were early. The Israelites were following the false gods of the Canaanites, and they needed to be told of their sin and urged to return to the way God desired.

## A. MIRIAM

### 1. The work

The nature of Miriam's work as a prophetess is revealed especially in Exodus 15:20, 21. Here the term *prophetess* (*nebhi'ah*) is used of her, and she is described as leading the women in an occasion of song. Israel had just crossed through the Red Sea and had reason for praise. The first eighteen verses of Exodus 15 give a song of praise that apparently was sung by Moses and the men of Israel. Then verse 20 states that "Miriam the prophetess, the sister of Aaron, took a timbrel in her hand; and all the women went out after her with timbrels and with dances." The song in which Miriam led the women was: "Sing ye to the LORD for he hath triumphed gloriously; the horse and his rider hath he thrown into the sea" (v. 21). This was the first refrain of the song which Moses and the men had sung (v. 1).

Because this is the one reference where Miriam is called a prophetess, it is likely that it characterizes her in that function. If so, her task was primarily the leadership of Israelite women. Moses was God's head leader of the people, but his dealings would have been primarily with the men, who were considered the heads of families. God apparently did not want the women left out and so directed Miriam to serve in giving them instruction and guidance.

## 2. The person

It has been indicated that Miriam was the older sister of Moses. She must have been considered responsible by her mother already when she was young, since she was given the task of watching over Moses when placed in the Nile River. According to Josephus, she became the wife of Hur and thus grandmother of the architect Bezaleel, who was placed in charge of the construction of the tabernacle.[2] Hur, it will be remembered, served with Aaron in holding up one of Moses' arms in the battle with the Amalekites (Exod. 17:10), and later was left in charge of the camp along with Aaron when Moses and Joshua went up into Mount Sinai at the time Moses was to receive the Law from God (Exod. 24:14). Following this, Hur is not heard from again, and he may have died soon after for certainly he was an important man on these two occasions.

### a. AN IMPORTANT PERSON

Miriam was an important person in her own right. That she led the women in song at the time just noticed shows her importance in respect to them, and later Moses, following the time of her death, referred to her in a way that shows the people considered her a leader (Deut. 24:9). Even more significant is the indication of God Himself when years later He spoke to the Israelite people through Micah in the following words: "I sent before thee Moses, Aaron, and Miriam" (Mic. 6:4). The leadership of Moses and Aaron is well known; it is significant that Miriam is placed with them. Her importance is demonstrated further by an action of the people when she along with Aaron rebelled against the leadership of Moses and as a result was made a leper. God took away the leprosy but only when she had been put outside the camp for seven days. In that regard, it is stated that for all seven days "the people journeyed not till Miriam was brought in again" (Num. 12:15). An

---

[2] *Antiquities* III.2.4; 6.1; IV.4.6.

ordinary person, no doubt, would have been left to straggle along as best he could, but for Miriam the entire camp waited until she could be restored to their number.

Miriam held a place of lesser importance than Moses, however. This is clear from the story in general and especially from her time of rebellion against Moses (Num. 12:1–16). She and Aaron attempted to assume the same level as Moses by saying, "Hath the LORD spoken only by Moses? hath he not spoken also by us?" (12:2).

The same occasion shows that Miriam held a lower place in respect to the office of prophet. The rebuke God gave to her and Aaron significantly included the following: "Hear now my words: If there be a prophet among you, I the LORD will make myself known unto him in a vision, and will speak unto him in a dream. My servant Moses is not so. . . . With him will I speak mouth to mouth, even apparently, and not in dark speeches; and the similitude of the LORD shall he behold" (12:6–8). In other words, in contrast to Moses with whom God spoke mouth to mouth and without use of intermediary means, God would communicate with Miriam and Aaron (and no doubt Miriam especially, since she alone is called a prophetess) only in a vision or dream. As a prophetess, then, Miriam did receive revelations, but they came by way of visions and dreams rather than "mouth to mouth" communications.

### b. Weakness of jealousy

The occasion when Miriam and Aaron rebelled against Moses shows also that Miriam had a weakness for jealousy. Holding a place of lesser importance than her younger brother, she clearly wanted a place of equality and tried for it in this manner. It is clear that she, not Aaron, was the leader in this occasion, too, because she was the one punished with leprosy. Apparently she suggested the idea and persuaded Aaron to go along with her. This says something regarding Aaron too, for, just as he had been pliable at an earlier time when the people were able to persuade him to make a golden calf, now he was pliable in the hands of Miriam to rebel against Moses.

The occasion for Miriam's jealousy was that Moses had recently married a Cushite woman; Zipporah, his first wife, apparently had died. It may be assumed that Miriam, his older sister, had filled in as a sort of feminine advisor during the years following Zipporah's death. The new wife could be expected to assume this role now. Apparently Miriam did not like this and became jealous. Accordingly she persuaded Aaron to go along with her and make complaint. God's marked displeasure at her attitude is shown by the sharp rebuke He pronounced and then by the imposition of the leprosy. Leprosy was considered a symbol of death and was employed as punishment only in cases where severe sin had been committed. Aaron's words as he besought Moses in her behalf are most significant: "Let her not be as one dead, of whom the flesh is half consumed when he cometh out of his mother's womb" (12:12).

But one should not let this weakness for jealousy cloud the fact that Miriam was otherwise an outstanding person in the camp of Israel. She apparently was thought of as roughly parallel to Aaron in importance, being the leader among all the women of Israel, the one to whom they looked for counsel and divine guidance through revelation. She must have been a true God-fearing person in order for God to have entrusted her with this important position.

## B. DEBORAH

### 1. The work

Deborah, the second person we notice, lived many years after Miriam, during the period of the judges. In fact she was one of the judges herself, the fourth in the illustrious line.[3] She is better known as a judge than a prophetess. She served as judge at the time of the Canaanite oppression over the Israelites, and it was she who selected Barak to lead in encountering this foe (Judg. 4:4-10). Before and no doubt after the encounter, she served as judge under a palm tree that was located between Ramah and Bethel in Mount Ephraim. Judges 4:5 indicates that Israelites came to her there "for judgment." The thought seems to be that at this place—no doubt well known to people of the region—Deborah served in giving advice, counsel, and judicial decisions in cases of disagreement among parties.

The verb *to judge* (*shaphat*), as used of the judges, meant more than merely to arbitrate. It carried the basic meaning of leadership, which may or may not have included arbitration as a major part of the work.[4] The implication regarding Deborah in her work as a judge is that it did involve arbitration in a major way, meaning that leadership as such played a minor role in her case. Perhaps the fact that she was a woman had something to do with this. Note that she called on Barak when need arose for military leadership to encounter the Canaanites in battle.

The nature of Deborah's work as a prophetess may only be conjectured. It appears that it actually began before her service as a judge (Judg. 4:4). It may be that it was a prime factor in leading on to her judgeship. That she was

[3]The first three had been Othniel, Ehud, and Shamgar (Judg. 3:9-31).
[4]For discussion and references see my *Distressing Days of the Judges*, pp. 4-6.

a prophetess suggests that she delivered messages to people that God had first given to her, and, doing this, she could have been led to give the counsel, advice, and judicial decisions noted above.

Though no revelation or message that Deborah either received or gave is included in the story, one may be sure that she was a devout person and appropriately fitted for prophetic ministry. Evidence to this end will be noted shortly. One may believe, therefore, that her work as a prophetess consisted in doing the two things that have been noted for other prophets: receiving revelations from God to answer people's questions, and giving forth God's word in a ministry of reformation. That she would have been interested in people reforming their lives and turning back to a life pleasing to God follows from the character she manifests. She would have been desirous that people obey God and do that which would lead on to a life of blessing.

## 2. The person

### a. Spiritual status

That Deborah possessed a high degree of spiritual maturity is without question. One indication comes from the fact that she, like Miriam, was accorded the privilege of being a prophetess. Not many women enjoyed this distinction. Another indication is found in the way she made her request of Barak that he go against the Canaanites. She did so in the name of God, stating, "Hath not the LORD God of Israel commanded" that this request be made of Barak (Judg. 4:6). Evidently God had instructed her to make this assignment, and she readily gave recognition of the fact. Further, when she later extended encouragement to Barak just before he was to launch his attack on the Canaanites, she did so believing God would deliver the enemy into Barak's hand and stated, "Is not the LORD gone out before thee?" (4:14). Troop strength had its place, but Deborah reminded Barak that victory depended on God's blessing, not the number of troops.

This reminder was much in order, for actually the two sides were very uneven in strength. The enemy, led by Sisera, probably had as many or more soldiers than Barak, and additionally had nine hundred chariots of iron (4:3). Further, Sisera had the level terrain of the Esdraelon Plain in which to use these chariots to advantage. Sisera had made his headquarters in the eastern end of this plain.[5] One must say, then, that Deborah and Barak showed unusual trust in God in being willing to come to this area to encounter their foe. Now with the battle at hand, Deborah wanted to remind

[5]At Harosheth of the Gentiles (Judg. 4:2). The city is best identified with modern Tell El-Harbej, a six-acre site on the south bank of the Kishon River, at the foot of Mount Carmel.

Barak that it was God who made the difference, not troops or chariot numbers.

Then, in writing her song in Judges 5, Deborah further showed her personal commitment to God, evidenced by the way in which she ascribed all praise to Him for the victory that had been won; she did not take glory either to herself or Barak. In Judges 5:3, for instance, she wrote, "Praise to the LORD God of Israel," and in 5:13, "The LORD made me have dominion over the mighty." Deborah clearly centered her thoughts in God and sought to exalt Him in her life and work.

### b. HER COMPASSION

Another matter to notice is that Deborah was a compassionate person. In her song of Judges 5, she states that she had seen a need in Israel, and had responded to that need by going to the aid of the northern tribes. She probably had learned of the need from people who had come to her from the north where the Canaanites were bringing hardship upon the people. Having had the need brought to her attention, she had not hesitated to give herself to it.

Deborah makes clear that this need was great. According to verse 6 of her song, though Shamgar, a prior judge (Judg. 3:31), had recently delivered Israel from six hundred Philistines, still Israelites feared to venture forth on highways, and those who found it necessary to travel did so on byways (secondary routes). In other words, people feared any possible meeting with the oppressing Canaanites. Then, according to verse 7, people who lived normally in the villages (literally, "people who lived in open country" where they were unprotected by hills) were not seen there any longer, apparently having fled for greater safety to hilly areas. And further, according to verse 8, weapons had become so few (no doubt due to the Canaanites' having disarmed the people) that no "shield or spear" was seen "among forty thousand in Israel."

Therefore, says Deborah, "I arose a mother in Israel." That is, she had assumed a position of watching over the people with maternal care, serving as judge. She had invited people to come with their sorrows and complaints, and she had given them courage and aided them in procuring justice. She had not turned a deaf ear but had shown compassion.

### c. ABILITY

Besides compassion, Deborah possessed ability for leadership in doing this work. Not just anyone could have assumed the position of a "mother in Israel." Having served in the capacity of prophetess, she had come to recog-

nize God's additional gift for counseling and guidance, and she had been
willing to assume the role. When she had, people apparently had come to her
in large numbers. Certainly Barak's willingness to respond as he did shows
his high respect for her. It is noteworthy, too, that numerous tribes showed
willingness to help against the Canaanites, as Deborah's song in Judges
5:14–18 makes clear, and one reason may well have been the debt people felt
to her for her help to them.

Deborah also displayed remarkable literary ability. This is evidenced by
the song she composed following Barak's victory over Sisera. The song is a
brilliant piece of work written under the inspiration of God. With fine dramatic sense, Deborah sets forth within it a series of separate scenes. The
language is powerful and full of meaning. Robert H. Pfeiffer calls it "the
finest masterpiece of Hebrew poetry" and states that it "deserves a place
among the best songs of victory ever written."[6]

One might think from an indication that immediately precedes this song
that Deborah had the help of Barak in composing it: "Then sang Deborah
and Barak." These words, however, are intended to say only that both
Deborah and Barak sang the song, not that they worked together in writing
it. That Deborah was the sole author is made clear in verse 3 from the use of
the first person singular pronoun in reference to her, and again in verse 7
where her name alone is used. Further in verse 12, Deborah is bidden to
"awake" and "utter a song."

d. Magnanimity

Deborah also displayed a magnanimous spirit. She was willing to put
herself out for the cause of the people of Israel. This is revealed in her
willingness to accede to Barak's request that she help him. Actually, in his
response to her, Barak made more than a request, he laid down an explicit
condition: "If thou wilt go with me, then I will go: but if thou wilt not go
with me, then I will not go" (4:8). Deborah might have refused to do as Barak
insisted. After all, she had her own important work to do, and he was a man
who should be able to take care of the task she had asked him to assume. She
had every right to refuse, but she did not. She overlooked her right so that
God's work might be done and the people benefited.

## C.  A PROPHET

The third person we consider is not designated by name, something that
is true also of others in the Old Testament, as will be seen.

---

[6]*Introduction to the Old Testament*, p. 326.

Why it is that God saw fit to give the names of some and not of others is not always clear. Sometimes those who are not named were called upon to do very important tasks. It was an important task that this man was assigned to do. We know him only as "a prophet."

## 1. The work

The account regarding this person comes in the general time of Gideon. In fact, his service is described prior to the event of Gideon's call (Judg. 6:7–10). The occasion involved the fourth of the oppressions the Israelites experienced. The first had come from the Mesopotamians, the second the Moabites, the third the Canaanites as just seen in connection with the story of Deborah, and now the fourth from the Midianites. The Midianite oppression was one of the most humiliating that Israel experienced. These people did not invade the country and then maintain a continuous occupation, as was true of the other oppressors, but they came only once a year, at the time of harvest, to appropriate the crops of the Israelites. They may have left a residual force in the land during the intervening months, but the main group came only to eat off the land until the harvest supply was exhausted and then returned to their own territory. The Midianites were a roving type of tribe, and they chose to do their roving in Israel at the harvest season.

By the time this prophet was called to bring his message, the Midianites had come in this manner for six consecutive years, and the seventh year was at hand. During these years, the Israelites had been very fearful of the annual invasion and had sought hiding places for their crops in dens, caves, and strongholds of the mountains (6:2). There had been no attempt to fight back in protection against the outrageous robbery committed, for the easterners came when they desired, took what they wanted, stayed as long as they wished, and left at their own pleasure. Surely, if any situation in the history of the period of the judges demonstrated abject weakness on Israel's part, this did.

The reason for this humiliating condition was the same as for the prior afflictions. The people continued to sin, and God permitted the condition as a way of discipline to bring the people back to Himself. The work of this prophet, then, may be easily ascertained. He was to call this situation to the attention of the people and urge them to give their allegiance back to God; they would then enjoy His blessing and not experience a continuation of this suffering.

Since Gideon was soon to be called to serve as Israel's deliverer (Judg. 6:11f.), the work of this prophet should be characterized as a preparation in anticipation of Gideon's service. In other words, God desired that someone precede Gideon and prepare the hearts of the people for the message he would bring and the deliverance he would effect. Thus this prophet was a type of forerunner, who prepared the way for another.

## 2. The person

Because very little is said regarding the man, not much can be concluded as to the kind of a person he was. Still there are a few implications that can be taken from the message he gave.

### a. SPIRITUAL STATUS

For one thing he must have been a person of relatively high spiritual standing. This follows first from the fact that God selected him as the prophet to come to the area of Ophrah at this time to bring the rebuke for sin. As indicated in the story of Gideon immediately following, Ophrah had turned strongly to Baal worship. In fact a task assigned to Gideon, before he could go against the Midianites themselves, was to tear down an altar to Baal there along with the pole to the goddess Asherah which regularly accompanied such an altar (6:25–28). Gideon did this and as a result the people of Ophrah wanted to kill him. It is shocking that people of God, Israelites, had so strayed in their worship that they wanted to kill a man who had torn down a false pagan center of worship. That this prophet was selected to come to such a place and bring God's message indicates that God saw him as a true and responsible servant. It has been indicated that at any given time in the period of the judges there were numerous prophets available. If God selected this man for this important task, one may believe that he stood high as a servant that God knew He could trust.

Then a second indication is found in the character of the message the prophet delivered. It is centered in God from beginning to end. It begins with the words, "Thus saith the LORD God of Israel," and continues by telling how God had brought the Israelites out of their bondage in Egypt into the Promised Land. It concludes by giving God's words to the people, "I am the LORD your God; fear not the gods of the Amorites, in whose land ye dwell." The prophet did not speak of himself or even of the sins of the people as such; his entire emphasis was focused on God's existence and what God had done for His people. To be thus God-centered in one's message means that the person is God-centered in his thinking, and this means in turn that he is a spiritually mature person.

### b. HISTORICAL ORIENTATION

The type of message given indicates that the man was historically oriented in his manner of thinking. The thrust of his message was that, because God had done so much for the people in the past, therefore they should be following Him now. In other words past blessings of the people should be a major factor in characterizing their present conduct. God had given Israel a marvelous deliverance from Egypt and had since driven out the inhabitants of Canaan so that they might have this fine place in which to live; therefore the people should be giving careful heed to God's requirements rather than diverting their allegiance to the false Canaanite god, Baal. It is true that the prophet was speaking a message God had first revealed to him, but still God uses men's minds and their own aptitudes in the type of message He imparts.

c. COURAGE

Still a third characteristic is that the man was courageous. One may know this because he was willing to respond to God's call to go to Ophrah and give this kind of message. If the people of Ophrah later were ready to take Gideon's life for destroying the Baal altar, one may be sure they were not ready to receive such a message as this prophet was assigned to give. Other prophets might have argued that the task was too dangerous or that harm might come to them, but this man went and obeyed the directive of God.

# 10

# Samuel

Our attention now turns to Samuel, a truly great man of the Old Testament. Samuel lived at the close of the period of the judges and actually served to introduce the time of the monarchy by anointing both Saul and David to their respective kingships. His story is found in the first twenty-five chapters of I Samuel.

Samuel is called "prophet" (*nabhi'*) twice (I Sam. 3:20; II Chron. 35:18), but several times "seer" (*ro'eh*) (I Sam. 9:11, 18, 19; I Chron. 9:22; 26:28; 29:29). As pointed out in chapter 4, however, the terms *ro'eh* and *nabhi'* were used for the same office. The difference lay in popularity of terminology rather than distinction of office. Whether Samuel was called a prophet or a seer, then, he held the office to which our concern is directed.

Samuel's day was characterized by grievous sin on the part of the people. It has been observed that sin abounded earlier in the period of the judges, for which reason the oppressions had been sent. The oppressions, however, had not caused the people to change. Instead, indications are that sin had become continually more serious. The degree of sin at any time was related closely to the extent of Baal worship observed by the Israelites. By the time of Gideon, Baal worship had been accepted so extensively that people were ready to take Gideon's life because he destroyed their Baal altar and Asherah pole. Then, by the later time of Jephthah, not only Baal, but the gods of several other countries were being worshiped.[1] Concerning his day,

[1] About 1100 B.C., three hundred years after the conquest (Judg. 11:26).

Judges 10:6 states, "And the children of Israel did evil again in the sight of the
LORD, and served Baalim, and Ashtaroth, and the gods of Syria, and the gods
of Zidon, and the gods of Moab, and the gods of the children of Ammon, and
the gods of the Philistines, and forsook the LORD and served not him." Sin,
therefore, was becoming very serious by Jephthah's time, and Samuel came
soon after.

Besides this general condition of wickedness, sin of a serious nature had
developed at the central tabernacle itself. Samuel's day was the day of Eli
when his wicked sons, Hophni and Phinehas, had taken over as the acting
priests. They perverted the sacrificial system so that people no longer wanted
to come and present their sacrifices. The two did this by illegally seizing
meat from animals brought for sacrifice (I Sam. 2:12–17), and also by having
immoral relations with women who served at the tabernacle (2:22). Actions
such as these quickly became known far and wide, and people not only no
longer wanted to come to the tabernacle, but they were influenced to commit
similar sin themselves. Rather than being examples for good, the tabernacle
priests actually became examples for wickedness.

In addition to this severe matter of sin in the land, Samuel's day was
characterized by a deep despair in terms of national morale. This was true,
first, because of a current oppression being imposed by the Philistines. This
oppression lasted forty years (Judg. 13:1), the longest of all the oppressions.
Then it was true also because of a disastrous battle fought with the Philistines
at Aphek just before Samuel began his time of judgeship.

By means of this battle, the Israelites had hoped to bring Philistine
oppression to a close. They did not succeed, however, but twice suffered
serious losses. At the first time, four thousand men of their troops died. At
the second, thirty thousand died, and included in the number were the two
priests, Hophni and Phinehas. Worse than this, the ark of the covenant was
taken by the Philistines. The ark had been brought to the battle by the
Israelites following the first defeat. This was a serious sin in the sight of God,
and He could not permit a victory under those conditions. Therefore, Israel
did lose, and the ark was taken by the Philistines back to their own land.
When news of the catastrophe reached Shiloh where Eli lived, he was so
shaken that he fell backward and broke his neck. With the two acting priests,
Hophni and Phinehas, killed in battle and now Eli dead with a broken neck,
the load of leadership in Israel fell on the shoulders of Samuel, who was now
of an age to assume it.

Still another factor making the day a dark one was a tendency on the part
of Israelites to unite their forces with the Canaanites. The danger of influence
by Canaanites was always present, but it was never more so than at this
crucial time. The reason for the coalition was that the Philistines were as
much an enemy of the Canaanites as of the Israelites. With the Philistines
being thus strong, a natural inclination of the two groups was to unite to-

gether in opposition against the common foe. When Israelites learned their precious ark had been taken and all the leaders at the tabernacle had been killed, their thoughts would have logically turned to such a cooperative effort. This, however, was the worst thing they could do in the sight of God, and Samuel, being a true man of God, knew it. There was need for quick and effective action, then, if the tribes were to maintain their distinctiveness.

## A. SAMUEL

### 1. The work

The nature of Samuel's work, as he assumed leadership following the disaster at Aphek, has to be reconstructed more on the basis of implication than direct statement in Scripture. The reason is that the Scriptures, rather than taking up this activity of Samuel, speak instead about the ark which had been taken by the Philistines. The fact that this is the subject dealt with in I Samuel 5 and 6—the chapters where one otherwise would expect Samuel's initial work to be detailed—is indicative of the importance God placed upon the ark and its protection.

There had been need for allowing the Philistines to capture the ark, since Israel had sinned in bringing it into battle. However, when it was so taken, the Philistines, pagan as they were, took this to mean that their gods were greater than the God of Israel. God could not have this, and so He took measures to protect His own honor, with the result that seven months after the ark was captured the Philistines were more than glad to be rid of it. The chapters indicated detail this significant story.

The little that Scripture has to say of Samuel's early work, however, should not be taken to mean he was inactive. On the basis of implications, in fact, one can know that Samuel was exceedingly busy. One implication arises from the severity of conditions in Israel, as has been indicated. Something had to be done by someone to save the situation. Another implication comes from the existence twenty years later of an entirely different set of circumstances. According to I Samuel 7, by that time the people had returned to God sufficiently so that an occasion of revival could be called by Samuel at Mizpeh, and the people in great number were willing to give their allegiance in a fresh way to God. Before the day ended, a complete defeat had been inflicted on the Philistines, as this enemy came thinking to defeat Israel again, but were soundly defeated themselves when God intervened with a timely thunderstorm (I Sam. 7:10).[2]

[2]There are three indications that the time of this battle was probably in the dry season. First, Samuel would likely have set a date for the revival in the dry season when there would be

Something had happened to bring about a major change of attitude on the part of the people; such a change does not come about by itself. Someone had to take charge as leader and perform with diligence and ability. There was one man who could give that leadership, and that was Samuel. One may be sure, therefore, that Samuel was used mightily by God during these intervening twenty years.

One of Samuel's first tasks was likely the movement of the tabernacle from Shiloh to Nob. It is known that the tabernacle was taken to Nob sometime following the Aphek defeat, for it was there when Saul later killed eighty-five priests in a cruel way (I Sam. 21:1; 22:16-19). The most likely time was immediately after the Aphek battle, because at that time the Philistines could be expected to have marched on Shiloh and captured also the tabernacle.[3] Someone must have moved it therefore and the most likely person was Samuel. He was at Shiloh at the time and had the interest, foresight, and recognized authority to order it done. His directive in this may have been his first as Israel's new leader. In fact, it may have constituted the first indication to the people at Shiloh—and later to others as they would have learned of it—that Samuel was willing to take over as the new leader.[4]

Samuel's main effort should be thought of in terms of stimulating priests and Levites to do the work God had assigned to them. The priests and Levites had sufficient numbers in personnel and maintained the closeness of contact with the people necessary to accomplish the change we have noted, but they first would have to be inspired to get busy. This would have meant personal contact with them in their respective forty-eight cities. Samuel would have had to put forth enormous effort in traveling from city to city to make so many contacts.

Samuel's word to these priests and Levites would have included such matters as the following: information that the tabernacle had been moved to safety at Nob and that the former God-approved program of priestly service would now be resumed; indication that Samuel had assumed leadership as judge and that he desired a direct reversal in attitude towards sin throughout

---

no danger of rain, since many people had to travel a great distance. Second, in view of II Chron. 35:18 it is likely the Passover was held at this time. This would include the fourteenth of Nisan, which came in the first half of April when the dry season would have just begun. Third, the thunder involved must have been highly unusual to account for the confusion of the Philistines. Apparently it came in the dry season when they did not expect it.

[3] Archaeological evidence seems to show that the Philistines did destroy Shiloh at this time. This was commonly believed a few years ago and then doubt was cast on the evidence. Recently, however, scholars have come to believe that the evidence is valid after all. For discussion of the subject, see Herschel Shanks, "Did the Philistines Destroy the Israelite Sanctuary at Shiloh?— The Archaeological Evidence," *The Biblical Archaeology Review*, 1 (June, 1975):3-5.

[4] It may be assumed that few people, if any, objected. Samuel already had achieved a fine reputation (I Sam. 3:20) and most persons would have been delighted that he was willing to give leadership at this time of desperate need.

the land, with full cooperation being given by priests and Levites; exhortation that the priests and Levites get busy in their God-assigned tasks of instructing and guiding the people in respect to God's Law (Lev. 10:11; Deut. 33:10); instruction that Canaanite influence toward Baal worship be discouraged and eliminated (I Sam. 7:3, 4); and direction that the dangerous tendency of joining in league with the Canaanites be nullified, since it would lead to a yet greater influence on the Israelites by these pagan neighbors.

Along with this demanding activity, Samuel would also have had to serve as judge of the day. It is directly stated that he did so serve (I Sam. 7:15), and one may imagine him involved in activity parallel to that of the judges before him. Since he was the new leader, people would have turned to him for direction naturally. One of his tasks would have been to get the high priesthood started again. Eli had died and another person had to be installed to take his place. The one he selected must have been Ahitub, son of Phinehas (I Sam. 14:3), because Ahimelech, Ahitub's son, served later in the time of Saul (I Sam. 21–22).[5] In all such matters Samuel would have served as the strong man of the day, on whom people could depend and to whom they could look for leadership.

Besides these tasks, there was still the work for Samuel of simply being a prophet. This would have entailed receiving revelations from God to answer people's questions, and preaching to the people a message of reform. The conclusion is unavoidable that Samuel became a very busy man.[6]

## 2. The person

### a. PREPARATION FOR SERVICE

Preparation for a work is always important. A person must be qualified for what he is to do. Samuel's preparation was arranged by God and was unique. It equipped him in just the way necessary to step into the demanding work just described.

Samuel's preparation took place at the tabernacle; there he was educated and there he encountered experiences that provided invaluable background information. Education of children was normally carried on at home, with the parents serving as teachers, but the situation was different with Samuel because of his mother, Hannah. She had been unable to have children, and,

[5] It is noteworthy that Samuel continued the line of Eli in this position even though God had earlier said it would end (I Sam. 2:27–36). No indication is given that God disapproved of Samuel in doing this. Apparently God had intended the change to come in Solomon's day at the time Abiathar was deposed in favor of Zadok (I Kings 2:27, 35).

[6] It will be indicated shortly that still another activity became his responsibility, namely, the starting and operating of an instructional program for new prophets.

in her prayer that God would grant her a child, she had vowed that if a son were born to her she would give him for service at the tabernacle. Samuel was born, and Hannah carried out her vow by bringing him to the tabernacle as soon as he was weaned.[7]

This means that someone at the tabernacle had to assume responsibility for Samuel, and the likely person was the high priest, Eli. He had been aware of Hannah's vow from the first, and the boy was presented particularly to him when he was brought to the tabernacle in due time (I Sam. 1:25–28). Also, the story shows that a deep attachment developed between the aged man and the young boy, such as could be expected if Eli personally assumed the task (see I Sam. 3:4-9). The challenge of doing so, when Eli had failed with his own sons some years before, may have carried a special appeal for him. The result in Samuel's life gives testimony that he became more than an adequate father and teacher this time. Eli, having been high priest and now well along in years, would have had an abundant store of knowledge regarding the Law and ceremonial activity to impart to the boy. Probably no one in all the land would have been able to serve in training Samuel as well.

More than this, Samuel, being raised at the central sanctuary, had the benefit of firsthand acquaintance with ceremonial activity. He grew up with the experience of seeing sacrifices and offerings presented every day. He did not have to learn about them merely by report of others, but he was able to see them in actual practice. This would have impressed him with their place and importance.

Another marked advantage would have been Samuel's access to copies of the Law for study. One may assume that a few copies of Moses' original writing had been made by this time—all produced laboriously by hand—but these would have been considered so precious that they probably were never permitted to leave the tabernacle. Here all the priests and Levites would have equal access to them, as they came for their times of service. Samuel, however, living right at the tabernacle, would have had immediate access to them, to read and to study as he wished. His teacher, Eli, could have actually made assignments for him from them. The benefit would have been twofold: the finest education in the Law the day could provide, and a special appreciation for the importance of God's requirements. Since Samuel had a native ability for learning—as evidenced by the general story—it may be concluded that Samuel came to be as well-educated as a man of the day could be for the task God had in mind for him to do.

That Samuel lived at the tabernacle provided him also with a firsthand acquaintance with the sinful conditions in the land. The tabernacle was a place to and through which such information regularly would have passed,

[7]Hebrew children were not weaned early; II Macc. 7:27 speaks of the age of three years.

since it was central in the land. It was the place also where priests and Levites came bringing such information with them. Besides this, Samuel was an actual observer of the terrible sin committed by Hophni and Phinehas. Following the time when these two took over in their perverted leadership, they probably even tried to influence the young boy, wanting his cooperation and possible help in their nefarious activity. If so, Eli was God's great counteracting influence, and Samuel was led by his counsel in the path of righteousness. He did not side with the two sons, but he followed the directions of Eli and the will of God.

Besides studying, Samuel assumed some actual work as he grew older. It is stated that he "ministered before the LORD" (I Sam. 2:18; 3:1). The probable meaning is that he performed some necessary functions around the tabernacle, such as sweeping, making wood available for the altar, and keeping water handy for drinking and cleaning. It is also indicated that he opened the "doors of the house of the LORD" in the morning.[8] Mention of this comes in connection with the occasion when God first revealed Himself to Samuel and told him of the demise portended for the house of Eli (I Sam. 3:15).

His place of sleeping was at the tabernacle near Eli's room. This is indicated by the fact that he was "lying down in the tabernacle of the LORD where the ark of God was" (literal translation) at the time when God first appeared to him. From his room he was able to run quickly to Eli's room (I Sam. 3:3–5).[9] As for dress, he is said to have been "girded with a linen ephod" (I Sam. 2:18), apparently in the style of the priests themselves (I Sam. 22:18), though his ephod (like that of the ordinary priests) was not made of the same ornate material as the ephod of the high priest (Exod. 28:6).[10] The term *girded* (*hagur*) is appropriate because the front and back parts of the ephod were drawn tight around the body with a sash or girdle. One may picture the young lad, then, busily engaged around the tabernacle, clothed in white linen like the regular priests.

## b. SPIRITUAL STATUS

There is abundant evidence that Samuel was a man of high spiritual standing. In a day of rampant sin among the people he must have stood out as

[8]These "doors" were no doubt the curtained openings into the court area of the tabernacle (Exod. 27:16). Evidently the curtains were closed at night and opened the following morning.

[9]Probably both Samuel and Eli slept in the court area of the tabernacle. The reference to the "lamp of God" (I Sam. 3:3) not having gone out is for the purpose of setting the time of the appearance. This "lamp of God" can hardly have been other than the golden lampstand of the Holy Place, which burned through the night until its oil was consumed (with this oil being replenished each morning—Exod. 27:20, 21; 30:7, 8). The thought is that God's revelation came to Samuel in the early morning hours before the oil was all consumed.

[10]The ephod of the ordinary priests was made of "linen" (Heb. *bad*), while the high priest's was of gold, blue, scarlet, and fine twined linen (Heb. *shesh*, meaning "linen").

a beacon light of influence for God. This follows from the fact that he did the great work that has been noted, and evidence exists also in concrete illustrations that call for notice.

From Samuel's early life, one illustration is found in his choice to do right, against the wrong influence of Hophni and Phinehas at the tabernacle. Being older than Samuel, these two would almost certainly have attempted to influence him in their direction and away from the instruction of their father. Samuel was a normal young boy and would have had normal inner emotions which enjoyed hearing some of the attractive things they told him. It is clear, however, that he did not follow their urgings but decided for truth and righteousness as taught by Eli. Deciding for the right in this way would have been a character-building experience already in young days.

Another occasion of significance was the time God remarkably revealed Himself to him during the course of a night. Samuel was still young at the time, perhaps about twelve years old,[11] and the event would have made a strong impression on him. God came to him and first simply called his name. The boy could think only of Eli and ran quickly to ask what he desired. This happened twice, and then on the third time Eli realized God was speaking to Samuel. Therefore, he told him now to respond, should the call come again, "Speak, LORD, for thy servant heareth." Samuel did this and God told him that Eli's house would not be allowed to continue in the high priesthood.

How much Samuel may have slept the rest of that night is hard to say, though it may have been more than Eli. Eli insisted the following morning that Samuel, still so young and untried, tell him exactly what God had revealed, clearly fearing that it concerned himself. It must have been an extremely hard thing for the young boy to do—to tell this kind of information to the aged and honored high priest—but he did. The experience for him would have been most maturing.

A third matter, directly related to Samuel's service as a prophet, is that God continued to appear to the young man. In I Samuel 3:21 we read, "And the LORD appeared again in Shiloh: for the LORD revealed himself to Samuel in Shiloh by the word of the LORD." Further, I Samuel 4:1 begins, "And the word of Samuel came to all Israel." In I Samuel 3:20 are the significant words, "And all Israel, from Dan even to Beersheba, knew that Samuel was established to be a prophet of the LORD." It is evident that God used Samuel in a prophetic capacity already in his early years. God apparently continued to appear to him in ways parallel to the appearance on that memorable first night, no doubt giving information pertinent for Israel in her time of serious sin and distress. Evidently Samuel moved out from the tabernacle to convey this information in various population centers, with the result that he became

---

[11]Josephus (*Antiquities* V.10.4) gives this as his age and it suits the story very well.

known as a prophet from the extreme north to the extreme south. God would not have so employed any person, much less one still young, unless that person had gained remarkable spiritual maturity.

A later occasion of marked significance was the splendid revival called at Mizpeh by Samuel (I Sam. 7:3–6). As noted earlier, this occasion came twenty years after the disastrous battle of Aphek (I Sam. 7:2).[12] At this time the people came in considerable number to Mizpeh for the purpose of renewing their promises before God. This was in marked contrast to their attitude twenty years before, when sin abounded and despair was everywhere. No one then wished for revival; the people were interested only in their own sinful pursuits. This shows that someone with a high spiritual message had been urging change upon them and had been sufficiently influential to bring it to pass. This man of course was Samuel, as God's spiritual leader and prophet among the people.

c. Ability

Like Moses and Joshua before him, Samuel must have been a man of remarkable ability in leadership. He apparently demonstrated this already as a young man, for in I Samuel 3:20 it is stated that he became known "from Dan even to Beersheba" as one "established to be a prophet of the LORD." As has been indicated, this must have come already at an early age as the result of receiving revelations from God and then relaying them to people in many parts of the country. He must have been a forceful speaker and naturally gifted for prompting people to respect his message.

The most remarkable evidence of his ability as leader, however, comes from the implied work of the twenty years between the battle of Aphek and the revival at Mizpeh. A great change certainly was effected during these years, and this would have required unusual effectiveness on Samuel's part. People do not leave their sin and take up righteous conduct easily. This is accomplished only when strong forces are brought to bear and dominant personalities lead the way. As noted, Samuel no doubt began by contacting strategically located priests and prophets, but it would have taken a strong personality to persuade them. He would have first had to convince them that a change had come at the tabernacle and that things were going to be different in the future, and then to inspire them to take this message out to their

---

[12]The "twenty years" mentioned in I Sam. 7:2 refers to the lapse of time between the return of the ark by the Philistines to Israel (I Sam. 6:21—7:1) and the revival at Mizpeh (I Sam. 7:5, 6). It does not refer, as it is often misunderstood, to the time the ark was at Kirjath-jearim. The ark remained at Kirjath-jearim until David brought it to Jerusalem, and this was seventy years later (c. 1074–1004 B.C.). (See II Sam. 6:1–3, where "in Gibeah" should be rendered "in the hill," as in I Sam. 7:1. Also, the name *Baale* is simply another name for Kirjath-jearim, as evidenced in Josh. 15:60; 18:14.)

various constituencies. Further, Samuel himself would have had to speak in many communities and contact numerous people. Elders of the various cities would have been key people to talk to. Again, they would have responded only if one of strong persuasive powers came to them.

Still a third matter showing Samuel's unusual ability is the continued recognition Saul gave to him all during Saul's reign. Saul had been anointed by Samuel (I Sam. 10:1), and later Samuel had played a major role in Saul's coronation (I Sam. 11:14, 15). Still later Samuel had the unpleasant task of twice telling Saul that he was rejected as Israel's continuing ruler (I Sam. 13:8–14; 15:28, 29). One might think that because of these two rejections Saul would have developed an animosity for Samuel. That he did not, however, is indicated by his visit to a medium, the woman of Endor, so that he might contact Samuel again even after Samuel had died (I Sam. 28:7–25). Had Samuel not been a strong personality and a true leader in his own right, Saul, the king of Israel, would certainly not have resorted to him in this way. The occasion speaks significantly of Samuel's ability and the high respect Saul had for him.

In another area Samuel seems to have shown less ability. This was his role as a father to his sons. When Samuel came to his declining years of life, he made his sons, Joel and Abiah, judges in the region of Beersheba. Apparently Samuel was no longer able to serve as much of the land as he had formerly, and so he sought in this fashion to have his work supplemented. The two sons did not follow his ways, however, but "turned aside after lucre, and took bribes, and perverted judgment" (I Sam. 8:2, 3).

This situation reveals two surprising facts regarding Samuel. One is that he had not raised his sons in the way he should have. They were not following in his footsteps but were leading in the sinful practices that he himself had been attempting to stamp out in the land elsewhere. Second, it shows that Samuel did not know this was true of his sons, for surely he would not have placed them as judges in Beersheba if he had known. Evidently they had been able to fool their father and keep their sinful ways secret from him.

This indicates that Samuel had not been the kind of father he should have been. It may be that he had become overly busy in his work as prophet and judge, so that he was away from home too much of the time and not able to give the attention his sons required. He provides a warning in this for all other fathers, for it is important that every parent give sufficient time to his family to insure that children are raised in a way pleasing to God. One has to be surprised that Samuel would have fallen short as a father inasmuch as Eli had fallen short in reference to his sons. Samuel had known firsthand concerning the deficiency of Eli; one would think that he would have taken special pains with his own sons. That he had not provides all the more warning that it is possible to neglect one's family and not realize it.

An area in which Samuel has been improperly accredited ability is military strategy. The thinking that he was militarily capable is based upon Samuel's leadership in the victorious battle against the Philistines at Mizpeh (I Sam. 7:7-14). It is questionable, however, whether this victory was due in any significant degree to strategy on Samuel's part. He had simply brought the people together at Mizpeh for a time of revival. The Philistines, learning about this scheduled time of gathering, had seized upon it for coming in battle against the assembled number. When the people learned of this invasion, they cried out in fear, and Samuel called upon God. God in turn "thundered with a great thunder on that day upon the Philistines and discomfited them" (7:10). The result was that the enemy was smitten before Israel, with Israel then pursuing the Philistines back toward their own land.

It is doubtful that the Israelites did any real fighting at this time. They had come to Mizpeh for revival, not to do battle. What weapons they may have had would have been very few. The battle apparently was won almost solely by God's work in their behalf, which prompted the Philistines to flee; about all the Israelites had to do was pursue and make sure the enemy returned to its own land. If this was the case, Samuel's part as a military strategist was very minimal. After all, he had not been trained in military matters but only in the things of God and in factors to make him a strong leader as a judge.

### d. PERSONALITY

*1) Strength, dominance.* A first matter to notice in respect to Samuel's personality is that he was a strong, dominant type of person. This has already appeared in the discussion above in respect to his ability as leader. In order to be such a leader, a person must have this kind of personality. He must be one who speaks forcefully and prompts people to listen and act in accordance with his directions.

*2) Obedience.* Though Samuel was strong and dominant he was altogether obedient to God, whom he recognized as his sovereign superior. As has been seen, this had been true of him already as a young man growing up at the tabernacle. He might have been influenced by Hophni and Phinehas to go in their way but he had not followed them. Rather, he had chosen the way he knew God desired.

This same obedience was shown later at the time Israel asked Samuel to provide them with a king (I Sam. 8:1-22). The people came to Samuel and informed him of his sons' wrong conduct at Beersheba and told him that they now wanted a king, instead of a judge, to rule them. This sounded to Samuel as though they were rejecting him and not showing appreciation for the great work he had done in the years past. He took the matter to God, and God told him that he should accede to their request. God indicated that the people were not really rejecting Samuel but Himself as God; in fact, they had been doing this all the time since they had left Egypt. At first, Samuel could only have been surprised at this response by God. He no doubt expected that God would tell him to go back to the people and refuse their request, but here God was instructing him to do just the opposite. Yet when God gave him the surprising instruction, Samuel did not object. He readily accepted it and told all that God said in his response to the people.

Another way in which Samuel showed commendable obedience was in conveying God's word of rejection to King Saul on the two different times noted. It would not have been easy for Samuel to do this, for he had a true love for Saul. In fact, we are told that following the second rejection, Samuel "mourned for Saul" continually when he was not able to see him any longer (I Sam. 15:35). There had been need both times, however, to bring the rejection. On the first occasion Saul had entered upon the priests' office in presenting a sacrifice, and this constituted serious sin in God's sight. At the second time, Saul had been told to slay all the Amalekites, but he had done so only up to a point; he had spared some of the animals and the Amalekite king. Because he had disobeyed a direct order from God, he was again guilty of serious sin and the second rejection was called for. Samuel brought it though it would not have been an easy thing for him to do.

Still another time of commendable obedience was the occasion God instructed Samuel to go to Bethlehem and anoint David as king (I Sam. 16:1-13). This was a dangerous assignment for Samuel, because Saul had just been rejected the second time and was naturally anticipating the possibility of a rival's being appointed in his place. Samuel knew that if Saul were told of the anointing of such a rival, his own life would be in jeopardy. When God told him to go, however, he did go, and of course God protected him. It took real obedience on his part to carry out the divine order, however.

*3) Courage.* Samuel was also a courageous person. This appears particularly in his willingness to take over as Israel's leader in the dark days following the disaster at Aphek. A lesser man would have refused to do this, thinking that the task was too great. The day was indeed dark, as has been noted. The national morale of the people was probably as low as it could be, and Samuel would have been keenly aware of this. He had been in the center of matters at the tabernacle, and he had been traveling the land in bringing his prophetic message. He might truly have despaired at ever bringing anything like order out of such conditions. That he did not despair shows both a great faith in God and a very courageous spirit. He had what it took to accept the challenge and perform the task that seemed impossible.

Another occasion showing courage was the time when the Philistines attacked at Mizpeh (1 Sam. 7:7–14). Twenty years had passed since the former disaster at the hands of this enemy at Aphek. Samuel had been enormously impressed with Philistine strength then, and must have been glad during the intervening years that this enemy had not struck again.[13] When he learned, therefore, that they were indeed coming again, his first reaction would have been one of fear and despair. The Philistines were coming, and the people were not ready. They had not come to fight a battle, they were not equipped with weapons, and he was not a military leader himself. Yet he did not flee or panic but rather turned in faith to God for His enablement. God responded by bringing terrifying thunder upon the Philistines and causing them to turn and run so that all the Israelites had to do was pursue. Samuel's courage must be highly admired.

*4) Persistence and hard work.* A last matter to notice is that Samuel was a persistent, hard-working person. Evidence for this comes again from the crucial twenty years between the time he took over as Israel's leader and the great revival at Mizpeh. The marked change in attitude on the part of the people has been noted, but it should be realized that this would have come only with great labor and persistent work. Actually, twenty years was not long to do so much, but at the time twenty years would have seemed a long time for the person who was carrying on the activity. And we may be sure that Samuel met with considerable opposition on the part of the people. Persons who had long been enjoying their sinful ways would not have been ready recipients of the type of message Samuel brought. He would have met with words of rebuke and closed doors. Even priests and Levites in their several cities would not always have been willing to receive him, for they too would have enjoyed their lax and sinful ways. The fact that such a change came, then, within only twenty years, indicates that Samuel showed remarkable determination in moving on in spite of all difficulties. He was persistent and hard-working; no other conclusion is possible in view of the remarkable results achieved.

All of this means that Samuel was an outstanding person. An interesting study is to analyze the way in which God throughout history meets needs. Many times, when conditions have been desperately dark, He has seen to it that a man of unusual ability was available to stand and move in to save the situation. This certainly was true at the time of Samuel. Perhaps no day in all Israel's history was any darker than the day when the ark was captured at the

---

[13]It may very well be that it was during these twenty years that God used Samson to deter the Philistines and caused their interest to be centered in him rather than in a further military attack on Israel. For discussion, see my *Distressing Days of the Judges*, pp. 303–304.

battle of Aphek. Samuel was God's man to do the work necessary. Samuel must be accorded one of the high places in sacred history.

## B. "THE SCHOOL OF THE PROPHETS"

One aspect of Samuel's work that has been mentioned only in passing now calls for treatment. It involves a "school of the prophets" that evidently he began at the time he took over as Israel's leader. Though the term *school of the prophets* is not found in the sacred record, another term, *company of prophets*, is mentioned in two significant texts involving Samuel (I Sam. 10:5-10; 19:20), and these texts connote a group which could well have constituted a type of school. In both passages the companies were clearly groups approved by Samuel, and in the second Samuel is pictured serving as their leader. It is commonly held that the company in each case was the same and that the members were students of Samuel. This parallels similar students under the headship of Elijah and Elisha in a later day (II Kings 2:3-7, 15-18; 4:38; 6:1, 2).

Samuel's interest in having such a group of students fits with the need of the hour. The task before Samuel was simply too great for one man as he took over as Israel's leader following the Aphek battle. Also, haste was necessary. The sooner the priests and Levites in their forty-eight cities could be contacted the better, so that they in turn could get busy among the people. But it would take one person many weeks to do this, and, when all cities had been visited once, the circuit would have to be made again to lend further encouragement and make a check on how well the first instructions were being carried out. Therefore, help was advisable, and it is quite clear that Samuel sought it in starting this informal type of school.

He probably gathered his students from concerned young men of the day, perhaps many of them Levites like himself.[14] He knew they would need training in what they were to do, which called for the idea of a school, and Samuel was the logical one to serve as teacher. It would have taken some of Samuel's valuable time to do this, but apparently he saw wisdom in taking that time so that the total task could be accomplished in a shorter period. It is possible, too, that Samuel did much of his instructing as he walked from one city to another. This would have saved time and the young trainees could have profited from seeing Samuel directly in action.

In the later day of Elijah and Elisha, similar schools seem to have been centered in three localities, Gilgal, Bethel, and Jericho (II Kings 2:1-5;

---

[14]Samuel was a Levite as well as being from the tribe of Ephraim (I Chron. 6:16-28). That he was from the tribe of Ephraim means simply that he was living in Ephraimite territory though he was of Levitic descent.

4:38–41). They probably had one or more buildings in these places where they met, for in II Kings 6:1f. an account is given of the prophets in training going to the Jordan to procure wood for a new building. This was the time when one of the young men lost an axe-head in the water and Elisha was called upon to save it by a miracle.

There is one clue that Samuel's school also had a building for its center of instruction. This comes in I Samuel 19:18, 19, where it is stated that David had fled to Samuel who was with his prophets at "Naioth in Ramah." The word *Naioth* means "habitations" or "buildings." The thought may be that David had come to Samuel who was in a building of this school located at Ramah, Samuel's home town. The date here, however, was well along in Samuel's life, many years after the inauguration of Saul as king. That Samuel may have had buildings for his school at this later time does not mean that he had them at first.

There is no way to know whether or not the schools Samuel started continued and became eventually the schools that Elijah and Elisha taught. Approximately two centuries had elapsed.[15] This is a considerable time for such schools to have continued, and there is no reference to them in between or before or after. It is interesting, however, that at least approximately the same geographical area was concerned. Samuel lived at Ramah and so would have had his center at this city, and Elijah and Elisha had their schools also in the mid-part of the country, at Gilgal, Bethel, and Jericho. This may have been pure coincidence, however, and not an indication that the schools continued.

It is also appropriate to notice that both periods of time—that of Samuel and that of Elijah and Elisha—were periods of great need for such schools, need which could have given rise to them. The need in Samuel's day has already been noted. The need in Elijah and Elisha's time was due to the wicked reign of Ahab and Jezebel. Their opposition to everything that pertained to the truth of Israel's God is well known, and certainly true prophets were few in number. Elijah and Elisha may well have started their schools to meet the need thus apparent.

The school in the day of Samuel is mentioned in two passages, both of which were noticed in chapters 3 and 6. The first is I Samuel 10, where Saul is described as meeting students as they came down from a high place, playing instruments and engaged in the act of praising God. Saul joined in with them, thus showing a changed personality. The other is I Samuel 19 which concerns a time several years later when David had fled to Samuel at Ramah to get away from the anger of Saul. At this time Samuel was standing as supervisor over the group of prophets, and again they were active in

[15]Samuel's time was around 1050 B.C. and the date of Elijah and Elisha about 850 B.C.

rendering praise to God. This was the occasion when three groups of messengers from Saul and later Saul himself came to arrest David and instead began praising God.

A few matters of significance may be noted in respect to these prophets as one studies the two times. First, they were a joyful group, given to rendering praise. This follows from the fact that both occurrences involve the rendition of praise. The first time the students were simply coming down from a high place, apparently marching along to their living quarters. They were voicing praise as they did so. The second time they were assembled together with Samuel and probably David at Ramah. Again they were rendering praise.

Second, Samuel was the head of this group. This is evident once more from both occasions. On the first occasion, though Samuel was not with the group, he knew where they would be and what their time schedule was so that Saul would meet them at a particular point as he returned home. This degree of familiarity with their activities suggests that Samuel himself had arranged the schedule. Then with the second instance it is definitely said that Samuel was "standing as appointed over them" (I Sam. 19:20), meaning that he was superintending the festive occasion. This manner of headship is in keeping with the idea already expressed that he had instituted the schools for the purpose of training young men to help him.

A third matter concerns chronology. These two occasions came approximately thirty-five years apart, thus showing that Samuel's schools continued at least this long. The first occasion happened at the time Saul was first told he would serve as king. This would have been a few months prior to the beginning of his forty-year reign (Acts 13:21). The second occasion came following the anointing of David, the occasion when David had come to play for Saul, and even the numerous attempts when Saul had tried to take David's life. The time when David was anointed must have been roughly twenty-five years after Saul began to reign. This is evident because David was thirty years old when he came to the throne, which means he was born ten years after Saul began his rule. His age when anointed by Samuel was probably about fifteen (in view of all attending circumstances). To account for the numerous events that had happened since that time, until this occasion when Saul wanted to take his life, calls for probably another five to ten years. That means no less than thirty-five years intervened between the two times. The schools that Samuel started may not have continued operating many years after Samuel's death, but at least they were kept active for this length of time.

# Section Two

# THE MONARCHY
# PROPHETS

# HISTORY CHART II

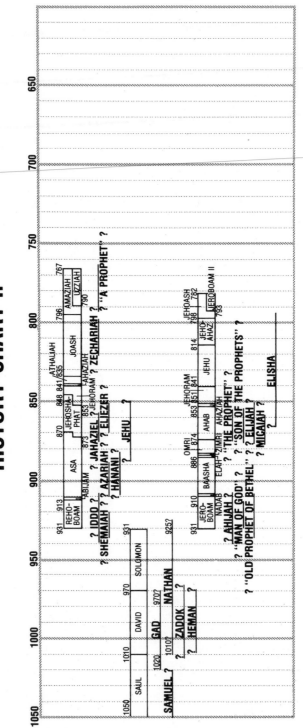

# 11

# The Reigns of David, Solomon, and Jeroboam

Our interest now turns from prophets of the period of the judges to those who ministered during the days of the monarchy prior to the first of the writing prophets. As indicated in chapter 8, many more prophets are named for this period than for the time of the judges, and the stress in their message differed also. In this chapter we confine our study to prophets that ministered during the days of David, Solomon, and Jeroboam. A brief historical survey is appropriate for seeing these prophets in the light of the circumstances that surrounded them.

The new monarchy did not get off to a good start under its first king, Saul. A first task that confronted him was to unify twelve quite independent tribes, and this was no easy assignment. Saul never really did accomplish it. For a while he seems to have made some progress, but then he disobeyed God and was rejected as king for the second time (I Sam. 15). At this the enabling Holy Spirit left him (I Sam. 16:14), and matters declined rapidly. Saul became emotionally disturbed as an evil spirit came upon him, and he grew jealous of David who he suspected would succeed him. He spent much of his closing years in pursuing David, until apparently his own people became disgusted. He finally died in battle at Mount Gilboa, before the onslaught of the enemy Philistines, and when he did he left his country in a weaker condition than when he began to rule. The reason was that now the

Philistines could come in and overrun the land, making a condition of great terror for the people.[1]

It is noteworthy also that Saul's relationship to religious personnel of the day was not happy. The one prophet was Samuel, and Samuel twice told Saul that he had been rejected from ruling (I Sam. 13:13, 14; 15:26). And as for priests, nothing is more significant than Saul's slaughter of eighty-five of their number at Nob, because the high priest, Ahimelech, had given some assistance to David (I Sam. 22:17–19).

David's rule stands in marked contrast to that of Saul. He took over leadership when the kingdom was divided and the Philistines were in charge, and he united the people and built the kingdom into a virtual empire. The story of David is a story of remarkable success. He became king at first only of the southern tribe of Judah, ruling at Hebron—the north was still under Philistine control. The people of the north in time made Saul's youngest son, Ish-bosheth, their king, placing him in charge at the city of Mahanaim, which was on the east side of the Jordan,[2] but he was assassinated two years after beginning to rule (II Sam. 2:10; 4:5–7).

When David had completed seven years at Hebron, the northern tribes came to ask him to be their king as well, and he complied. A prime task then facing him was to defeat the Philistines, and he did this in two short battles (II Sam. 5:18–25). The people were no doubt surprised that he was able to solve their major problem so quickly, but certainly they were also happy. David formed a fine army, and, when conflicts arose (seldom due to any offensive action by David), he was able to win on each occasion and gradually enlarged Israel's borders. Finally the boundary stretched as far north as the region of Hamath, which really meant all the way to the Euphrates River, in keeping with God's promise to Abraham many years before (Gen. 15:18).

David was not without his faults, as seen particularly in his sin with Bathsheba and her husband, Uriah (II Sam. 11:1–27). Not only did he take this woman when he had no right to her, but when she became pregnant by him he had her husband killed in battle so that he might marry her. It was as the result of this great sin that David had continuing trouble in his own family. An aspect of this trouble was a major revolution instigated by Absalom, his third son, who attempted to take over the kingdom. David actually had to flee from his throne before he could engage the young man in battle and defeat him.

In contrast to Saul, David had a good relationship with religious person-

---

[1] It is significant that it was as the result of this defeat that Mephibosheth was dropped by his nurse in the capital, Gibeah, which was far south of the actual battle scene. The nurse was running in panic at the news of the catastrophe in the north (II Sam. 4:4).

[2] The fact that his capital was made at Mahanaim signifies that he did not dare make it at Gibeah or any of the cities on the west of the Jordan due to the Philistine danger.

nel. The two prophets of his time were Gad and Nathan. Both of them were used of God to advise David, and both were also used to rebuke their king. As for priests, David organized them into twenty-four courses, with one course serving at the central sanctuary one week in turn. There were so many priests and Levites that it was impossible for all to be in attendance at one time. He also brought the ark from Kirjath-jearim, where it had been since coming back from the land of the Philistines (I Sam. 7:1), to the city of Jerusalem, where he placed it in a temporary tent until the permanent temple could be built.

The third king, Solomon, was once more a different type of person and one who ruled in a different way than either Saul or David. Whereas Saul and David both rose from a farm life, where hardship and difficult labor were commonplace, Solomon was born and raised at the court and knew only luxury all his life. He had a natural taste for fine things and lavish provisions. Accordingly, his life was characterized by a desire to satisfy this taste, and this called for enormous expenditures. In fact, one day's supply of food for his court consisted of "thirty measures [kor] of fine flour, and threescore measures of meal, ten fat oxen, and twenty oxen out of the pastures, and an hundred sheep, besides harts, roebucks, and fallow deer, and fatted fowl" (I Kings 4:22, 23).

Moreover, Solomon was not a man of war but of peace. He did not fight battles on foreign soil as did David.[3] Instead he built strong cities of defense (I Kings 9:17–19) and formed large units of chariotry to man them. In Solomon's closing years, he fell into a disobedient way of life, due especially to the influence of many foreign wives (I Kings 11:1–8). The consequence was that God's blessing was lost and Solomon suffered severe difficulty both at home and abroad (I Kings 11:11–39). By the time of Solomon's death, he had lost much of the empire that he had inherited from his illustrious father.

As to Solomon's relationship to religious personnel, it was both good and bad. It was good in that Solomon built the temple and instituted the sacrificial program that God had commanded through Moses years before. At that time Solomon was yet conducting his life properly, and he even led in the ceremonial activity at the dedication of the temple, offering a fine prayer and presenting a splendid sermon of admonishment to the people (I Kings 8:12–53). It was bad in that at the close of his life one of his sources of trouble arose when the prophet Ahijah told a young worker of Solomon named Jeroboam that he would become ruler of a division of Solomon's kingdom, including no less than ten of the twelve tribes (I Kings 11:26–39).

Jeroboam did become king of the new northern kingdom of Israel in due

[3]With the exception of a campaign against Hamath-zobah, followed by the building of Tadmor (Palmyra) east of Hamath-zobah (II Chron. 8:3, 4; cf. I Kings 9:18).

time. Solomon's son was named Rehoboam, and the people of the north had become so weary of high taxation under Solomon that they asked Rehoboam at the beginning of his rule if this taxation might be reduced (I Kings 12:1–15). Rehoboam would have been wise if he had acceded to the request, but he followed the advice of young men who also liked lavish ways, and refused. The result was a secession on the part of ten tribes and the establishment of a new kingdom called Israel. Jeroboam, who had fled from Solomon to Egypt, was now recalled, and he was made the new king according to the prophecy of Ahijah. He had been promised great blessing from God if he would obey God after he became king, but Jeroboam forgot the admonishing words of Ahijah and became disobedient.

One of Jeroboam's most flagrant sins was the establishment of substitute worship for his northern people (I Kings 12:26–33). He reasoned that if he did not do this the people, on returning to Jerusalem to worship, would be attracted to a reunion of the two countries. He established new worship centers at Dan in the north and Bethel in the south. As symbols for the new program, he erected gold images of calves at each center. The intent was still to worship the true God but in a new way. He built a temple ("house of high places") presumably to house the image and an altar (I Kings 12:31, 33) at each center, and he appointed priests from the common people (non-Levites) to serve them. One reason for not using Levites, as required in the Mosaic Law, was that many Levites, perhaps most, had left for Judah, evidently in rebellion at these innovations (II Chron. 11:13, 14).

As a result of these and other sins, Jeroboam did not enjoy the blessing of God. He lost much of the territory that he had received on becoming king. It may be assumed that the entire area Solomon had controlled, apart from that retained by Judah, came under Jeroboam's jurisdiction at his inauguration. If it did, significant sections were lost during the reigns of early Israelite kings, and much during that of Jeroboam. One such section was in the north, the Damascus region. Substantial loss in degree of control had occurred there already while Solomon reigned, because of vigorous opposition by a man named Rezon (I Kings 11:23–25), but during Jeroboam's rule the region itself was lost.[4] Another section was in the southwest where the Philistines now became active again, reclaiming some of their lost territory. Nadab, Jeroboam's son and successor, found it necessary to try to regain the city of Gibbethon from them in his reign, though without success (I Kings 15:27). In the east, at least Moab was lost, for the Moabite Stone records Moab's later reconquest by Omri, Israel's sixth king.[5]

---

[4]For evidence and general discussion of Aramaean history at this time, see Merrill F. Unger, *Israel and the Aramaeans of Damascus*, pp. 38–57.

[5]For text and discussion, see *Ancient Near Eastern Texts*, ed. James B. Pritchard, p. 320; for discussion and a picture, see *Documents from Old Testament Times*, ed. D. Winton Thomas, pp. 195–199.

Jeroboam died a natural death after twenty-two years of rule. He had shown ability but forfeited God's blessing because of sin. He gave the new country its start, but he fell short of moving it on to become a strong, vigorous state. Indeed, he left the country with seeds of discontent, which were to sprout in royal assassinations, rapid succession of kings, and serious weakness of rule.

The prophets from the period of time just surveyed were Gad, Nathan, Zadok, Heman, Ahijah, a "man of God," and an "old prophet in Bethel." Each will now be discussed in turn.


## A. GAD

The first prophet is Gad. He lived during the time of Saul and David, though he is never associated with Saul in the scriptural account, but only with David. He is first noted as he came to David while David was a fugitive from Saul (I Sam. 22:5), and he apparently stayed with David from that time on. Hence, we speak in this chapter only of the reigns of David to Jeroboam, rather than Saul to Jeroboam. The one prophet related to Saul was Samuel, and he has already been considered.


### 1. The work

In I Chronicles 21:9, Gad is called "David's seer," which suggests that a principal work of Gad lay in serving David. Calling Gad a seer[6] in this significant context, rather than a prophet, indicates that God used him mainly as an instrument to convey divine revelations to the king. The time when he first came to David is not revealed. The first mention of him comes from David's early life as a fugitive when he was in Moab (I Sam. 22:5), but the manner of mention implies that Gad had already been with David for some time. He may have joined him when the four hundred had come to David at the cave of Adullam. It is also quite possible that he had been trained in Samuel's school.

At the time of this first mention, David had left Judah and gone to the eastern country of Moab, taking his parents with him. He feared that Saul might do them harm because of himself. He asked asylum for them from the king of Moab, and this was granted. David himself took up a position in what is called "the hold" (*metsodah*). This was probably at the top of one of the mountain peaks of Moab, from which he could see in any direction to know

---

[6]See discussion in chapter 4.

of possible pursuit.[7] It was while David was here that Gad brought his first word of advice, counseling that David "abide not in the hold" but go "into the land of Judah" (I Sam. 22:5). The reason for the advice is not given, but presumably Gad had divine revelation to this effect. David carried out the advice, probably leaving his parents in Moab.

A much later time of contact between Gad and David is recorded in II Samuel 24:11–19 (cf. I Chron. 21:9–19). The occasion followed David's grievous sin involving the numbering of Israel. The reason why this sin was considered so serious is not revealed, but it is significant that even Joab, hard as he was in his own personality, did not wish to carry out this order of David. But David insisted, and when the census had been taken, God sent Gad to David to give him a choice of three punishments. One was seven years of famine in the land, another was three months of flight before David's enemies, and the third was three days of pestilence bringing death on the people. David chose the last, and the result was that seventy thousand men died (II Sam. 24:15).

A particular area of work by Gad is suggested in II Chronicles 29:25, which says that King Hezekiah set Levites in their work of service in the temple "according to the commandment of David, and of Gad the king's seer, and Nathan the prophet." It is well known that David did much in organizing the ministries of the priests and Levites, a work which seems to be in reference here, and the inclusion of the names of Gad and Nathan shows that they helped in this effort. Both men probably worked closely with the king in determining the best policies and making suggestions for the organization.

## 2. The person

### a. SPIRITUAL STATUS

One factor may be noticed that shows a relatively high standing for Gad in spirituality. It is that he is called "the king's seer" (II Chron. 29:25). The designation *seer* must be taken as significant here because in the same verse Nathan is called "the prophet." It would seem, then, that Gad was considered more a "seer" while Nathan was more a "prophet." Since "seer" connotes one who receives revelation in distinction from "prophet" indicating one who speaks, this suggests that Gad was used in a special sense to bring divine messages of revelation to the king. The point to notice is that God would not have used a person to receive revelations in this way unless he was considered spiritually mature and able to receive them properly.

[7]Aharoni believes the reference is to the stronghold of Masada just on the west of the Dead Sea, across from Moab at the Lisan (Yohanan Aharoni and Michael Avi-yonah, eds., *The Macmillan Bible Atlas*, map 92).

## b. COMMAND OF RESPECT

It is evident that Gad was a man who commanded the respect of others. For instance, when he advised David while in Moab to move back to Judah, David seems to have done so without hesitation. One has to wonder why Gad gave this advice, and surely David must have wondered at the time. Gad must have spoken with a ring of authority for David to have followed the counsel directly. Then later, when Gad brought the three choices of punishment to David, David again accepted what he said as authoritative. He did not argue with the prophet but made his selection from the three. Then still later, when Gad indicated that David should purchase the threshing floor of Araunah for the purpose of offering sacrifice, David also did this. If the king himself gave this kind of respect to Gad, it follows that others did the same.

## c. COURAGE

The same occasions show that Gad was a courageous person. When David was a fugitive from Saul, he already had gained a high reputation. Gad must have respected him accordingly. For Gad to come to David, then, and advise him to return to Judah when he had just recently arrived in Moab took courage on his part. David, with his four hundred men in support, might have responded with a word of rebuke, thus bringing humiliation upon the prophet in front of the others. He did not, but this in no way detracts from the fact that such a word from Gad took courage in that situation. The same is true in respect to bringing the three choices of punishment. By this time David was king of the land. In fact, his time of rule was well along in years, and David was an established monarch, probably the most important ruler in the world of the day. Gad, however, did not hesitate in going to him with this very unpleasant message.

## d. MAN OF JUDGMENT

There is one clue that David respected Gad as a man of judgment. This is found in II Chronicles 29:25, which indicates that Gad assisted David in organizing the Levites. Nathan also helped in this, showing that he too was highly regarded. One may imagine David calling in the two when he wanted to do this work and having them offer suggestions and perhaps even formulate guidelines. He would not have done this if he had not had a high respect for both of them.

## e. LITERARY ABILITY

The fact that Gad wrote a book which included the "acts of David" shows that he must have had some measure of literary ability.

## B. NATHAN

### 1. The work

Though Gad is depicted as having been with David earlier than was Nathan, more is said regarding Nathan than his counterpart. There is no way to know when the first contact was made by Nathan with the king, but the first recorded is given in two different passages, II Samuel 7:2-17 and I Chronicles 17:1-15. The occasion concerned God's response through Nathan to David's desire to build the temple. The time was probably comparatively early in David's rule at Jerusalem, though it could not have been in the very first years because II Samuel 7:1 says it happened when "the LORD had given him [David] rest round about from all his enemies." David's earlier battles evidently had been fought prior to this time.

David had brought the ark into Jerusalem and now wished to build a fine temple in which to house it. This desire was not wrong, and Nathan's first response when David spoke of the idea was that David should proceed. That night, however, God revealed to Nathan that David should not do this, and Nathan then brought God's word to David. The essence of the message was that, rather than David's building a physical house for God, God was going to build a continuing house for David, that is, a dynasty on Israel's throne. He also indicated that the matter of building a physical temple would be accomplished by the son of David who would succeed him.

A second major contact with the king was made following the sin of David in taking Bathsheba, the wife of Uriah. While walking on the roof of his palace, David had seen Bathsheba bathing and had called for her and taken her. When he later learned that she was pregnant by him, he called for her husband Uriah to be returned from the battle front so that he might be with his wife. Uriah did return but refused to go to his wife; David then had him put in the most dangerous part of the battle so that he would surely be killed. Thereupon David took Bathsheba as his wife. In all this David acted very reprehensibly.

Accordingly, God gave Nathan a message of reprimand to bring to David. This was done after the son was born, meaning that several months had intervened. The thrust of the message was that David had severely sinned in this action and would be punished. The punishment would involve, first, the death of the little child now born and, second, a continuing problem in David's family. Subsequent history shows that this punishment was duly carried out much to David's sorrow.

A third contact of Nathan with David involved one aspect of this punishment being carried out. It was the occasion when Adonijah, fourth son of David, tried to take over the throne for himself. Earlier Absalom, the third son, had sought to do this and had failed.[8] Adonijah now made a similar attempt and received the support of Joab, the head of David's army, and Abiathar, one of the two high priests then living. David, however, had earlier designated Solomon as his successor, though apparently he had not made this generally known. Nathan knew of the designation and now set in motion a plan to thwart the endeavor of Adonijah. He persuaded Bathsheba, the mother of Solomon, to go directly to David and tell him of Adonijah's attempt, and then he himself went before David. David was now persuaded that quick action was necessary, and he directed that Solomon be crowned immediately at the pool of Gihon. Nathan apparently superintended in this and, with the help of Zadok, the other high priest, and Benaiah, the leader of David's bodyguard, the Cherethites and the Pelethites, succeeded in doing so.

In two other activities Nathan resembled Gad. He helped in advising David regarding the organization of the Levites (II Chron. 29:25). And he wrote a book concerning the "acts of David" (I Chron. 29:29). Apparently his book was longer, because it included as well the "acts of Solomon" (II Chron. 9:29).

## 2. The person

### a. Spiritual status

Though Nathan apparently was not used for revelation purposes to the degree that Gad was, there is reason to believe that he was no less spiritually mature. He was used primarily for declaration purposes. Two of the times of giving declaration were unusually important. The first, as noted, concerned denying David the privilege of building God's temple and telling him that instead God would build for him a continuing dynasty. The importance of such an announcement is obvious. The second concerned bringing rebuke to David regarding his great sin with Bathsheba and Uriah. This also was a crucial occasion in David's life, and the announcement concerning it was of major importance. Both occasions called for a prophet who could be entrusted with messages of this kind.

### b. Command of respect

Like Gad, Nathan commanded respect when he spoke. Three times he had an important contact with David, with each involving a significant mes-

---

[8]Absalom earlier had killed the first son Amnon (II Sam. 13), and the second son Chileab had apparently died early, thus leaving Absalom as the oldest living son and therefore proper heir to the throne. When Absalom was killed as a result of his rebellion, Adonijah became the next in line.

sage. David listened each time, and in no way brought rebuke to the prophet nor showed an attitude manifesting anything but respect.

When Nathan told David he could not build the temple, certainly David was very disappointed. The king might have issued a sharp retort to the one who addressed him, but David did not do this. Again, when Nathan rebuked him for his sin with Bathsheba and Uriah, David might have responded sharply, but he did not. The third time, concerning Adonijah's attempt at assuming the throne, David would have been affected somewhat differently, but still he did not respond in any way to show a lack of respect for the prophet. In contrast, when persuaded to act quickly in having Solomon anointed, he designated Nathan to head in the activity. The fact that he did not say anything about Gad at the time may indicate that Nathan was accorded a higher place in David's estimation than Gad.[9]

c. COURAGE

Like Gad again, Nathan showed outstanding courage in bringing his messages to David. As has been noted, all three messages were important; this was especially true of the first two. Both were messages which could affect the king in a very adverse manner. Certainly it was not easy to tell the king that he could not build the temple or that he had sinned grievously in the sight of God. Nathan could have thought of many other tasks more pleasant to do. Since God had instructed him to bring these messages, however, he did so even though the king was the one being addressed.

It might be thought that Nathan showed less courage in respect to the third contact. He worked through Bathsheba this time rather than going to the king directly. But one need not take this as a lack of courage on his part. Courage was unmistakably demonstrated the first two times, and there was not the same danger this third time. Rather the reason for going through Bathsheba is to be found in Nathan's desire that the king act quickly. He apparently believed that if both Bathsheba and he himself told the king this message, the king would be impressed to act more quickly than if only one came and gave the word.

d. LOYALTY

Gad was probably loyal to David, too, but there are special features in connection with Nathan's contacts which show this fine trait in a particular way. Perhaps the most significant was his desire that David's wish for Solomon to succeed him be carried out. Adonijah wanted the kingship for

[9]It may also indicate that Gad, who certainly was older than Nathan, had died by this time.

himself, but Nathan knew that David had designated Solomon. The fact that Nathan had earlier brought two unhappy messages to David, one of denial and one of rebuke, did not mean that he was not a true friend of the king. Therefore, when he learned of the attempted coup by Adonijah, he did not hesitate to go quickly to tell the king about it.

In keeping with this thought is the fact that Nathan demonstrated an unusual intimacy in knowing the king's affairs. For instance, he knew that Solomon had been designated by David as his successor. It is quite clear that this was not generally known. Also, regarding the rebuke of David in respect to his sin with Bathsheba, the message concerned a very intimate subject in the king's life. No doubt many other people knew of the sin, for something like this could not have been kept quiet, but it would have taken someone well known to the king, intimate with him and knowledgeable of family affairs, to properly bring a message of rebuke. God saw fit to use Nathan. It seems safe to say that Nathan was considered by David his close friend and intimate confidant. This apparently was true of Nathan more than it was of Gad.

### e. JUDGMENT

The same may be said of Nathan as of Gad in respect to judgment. Both men were asked by David to advise and assist in organizing and giving instructions to the Levites regarding their work (II Chron. 29:25).

### f. LITERARY ABILITY

Once more like Gad, Nathan was a man of literary ability. One may say that possibly his ability was greater, for Gad is said to have written of the acts of David, but Nathan of both the acts of David (I Chron. 29:29) and the acts of Solomon (II Chron. 9:29). The reason for this, however, may be that Nathan simply outlived Gad. Fitting in with this chronological possibility is the fact that Gad had been with David already during his fugitive days, and Nathan is not heard from until well after David had established his rule.

## C. ZADOK AND HEMAN

Two other persons from the time of David and Solomon are called seers (one time only). The first was Zadok, who was one of the two high priests, and the other Heman, a musician in the temple.

## 1. Zadok

The passage where the term *seer* is used of Zadok concerns the time when David fled from Jerusalem before the rebellion of Absalom. As the king left the city, Zadok, accompanied by numerous Levites bearing the ark of the covenant, followed along. David noticed this, turned to Zadok, and urged him to return to the city and take the ark back with him. He then spoke the words, "Art not thou a seer? Return into the city in peace and your two sons with you, Ahimaaz thy son, and Jonathan the son of Abiathar" (II Sam. 15:27). David's thinking seems to have been to have Zadok remain in the city where he might learn the plans of Absalom and report to David in his flight so that David could better plan his own actions. Later, the counselor, Hushai, also came to the king (15:32–37), and David asked him to return and counter advice given by Ahithophel, and so persuade Absalom to act in a way which would be more to David's advantage.

The use of the word *seer* (*ro'eh*), however, may well be used here of Zadok only in the sense of one who could consult the Urim and Thummim. Zadok, being high priest, did have the use of this instrument of revelation. David may have been thinking of Zadok as one who had a way of contacting God by this device, if the need should arise for David to do so. If this is the correct interpretation of this reference, Zadok was not considered a prophet by David, but only one who could hear from God in some manner.


## 2. Heman

The situation clearly was different regarding Heman, however, who is called a "seer" (*hozeh*) in I Chronicles 25:5. Since he was not a high priest as was Zadok, the usage of the term here must be in the sense of one who heard from God in the capacity of a prophet.

The term is used in a context where the sons of Asaph, Jeduthun, and Heman are listed as singers for the ceremonial services. In this context, the words appear, "All these were the sons of Heman, the king's seer, in the words of God, to lift up the horn." The notation that Heman was the "king's seer" is not pertinent to the context. Its usage is simply to the end of appropriately identifying him. This means that he was known as a seer for the king.

In view of the meaning of "seer" as set forth especially in chapter 4, one may believe, therefore, that Heman was used of God to receive and convey revelations to David somewhat in parallel to the prophet Gad. Since Heman is not depicted by illustration in the capacity of doing this as Gad is, probably he was not used as much as Gad. Because he was a musician, it may be that revelations pertaining to ceremonial services involving music were given particularly through him.

## D. AHIJAH

A prophet who is given greater notice is Ahijah, called "the Shilonite," evidently being from the town of Shiloh (I Kings 11:29). Events that are described regarding him concern his contact with Jeroboam, the first king of the northern kingdom of Israel. There are clues, however, that he ministered during much of the reign of Solomon and may have had contacts also with him. These will be noted in due time. For some reason God did not see fit to record in Scripture any contact between Solomon and a prophet. Nathan, of course, led in the crowning of Solomon and probably lived on into the time of Solomon for most of his reign since he wrote a history of it. No other contact between the two is mentioned, however, nor between Solomon and Ahijah.

### 1. The work

Ahijah's first contact with Jeroboam came during the reign of Solomon, when he told the young man that he would take over the rule of ten of the tribes (I Kings 11:29–39). At this time, Jeroboam was serving as superintendent over a work project Solomon was carrying on in the city. He had achieved this fine position as a reward for demonstrated ability. Ahijah found him one day when Solomon was outside the city, and he took a new garment that he was wearing and tore it into twelve parts. Then he took ten of the parts and gave them to Jeroboam with the words, "Take thee ten pieces: for thus saith the LORD, the God of Israel, Behold, I will rend the kingdom out of the hand of Solomon and will give ten tribes to thee" (I Kings 11:31). He went on to tell the young man the reason for this portended division of the kingdom: the people had begun to worship the gods of the Zidonians, the Moabites, and the children of Ammon and so were not walking in the ways of God to please Him. He added that the full kingdom would not be taken from Solomon, because of the promise to David that he would have a continuing dynasty. He stated further that if Jeroboam would follow God truly, like David before him, God would give Jeroboam a continuing house as he had promised to David.

A matter of interest in this statement is that Ahijah spoke of giving Jeroboam ten of the tribes and later of keeping only one tribe for the line of David (11:32, 36). Earlier he had torn the garment into twelve pieces representing all twelve tribes, which leaves a question concerning the twelfth tribe, or the twelfth piece of garment representing that tribe. The answer of later history is that this twelfth tribe was Benjamin. It came to join the one tribe of Judah to make up two principal tribes for the southern kingdom. Ahijah was not led of God to speak of two tribes probably for two reasons: first, Judah was the more important of the two tribes; and, second, Benjamin did not immediately unite with Judah so that, at the beginning of the southern nation, only the one tribe of Judah constituted it.

The second main episode involving Ahijah concerned a message of rejection he gave to Jeroboam towards the close of Jeroboam's reign (I Kings 14:2–18). Many years had elapsed since the first occasion, probably more than twenty-two, since Jeroboam reigned this number of years (I Kings 14:20), and the first prophecy was given well before he began his rule.

The occasion involved a time when Jeroboam was worried over his son Abijah, who was ill. He instructed his wife to go to Ahijah and ask if the boy would get well. It is likely that Abijah was his oldest son and heir apparent to the throne, and therefore he was the more concerned. Jeroboam remembered that Ahijah had earlier promised the kingdom to him and so he expected a good word now. Whether there had been any contact between Ahijah and Jeroboam during the intervening years is not indicated. It is quite possible there had not been, since Jeroboam had persisted in sin and would not have welcomed visits by the godly Ahijah. It is in keeping with this suggestion that Jeroboam now told his wife to disguise herself so that Ahijah would not know who she was. God revealed to Ahijah, however, prior to her arrival at his door, that she would be coming. Therefore Ahijah knew her and greeted her as "thou wife of Jeroboam" (14:6). In conveying God's message to her, he did not speak at first regarding the son Abijah but referred to the evil ways that Jeroboam had followed since taking over as Israel's king, saying that God would bring evil on him as a result. Then he did indicate that when Jeroboam's wife returned to her home city the child would die. He further warned that God would raise up a king to destroy and replace Jeroboam's line. Jeroboam's wife then left and returned to the capital city of Tirzah, and as she approached the palace the child did die just as Ahijah had indicated.

Ahijah's work both times was the same, that is, he served as a prophet in bringing God's message. In contrast to the first time, however, the second message was a very unhappy one. In the first instance, he announced that Jeroboam would reign, but now he indicated that his reign would be taken away and his entire house destroyed by a succeeding king.

As noted there are clues that Ahijah ministered also during the time of Solomon. One is that he is said to have been old at the time of giving the second message regarding the destruction of Jeroboam's household (I Kings 14:4). This suggests that he had already lived a number of years by the time he gave his first message. Then it is possible that he is the one who gave two recorded messages to Solomon, without his name being mentioned. The first involved God's word to Solomon concerning the building of the temple (I Kings 6:11-13), and the second God's direct word that Solomon was rejected as king due to his sin (I Kings 11:11). Both messages were probably given by a prophet,[10] who could easily have been Ahijah. The second message especially would be in keeping with this thought, since Ahijah was the one who soon after told Jeroboam that he would be the person to receive the ten parts of the kingdom just denied to Solomon.

One other work of Ahijah was that he, like Gad and Nathan, wrote a history. This history concerned the acts of Solomon (II Chron. 9:29).

## 2. The person

### a. SPIRITUAL STATUS

The comparatively high spiritual status of Ahijah is evidenced by the importance of the messages God entrusted to him. The first message really involved two significant facts regarding the nation of Israel: first, Solomon's family was rejected as the continuing line to rule all the country, and, second, Jeroboam was God's selection to be the first king of the new northern division. It was an announcement that the kingdom would be divided and an indication as to the identity of the new ruler. One could hardly find a more important message than this. The second message concerned an announcement of somewhat less importance, but still it was vital to the northern nation. It was that Jeroboam's line would not continue to rule. Both messages were of a kind that God would not have entrusted to a prophet spiritually immature.

The fact of close intimacy between God and Ahijah is suggested also by the revelation God gave to the prophet in respect to the wife of Jeroboam. She had come in disguise so that Ahijah would not know who she was. God, however, did not permit this type of deception to succeed and told Ahijah beforehand of her coming. That God found Ahijah an appropriate recipient of this kind of immediate revelation is further indication of his spiritual maturity.

---

[10]Evidenced especially by two lines of thought. First, though on two other occasions God appeared to Solomon by a dream (I Kings 3:5; 9:2; II Chron. 7:12), this is so designated either directly or indirectly. But there is no such designation here. Second, God normally spoke to kings through prophets. God used Gad and Nathan to bring His messages to David, and on occasions when this did not happen it is stated specifically that David enquired of God (II Sam. 2:1; 5:19; 21:1). At these times he probably went to the high priest and enquired through the Urim and Thummim.

## b. Courage

Both messages by Ahijah show that he was a man of courage. When he gave the first message, he must have recognized that Solomon would be very displeased. This could easily lead to a dangerous situation for himself as Solomon might seek to do him harm. As matters developed, danger existed only for Jeroboam, who had to flee to Egypt. Ahijah, however, could not have known but what Solomon might take action toward him, and therefore one must see him as demonstrating courage in giving the message.

The same must be said regarding the later message. Ahijah's first message to Jeroboam had been pleasing to the young man, for it told him that he would reign. But this time it would have been very displeasing. Therefore the same danger could now develop for Ahijah from Jeroboam that could have developed from Solomon the first time. In fact, the danger really was greater because this prediction was directly to Jeroboam himself (through his wife who would quickly report), and there was no third party on whom the king could vent his anger.

## c. Command of respect

As true of both Gad and Nathan, Ahijah commanded respect when he spoke. He did the first time in speaking to Jeroboam directly. This is not evidenced so much in that Jeroboam received his message but that Solomon was impressed by it. Solomon did not challenge Ahijah, nor did he disbelieve what Ahijah said. Rather he soon sought to take the life of Jeroboam, indicating he did believe the prophet. In the second message, the wife readily accepted Ahijah's unpleasant message and later so did Jeroboam. Neither one challenged the prophet nor indicated any disbelief of what he had said. Simply because Ahijah had given the words, they accepted them as authoritative.

## d. Literary ability

Ahijah was like Gad and Nathan also in having literary ability. It is said of him that he wrote "the acts of Solomon" (II Chron. 9:29). He is listed along with Nathan the prophet and Iddo the seer as having written such a history.

# E. "MAN OF GOD"

The next prophet to consider is not given a name in Scripture but only the designation, "man of God." He appears in one story only (I Kings 13:1–

24), a story closely intertwined with the last prophet we will consider in this chapter, known as an "old prophet in Bethel" (13:11).

## 1. The work

This "man of God" was sent north from Judah to the false altar that Jeroboam had erected at Bethel. Jeroboam the king was there himself when the prophet arrived. The prophet did not hesitate because of the monarch's presence but cried out against the altar, "Oh altar, altar, thus saith the LORD: Behold, a child shall be born unto the house of David, Josiah by name; and upon thee shall he offer the priests of the high places that burn incense upon thee, and men's bones shall be burnt upon thee" (13:2). Jeroboam, standing by, was infuriated at these words, stretched forth his hand toward the prophet, and directed those near at hand to "lay hold on him." At that, Jeroboam's hand was "dried up, so that he could not pull it in again to him" (13:4), and the altar was broken so that the ashes poured out, in keeping with further words of the man of God.

With both supernatural events having transpired, Jeroboam became completely changed in attitude and asked the prophet's help in respect to his hand. He cried out, "Entreat now the face of the LORD thy God, and pray for me, that my hand may be restored me again" (13:6). The man of God did so, and God did restore Jeroboam's hand. The king then wanted the man to go to his home where they might eat together. The man of God replied, "If thou wilt give me half thine house, I will not go in with thee, neither will I eat bread nor drink water in this place" (13:8). He then added that God had forbidden him to eat bread or drink water in Bethel but commanded him to return immediately to Judah whence he had come. Having said this he started his return homeward.

Until this point the prophet had acted very well, but now there came a change. An "old prophet in Bethel" had learned of his visit and followed after him. He caught up with the younger man as he was resting under an oak. The old prophet told him that he too was a prophet and that he had been instructed by God to bring the younger man back to his house where he might eat bread and drink water. He was not telling the truth, but the younger man did not know this. In disobedience to the word of God the younger man returned to Bethel. Then as the two sat eating together the old prophet rebuked the young man for returning and told him that, when he left now and started home, he would be killed (13:22). The young man left and as he was on his way a lion met him and killed him, and his body was left by the roadside where later the old prophet found it and gave it an appropriate burial.

## 2. The person

### a. SPIRITUAL STATUS

This prophet displays some marks of spiritual maturity but also some of immaturity. He cannot be placed on the same level with Gad, Nathan, or Ahijah. In his favor is the fact that he was chosen of God to go north from Judah to speak against the altar in Bethel. There must have been other prophets in Judah that God might have selected, and therefore, that he was the one speaks well for him.

Further, evidence of his spiritual maturity is the twofold fact that God gave a prediction and worked a miracle through him. The prediction was a remarkable one, that Josiah (who lived approximately three hundred years later) would one day offer the bones of the priests of the altar upon that altar.[11] He even gave Josiah's name, making this one of the more remarkable predictions of Scripture. He also stated that the altar would be broken and its ashes poured out, and this happened even while he was there. The miracle concerned the restoration of Jeroboam's hand. The king had stretched his hand out in anger and God had caused it to wither. When the prophet prayed, the hand was restored. It was a definite and remarkable miracle performed through the young man.

It should also be observed in the young man's favor that at first he obeyed God in respect to returning home without eating or drinking in the sinful town of Bethel. There would have been attraction, too, in being invited to dine with a king. The man must be credited for having refused.

The one factor to the man's discredit was his disobedience of God after he started home. When the old prophet in Bethel caught up with him and told him the lie, the young man was too easily convinced and went directly against God's clear instruction. This indicates that he did not realize God never contradicts Himself. The old prophet's deception was wrong, but it gave no excuse for the younger man to do as he did. The result of the disobedience was that he suffered severe punishment in being killed by a lion.

### b. COURAGE

Still, one must accord this man real courage in going to Israel and speaking in the way he did against Jeroboam's altar. It would have taken courage for him just to leave home in the first place and go to a foreign

---

[11]The date here was in the late tenth century and Josiah lived in the late seventh century.

country to speak against one of its sacred centers. One may believe that, when he had left, he hoped for the best possible conditions when he arrived. Thus, in that he found Jeroboam himself present, one can imagine that he had thoughts of returning home without carrying out his mission. This would have been only natural. He did not return, however, but spoke his message no matter how displeasing it would be to Jeroboam. This took real courage.

### F. "OLD PROPHET IN BETHEL"

The last prophet to be considered here is the old prophet already noted. What sort of a man was this person who would so deceive a younger man? Was he a false prophet who had earlier been a true prophet? Or had he been a false prophet all along? These questions will be answered as we proceed.

### 1. The work

This old prophet also appears only once in Scripture. He is not known by name nor is he mentioned elsewhere. When he learned that the younger man had spoken against the altar in Bethel, he asked his sons to discover which way the young man had started on his way back to Judah. Then he had his sons saddle his own animal that he might make pursuit. He caught the young man and persuaded him to return to Bethel and his own home. The story gives no reason for his wanting to do this but says only that he did and that he had to state a falsehood to the young man to persuade him to return to Bethel.

When the two had returned to the old prophet's home, however, a true word from God came to him in respect to the young man, and he conveyed it to him. "Thus saith the LORD, Forasmuch as thou hast disobeyed the mouth of the LORD, and hast not kept the commandment which the LORD thy God commanded thee, but camest back, and hast eaten bread and drunk water in the place of which the LORD did say to thee, Eat no bread and drink no water; thy carcass shall not come unto the sepulchre of thy fathers" (13:21, 22). Later on, learning from travelers that they had seen the carcass of the young man by the side of the road and a lion standing by it, the old prophet set out again with his animal, this time to find the body. He picked it up, put it on his donkey, brought it back to Bethel, and buried it in his own grave. Then he turned to his sons and requested that he be buried in the same sepulchre when he died.

2. The person

a. A TRUE PROPHET

It is well first to establish that this man was a true prophet. Some have thought of him as a false prophet, inasmuch as he acted as he did. There are definite clues, however, that he was a true prophet.

There is first the fact that in the middle of the story God did truly reveal through him. After he had brought the young man to his house, God told him to give a word of warning to the younger man. This word concerned a prediction of the young man's death, and later this prediction came to pass. Such a word was certainly from God and God did not give such words through false prophets. Further, the prophet showed respect for the young man. On learning that he had been killed, he went to where he was, picked up his body, returned it to the city, and buried it in his own grave. He even told his sons that he wished to be buried in the same grave. Still further, he gave personal confirmation to the declaration the young man had made regarding the eventual destruction of the Bethel altar. This shows that he approved of the denouncement and believed that the destruction would come to pass.

b. SPIRITUAL STATUS

At the same time it is clear that the man definitely was spiritually deficient. He deliberately deceived a younger man. Though the reason he did so is not given, one may conjecture its nature. The old prophet, living right in Bethel where Jeroboam had erected the false altar, quite clearly had not given any denouncement of that altar himself. He probably had long felt some shame at not having done so. Thus, learning of the young man's courage in coming even from Judah to do this, he sought some measure of spiritual strength for himself by a contact with the younger man. In order to procure it, he apparently believed the use of a lie was justified and stooped to this level to accomplish the end he desired.

The extent to which this man may have been used of God for good in earlier days is not revealed. One has to believe that it was never of great amount in view of his action here with the young prophet. Still one must allow for the possibility of significant change in the extent of his ministry at the time of his silence when Jeroboam first instituted the false worship.

c. A MAN GIVEN TO DECEPTION

The fact that the old prophet sought to bring the young man back to him by deception suggests that he had been given to such behavior in earlier days.

One does not often lower himself to such an action late in life when he has not employed it earlier. Deception is a serious sin in God's eyes, and it may have been one reason why this old prophet had not been used more in former times.

It has been suggested by some that God did not see this old man's sin as very serious, since it was the younger man who was punished. It is true that it was the younger man who was killed by the lion, but this is not to say that the older man did not experience punishment. He did experience it, in the form of shame and remorse over his action regarding the young man. This is implied in his going after the young man's body, bringing it back, putting it in his own grave, and requesting that he be buried there himself. Very likely the rest of his days were spent in sorrow over his action regarding the fine young prophet whom he thus had spoiled. It should also be noted that a reason for God's bringing the outright punishment on the younger man was that God was dealing particularly with him and not with the old man. It was the young man whom God had sent north to Bethel and who had disobeyed God's clear order. He was the one, then, to be disciplined in this pronounced manner.

# 12

# The Reigns of Rehoboam, Abijam, Asa, Jehoshaphat, and Baasha

In this chapter we consider prophets who served during the reigns of five kings, the first four consecutively in Judah and the fifth in Israel. Baasha, the fifth, while not the immediate successor of Jeroboam in Israel, was the one who destroyed Jeroboam's house and then ruled himself twenty-four years (I Kings 15:33).

Much of the period was occupied with warfare between the two divisions of the kingdom. The period began in an atmosphere of conflict, when the ten tribes seceded from the union ruled over at the time by King Rehoboam. Early in Rehoboam's reign the northern ten tribes asked him to come north from Jerusalem to Shechem where they requested relief from the severe taxation Solomon had placed upon them. Rehoboam asked three days in which to consider the matter and, after consulting with both older and younger advisors, he followed the counsel of the latter and refused the request. He even said that he would tax the people harder than his father had. The result was that the northern tribes did secede and established Jeroboam as their first king. Rehoboam's initial response was to raise an army to force them back into his kingdom, but through a prophet God told him not to do this since this division of the kingdom was His doing.

Rehoboam had taken over as king at the age of forty-one and he ruled for seventeen years (931–913 B.C.). He followed in the evil ways his father had pursued in the latter part of his reign. He built high places, set up images and Asherah poles, and even permitted male prostitutes to live in the land (I Kings

14:23, 24). He had military encounters with two main enemies, Jeroboam of Israel and Shishak (Sheshonq I) of Egypt. With the first he was generally successful, but with the second he suffered tragic loss, said to have been God's punishment for his religious defection.

Rehoboam had almost continual conflict with Jeroboam (I Kings 14:30). There is no indication that this was violent warfare, but it seems to have centered in repeated border disputes, especially involving the area of Benjamin. Rehoboam felt that Judah needed Benjamin as a buffer zone, and Jeroboam wanted the area also. In that Benjamin came to be associated with Judah in due time, it follows that Rehoboam won in these disputes more often than Jeroboam. The victories would have resulted from both military clashes (defeating Jeroboam's border guards) and psychological persuasion (bringing Benjaminites to a willingness to side with the southern nation).

The Egyptian king, Shishak, founded Egypt's twenty-second dynasty and was the person who had given asylum earlier to Jeroboam, when he had fled from Solomon. Now in Rehoboam's fifth year Shishak made a strong attempt to reassert Egyptian supremacy in Palestine. He left a list of 150 cities which he overran in this campaign.[1] Many are located in southern Judah and still further south in Edom. No cities of central Judah are mentioned, a strange omission in that the biblical record speaks of Shishak's taking vast treasures from Jerusalem itself (I Kings 14:26; II Chron. 12:9). It may be that Rehoboam simply gave this treasure as tribute to Shishak to keep him from destroying Judah proper. It should be added that the northern kingdom felt Shishak's power also. Megiddo gives testimony of his destruction in the form of a victory monument bearing Shishak's name. The Egyptian army even crossed the Jordan River into Gilead, and numerous cities from that region are listed by the Egyptian. All this means that Shishak covered a wide area in his campaign but there is no indication that he held it long. Rehoboam, however, did suffer greatly.

The son and successor of Rehoboam was Abijam,[2] who ruled three years (913–911 B.C.). He continued in the sin of his father. He also continued his father's struggle with Jeroboam and evidently with greater success. In one major battle (II Chron. 13:3–19) in the area of Ephraim near Mount Zemaraim (likely east of Bethel), Abijam, though having a smaller force, gained control even over Bethel, the important southern religious center of Israel. In addition he took less important Jeshanah and Ephron nearby. This

---

[1]On the exterior south wall of the Temple of Amon at Karnak, Shishak is pictured smiting the Asiatics and the god Amon presents to him ten lines of captives, who symbolize the cities listed. See *The Ancient Near East in Pictures*, ed. James B. Pritchard, fig. 349, for a picture. For a translation, discussion, and bibliography of publications, see J. Simons, *Handbook for the Study of Egyptian Topographical Lists Relating to Western Asia*, pp. 90–101, 178–186.

[2]Called Abijah in II Chron. 13:1f. Abijam means "father of the sea" and Abijah, "father is Yahweh." Apparently he was called by both names.

advance did not last long, however, for Asa,[3] his son and successor, was soon hard pressed by Baasha, who moved for a time as far south as Ramah, just four miles from Jerusalem, with an occupying force.

Asa ruled forty-one years (911–870 B.C.) and was the first of the religiously good kings of the southern kingdom.[4] Asa put away male prostitutes and idols out of the land, and he removed his (grand)mother from being queen mother because she had made an idol to the goddess Asherah. At one time he called for a great assembly of people, inviting even Israelites from the northern tribes of Ephraim, Manasseh, and Simeon, to renew their covenantal promises with God (II Chron. 15:9–15). But one thing he did not do was remove the old Canaanite high places.

Asa had important contacts with foreign powers on two occasions. The first was a conflict with an Egyptian army led by Zerah of Ethiopia (II Chron. 14:9–15). The battle took place near Sharuhen in southwestern Palestine and ended with a marked victory for Asa. The reason for the victory was that Asa trusted in God for assistance, and God enabled him to defeat the larger foreign force. The second contact was with Baasha, king of Israel, and its nature was more economic than military (II Chron. 16:1–10). Baasha had penetrated the northern border of Judah for the purpose of fortifying Ramah, four miles north of Jerusalem, that he might establish control over the north-south caravan route into Jerusalem. In retaliation Asa, rather than seeking guidance from God, relied on his own cleverness and sent for help to Ben-hadad I of Damascus. Ben-hadad, just rising to a position of power, was happy to comply and test his strength against Israel. He attacked certain northern cities of Baasha, and the Israelite king had to desist at Ramah and protect his own interests. Thinking himself wise in this maneuver, Asa was quite taken back when Hanani, a prophet, did not praise him but brought stern rebuke for his procedure. The prophet told him that what he had really accomplished was to bring Judah under obligation to a foreign power and to set the stage for further conflict, rather than to achieve true benefit as Asa had thought. It is clear that Asa did not act nearly as commendably on this second occasion as on the first.

Baasha, as just mentioned, was king of Israel, contemporary with Asa.

[3]Because Abijam and Asa are said to have had mothers and grandmothers of the same name (I Kings 15:2, 10; II Chron. 15:16), some scholars believe they were brothers and not father and son, as indicated in I Kings 15:8 and II Chronicles 14:1. Though Abijam ruled only three years, he still was old enough to have sons himself (indeed, according to II Chronicles 13:21 he had twenty-two sons and sixteen daughters by fourteen wives). It is likely that his mother Maachah and grandmother Abishalom were really grandmother and great-grandmother to Asa. Because of Abijam's short reign, Maachah had carried over as queen mother and she it was who was deposed by Asa for worshiping a false idol (I Kings 15:13; II Chron. 15:16). For discussion, see William F. Albright, *Archaeology and the Religion of Israel*, p. 158.

[4]Eight of Judah's total nineteen kings are said to have been good in God's sight, a marked contrast to the kings of Israel where none out of nineteen are described as good.

He ruled for twenty-four years (909–886 B.C.). Little is recorded from his reign except that he continued in conflict with Judah to the south. The only particular episode described is the one just mentioned involving Asa. Religiously, Baasha continued in the way of Jeroboam and Nadab. Jeroboam had been warned by Ahijah that his family would be destroyed, and though this did not happen in Jeroboam's own reign it did in that of his son Nadab. Baasha killed Nadab, after Nadab had reigned only two years (910–909 B.C.). Because of Baasha's religious deficiency, he was warned through Jehu, the prophet, that his house would suffer a fate similar to that of the house of Jeroboam (I Kings 16:1–7).

In the southern kingdom of Judah, the son and successor of Asa was Jehoshaphat, who ruled twenty-five years (873–848 B.C.). Religiously, Jehoshaphat was the second good king of Judah. He followed his father in ridding the land of Baal's cultic features, even removing the high places to some degree.[5] Further, he gave special orders to Levites and others to teach the "book of the Law" throughout all Judah. A prime task of the priests and Levites from the beginning had been such teaching, but apparently they had become lax in this assignment. Jehoshaphat sought to correct this.

An illustration of Jehoshaphat's commendable faith in God is seen in connection with an attack made against him by an alliance of Moab, Ammon, and Edom (II Chron. 20:1–30). Learning of the invasion, Jehoshaphat did not despair but called for a time of fasting and prayer in Jerusalem. God gave a remarkable victory to Jehoshaphat, and the occasion resulted in his own army merely having to pick up the booty of the enemy, and there was so much that it took three days to do so. Jehoshaphat actually had a strong army consisting of five divisions, three from Judah and two from Benjamin. At one time, in fact, because of this strength, the Philistines and Arabians sought to maintain his good will by bringing valuable presents. Jehoshaphat also took steps to improve juridical procedures in the land. Apparently the people had become lax in respect to matters spelled out in the Mosaic Law, and Jehoshaphat called for correction to be made.

It is quite clear that Jehoshaphat allied himself with Ahab and Ahaziah of Israel (I Kings 22:44, 48, 49; II Kings 3:4–27; II Chron. 18:1—19:3; 20:35–37). This alliance probably had some economic and military value for both countries, but resulted in a great loss for Judah religiously. This was true for one major reason—it involved the tragic marriage of Jehoshaphat's son, Jehoram, to Ahab's daughter, Athaliah, who followed in the ways of her mother, Jezebel. Jehoshaphat had abundant reason to regret this marriage in years to come.

On three different occasions Jehoshaphat himself suffered severely as a

---

[5] Both I Kings 22:43 and II Chron. 20:33 state that the high places were not removed, while II Chron. 17:6 says they were. The situation likely was that the better-known high places were, while those where many of the common people worshiped (I Kings 22:43) were not.

result of the alliance. At one time he helped Ahab in his battle with Ben-hadad at Ramoth-gilead and was nearly killed for his trouble (I Kings 22:29–33; II Chron. 18:29–34). Later he joined Ahab's eldest son, Ahaziah, in shipbuilding at Ezion-geber on the Gulf of Aqaba, and every ship was destroyed before its maiden voyage (I Kings 22:48, 49; II Chron. 20:35–37). He also allied himself with Ahab's second son, Jehoram, in a military offensive against Moab, to coerce tribute-paying to Israel, and he nearly perished for lack of water (II Kings 3:4–27). Prophets of God were involved in each instance as will be noted.

## A. IDDO

The prophet Iddo is mentioned three times in the Old Testament (II Chron. 9:29; 12:15; 13:22), and none of these depict him as involved in any event. Rather all three references speak of him as writing books. This means that little is known of the man, but information given regarding him in respect to the writing, as well as the things of which he wrote, is suggestive of certain matters.

### 1. The work

Two general matters are revealed regarding Iddo's work. The first is that he was indeed a writer. According to II Chronicles 9:29,[6] he recorded visions "against Jeroboam, the son of Nebat," which involved information regarding "the acts of Solomon." In 12:15 it is stated that he wrote a book concerning genealogies that included historical notices regarding "the acts of Rehoboam." And in 13:22 it is indicated that he wrote a story (*midrash*, meaning "commentary") concerning the acts, ways, and sayings of Abijam (Abijah).

This means for one thing that he lived during the reigns of Jeroboam who ruled over Israel in the north, and his contemporaries, Rehoboam and Abijam, who ruled over Judah in the south. It means further that he had an interest in history, apparently making note of the actions of these three kings and recording this history in the books indicated.

A second matter to notice is the designation given to Iddo in two of these three passages. In 9:29 and 12:15 he is called "the seer" (*hozeh*) and only in 13:22 "the prophet." Since the designation *seer* is used sparingly in the Old Testament, its employment twice with Iddo must be taken as significant. Like Gad before him, apparently he was used of God especially in the

---

[6]His name here is spelled *Ye'do* whereas it is spelled *iddo* in 12:15 and 13:22. There is general consensus among expositors, however, that the same person is in view.

capacity of receiving revelations to convey to others. In keeping with this thought is the fact that 9:29 speaks of his writing "visions" against Jeroboam. The implication is that God gave Iddo revelatory visions regarding Jeroboam and the judgment God was going to bring upon him for his sin. No indication is given that he relayed the content of these visions to Jeroboam but it is probable that he did so.[7]

Since the first of Iddo's writings concerned information from the time of Solomon, this man must have served for twenty years or more. He wrote of both Rehoboam and Abijam, whose combined rule totaled twenty years, and he must have served a few years of the earlier time of Solomon. This means he served for a comparatively long period.

## 2. The person

### a. SPIRITUAL STATUS

Two matters suggest that Iddo was a man of spiritual maturity. One is the long service God gave him. The fact that he wrote regarding so many kings shows that God continued to use him during these years. In other words, there was no time when his ministry was brought to an end due to sin in his life. The other factor is that he was used of God to receive revelations. As was noted regarding Gad, those who were so used had to be proper recipients to qualify.

### b. KNOWLEDGE

That Iddo wrote three different accounts regarding kings of both Israel and Judah shows that he was a man of knowledge. One cannot write without knowing what he is writing about, and, since Iddo's material concerned both kingdoms, he must have been informed regarding both. This means that he was active in his day, contacting people who would have information regarding both kingdoms and recording what he learned.

### c. LITERARY ABILITY

Iddo seems to have written more than any of the prophets noted thus far. Therefore, if these men are to be credited with literary ability, the same

[7] The tradition that Iddo was the young disobedient prophet who brought the message against Jeroboam noted in 1 Kings 13 is probably incorrect. That young man died on the way home from Bethel. Likely he had brought this message rather early in Jeroboam's reign, shortly after the false altar had been instituted. Iddo, however, must have lived for many years longer than this in order to record the history of both Rehoboam and Abijam in Judah to the south.

must be said of Iddo. The notice in II Chronicles 13:22 is particularly significant. It says that he wrote "a story" concerning the acts, ways, and sayings of Abijam. The word for "story" is *midrash*, which means "commentary." It is noteworthy, further, that Iddo wrote this commentary regarding the acts, ways, and sayings of Abijam. This was not, then, merely a history concerning Abijam. It was an evaluation of what he both did and said so as to form a commentary on his life. This means that Iddo had an interest in such evaluations and a willingness and desire to record the judgments he made.

## B. SHEMAIAH

Shemaiah was a contemporary of Iddo, but perhaps he did not minister as long for accounts regarding him relate only to Rehoboam of Judah. From this time, however, two brief stories are recorded.

### 1. The work

The first story concerns the time early in Rehoboam's reign when the ten tribes seceded from the kingdom. Following the announcement of this secession, Rehoboam returned from Shechem to Jerusalem and set about gathering an army to go against the northern tribes to thwart the secession endeavor. He had succeeded in gathering 180,000 men from both Judah and Benjamin when he was stopped by Shemaiah. God had instructed Shemaiah that Rehoboam should desist in his efforts, since the secession had the approval of God. It was to Rehoboam's credit that he listened to the words of Shemaiah, and, in spite of his disappointment and the enormous effort he had put forth, he did desist and left the northern kingdom to establish itself as it desired.

The second story transpired in the fifth year of Rehoboam. This was the time when Shishak, king of Egypt, came against the land in an attempt to recover it for Egypt. When Rehoboam learned that Shishak was coming, he assembled his leaders in Jerusalem to plan how to counter the enemy. When he did so, Shemaiah came and spoke an unpleasant message from God, "Thus saith the LORD, ye have forsaken me, and therefore have I also left you in the hand of Shishak" (II Chron. 12:5). Again Rehoboam acted properly as both he and the leaders humbled themselves, saying, "The LORD is righteous" (12:6). Because of this, God gave a further word to Shemaiah: "They have humbled themselves; therefore I will not destroy them, but I will grant them some deliverance; and my wrath shall not be poured out upon Jerusalem by the hand of Shishak" (12:7).

The meaning of this message seems to be that, as a result of the humbling of Rehoboam and his leaders, God would not bring punishment as severe as He would have otherwise. It could not mean that Judah was to escape from Shishak entirely for, as noted earlier, Shishak did come and devastate many cities of the country. It was noted, however, that cities in the area of Jerusalem are not listed by Shishak as having been overrun, and it may be that the reprieve God gave involved His deliverance of these central cities from the hand of the enemy. It is true that II Chronicles 12:9 indicates that Shishak did come against Jerusalem and take "away the treasures of the house of the LORD, and the treasures of the king's house," including "the shields of gold which Solomon had made," but, as indicated, it is possible that Rehoboam gave these monetary considerations to the Egyptian as a way of keeping him from destroying Jerusalem and the cities of central Judah. God may be thought of as inclining Shishak to accept the exchange. It is certainly significant that Shishak did not list cities of central Judah as taken when he did list cities of southern Judah, Edom, and Israel, and even some from Transjordan.

One further aspect of Shemaiah's work is that he also wrote. Second Chronicles 12:15 speaks of the "book of Shemaiah the prophet" as another of the sources of Chronicles.

Shemaiah's work, then, seems to have been principally involved in declaring God's word, rather than receiving it. Though it is true that both messages to Rehoboam were first received from God, the stress of both stories is on declaration rather than reception, and Shemaiah is called in both instances a prophet and not a seer. Apparently the seer of the period was Iddo while Shemaiah was the prophet, a situation somewhat comparable to that of Gad and Nathan in the earlier time of David.

## 2. The person

### a. SPIRITUAL STATUS

There seems adequate evidence from the character of the messages God gave to Shemaiah to believe that he was a spiritually mature person. Both messages were of great importance for Rehoboam and the history of Judah. The first involved the stopping of a civil war between Judah and the newly-organized kingdom of Israel, and certainly this was of great importance. The second involved a partial reprieve for Judah and the sparing of many of Judah's cities from the onslaught of the Egyptian, Shishak. From the numerous prophets that no doubt lived at the time, God selected Shemaiah to bring these messages, and one may conclude that God considered him a prophet of high standing in His sight to be thus chosen.

## b. COMMAND OF RESPECT

The fact that Rehoboam and his leaders gave remarkable respect to Shemaiah when he spoke in both instances is noteworthy. In the first instance, a great effort had already been put forth to assemble as many as 180,000 men. No doubt, elaborate plans had been made and provisions gathered for making the attack on the northern nation. One is not easily dissuaded when he has put forth this much effort. Yet when Shemaiah came and told Rehoboam to desist, he did so and apparently without any real hesitation. One is almost surprised at the way in which he was willing to accede to the words Shemaiah gave.

Then the same was true regarding the oncoming campaign of Shishak. Rehoboam was worried concerning it and had assembled his leaders to plan how to make countermeasures. At this point Shemaiah arrived and gave his words of rebuke, when certainly Rehoboam was in no mood to receive such a message. He might have retorted harshly, but he did not. Rather, he and his leaders humbled themselves before God and gave full respect to the words of Shemaiah; then God gave His message of reprieve through the prophet. Shemaiah clearly was a man who spoke his messages with authority so that even the king gave responses of this kind.

## c. COURAGE

The two messages Shemaiah brought would have taken courage to speak. That he voiced them with commanding authority in no way discounts the fact that it required courage to do so. Shemaiah would have realized that both would be unpleasant for the king to hear, and he might have feared to bring them. He still did, though, and he must be commended.

## d. LITERARY ABILITY

Shemaiah also wrote a book and although he did not do as much writing as his contemporary Iddo, he had some interest in this area and certainly some literary ability.

## C. AZARIAH

In coming to consider the prophet Azariah, we move into the reign of Asa, the third king of Judah. As noted, Asa was the first of the religiously good kings of the southern kingdom. It is logical to believe that life for the true prophets was more pleasant under kings of this kind.

Azariah is mentioned in only one passage, II Chronicles 15:1-8. A problem exists in verse 8. The first seven verses record a message given by Azariah to King Asa, and then verse 8 says, "And when Asa heard these words, and the prophecy of Oded the prophet, he took courage. . . ." These words seem to indicate that Oded had given this prophecy rather than Azariah, an apparent conflict with verse 1 where Oded is called the father of Azariah. It is probable that some error has crept into the text of verse 8 through transcription. Two possible explanations exist. First, the words "of Oded the prophet" may be an inserted gloss so that the original reading was, "And when Asa heard these words and the prophecy, he took courage. . . ." The other is that a phrase such as "Azariah the son of" was omitted. Thus: "And when Asa heard these words, and the prophecy of *Azariah, the son of* Oded, the prophet, he took courage. . . ." These words are inserted in the Syriac and Vulgate versions, as well as the Septuagint, as represented in the Alexandrinus manuscript. Whatever the correct explanation, there seems little question but what the words of the first seven verses were spoken by Azariah and not by his father, Oded.[8]

## 1. The work

The one recorded instance when Azariah prophesied came following the victory of Asa over Zerah, an Ethiopian conqueror from Egypt. Approximately thirty years had elapsed since Shishak's attack, assuming that Zerah's campaign came in Asa's fifteenth year, which is likely.[9] Zerah attacked presumably in an attempt to do what Shishak had failed to do the earlier time. Zerah, like Shishak, launched his campaign in the general region of Sharuhen, involving specifically the cities Mareshah and Gerar. Asa looked to God for assistance and received it, God enabling him to defeat the larger force and take much spoil for Israel.

On returning home, Asa was met by Azariah with the message here concerned. It was a message of encouragement, comfort, and warning. Asa was commended for trusting in God, with the indication that Israel had long been without such trust. The nation had not looked to the true God, the priests had not done their proper work of teaching, and the people had not followed the Law as they should. The result had been that trouble had ensued, and God's blessing had been withheld. In view of this, the prophet

---

[8]The tradition that this Oded was identical with the Iddo mentioned above carries some possibility in that the names are similar. Chronologically, the two would at least have lived at the same time.

[9]See E. R. Thiele, *The Mysterious Numbers of the Hebrew Kings*, pp. 57-62.

urged Asa, "Be ye strong, therefore, and let not your hands be weak; for your work shall be rewarded."

## 2. The person

### a. SPIRITUAL STATUS

There is reason to believe that Azariah was also a man of spiritual maturity. The evidence, however, is of a different kind than what we have seen for the prophets studied thus far.

Azariah was probably not a full-time prophet. It is stated in 15:1 that "the Spirit of God came upon Azariah," which, according to the discussion given in chapter 6, is an indication that he was only a part-time prophet. Full-time prophets were empowered continuously by the Holy Spirit, and only those who were part-time had the Spirit of God come upon them for a particular assignment. If this line of thinking is correct, one must think of Azariah as a lay person of the day, who was sufficiently spiritually-minded that God saw fit to call him and use him in this one instance to bring a word of encouragement to Asa. He must, then, have been a man of close walk with God, ready to be used and willing to accept if and when called. Also, the fact that the Spirit of God came upon him to enable him for the occasion shows that he was a proper recipient to receive such special empowerment for a task.

Besides this, the message he brought to Asa was centered in the idea of obeying God. He indicated that, because the nation in prior days (thinking no doubt of the last days of Solomon and the days of Rehoboam and Abijam) had not followed God closely, difficulty and problems had arisen. So it was altogether to Asa's benefit to continue to trust God as he had in the case of Zerah.

### b. COMMAND OF RESPECT

Though Azariah was apparently not a full-time prophet, he was a man who evidently spoke with authority. At the time here in view, Asa not only listened to what Azariah had to say, but when the prophet had finished, he put into action the counsel given. He "put away the abominable idols out of all the land of Judah and Benjamin, and out of the cities which he had taken from Mount Ephraim, and renewed the altar of the LORD that was before the porch of the LORD" (15:8). He further gathered a large assembly of people, both from his own country and several of the northern tribes, for a time of sacrifice, thus entering "into a covenant to seek the LORD God of their fathers with all their heart and with all their soul" (15:12).

## D. HANANI

The prophet Hanani also served during the extended reign of Asa. Only one story is told from his ministry, though he is mentioned as the father of Jehu in four other places (I Kings 16:1, 7; II Chron. 19:2; 20:34).

### 1. The work

The one recorded occasion concerned a time when Hanani rebuked King Asa. Asa had suffered from an economic ploy against him by Baasha, king of Israel. Baasha had come south to occupy Ramah, just north of Jerusalem, and thus control north-south caravan travel into the capital city. In retaliation Asa had sent north to Ben-hadad in Damascus, asking that he attack the northern part of Israel so that Baasha would have to defend his own cities. The plan seemed to work, for Baasha did leave off from his endeavor at Ramah, and then Asa was able to take the building material Baasha had assembled at Ramah and use it to enlarge two of his own cities, Geba and Mizpeh. This made Asa proud of what he believed was a brilliant piece of strategy, and therefore he expected plaudits from others who might come to him. Hanani did come but not to bring plaudits; rather he brought a stinging rebuke. The rebuke was that Asa had relied on his own judgment and gone to a foreign king for assistance rather than relying on God. In this he had acted foolishly, for he had brought himself under obligation to the foreign king; and, as a result, he would have continued wars. Hanani also reminded Asa of the former time when Asa had trusted in God and had defeated Zerah the Ethiopian. He then added the important words, "For the eyes of the LORD run to and fro throughout the whole earth, to show himself strong in the behalf of them whose heart is perfect toward him" (II Chron. 16:9). The thought is that God would have helped Asa this time against his enemy Baasha, as God had against Zerah the Ethiopian, if Asa had simply trusted God now as he had then.

People do not like to receive rebuke when they expect plaudits, and Asa did not in this case. As a result, he ordered that Hanani be placed in prison, and this was done. One finds it hard to believe that Asa, who otherwise was a good king, would have so acted when his conduct had been very exemplary just a year or so before in connection with the Egyptian encounter.

## 2. The person

### a. SPIRITUAL STATUS

Evidence that Hanani was a spiritual person is of the same kind as the evidence concerning Iddo and Gad. He is identified as a seer three different times (II Chron. 16:7, 10; 19:2) and never as a prophet. It is quite clear, therefore, that his primary work consisted in receiving revelations from God to relay to people. As was noted earlier, such a person had to be spiritually mature in the sight of God.

It is noteworthy besides that the one message recorded from Hanani's lips is focused in a God-centered emphasis. Asa had erred in depending on his own strategy rather than trusting in God, and he was reminded that if he had trusted, God would have provided for him at this time just as he had earlier.

### b. WILLINGNESS TO SUFFER

The result for Hanani in bringing his rebuke to the king was that he was put in prison. It should be realized that prisons of the day were not clean places, but were often vermin-infested and foul-smelling. The thought of being confined in one could only have been revolting. It might be argued that Hanani did not know ahead of time that he would be so treated, and therefore to speak of him as willing to suffer punishment is to speak of him in a way not warranted by the story. However, he must have recognized the possibility of such confinement, for certainly to rebuke a king when he expects plaudits is always dangerous. Imprisonment was definitely a possibility he had to contemplate.

### c. IMPORTANCE

There is evidence that Hanani was well known in his day. This appears from the fact that his son, Jehu, is identified as "the son of Hanani" four of the five times that Jehu is mentioned. Since this degree of parental reference was not ordinary for the prophets, one must conclude that Hanani must have been unusually important for Jehu to be known especially as his son.

## E. JEHU

We come now to speak of Jehu himself, the son of Hanani. He had contact with King Baasha of Israel, the opponent of Asa, and with King

Jehoshaphat of Judah, the son and successor of Asa. He is mentioned more often than his father, but, in that he is identified so often as the son of Hanani, one should not think that he was more important as a prophet than was his father. One should not conclude either that because these two prophets have the relation of father and son the sons of prophets ordinarily followed their fathers in becoming prophets. Actually the situation of a son following his father in office is relatively infrequent. Jehu is also different from most other prophets in that he served in both Israel and Judah.

### 1. The work

Jehu's contact with Baasha consisted in a rebuke much in the pattern of his father in respect to Asa. The rebuke was due to the disobedience of Baasha, as he followed in the way of Jeroboam and Nadab before him. God had permitted Baasha to destroy the house of Jeroboam because of Jeroboam's sin, but Baasha then did no better. Jehu came to him and brought a severe rebuke. He told the king that God would "take away the posterity of Baasha, and the posterity of his house," and would make his house "like the house of Jeroboam, the son of Nebat" (I Kings 16:3). This must have been rather early in the ministry of Jehu, because he had his contact with Jehoshaphat at least thirty years later. Baasha died in 886 B.C., and the contact with Jehoshaphat came following Jehoshaphat's assistance to Ahab, which likely was in 853 B.C.[10] Jehu evidently served as a prophet over many years.

Jehu's contact with Jehoshaphat also consisted in a rebuke. Jehoshaphat had just helped Ahab, with whom he had made alliance, in his conflict with the Aramaeans of Damascus at Ramoth-gilead (II Chron. 18:28–34; cf. I Kings 22:29–40). In this he had displeased God, and Jehu met him on his return with the words, "Shouldest thou help the ungodly and love them that hate the LORD? Therefore is wrath upon thee from before the LORD" (II Chron. 19:2). He added, however, that God recognized some good things in Jehoshaphat, particularly that he had put away the cultic carved poles unto Asherah out of the land of Judah. If either Baasha or Jehoshaphat gave a response to Jehu's words, it is not recorded.

Because Jehu is called a prophet, rather than a seer like his father, and because he is depicted as declaring God's word on these two occasions, it appears that he differed from his father in being primarily a prophet to speak forth God's word rather than a seer to receive it.

[10]For discussion of this date see my *Survey of Israel's History*, p. 312.

## 2. The person

### a. Spiritual status

Jehu shows spiritual maturity in that he was entrusted with these two important occasions of rebuke for a king. Of all types of messages that prophets were called upon to bring, certainly the most difficult and unpleasant were messages of rebuke. No one likes to receive rebuke. God would not have called upon one who was considered spiritually immature to give this type of a message.

### b. Courage

That Jehu was willing to bring two such rebukes shows that he was a man of courage. This is all the more true in that his father, Hanani, had suffered imprisonment for bringing a rebuke to Asa. Certainly Jehu was well aware of the consequences such action could bring to himself.

### c. Literary ability

Jehu was also a prophet who had literary ability. He is said to have written a book which contained the "acts of Jehoshaphat" (II Chron. 20:34). Because this book is the only one mentioned as source material for the history regarding Jehoshaphat, it follows that Jehu must have lived during his entire reign. This means that he ministered over many years, having begun as early as the last years of Baasha and continuing through all twenty-five years (I Kings 22:42) of Jehoshaphat.

## F. JAHAZIEL

Jahaziel is mentioned only once in Scripture (II Chron. 20:14–17), and the reference involves again the reign of Jehoshaphat. Because of the circumstance and because Jahaziel also is said to have had "the Spirit of the LORD" come upon him, he must be thought of in the same category as Azariah noted above. That is, he was a part-time prophet, possibly used to bring a message this one time only. Actually the term *prophet* is not employed regarding him, but the fact that he was used to bring a word of prophecy in a crucial time in Israel's history shows that he is properly included in the illustrious group.

## 1. The work

The occasion of Jahaziel's work concerned a time in Jehoshaphat's rule when the country of Judah was being invaded by a threefold army. It was made up of troops from Moab, Ammon, and Edom (II Chron. 20:1, 10). On hearing of this invasion, Jehoshaphat called for a fast in Judah and then rose to pray as his people gathered in Jerusalem. He called upon God to give them help in this time when they did not have sufficient troops of their own to meet a large invading enemy. As he finished praying, the Spirit of the Lord came upon Jahaziel and he rose to give God's response in view of Jehoshaphat's splendid prayer. He said, "Thus saith the LORD unto you, Be not afraid nor dismayed by reason of this great multitude; for the battle is not yours, but God's" (20:15). After giving some instructions on procedure, he added the stirring words, "Set yourselves, stand ye still, and see the salvation of the LORD with you" (20:17).

With this message of instruction and encouragement given, Jehoshaphat set out with his troops to meet the enemy, placing Levites in the forefront to sing, "Praise the LORD; for His mercy endureth forever" (20:21). When they reached the enemy, they found that the three armies, apparently in jealousy, had killed each other off and all that Jehoshaphat's troops had to do was pick up the booty that was left. This was indeed a great day for the people of God.

## 2. The person

### a. SPIRITUAL STATUS

Like Azariah before him, Jahaziel must have enjoyed a high spiritual status to have been selected out of a large audience to give God's word to Jehoshaphat and those assembled. Certainly God did not choose just anyone. Jahaziel must have been seen as a proper recipient for the Spirit of the Lord to come upon and to give the message. It was a fine message, too, reminding the people that the battle was really not theirs but God's. A God-centered message of this kind reveals that the one giving it is God-centered in his own life and thought.

### b. ABILITY TO SPEAK

It follows that Jahaziel possessed ability to speak. Clearly the assembly that had gathered was large, and therefore not everyone would have had the courage to rise and give this sort of message. Jahaziel, then, had to be capable and confident in terms of expressing himself in clear speech. He probably had little surmised how God was to use him as he gathered with the others, but God saw him as the proper vehicle to bring the stirring message.

## G. ELIEZER

Still another who prophesied during the reign of Jehoshaphat was Eliezer. He is mentioned only once (II Chron. 20:37) and this briefly, so very little is known regarding him. His home town is indicated as Mareshah, which was located in the western hill country of Judah.

### 1. The work

The occasion of this mention of Eliezer involved the second time when Jehoshaphat allied himself with the house of Omri in a joint venture. It was pointed out earlier that he had made a treaty with the northern dynasty and that three times this led him into dangerous and unhappy occasions. This second alliance was with Ahaziah, Ahab's oldest son, in a maritime venture. The two built ships at the port of Ezion-geber, for the purpose of sailing down the Red Sea to engage in trading. While the ships were being built, Eliezer warned Jehoshaphat, "Because thou hast joined thyself with Ahaziah, the LORD hath broken thy works" (II Chron. 20:37). The ships were built, but they never left port. In some way they suffered destruction so that the trading endeavor ended in complete disaster.

### 2. The person

#### a. SPIRITUAL STATUS

Though little can be said regarding Eliezer as a person, one clue exists to show that he stood relatively high in spiritual stature. The message he gave to Jehoshaphat was again one of rebuke. As has been noted, God could hardly entrust such a message to one who was not truly devoted to Him.

#### b. COURAGE

The same fact shows that Eliezer was a man of courage. Certainly Jehoshaphat and Ahaziah had invested considerable effort and money in this venture, when Eliezer brought his warning. It would have taken courage to tell them that the venture would end in disaster.

# 13

# The Reign of Ahab: Elijah

No prophets are mentioned between the reigns of Baasha and Ahab (about twelve years), when Elah, Zimri, and Omri ruled. This brings us to the reign of Ahab when the great prophet Elijah ministered. The Scriptures give this prophet a very prominent place, though he was not one of the writing prophets. Accordingly, this chapter is devoted entirely to him.

The reign of Ahab followed the strong rule of his father Omri. Though Omri did not rule long, he was probably the most capable king northern Israel had until his time. One thing he did, however, resulted in a tragic loss for Israel religiously. This was the formation of an alliance with Phoenicia to the north, which involved the marriage of his son Ahab to the Phoenician princess, Jezebel. Such marriages were commonplace when alliances of this kind were made, and normally, when the princess came into the foreign palace, she was hardly heard from again. This was not to be, however, with the proud and self-willed Jezebel. She brought with her the foreign worship of Baal-Melqart.[1] Worship of Baal, the Canaanite deity, had been observed among Israelite tribes in premonarchial days. Samuel had fought vigorously against it, and David had finally succeeded in ridding the land of it. Now it was brought back in this worship of the Tyrian Baal-Melqart.

Jezebel, persistent and dominant as she was, was not content with hav-

[1]This Tyrian god was called Melqart. Melqart, however, corresponded to the older Canaanite god Baal in idea, being the Tyrian counterpart to Baal. So he is called Baal in the biblical account.

ing her religion merely co-exist with that of Israel's God. She wanted it to supplant what had been before, and lent strong effort to this project, with Ahab doing little to stop her. She came near to accomplishing her purpose, too, as indicated by her vicious slaughter of the native prophets of God (I Kings 18:4), something she, being the foreigner, would not have dared to attempt unless she had already been well in command of religious matters. The earlier sin of Jeroboam, establishing the golden calf worship, had been serious enough, but this introduction of the Baal cult was much worse. It involved an outright substitution of deity as well as degrading, licentious observances including religious prostitution.

Though Ahab permitted this religious defection, he was otherwise a capable ruler, seeking to follow the pattern of his father. For one thing he continued building activity. Excavation at Samaria, his capital, has revealed an inner and outer wall of fortification which Ahab constructed around the general court area of the palace Omri had built. Imposing foundations of a large structure located near Omri's palace have been identified as Ahab's "ivory house" (I Kings 22:39; cf. Amos 3:15; 6:4). The walls of this structure were faced with white marble, thus giving the appearance of ivory, and more than two hundred real ivory figures, plaques, and small relief panels were found in a storeroom.[2] Ahab also built certain cities for his people (I Kings 22:39).

## A. THE WORK OF ELIJAH

It was during the reign of Ahab and Jezebel that Elijah was called to serve. The Bible speaks of their reign as being the worst in all Israel's history up to that time (I Kings 16:30), and perhaps this is the reason why God raised up one of his greatest prophets as a countermeasure.

### 1. Unusual importance

The Bible accords Elijah a place of unique importance in three ways. The first is that he was one of two men who did not have to die. Enoch was the other, of whom it is said, "Enoch walked with God, and he was not; for God took him" (Gen. 5:24). God honored Elijah by providing a special arrangement so that he "went up by a whirlwind into heaven" (II Kings 2:11). A second is that he was one of two that God permitted to appear on the Mount of Transfiguration, when Jesus was there with three of His disciples

---

[2]For discussion see Jack Finegan, *Light from the Ancient Past*, pp. 187–188.

(Matt. 17:1–13; cf. Mark 9:2–13; Luke 9:28–36). The other person was Moses, and of course the importance of Moses needs no elaboration. The third is that when Jesus asked the disciples concerning the identity people attributed to Him, one of the answers regularly was "Elijah" (Matt. 16:14). That people gave this answer shows the importance Elijah played in their thinking, and it indicates also their remembrance of God's prophecy through Malachi, "Behold, I will send you Elijah the prophet before the coming of the great and dreadful day of the LORD" (4:5). God thus gave Elijah an important position in prompting Malachi so to speak of him.

### 2. Prediction of famine

Elijah's first action, as set forth in I Kings, was the prediction of famine to King Ahab. He told the king, "As the LORD God of Israel liveth, before whom I stand, there shall not be dew nor rain these years, but according to my word" (17:1). From James 5:17, it is evident that Elijah had earlier prayed that this famine might occur. The reason he did so was his distress over the false religion being brought into the land by Jezebel. Though Elijah lived on the east of the Jordan in Gilead (I Kings 17:1), the influence of her attempts evidently had moved that far, and Elijah had become sufficiently concerned to make this serious request in prayer.[3] Apparently God then informed Elijah that He would do as Elijah had requested and instructed the prophet to carry the message to Ahab. Elijah is seen doing this as the story opens in I Kings.

### 3. Hiding at the brook Cherith

With the announcement given to the king that the famine would come, it was necessary for Elijah to hide. God came to him soon to tell him to do this at the brook Cherith. It is believed that Cherith was one of several streams which thread their way down into the Jordan valley making sharply chiseled gorges as they go.[4] These gorges have numerous recesses and dark caverns which the prophet could easily have used for effective concealment. While Elijah was at Cherith Ahab tried to find him, looking not only throughout his own land but even foreign countries (I Kings 18:10). It was probably only after the intensity of this search had ceased that God came to Elijah and told him to move from Cherith north to the village of Zarephath.

[3]God had long before indicated that famine would be a last extreme of punishment He would bring if the people failed to follow Him properly (Deut. 11:17; 28:23; cf. I Kings 8:35).

[4]Wadi Kelt is traditionally identified as the stream, but it flows from the west rather than the east, and many believe that a stream flowing from the east is more likely.

Zarephath lay between Tyre and Sidon, eight miles from Sidon to the north and twelve miles from Tyre to the south. Here he stayed in the home of a widow, and God fed the two of them miraculously by continually keeping a supply of meal in a jar and oil in a jug. It was while Elijah was here that the little son of the woman fell ill, and God wrought a miracle through the prophet to raise the boy back to life (I Kings 17:17–24).

### 4. A contest arranged

When the three-and-a-half years of famine (Luke 4:25; James 5:17) were drawing to a close, God told Elijah to go back to Israel. The purpose was to arrange a contest that would properly bring to a climax the lesson God had been intending by the famine. Through the hesitant assistance of one of Ahab's servants (18:7–16), Elijah made contact with the king and the contest was arranged (18:17–20). He asked the king to have the 450 prophets of Baal present on Mount Carmel, along with the 400 prophets of Asherah who ate at Jezebel's table. He also wanted him to gather together people from all Israel to the mountain, so that they might see what the contest would reveal. It was necessary that Ahab give this invitation to the Israelites, because the leaders would hardly have dared come otherwise, when Jezebel had such a hold on religious matters in the land. Ahab did as the prophet requested, and the reason was that he wanted rain to be sent so badly. The idea of the contest was to provide a way to prove before the people who was Israel's true God, whether Baal or Jehovah.

In this connection it is well to notice that another contest had been in progress since the time that the famine had started. Inasmuch as Baal, whom Jezebel had brought into the land, was thought to be the god of storm and rainfall, the announcement by one of God's true prophets that it would not rain had amounted to a challenge to the priests of Baal to make it rain by the power of Baal. When three-and-a-half years had gone by and it had not rained, this could have meant to the people only that Baal was not living up to what he was supposed to do. All this time, then, it would have become increasingly apparent that Baal was not all that Jezebel had said he was. Therefore, to bring this contest to a close by a new one concerning fire on Mount Carmel would be a suitable manner to present climaxing evidence that Israel should follow Jehovah and not Baal.

### 5. The contest

Ahab did as Elijah desired, so that on the day of the contest both the people and the prophets of Baal were on hand. We are told that there were

450 prophets of Baal (18:22), but nothing is said about the 400 prophets of Asherah. Apparently Ahab was able to arrange for the one group to come but not the other; it may be that Jezebel objected sufficiently to keep the one group away. However, 450 comprised a large number, and no doubt Elijah was pleased that at least these were present. The number of spectators must have been still greater, for later on, when Elijah asked them to see to it that none of the 450 prophets of Baal escaped, they were able to carry this out. It should be realized, too, that these would have been important people of the land, not just anyone. Elijah would have wanted important people, for they would be the most influential on returning home to persuade others to follow the true worship of God. That was the reason why Ahab's personal invitation had been necessary, so people of influence would be willing to come.

When all were present, Elijah began to speak and outline the manner of contest that was to be held. The prophets of Baal were to call upon their god to light miraculously a fire on an altar to Baal, and later Elijah would do the same in respect to an altar to the God of Israel. The God who would answer by fire would be proven the true God. Elijah also told the prophets of Baal they could select the animal they wanted to sacrifice and proceed first. The prophets of Baal then sacrificed their animal, and began to call upon Baal to send fire. They continued to call through the morning hours until noon, and then in the afternoon, at Elijah's mocking, they called still louder and even cut themselves with knives to bring blood on their bodies. All was to no avail, however, as the afternoon wore on; Baal did not answer.

Late in the day Elijah called the people over to a place where there had been a small altar unto Jehovah. He repaired it, using twelve stones, one representing each of the tribes of Israel. This would have been a rather insignificant altar to look at, in comparison with the large altar that the Canaanites had used.[5] Elijah also dug a trench about his altar and then called for a total of twelve containers of water to be poured over it. This drenched the altar completely, proving that there could not possibly be any fire secretly hidden underneath. Elijah then offered a brief prayer, recorded in only two verses (18:36, 37), and God answered with the fire. The fire that fell was so intense that it consumed the wood and the sacrifice, the stones of the altar, and even licked up the water in the surrounding trench. No doubt, the people standing nearby had to move back to get away from the heat of such a blaze.

The result was that the people immediately cried out, "The LORD, he is the God; the LORD, he is the God" (18:39). The demonstration had been unmistakably convincing, and the people were ready to acknowledge it.

[5] A Canaanite altar, dating yet earlier than this, was found at Megiddo, measuring some twenty-six feet across and roughly four-and-a-half feet high, made of hundreds of stones cemented together with mud. This altar on Mount Carmel may have been smaller but doubtless was still sizable in comparison with the small one Elijah now used.

They had been prepared through the prior three-and-a-half years by the contest for rain, and now they were persuaded by this contest for fire. Elijah quickly followed up on this acknowledgment by calling for the people to make sure that none of the prophets of Baal escaped. They were herded down the side of Mount Carmel to the brook Kishon, where they were slain. It should be realized that this was a key matter in the day's activity. These prophets were the favorites of Jezebel, and therefore anyone who had a part in taking their lives would immediately endanger his own life before her anger. Elijah recognized this and called for action on the part of all spectators present so that they would be definitely placed on his side for returning to the worship of Israel's true God.

That same evening Elijah climbed again to the top of Mount Carmel for the purpose of asking God to send rain. We are told that he bowed down as he did so, probably near the smoldering pile of ashes, since this was the place where God had answered so marvelously earlier in the afternoon. Having asked God to send the rain, he sent a servant who was with him up to a higher point to look toward the west for an answer in the form of a cloud. The servant came back and reported there was none. Elijah did not desist, however, but continued to pray and ask again and again, with the servant each time reporting negatively. Finally, the seventh time the servant said there was indeed a small cloud rising out of the sea, and Elijah responded that this was the answer. He also told the servant to go quickly and warn Ahab to start for home in his chariot, since it was going to rain hard. Apparently the rain started before Ahab was able to get under way, and Elijah then made the strenuous effort of running before his chariot all the way to Jezreel, a distance of approximately twelve miles. It may be that the brook Kishon overflowed from the pouring rain so that Elijah had to lead Ahab over higher ground that he might get home safely.

### 6. Flight from Jezebel

On arriving at his own quarters in Jezreel, Elijah in his wet and exhausted condition received a threatening message from Jezebel. She had learned from her husband what had transpired out at Mount Carmel. Her message read, "So let the gods do to me, and more also, if I make not thy life as the life of one of them by tomorrow about this time" (19:2). Those she referred to as "them" were the 450 prophets who had been killed. Elijah, so strong when out at Mount Carmel, now showed weakness as he wrongly fled from his house yet that night as a result of the message. The statement is that "he arose and went for his life, and came to Beersheba, which belongeth to

Judah, and left his servant there" (19:3). He evidently hardly stopped to eat and sleep as he moved quickly to get away from the danger of this wicked woman. Then, leaving his servant in Beersheba, at the far south of the land, he went on alone and, sitting down under a juniper tree, asked God to take his life, saying, "Oh LORD, take away my life; for I am not better than my fathers" (19:4).

God did not accede to Elijah's request, however, but sent His angel to minister to the prophet. The angel awoke Elijah from his sleep and told him to eat and drink of provisions that were suddenly there before him, a jug of water and cakes freshly baked on a fire. These evidently were provided miraculously. Elijah did eat and drink and then lay down to sleep again. After a time the angel once more awoke him and directed him to eat and drink, and Elijah did. Then with the strength thus received, Elijah made his way further south through the Sinai Desert until he came to Mount Horeb, where the Law had been given to the Israelites many centuries before.

### 7. Restoration

Finding a cave in which to dwell on Mount Horeb, Elijah soon was contacted by God with the words, "What doest thou here, Elijah?" (19:9). This question must have been very penetrating to Elijah's mind. In effect God was asking Elijah why he was down here at Mount Horeb when the contest had been arranged up in Israel, where there had been such success in turning key people to God that memorable afternoon. In other words, Elijah had fled when he had not needed to, and now he was not where God wanted him to be.

Elijah tried to defend himself by indicating he had been jealous for God and had done his best to maintain God's word, but that it had been impossible and that he had just managed to save his life under difficult conditions. At this, God told him to go forth out of the cave and observe what was about to happen. As he did so, God caused three great object lessons to transpire. The first was the formation of a strong wind that blew sufficiently to cause rocks of the mountain to break in pieces. Then He stirred up an earthquake that shook the entire mountain. And, thirdly, He kindled a fire in front of where the prophet stood that apparently blazed with a ferocity parallel to that of the wind and earthquake. When these mighty displays were completed, God caused Elijah to hear a still small voice, which came in complete contrast to the terrible devastating actions of the earlier demonstration. The indication is given that God had not been "in" the three mighty actions, thus implying that He was in the still small voice.

Three lessons appear to have been intended by this occasion. Two of them concern primarily the large and powerful displays, and the third the still small voice. The first was that Elijah had not needed to run from Jezebel that night because God could stir up such things as a great wind, a strong earthquake, or a burning fire to destroy her completely so that she could not touch God's prophet. In other words Elijah had shown a lack of faith in not recognizing the ability of God to protect him in spite of the threatening message.

The second was that God's method by which now to deal with Jezebel was not to be such destructive measures as these. Likely, as Elijah had moved south through the Sinai Desert, his thinking had been that the only way to solve the problem in Israel was for Jezebel to be destroyed, and he may have tried to think of ways in which this could be done. God now showed him that there were three ways that it might be done. As successively the wind blew, the earthquake rocked, and the fire burned, Elijah may well have responded each time with the thought, "Yes, Lord, this will do very nicely." God, however, was saying, "No, Elijah, this is not the way we will do it. We will not destroy her either by wind, earthquake, or fire, but we will work by a still small voice."

The third lesson was that Elijah should know that God's way of carrying on His work was not only or even normally by violent and sensational methods but rather by simple hard work, symbolized by the still small voice. Until this point Elijah had worked only with the big and sensational and apparently had thought this was the only way. When the big contest had not worked out in total victory, therefore, Elijah had believed that all was fruitless and the only thing left for him was to die. God was now saying that all was not over, that the battle had not been lost, and that Elijah did not need to die because thus far he had tried only the unusual methods in changing Israel back to God. What was left was actually the more normal activity, the "still small voice" such as prophets ordinarily followed. Elijah, then, was to return to the land and get under way in this further work, in contrast to what he had done earlier, and so to see what God could do in this manner.

How soon these lessons registered in Elijah's mind is hard to say. It may have been some time before he recognized them fully, but that he did so in part almost immediately is indicated by his willingness to return. He was to do three things (19:15–17): anoint Hazael as king over Syria, anoint Jehu as king over Israel, and summon Elisha as a prophet to serve in his own place. The first two matters were not possible for Elijah personally to carry out, but later Elisha would act in his place (see II Kings 8:7–13; 9:1–10). The third direction, however, Elijah could carry out and he did as soon as he returned to the land.

## 8. The call of Elisha

Elisha lived at Abel-meholah, located in the Jordan valley a few miles south of the Sea of Galilee. He may have come from an affluent family, for it is said that when Elijah called him he was plowing in a field where twelve yoke of oxen were working ahead of him. Elijah came to him and cast his mantle upon him. Elisha evidently realized the significance of the action, for he quickly ran after Elijah and asked permission first to say farewell to his parents before following the prophet. Elijah granted the permission, and Elisha made a feast using the oxen he had been plowing with for the meat and the plow and equipment for the firewood. Then at the feast he bade farewell to his parents and friends and went after Elijah. The two apparently ministered together until the day of Elijah's departure, probably a period of about ten years.[6]

## 9. Rebuke of Ahab

The stories given thus far regarding Elijah are all recorded consecutively in I Kings 17–19. Three other episodes are presented later on. The first concerns a direct rebuke of Ahab for wrongly procuring the vineyard of one named Naboth.

The vineyard of Naboth was near Ahab's palace in Jezreel. Ahab wanted it and asked Naboth to sell it to him, but Naboth refused on the basis that it was a part of his patrimony. Jezebel noted that Ahab was sad as a result, and, finding out the difficulty, arranged for Naboth to be killed. She instructed the leaders of the city to hold a feast and have false witnesses charge Naboth with blasphemy against God and the king. This was done and Naboth was carried out and stoned to death. When Jezebel learned of it she told Ahab to claim the vineyard, for Naboth no longer lived.

When Ahab went to do this he was met by Elijah who had been instructed by God to bring rebuke. Elijah told him that, because of what had just been done, his house would be completely destroyed like the "house of Jeroboam, the son of Nebat, and like the house of Baasha, the son of Ahijah" (I Kings 21:22). He said further regarding Jezebel specifically, "The dogs shall eat Jezebel by the wall of Jezreel" (21:23).

As a result of this solemn message, Ahab remarkably humbled himself and repented before God. God, therefore, gave Elijah a further word to the

---

[6]Though this figure is not given it is likely in view of the events that transpired while the two were together.

king, that, in view of Ahab's repentance, the evil indicated would not come in his own day but in the day of his son. It was effected in the reign of Jehoram, Ahab's second son (see II Kings 9:14—10:11).


## 10. Rebuke of Ahaziah

The second episode concerns Elijah's rebuke of Ahaziah, Ahab's first son and immediate successor (II Kings 1:1-16). Ahaziah had met with an accident, falling "through a lattice in his upper chamber" (1:2).[7] He sent messengers to enquire of Baal-zebub,[8] god of the city of Ekron, as to possible recovery. The angel of the Lord told Elijah to intercept the messengers, give rebuke to the king through them for seeking information from this false god, and predict Ahaziah's death. Elijah did so, and, when Ahaziah received report of this, recognizing Elijah from a description by the messengers, he sent fifty men to bring Elijah to the capital. Elijah called destroying fire down from heaven upon this company and then upon another sent by Ahaziah before a third group came humbly entreating for their lives. The prophet then went with them to see the king. When Elijah came to the king, he simply reiterated the message he had already given to the men Ahaziah had sent at the first. It was to the effect that Ahaziah had done wrong in sending to a foreign deity and not consulting the true God of Israel. He also indicated that Ahaziah would die from the wounds he had received. The result was that Ahaziah did die shortly, after reigning less than two years.


## 11. Elijah's miraculous homegoing

The final account concerns Elijah's unique and honored departure for heaven. He did not die but was especially transported.

God had told Elijah ahead of time that his homegoing would be unique. It is quite clear that he also told Elisha and the prophets in training in Elijah's schools that this would happen. Elijah did not know that these others had been told. Proceeding on a final visit to the schools, Elijah urged Elisha three times, first at Gilgal, and then at the schools of Bethel and Jericho, not to accompany him, but Elisha persisted. At each school the prophets in training told Elisha they knew of Elijah's impending departure and wondered if

---

[7]The word translated "lattice" (*sebakah*) is often translated "network" in connection with the temple construction (I Kings 7:17, 18, 20, 41, 42). It was probably something like a window screen—only with larger openings—through which the king fell, perhaps to the ground some distance below.

[8]The name *Baal-zebub* means "Lord of flies." It is conjectured that this god was symbolized by a fly and reputed to have predictive power.

Elisha did. Elisha said he did and asked them not to speak further of the matter, apparently not wanting Elijah to learn that others knew. Elisha then continued with Elijah until they reached the Jordan.

Here Elijah struck the water with his mantle and the waters divided to make a dry path. People normally crossed the Jordan at shallow fording places, and certainly Elijah usually did too. The reason for dividing the water this time was apparently to provide a lesson of faith for both Elisha and the fifty prophets in training who were following behind. On crossing the Jordan, Elijah, who now realized Elisha knew of his homegoing, asked the younger man what he wished to have before Elijah left him. Elisha asked for a double portion of the Spirit that indwelt Elijah; Elijah indicated that he could not give this, but if Elisha saw him as he left, he would know that God would grant it. Elisha watched closely until Elijah was caught up from him, and then he took up the mantle that fell from Elijah's shoulders and put it on himself. Returning to the Jordan, he took the mantle and struck the water and saw it divide. This proved that indeed the same Spirit now dwelt upon him, and he walked back into the land to carry on the work that Elijah had left to him.[9]

## B. THE PERSON

### 1. Spiritual status

There is abundant evidence that Elijah was a spiritually strong prophet. This is indicated first by his prayer life. It was noted that he prayed that God would send famine because of the sin in the land, and God responded by turning off the rain for three-and-a-half years. What Elijah asked for was no small thing, but God still answered. Elijah was a man of prayer, who knew what it is to ask big things from God and receive them. The same was true later when he asked God to send fire as the crowd of people watched on Mount Carmel, and then as he asked for rain while alone on the same mountain top.

Elijah's spiritual maturity is also evident in his keen consciousness of sin. This after all was the reason why he prayed for the famine. He was not interested in people suffering but that people turn from their sin. He evidently knew that God long before had warned that He would use famine as a final resort if the people persisted in rebelling against Him (Deut. 11:17; 28:23). Elijah asked for this most severe measure now to be brought, because

---

[9]For significance of this account regarding the Spirit, see chap. 6, pp. 86, 88.

he was so concerned regarding the sin that was coming into the land. Such a consciousness of sin is a clear mark of a high spiritual standing.

A third indication is found in the many miracles God permitted Elijah to perform. It was noted in an earlier discussion that not all prophets performed miracles, and surely that they did not was not in itself an indication that they were not spiritually mature. It simply was not God's will that miracles be performed at just any time. However, when it was His will, certainly He did not perform them through persons who were not spiritually approved. After all, the performance of a miracle was a great trust. One who was not suitable as an instrument through whom to work might become proud of the work effected. Elijah, however, was worthy and was used to perform numerous miracles.

Still another indication is the fact that God restored Elijah to service after Elijah had run from Jezebel. One might expect that Elijah had forfeited all right to continue as a servant of God. The revival had been going so well on Mount Carmel, but Elijah had spoiled it all when he ran from the queen. God, however, did not cast Elijah aside but taught him lessons down on Mount Horeb and restored him to service. This restoration was genuine, for at the close of Elijah's life God saw fit to honor him by the special entrance into heaven. Certainly this was a result primarily of his work during the years of his "still small voice" activity, rather than the earlier efforts which had been spoiled by Elijah's flight. If God so restored Elijah, God surely saw him as a man of spiritual strength who could still be used if brought back into service again.

## 2. A man of faith

In his spiritual maturity Elijah was outstanding as a man of faith. Other prophets already studied showed real aspects of faith, too, but perhaps Elijah demonstrated faith in even more pronounced ways. He showed it in his prayer that God would send the famine, believing clearly that God could and would do so, and God as a result did that very thing. He showed it in telling Ahab the king that there would be no dew nor rain until Elijah gave the word. Certainly this took great faith because there is nothing more impossible for man to do than to control the elements of nature. Yet Elijah believed God would work through him to stop rainfall, until Elijah gave the word for it to rain again.

He showed it, thirdly, in his belief that the little son of the widow of Zarephath would live again. This is the first recorded occasion of resurrection in the Bible, so Elijah had no prior event on which to base this faith. Certainly it took more faith for him to believe in resurrection here than it did, for instance, for Elisha later when he was asked for the Shunammite's son to be raised (II Kings 4:32–37). Elisha then had the prior example of Elijah. Elijah simply had to believe that God would do this because he was certain that God would not bring further problem and harm upon the widow of Zarephath.[10]

Great faith was demonstrated by Elijah later when he called on God to send fire upon the altar on Mount Carmel as all the people looked on. The prophets of Baal had tried for many hours earlier in the day and had failed completely. Now all the people were watching as Elijah's turn came. It took faith on his part to believe that God would answer him, when the prophets of Baal had failed so miserably.

Perhaps a still greater display of faith occurred in connection with his prayer for rain that evening. On the way back to the top of Mount Carmel to offer the prayer, Elijah noticed Ahab apparently with a downcast countenance. He went to him and said, "Get thee up, eat and drink; for there is a sound of abundance of rain" (I Kings 18:41). At the time there was not a cloud in the sky, and forty-two months had elapsed since rain had fallen. Elijah knew that Ahab wanted rain and here, even before going up the mountain to ask for it, he went out of his way to promise that it would come.

It is noteworthy also that he talked about an abundance of rain. In other words, he told Ahab that it would do more than merely sprinkle or rain in an ordinary manner, but that a great quantity would fall, such as the land needed to really benefit. Elijah could not have been basing this bold statement on a prior revelation of God regarding rain falling that evening, either, for if he had there would have been no need for him to pray that it would come. Not only did he pray, but God let him make his request seven different times before He answered. Moreover, in James 5:17, 18 this prayer, along with Elijah's earlier prayer that it stop raining, is made an example of true effective prayer. Certainly James would have used as an example only a prayer that was a genuine demonstration of faith.

## 3. Courage

Elijah also demonstrated courage on many occasions. He did so in coming to Ahab the first time. He must have known that Ahab would not like to hear a message that famine was to come on his land. Kings feared few things more than famines, because they meant terrible suffering for the people. It

---

[10]She had earlier lost her husband and had apparently stood alone against almost certain opposition in northern Zarephath, which was the center of Baal worship. In view of her difficult situation prior to the coming of Elijah, she must have gone through great suffering in maintaining a faith in God.

took courage for Elijah to bring this kind of message, but he brought it. It took courage to come to Ahab again much later when he rebuked Ahab for taking Naboth's vineyard. He must have known that Ahab already felt guilty because of having obtained the vineyard in the way he had, and when a person feels guilty he is in no mood to be rebuked for that guilt. Elijah, having been instructed of God, did go and give the message in spite of the danger. Then, courage was involved in Elijah's going to King Ahaziah, the son of Ahab. Ahaziah had sent messengers to Baal-zebub of the Philistines. Elijah, however, had intercepted them and sent back word to the king which again was a word of rebuke. Certainly Ahaziah was in no mood to receive such a communication, and Elijah would have known this. But Elijah sent it and finally went himself.

## 4. Obedience

Elijah was an obedient person, showing this on numerous occasions. One was the time when he went to Ahab with the message regarding the famine. He had already prayed for the famine. God evidently had told him He would accede to that request and then instructed Elijah to go and tell Ahab that it was to happen. That Elijah did this, in spite of possible anger on Ahab's part, shows that he was obedient to God.

Obedience was remarkably demonstrated when Elijah moved from the brook Cherith to Zarephath. Elijah probably had been at the brook Cherith about one year at the time, and all the while he had been completely hidden from people. Now the instruction was to go where people would be, even to a city called Zarephath. There he was to dwell with a widow in this time of famine. Elijah knew that widows suffered more during times of famine than did others, since there was no breadwinner to provide food for the table. He must, then, have wondered at these instructions from God and could well have asked God to explain them before moving to obey. We do not read that he hesitated, however, but simply that he "arose and went to Zarephath" (I Kings 17:10).

It may be added that, if Elijah had asked, God could have given him assurances. Zarephath, being a port city on the Mediterranean, would have been visited by many foreign people and therefore any new foreigner, such as Elijah from Gilead, would not have been conspicuous. Also, God was going to provide for Elijah and the widow through a miracle—containers of oil and meal would never run dry. God was going to take care of the woman, then, as well as Elijah, in this miraculous way.

Another act of noticeable obedience was that Elijah returned to Israel and to service for God following God's instructions to him on Mount Horeb.

Earlier he had asked to die, thinking that his work was done, but, when God showed him that it was not and that there was more for him to do, he did go back and accept the further assignment. He showed obedience in doing so.


## 5. Command of respect

Like prophets before him, Elijah commanded respect when he spoke. Certainly Ahab gave respect to his words when Elijah first came and announced the famine. We are told that as a result of those words Ahab looked for Elijah all through Israel and even in foreign lands (18:10). Later, on Mount Carmel, the 450 prophets as well as the spectators listened to Elijah. They let him dictate the terms of the contest and then took first chance at choosing an animal to sacrifice when Elijah gave them opportunity. At the noon hour, when Elijah mocked them, they gave notice to his words and did cry louder and even gashed themselves with knives in their endeavor to get the notice of their god Baal.

Later on, Ahab listened to Elijah as he rebuked him for seizing Naboth's vineyard. In fact he listened so well that he humbled himself and repented before God with the result that God gave him some reprieve from the words of catastrophe Elijah spoke. Still later, Ahab's son, Ahaziah, gave respect to Elijah's words. His messengers, who had been sent to Baal-zebub and were intercepted by Elijah, returned to tell Ahaziah what Elijah had said. When Ahaziah realized who had sent the words, he commissioned three groups of fifty men each to go and bring Elijah to him. He sent them one after the other even though the first two were burned by fire from heaven. Certainly Ahaziah respected the words that Elijah spoke.


## 6. Human frailty

At the same time that Elijah possessed so many commendable traits, he still was subject to human frailty, as is true of all individuals. He showed this especially at the time he ran when he received the threatening message from Jezebel. He had acted with great strength of courage out on Mount Carmel earlier, yet when he received the message he ran for his life.

Probably one reason that he did was that he was very tired, and tiredness regularly makes a person subject to poor decisions. He had experienced an exhausting day on Mount Carmel and had just run twelve miles to lead Ahab back to Jezreel through pelting rain. Had the message arrived the following morning, after a few hours of rest, Elijah's reaction might have been quite different. Another reason may be that Elijah did not have a companion with whom to consult. It is true that he apparently had his servant with him, but this servant may have been more a hindrance than a help. Since God later told Elijah, when down at Mount Horeb, to go and procure the assistance of Elisha, it may be that God was saying Elijah had needed an Elisha with him that night to help him decide aright. Another reason is probably that Elijah had not planned on such a development. He should have realized that Jezebel would not accept the victory he had gained out on Mount Carmel without a retort. He should have had a plan in reserve for countering her move. In view of his action, however, it is quite clear that he did not. Had he planned better, he would have been able to act more wisely.

Then another weakness of Elijah was that he could become despondent. A period of despondency came soon after his sin in running from Jezebel. When he arrived in the desert south of Beersheba, he wanted to quit his work and have God take his life. This was not God's will, for God wanted him to return to service again. Elijah was wrong and he showed frailty in his thinking when he made the request. He gave as his reason that he was not better than his fathers. Apparently, he had once thought he would be able to work a revival in Israel though prophets that preceded him had not been able to do so. That he had not succeeded had thus brought him to a place of defeat. Actually he should not have believed that he was more capable than his fathers in the first place. This additional sin of pride led him to despondency. But one should not let these weaknesses cloud his recognition of Elijah's outstanding character. He must be accorded a leading place among Israel's great prophets.

# 14

# The Reigns of Ahab, Joash, and Amaziah

Five prophets are to be studied in this chapter. Three served in Israel along with Elijah during the reign of Ahab, and two later in Judah during the reigns of Joash and Amaziah. Elisha, the last to be studied in this section, who ministered in Israel from the time of Jehoram through that of Jehoash, will be considered separately in the following chapter.

It should be understood that a slight overlap in time exists between these prophets and the first of the writing prophets to be considered in the next section. As will be seen, both Obadiah and Joel, who were the first of the writing prophets, are best placed during the reigns of Jehoram, Ahaziah, Athaliah, and the early years of Joash, all rulers of Judah. This means they preceded the last two prophets to be considered in this chapter, who ministered in the latter part of Joash's rule and in the time of Amaziah.

Accordingly, in respect to background history, events pertaining to the reigns of Jehoram, Ahaziah, and Athaliah will be reviewed when we consider Obadiah and Joel, and only the history involving Joash's latter days and the time of Amaziah will be taken up in this chapter. Further, in respect to Ahab, much has already been said regarding his rule in the previous chapter involving Elijah. Only those additional factors which pertain especially to the ministry of the three prophets to be considered herein will be given further notice.

Following their attack on Israel during the reign of Baasha (II Chron. 16:1-9), the Aramaeans of Damascus refrained from further contact until the

latter years of Ahab. The king who made the earlier attack was named
Ben-hadad, and a Ben-hadad is named as the person who pressed further
attacks in Ahab's later days. Whether this was the same man or a successor of
the same name is impossible to determine.[1] The power of Damascus had
been growing stronger during the intervening years, and now Ben-hadad
made two different attacks against Israel. This was almost certainly after
Elijah had returned from Mount Horeb to resume his work. The story is told
in I Kings 20.

Ben-hadad came against Ahab's capital, Samaria, along with thirty-two
allied kings. On arrival he laid claim to all Ahab's silver and gold as well as his
wives and children, and to this exorbitant demand Ahab did accede because
he was fearful of the might of the foreign ruler. Then Ben-hadad went
further and insisted that his servants be permitted to search the capital of
Israel and take whatever they wanted. Now Ahab objected and said he would
not comply. As a result, Ben-hadad declared he would attack and completely
destroy the city. He did not succeed in doing so, however, for God intervened to stop him, working through one of the prophets we consider in this
chapter.

The following year Ben-hadad made another attempt, again with a great
army. But as before, God intervened in behalf of Israel, working once more
through the prophet. Ben-hadad this time was forced to surrender to Ahab,
though Ahab let him off with easy terms, much to the displeasure of a second
prophet we will consider.

Ahab's motive in being lenient with the Damascus ruler may be found in
a threat then being posed by the great Shalmaneser III (859–824 B.C.), king
of Assyria. If Ben-hadad were to be helpful to Ahab and other rulers of the
West in resisting this greater and common foe, he should not be deprived of
his army. Chronological considerations indicate that the well-known battle of
Qarqar, between allied kings (including Ahab and Ben-hadad) and Shalmaneser III, did take place very soon after this second attack on Israel by
Ben-hadad.[2] The battle seems to have ended in a draw, with Shalmaneser III
going back to Assyria, and Ahab, Ben-hadad, and the allies returning to their
home countries.

It was probably still the same year[3] that Ahab again fought with Ben-

---

[1] See Merrill F. Unger, *Israel and the Aramaeans of Damascus*, chaps. 5–10.

[2] It was in 853 B.C. that both Ahab and Ben-hadad joined a northern coalition to stop
Shalmaneser at Qarqar on the Orontes River. To this coalition, Ahab contributed 2,000 chariots
and 10,000 soldiers, and Ben-hadad 1,200 chariots, 1,200 horsemen, and 20,000 soldiers. For the
text from Shalmaneser, see George Barton, *Archaeology and the Bible*, p. 458; *Ancient Near Eastern
Texts*, ed. James B. Pritchard, pp. 278–279; or *Documents from Old Testament Times*, ed. D.
Winton Thomas, pp. 46–49.

[3] See E. R. Thiele, *Mysterious Numbers of the Hebrew Kings*, p. 66, note 7, for an explanation of
both battles occurring the same year.

hadad, this time at Ramoth-gilead,[4] and was killed, thus fulfilling a prediction and warning of the fearless Micaiah, a third prophet we will consider. Jehoshaphat, king of Judah, had allied himself with Ahab for the battle, and he was nearly killed himself when mistaken for Ahab by the enemy. Ahab had disguised himself in view of Micaiah's prediction, but was killed in spite of the precaution.

Leaving now the northern kingdom of Israel and turning to the southern kingdom of Judah, and also moving along in time twenty years, we come to the day of the other prophets to be considered in this chapter. Ascending the throne of Judah in 835 B.C. was young Joash, only seven years old at the time. He was installed as king by the great high priest, Jehoiada, so that the land could be rid of the wicked rule of Athaliah (II Kings 11:4–16; II Chron. 23:1–15). Because the new king was so young at his crowning, the real leader of the land for several years was Jehoiada, and the fine record made by Joash during these years must be credited primarily to this godly high priest.

One thing that was needed following the apostate innovations of Athaliah was religious reform. Religious articles introduced by her were destroyed, including the Baal-Melqart temple, its altars, and images. The Baal priest, Mattan, was killed, and the personnel and offerings prescribed in the Mosaic Law were reinstituted. True worship of God was again observed, though some of the high places still continued to be used.

As long as Jehoiada continued as high priest, Joash remained a true follower of God; when he died, however, the king changed. This development came some time after Joash's twenty-third year, for it was then that he gave a fine order relative to repairing the temple. Jehoiada died at the age of 130 (II Chron. 24:15), which was sometime in the latter part of Joash's reign. Following the great man's demise, the king began to listen to new advisors who were more sympathetic to the deposed cult of Baal-Melqart (II Chron. 24:17, 18).

Because of the sin that now resulted, God's hand of blessing was withdrawn, and serious defeat was experienced at the hand of Hazael, a new king of Damascus. Hazael first brought a crushing blow upon Israel to the north and then turned south as far as Gath in Philistia and seized this city. After that he turned toward Jerusalem and brought destruction on Judah generally, taking many lives including those of a number of princes (II Chron. 24:23, 24). Only by giving Hazael large tribute[5] did Joash succeed in persuading him to spare Jerusalem from complete destruction (II Kings 12:17, 18).

---

[4]Identified with Tell-Ramith, some twenty-eight miles east of the Jordan and fifteen miles south of the Sea of Galilee. See Nelson Glueck, "Ramoth-gilead," *Bulletin of the American Schools of Oriental Research*, 92 (Dec. 1943):10–16.

[5]Described as all the "sacred treasures" of his fathers and of himself, in addition to all the gold deposited in the temple treasury and in the palace.

As further punishment, Joash died by assassination at the hands of conspirators (II Kings 12:19–21; II Chron. 24:25–27). Even his own servants took part, prompted apparently by their disapproval of his reversal in policy after Jehoiada's death. To die in this manner must have been a bitter experience for Joash, especially when his earlier years had been a cause for rejoicing.

The successor of Joash was his son Amaziah (796–767 B.C.; II Kings 14:1–20; II Chron. 25). Amaziah was approved by God in his life and reign, as his father had been. One of Amaziah's first actions was to punish the conspirators who had brought about his father's death (II Kings 14:1–6).

Two major battles were fought by Amaziah. The first was with Edom to the south. Amaziah made ambitious plans to gain control of the country, and even hired soldiers from Israel to help him, paying one hundred talents of silver. Rebuked by God for doing so, however, he sent these troops home. He found he did not need them anyway for he went on to win a complete victory over Edom with his own army. Then, following the victory, he greatly displeased God by bringing images of Edom's false gods back to Judah and worshiping them.

The second battle was with Israel. Amaziah, made proud and self-confident by the Edomite victory, challenged Jehoash of Israel. Jehoash tried to dissuade Amaziah from his intention, but the Judean king insisted and war did ensue near Beth-shemesh, west of Jerusalem. Judah was fully defeated and Jehoash then moved on Jerusalem, destroying six hundred feet of the city wall and seizing substantial booty and many captives. It is likely that among these captives was Amaziah himself (II Kings 14:13). If so, this was a humiliation for him of the greatest kind. It is likely that the king was kept in Israel as long as Jehoash of Israel lived (II Kings 14:17) and was then allowed to return to resume the rule of Judah.[6]

No information is given regarding Amaziah's rule after he returned except the unhappy note that he too, as his father, saw a conspiracy form against him. He tried to escape death by fleeing to Lachish, but was followed and killed there. His body was returned to Jerusalem for burial.

### A. "THE PROPHET"

The first prophet we notice is not designated by name even though specific reference to him is made three times. The first time he is called "a prophet" (*nabhi' ehadh*, "a certain prophet"—I Kings 20:13); then he is called "the prophet" (*ha-nabhi'*—20:22); and finally "a man of God" ('*ish ha-*

[6]See Thiele, *Mysterious Numbers*, pp. 83–87.

'elohim—20:28). The suggestion has been made that the person in view was Elijah, since this was the day of Elijah. This is not likely, however, since Elijah is identified by name in every other instance where he is mentioned.

## 1. The work

The three references to this prophet come in connection with the two occasions when Ben-hadad of Damascus was defeated by Ahab (I Kings 20:1-34). The prophet had a definite part in these defeats. In respect to the first occasion, the prophet came to Ahab following Ben-hadad's warning that he would attack the city of Samaria. All looked hopeless at the time, since Ben-hadad's force so outnumbered that of Ahab. The prophet said to Ahab, "Thus saith the LORD, Hast thou seen all this great multitude? Behold, I will deliver it into thy hand this day; and thou shalt know that I am the LORD" (20:13). He further indicated that the victory would be won primarily through "the young men of the princes of the provinces" and that Ahab should lead in the battle (20:14).

As a result of this encouragement, Ahab led his troops out, headed by the "princes of the provinces," and came upon the enemy king as he was "drinking himself drunk in the pavilions" (20:16). A battle ensued, and Israel's troops were fully victorious, putting the Aramaeans to flight. Following the victory the prophet came to Ahab again and told him to strengthen his forces and be on the watch, for at the turn of the year the king of the Aramaeans would come against him again.

Meanwhile in Damascus, Ben-hadad's advisors told him that Israel's God was a God of the hills and not of the plain, and if he would now attack Israel in the plain, he would surely win the battle. They said he should also replenish his army and make it just as strong as the first time. Ben-hadad did so, and in the following year he attacked again. Ahab went out to meet him, once more with troops much fewer in number, "like two little flocks of kids" (20:27).

At this point the prophet came to Ahab and said, "Thus saith the LORD, Because the Syrians have said, The LORD is God of the hills, but he is not God of the valleys, therefore will I deliver all this great multitude into thine hand, and ye shall know that I am the LORD" (20:28). For seven days the armies faced each other, and then the battle was joined, with Israel once again achieving victory. Ben-hadad was not able to escape this time, and he had to sue for peace. It was at this time that Ahab gave him lenient terms. He was required only to return the cities that his father had taken from Israel and to permit Ahab to "make streets . . . in Damascus" as Ben-hadad's father had made in Samaria (20:34). These "streets" were probably places of trade.

The significance of God's work through this prophet is noteworthy. Apart from God's intervention, Israel would have had no chance for victory against the opposing superior force. Also, Ahab otherwise was not a person to draw God's approval and therefore His blessing. One can account for the victories only on the basis that God wanted to teach Ben-hadad a lesson and show the superiority of Israel's God over the gods of the Aramaeans. The two victories were given to Ahab, then, in spite of his sinfulness and in no way because of it.

## 2. The person

### a. SPIRITUAL STATUS

This prophet may have enjoyed a high spiritual standing in God's sight as other prophets that have been studied, but evidence to this end is not as clear. His messages, for instance, were characterized by hope and encouragement rather than rebuke, and it has been seen that such messages did not take the same degree of dedication to give. This is not to say that he was wrong in giving them, for they were divinely revealed to him by God, but only that, since the messages were of this kind, they do not of themselves give indication as to his spiritual stature. One matter that does speak in his favor is that he received these revelations from God. This is evidenced by the words prefaced to his messages, "Thus saith the LORD." This means that God saw him as one to whom He could entrust revelation.

Why God used this prophet and not Elijah to bring these words to Ahab may be that they were not of a kind that Elijah had been giving to the king. Elijah's words had from the first been characterized by rebuke, and God may have seen these messages of hope and encouragement to be so much in contrast that it would be better for another prophet to speak them. Ahab might otherwise mistake them as an indication of a change in Elijah's (and God's) evaluation of his kingship.

### b. AVAILABILITY FOR ASSIGNMENT

It can also be said in favor of this prophet that he was available for assignments that God might give him. Three times God summoned him, and each time he complied and delivered messages of considerable importance to the Israelite ruler. Readiness to obey when God calls is always commendable even if it is only to deliver messages of hope and encouragement. The prophet should be thought of in a favorable way, though hardly in a class with some of the great prophets that have been studied.

## B.  A SON OF THE PROPHETS

A second prophet we notice is not designated by name either (I Kings 20:35–43). He is called once "a certain man of the sons of the prophets" (*'ish ehadh mibbene ha-nabhi'im*—20:35), and once merely "the prophet" (*ha-nabhi'*—20:38). Mention of this prophet comes as a result of the lenient terms Ahab gave Ben-hadad when he defeated him the second time.

### 1.  The work

The work of this person consisted in bringing rebuke to Ahab for making these lenient terms. He did so by way of an object lesson. He first asked another person to strike him so as to wound him. This person refused and he asked another person to do so. This man did as asked, and then the young prophet waited along the way where the king was expected to pass, having disguised himself by putting ashes upon his face. As the king rode by, he cried out, "Thy servant went out into the midst of the battle; and behold, a man turned aside, and brought a man unto me, and said, Keep this man: if by any means he be missing, then shall thy life be for his life, or else thou shalt pay a talent of silver" (20:39). He added that while he was busy the person put in his charge escaped. The king of Israel responded that he should be punished for having let the man get away.

At this the prophet took away his disguise, thus letting the king know that he was one of the prophets, and gave this appropriate message: "Thus saith the LORD, Because thou hast let go out of thy hand a man whom I appointed to utter destruction, therefore thy life shall go for his life, and thy people for his people" (20:42). The king recognized the meaning intended and was "displeased." But whether he repented in any way or felt he had done wrong is not indicated. As noted earlier, the reason for the leniency may have been the impending battle against the Assyrian conqueror, Shalmaneser III. If so, Ahab may have thought himself justified in doing what he had, though God clearly did not.

### 2.  The person

This person, being called a son of the prophets, was quite clearly one of the prophets in training of the day. The term *son of the prophets* was used for these individuals (cf. II Kings 2:3f.; 4:1f.; 6:1f.; 9:1f.). He may well have been a student in Elijah's school.

### a. SPIRITUAL STATUS

In terms of spiritual maturity, the young man gives evidence of standing relatively high. For one thing the message he brought was one of rebuke. Ahab had given lenient terms to Ben-hadad, and the prophet told him that he had grievously sinned in doing so. It would have taken a true sense of obedience and courage to voice such words. Then a second indication comes from his willingness to suffer a wound in order to bring the message forcefully in the way of an object lesson. Certainly this was not pleasant either, but apparently the young man was ready to do whatever God directed, no matter the cost.

### b. VIOLENCE NOT NECESSARILY A PART OF HIS CHARACTER

One might think of him as a violent person, since at the time the first man refused to smite him he spoke the words, "Behold, as soon as thou art departed from me, a lion shall slay thee" (20:36). The result was that the man was killed by a lion soon after. One must believe, however, that the prophet spoke these words by the command of God, since God carried them out so quickly. God no doubt wanted to teach by this example that when His prophets spoke, people were to do as told and not refuse as this man had done.

### c. NO MARK ON THE FOREHEAD

As was noted in chapter 1, some scholars believe this episode gives reason for thinking of prophets as having a special mark on their face. The theory is that it was this mark that the prophet uncovered to make his identity apparent to Ahab. This conclusion does not follow, however, for the prophet simply wanted to disguise himself as he told the allegorical story to the king. He apparently did not want the king to know who it was doing the telling. Why the king did recognize him when he removed the disguising ashes is not revealed. It may be that he was known otherwise to the king, so that Ahab simply saw him as a person of past acquaintance. The story says nothing regarding any special mark on his face or forehead, as is true also of all the other stories concerning prophets.

### d. COMMAND OF RESPECT

It may be added that, though this prophet was likely young, still the king gave respect to his message. He did not rebuke the young man for bringing it nor deny its force; but he was in fact displeased and sullen as he turned away, realizing the impact of what the prophet had said.

## C. MICAIAH

The third prophet from Ahab's day is Micaiah, who came into our discussion regarding true and false prophets in chapter 7 (I Kings 22:1–39; II Chron. 18:1–34). Mention of Micaiah comes regarding the third contact of Ahab with the Aramaeans to the north. Though Ben-hadad had been severely defeated at the time of the second contact, he came against Israel once more. Ben-hadad was in a sufficiently strong position to wage this further war, probably because Ahab had been so lenient at the time of the second defeat.

### 1. The work

The basic outline of the story was set forth in chapter 7. Jehoshaphat, the good king of Judah, had come north to Israel to visit Ahab. While he was there, Ahab, remembering his earlier victory over Ben-hadad, suggested that the two of them go together in an offensive battle to recover the city of Ramoth-gilead and its surrounding area from control by the Aramaeans. Jehoshaphat said he was willing but that he desired enquiry be made as to the will of God. Ahab called his four hundred prophets together to ask their counsel, and they indicated that he should go ahead with his plans. Jehoshaphat apparently realized the kind of prophets these were and asked if there was not "a prophet of the LORD besides, that we might inquire of him" (I Kings 22:7). Ahab said there was, namely, Micaiah, but that he didn't like him since the man never prophesied good concerning him. Jehoshaphat insisted that Micaiah be called.

When Micaiah first arrived, he pretended to speak as he knew the king desired, but immediately Ahab recognized insincerity on his part and told him to say "nothing but that which is true in the name of the LORD" (22:16). Micaiah then replied, "I saw all Israel scattered upon the hills, as sheep that have not a shepherd" (22:17), indicating that Ahab would be defeated and killed if he carried out his plan. He continued by telling Ahab how he knew this was God's true word. He said he saw God in heaven ask the host of heaven, "Who shall persuade Ahab that he may go up and fall at Ramoth-gilead?" (22:20). He said further that he saw a spirit come forth and say that he would be "a lying spirit in the mouth of all his prophets." God indicated that He approved this suggestion.

Zedekiah, one of the four hundred false prophets, now stepped forward to strike Micaiah on the cheek and say, "Which way went the Spirit of the LORD from me to speak unto thee?" (22:24), indicating his displeasure at Micaiah's words. Ahab also was angry and responded that Micaiah should be taken away and placed in prison until Ahab came home safely from the battle. To this Micaiah replied, "If thou return at all in peace, the LORD hath not spoken by me" (22:28). Ahab and Jehoshaphat then went to battle, with the result that Jehoshaphat was nearly killed and Ahab did suffer a fatal wound.

Though this is the only reference to Micaiah in Scripture, the story gives evidence that Micaiah had spoken to Ahab prior to this and probably on several occasions. When Jehoshaphat asked if there was not another prophet that they might look to, Ahab readily knew of Micaiah and also of the type of message Micaiah would give. Apparently the messenger that was sent for Micaiah also knew of him because he tried to persuade him ahead of time to speak favorably, rather than the way he knew Micaiah normally spoke. One should think of Micaiah, then, as a prophet who was ready to give God's true word to Ahab whenever asked, and who did so at least on several occasions.

## 2. The person

### a. SPIRITUAL STATUS

Micaiah was definitely a man of high spiritual standing. This is indicated by the kind of message he brought to the king. It was an unwanted message that was sure to displease the ruler. The type of person who would have been entrusted with such a word and been willing to give it must have been a true man of God. Further, Micaiah was ready to suffer imprisonment for the word God gave him. Ahab indicated that because of the message, Micaiah should be put in prison until the battle was won; Micaiah's sole response was that if Ahab returned from the battle in peace, then God had not spoken by him.

Another indication comes from the nature of the revelation God gave to Micaiah. Micaiah, apparently in a vision, had been privileged to view an actual scene in heaven where God had directed a spirit to go and be a lying spirit in the mouth of Ahab's prophets.[7] One may be certain that no prophet who was spiritually immature would have been granted such an intimate glimpse of the heavenly realm.

[7]This spirit was likely a demon whom God permitted to carry out this mission. The story of Job is clear that Satan (and probably his hosts) does have access to heaven. Evil spirits, not the angels of God, tell lies.

The story of Micaiah leads us to question where Elijah was at this time. Since Ahab did not like either man, why did he think only of Micaiah, and why did he speak of Micaiah as being the "one man" in Israel that would satisfy Jehoshaphat? The question can be asked also in reference to the unnamed prophet, who had earlier spoken words of encouragement to Ahab in connection with the two campaigns of Ben-hadad. The answer is probably found simply in the matter of the proximity of each to the city of Samaria. Micaiah quite clearly lived right in the city, so that the messenger was able to summon him without any great lapse of time. Elijah, however, probably lived in the area of his schools—located at Gilgal, Bethel, and Jericho—and the unnamed prophet may well have lived outside the capital city also.

## b. COURAGE

Micaiah was a man of courage. He had been so earlier, as he had gained his reputation with Ahab for being a prophet who did not speak well concerning him; and he continued in this vein in the instance here set forth. Though four hundred prophets had spoken a message that was pleasing to the king, and though Micaiah knew Ahab wanted to hear a similar message from him, Micaiah still gave the contrasting word God desired. Micaiah's courage was sufficient not only to give the message but also to suffer imprisonment in behalf of it should this be necessary, as it proved to be.

## c. LOYALTY TO THE KING

Contrary to what Ahab thought, Micaiah was loyal to him as a proper subject. Because Micaiah had earlier spoken words which did not please the king, Ahab had thought he was against him. And now, after Micaiah gave his word that Israel would be scattered as sheep without a shepherd, Ahab again complained to Jehoshaphat that Micaiah was against him. But this was not so. In his reply Micaiah explained why he had said what he had.

He began his statement with the words, "Hear thou therefore the word of the LORD" (22:19). The word *therefore* (*lakhen*) is significant. By it Micaiah was saying that, because the king thought he was speaking intentionally against him (which was not true), Micaiah would tell him why it was he had to speak as he had. He did not have to give this reason; the fact that he did indicates he wanted the king to realize that God had indeed given him the word and that it was not just himself speaking. Actually he was more loyal to the king than were the four hundred prophets, for what he said was true: Ahab would indeed be killed if he went to battle. The prophets, who said he would not, really were not his friends.

### d. APPRECIATION FOR LITERARY FORM

There is reason to believe that Micaiah had an appreciation for literary form. Three of his replies show this. In verse 17, where he indicated that Ahab would die, rather than stating this directly he spoke of it by using a metaphor, "I saw all Israel scattered upon the hills, as sheep that have not a shepherd." Ahab knew the meaning, but Micaiah had said it in a poetic way. In fact, Micaiah may have been referring to Numbers 27:16, 17, where at the time of the appointment of Joshua, Moses urged God to select a man who would lead Israel so that they would "be not as sheep which have no shepherd."

Then in verse 25, Micaiah answered Zedekiah, one of the false four hundred, with the words, "Behold, thou shalt see in that day, when thou shalt go into an inner chamber to hide thyself." He might have responded to Zedekiah quite differently when the false prophet asked, "Which way went the Spirit of the LORD from me to speak unto thee?" Micaiah spoke, however, in this poetic way, indicating that Zedekiah would know the truth of the matter in the day when danger came upon him so that he would have to hide in order to save himself. The Scriptures do not record the day on which this happened, but no doubt in due time all these false prophets did perish in punishment for the way they brought the purported message of God to Ahab.

Still further, in verse 28, Micaiah replied to Ahab in the following words, "If thou return at all in peace, the LORD hath not spoken by me." Ahab had just given directions for Micaiah's imprisonment, and one might expect the prophet to have stated directly that he would not change his words just because the king had ordered his imprisonment. He used, however, a poetic expression to give the response, which said all that was necessary.

## D. ZECHARIAH

We now leave the kingdom of Israel in the north and go to Judah in the south, to the reign of Joash, who followed Ahab by about twenty years. The prophet in view is Zechariah, who ministered in the closing years of the reign of Joash. It should be understood that this Zechariah is not the same as the postexilic writing prophet, who wrote the Book of Zechariah.

### 1. The work

Zechariah is mentioned as he brought a word of rebuke to King Joash (II Chron. 24:17–22). By the time in view, the great high priest, Jehoiada, had died, and Joash, now ruling by himself, had come under the influence of wrong advisors. This king, who had ruled so well as long as Jehoiada had lived, now actually turned from God to serve false deities. The result was that "wrath came upon Judah and Jerusalem for this their trespass" (24:18).

God then sent prophets to give warning to the king and his advisors, and among them was Zechariah. He was the son of the high priest, Jehoiada, and apparently followed closely in his father's footsteps. It is stated that "the Spirit of God came upon" him at this time and he "stood above the people, and said unto them, Thus saith God, Why transgress ye the commandments of the LORD, that ye cannot prosper? because ye have forsaken the LORD, he hath also forsaken you" (24:20). The phrase, "stood above the people," is explained in verse 21, which indicates that he was in the "court of the house of the LORD." The people he addressed apparently were standing in the lower outer court, and he took a position on the steps which led up to the higher inner court as he spoke to them.

Because of these words of rebuke, the king gave an order that Zechariah should be stoned, and the people did stone him, even in the court of the temple. It is hard to believe that Joash, who had earlier given the splendid orders for repairing the temple, actually gave this shameful directive. It is even more surprising since Zechariah was Jehoiada's son. Joash had been so dependent upon Jehoiada all during his reign, and now he treated his son in this manner. Certainly the power of sin and the hold Satan can have on a person are demonstrated here most forcefully. Accordingly, verse 22 indicates, "Thus Joash the king remembered not the kindness which Jehoiada his father had done to him, but slew his son."

That God held this action by Joash and the people strongly against them is revealed by Jesus' words regarding the occasion in Matthew 23:35 (see Luke 11:51). Here Jesus referred to the "blood of Zacharias, son of Barachias, whom ye slew between the temple and the altar."[8] Jesus specifically identified the place of Zechariah's death as being "between the temple and the altar." The thought is that it occurred between the temple proper, where the Holy of Holies and the Holy Place were located, and the great brazen altar just outside. This means the murder transpired in a very sacred area of the temple. No doubt this added to its blameworthiness and constituted a main reason why Jesus used it as an illustration in his denouncement of woe upon the Pharisees of His day.

When Zechariah died he said, "The LORD look upon it and require it"

---

[8]That this was the occasion Jesus had in mind is made highly probable by the description of the spot where the murder took place. That Zechariah is called the "son of Barachias" here rather than the son of Jehoiada may be explained in one of two ways. Jehoiada may have had more than one name, or this Barachias could have been the immediate father of Zechariah and Jehoiada his grandfather, something made quite possible since Jehoiada was 130 years old when he died.

(24:22). The vengeance he thus called for was brought upon King Joash in two ways: first by his defeat shortly after by the Aramaeans of Damascus (24:23, 24), and second by his own death as a result of a conspiracy on the part of his servants (24:25).

There is a clue that Zechariah may not have been a full-time prophet. The "Spirit of God" is said to have come upon him to give the message that he delivered. According to the discussion of chapter 6, this is an indication that the prophet concerned was not filled by the Spirit continually, as normal for full-time prophets, but needed this experience for only one occasion. Zechariah, being a son or possibly grandson of Jehoiada, was a priest, and no doubt this was his primary work. It may well be that God used him only on this one occasion in the capacity of a prophet. Perhaps the fact that he was the son of the great Jehoiada was a reason for God so employing him at this time.

## 2. The person

### a. SPIRITUAL STATUS

There are again definite marks of spiritual strength that appear in Zechariah. For one thing the message he brought was a message of rebuke. The ungodly advisors of Joash had persuaded the king to act in a sinful way and Zechariah arose to give reprimand. This was not an easy assignment, and God would not have entrusted it to just anyone.

There is also the indication that the Spirit of God came upon him in the instance concerned. This is similar to what was seen earlier in respect to Azariah and Jahaziel, and a similar conclusion can be made. Zechariah would not have been empowered if God had not considered him a choice servant. Still further, since regular prophets were available to bring the message (see 24:19), God evidently saw Zechariah as particularly suitable for the task. If God by-passed prophets, the man He chose must have had special qualifications, and among these must have been a high spiritual standing.

### b. COURAGE

The work Zechariah did points to remarkable courage on his part. It would not have been easy to stand before this assembly of people, all of whom were opposed to what he was to say, and indicate God's word of rebuke. And he did not position himself in a way so that only a few would hear him; rather he stood above the people where all could see him. Thus he took a fearless position, one in which he could be well heard and understood. Courage truly was displayed.

c. WILLINGNESS TO SUFFER

This act of courage was great enough to include a willingness to suffer. Zechariah did not know when he arose before the assembly what the result would be, but he found out as soon as he had finished. The people together, at the command of the king, stoned him with stones. In that this stoning took place within the very sacred court of the temple, the people clearly moved from the lower outer court where they were at the time of hearing Zechariah's speech into the inner court for the actual stoning. One has to be amazed at the brazenness demonstrated. Though numerous prophets suffered imprisonment for their ministry, Zechariah is one of few who experienced actual death.

## E.  A PROPHET

The last prophet to consider in this chapter is also not designated by name. He is referred to by two general designations—"a man of God" (*'ish ha-'elohim*) and "a prophet" (*nabhi'*). The story regarding him falls in the reign of Amaziah and concerns the occasion when Amaziah went to war against the Edomites to the south of Judah (II Chron. 25:5–16; cf. II Kings 14:1–7). It is possible that two different persons are in mind, since the designation *man of God* comes in the early part of the story and *a prophet* towards its close. Since, however, both designations are involved in the one continuing story, and since prophets otherwise have been found to be designated by differing forms of reference, it seems likely that the same person is in view.

### 1.  The work

The work of this prophet consisted in giving a word of instruction to Amaziah and later one of rebuke. Amaziah, desiring to go in strength against Edom to the south, hired one hundred thousand mercenary soldiers from Israel to the north, paying one hundred talents of silver. The prophet approached the king and said that he should not have done this and should now let them all go home, for God would grant him a victory without them. When Amaziah asked what he should do in respect to the money he had spent for them, the prophet simply said that God was able to give him much more than this if he would obey.

Amaziah followed the prophet's advice and sent the Israelites home. Then he moved to the warfare with his own troops. He was successful and defeated the Edomites, killing ten thousand and taking ten thousand captive;

on the way home he even killed these, throwing them from the top of a cliff. Along with this success, however, he sinned in bringing home some of the idols of the Edomites and setting them up for himself to worship, even bowing down and burning incense to them (II Chron. 25:14).

This occasion called for the rebuke of the prophet. The anger of God was stirred, and He sent the man to Amaziah with these words, "Why hast thou sought after the gods of the people, which could not deliver their own people out of thine hand?" (25:15). In other words, Amaziah had not only sinned in bringing idols home to worship but he had acted foolishly. He had honored so-called gods who could not deliver their own country from the power of Israel's God. The question posed through the prophet was a telling one that Amaziah could not answer. Not being able to answer, he rebuked the prophet for presuming to give counsel to the king. The prophet then ceased speaking, but not before adding the words, "I know that God hath determined to destroy thee, because thou hast done this, and hast not hearkened unto my counsel" (25:16).

## 2. The person

### a. SPIRITUAL STATUS

This prophet also shows a clear mark of spiritual strength. He brought a message of sharp rebuke. He told the king directly that he had done wrong in bringing false gods back to Israel. The situation made this rebuke dangerous, too. The king had just been successful in Edom and would have been in a mood to receive plaudits, not rebuke. The prophet must have realized this, but still, at God's command, he brought the straightforward reprimand. Again one must say that God would not have entrusted such a responsibility to a prophet who was not highly approved.

### b. COURAGE

This prophet showed courage in the message he brought. This is indicated first by the type of instruction he gave Amaziah at the beginning of the story. Amaziah had spent a hundred talents of silver to hire soldiers from Israel. This had taken considerable effort and work on his part as well as the large expenditure of money. He surely was not inclined to send all these home and lose the money, but still the prophet came and gave him that word. Besides this, the message of rebuke just noted took great courage. The prophet would have known the danger involved in bringing such a word, when the king had just won a victory, but this did not stop him. In fact, when the king warned him, he still told Amaziah directly that God had determined to destroy him for his sin.

### c. COMMAND OF RESPECT

The fact that Amaziah carried out the instructions of the man, when he told him to send the hundred thousand soldiers of Israel home, shows that the king respected his word. He must have been a man who spoke with authority. It would not have been easy for Amaziah to send these men back home, not only because he would be losing money but also admitting that he had made a mistake in hiring them. No one likes to admit mistakes and surely not kings.

In the word of rebuke as well, respect was shown to the prophet in that the king did not attempt to answer the penetrating question the prophet asked. He simply resorted to a word of warning not to speak in this way. Had he not respected the significance of the question and especially the forceful-ness of the prophet in asking it, he would have no doubt attempted to defend himself. He did not do this, but merely resorted to a display of kingly authority in giving warning to the man who dared thus to speak.

### d. WILLINGNESS TO SUFFER

This prophet also gives evidence of willingness to suffer. Even though the king warned him of possible harm for his word of rebuke, the prophet continued to speak long enough to tell the king that God was determined to destroy him. He thus demonstrated his conviction that it was more important to deliver God's word than to escape punishment. This man also is to be highly commended.

# 15

# The Reigns from Jehoram to Jehoash: Elisha

Our attention now reverts to the northern nation and to the prophet Elisha, who followed Elijah. Elisha's ministry began with the translation of his master Elijah, early in the reign of Jehoram. Jehoram was the second son of Ahab, succeeding Ahaziah, the first son, who ruled only two years. The scriptural account of Elisha is presented in the form of eighteen short stories, all but two of which transpired in the reign of Jehoram, who ruled twelve years (II Kings 3:1). The two stories not from Jehoram's time fell in the reign of Jehoash. In between, both Jehu and Jehoahaz ruled but nothing is told about Elisha during their time. In giving scriptural background for the ministry of Elisha, then, it will be in order to dwell mainly on the reign of Jehoram and then a little on the reign of Jehoash.

Religiously, Jehoram continued in the worship of Baal as his father and mother had done. One might think otherwise from a notice in II Kings 3:2, which says he removed an image of Baal that his father had made. But other matters indicate that this was only the removal of an image and not the removal of Baal worship itself. At a later time, for instance, Jehoram was ironically bidden by Elisha to seek help from the prophets of his father and mother in a time of need, implying that this was his normal practice (II Kings 3:13). Also, Jehu, his successor, later found it necessary to slay the prophets of Baal when he came to the throne (II Kings 10:19–28). That Jehoram could be expected to have continued the Baal cult follows from the fact that his domineering mother, Jezebel, still lived throughout his rule (II Kings 9:30, 33).

A historical matter to notice from Jehoram's reign relates to a military engagement with Moab located east of the Dead Sea. Mesha, Moab's king, refused to send tribute that had been imposed years earlier by Omri. Jehoram missed the economic advantage the tribute afforded and took steps to force its continuance, seeking the aid of Jehoshaphat, king of Judah. As the combined armies rounded the southern end of the Dead Sea, apparently seeking to attack Moab by surprise from the south, they ran out of water. Only by Elisha's timely intervention were they spared. The armies were successful against Moab for a time but then, through a dramatic sacrifice of Mesha's eldest son, Jehoram and Jehoshaphat were somehow forced to withdraw without accomplishing their objective.[1]

Jehoram also had numerous encounters with the Aramaeans of Damascus to the north. At one time the Aramaeans came in large number and laid siege to the capital city, Samaria. Being maintained for some time, the siege brought starvation conditions to the city (II Kings 6:28, 29). Elisha was blamed by Jehoram, likely because of some earlier warning that the prophet had given, but the prophet then revealed that everyone would have all the food he desired on the following day. This came true when God caused the Aramaeans to flee in the night and leave behind abundant food and other goods. The result was that the people did in truth have the nourishment they needed, just as Elisha had predicted.

A final contact with the Aramaeans led to Jehoram's death. Like Ahab his father, he met the Aramaeans in battle at Ramoth-gilead, and like him too he had help in the encounter from a king of Judah, now Ahaziah, suggesting that the formal alliance between the two countries still existed. Jehoram was seriously wounded and returned to Jezreel to recover. Later, Ahaziah, who had returned to Judah after the battle, came to Jezreel to visit him, and while he was there he became involved in a storm of destruction brought by Jehu, which resulted in the death of both kings.

To understand the kingship of Jehoash, background must be taken from the previous reigns of Jehu and Jehoahaz. During the reign of Jehu, the relatively strong position of the Omri dynasty was lost. Jehu slew great numbers of the leaders of that dynasty, leaving him apparently with second-rate help in governing his kingdom. As a result, his twenty-eight years of leadership were marked by continued unrest and turmoil. Hazael, new king in Damascus, succeeded in taking over from Israel all its territories across the Jordan and in apparently invading much of Israel proper on the west of the Jordan. By the time of Jehoahaz, in fact, the Aramaeans had brought suffi-

[1]This occasion is documented by the Moabite Stone: for text and discussion see *Ancient Near Eastern Texts*, ed. James B. Pritchard, p. 320; for the same and a picture see *Documents from Old Testament Times*, ed. D. Winton Thomas, pp. 195–199.

cient humiliation to be able to dictate how many horses, chariots, and footmen Israel's king could have in his army (II Kings 13:7).[2]

During Jehu's reign also, Israel suffered greatly from an invasion by the Assyrians.[3] For the sixteenth time, Shalmaneser III crossed the Euphrates in a military campaign. He succeeded in leading his army all the way to Damascus, effecting extensive damage to the city though without actually capturing it. He then was able to force Jehu in Israel to pay heavy tribute. On his famous Black Obelisk,[4] found in 1846 in Nimrud, Shalmaneser lists the tribute and depicts in bas-relief the Israelite king bowing low in submission presenting his payment. Though Shalmaneser did not bring actual destruction on Israel, the heavy tribute he demanded was humiliating and economically oppressive.

Jehoahaz succeeded his father and reigned seventeen years. Little is said regarding him except some intimations that he suffered further humiliation before Hazael for a time, but then began to make a recovery in national strength. This recovery came as a result of a military campaign by the Assyrian, Adad-nirari III, who almost completely destroyed the city of Damascus in the year 803 B.C.[5] By the time of this attack, Ben-hadad III, son and successor of Hazael, had ascended the throne in Damascus. Israel also was forced to pay tribute to Assyria but did not suffer the same physical loss as Damascus. The result was that Israel was able to recover some of the land lost to the northern neighbor.

The son and successor of Jehoahaz was Jehoash. During his rule, Israel made rapid strides on the road of recovery in strength. Soon after assuming office, Jehoash was promised a resurgence in military position by Elisha. This promise will constitute one of the last episodes we will notice from Elisha's life. As the result of the promise, Jehoash was enabled to bring defeat on the Aramaeans three different times and recover all the cities that Damascus had taken earlier from Israel (II Kings 13:25).

## A. THE WORK OF ELISHA

Elisha's work was basically the same as that of Elijah: resistance to the worship of Baal-Melqart. It was suggested earlier that Elisha may have come

[2]He was permitted only fifty horsemen, ten chariots, and 10,000 footmen, a marked contrast to the 2,000 chariots Ahab had brought to Qarqar.

[3]This is known only from Assyrian records left by Shalmaneser III. For his inscription see *Ancient Near Eastern Texts*, pp. 276–281.

[4]This four-sided black limestone pillar stands six-and-a-half feet high, with five rows of bas-reliefs and explanatory inscriptions on all sides. In the second row of one side appears Jehu, the only extant representation of an Israelite king. For text, see *Ancient Near Eastern Texts*, p. 280; for pictures see *The Ancient Near East in Pictures*, ed. James B. Pritchard, figs. 351–355.

[5]For the text of Adad-nirari III, see *Ancient Near Eastern Texts*, pp. 281–282; also *Documents from Old Testament Times*, pp. 50–52.

from a rather wealthy family, since he was plowing with a team of oxen in a field where twelve other teams preceded him at the time of his call. If so, he contrasted on this count with his master, Elijah, who had been raised in the poor area of Gilead near the desert. Elisha's decision to follow Elijah was final and decisive. He killed his own oxen to prepare a farewell feast for relatives and friends, and he used the wood from his tools as fuel for the fire (I Kings 19:21). Clearly, he did not plan to come back to use them again.

Though having the same objectives in view as Elijah, Elisha's manner in reaching them was somewhat different. In keeping with his contrasting background, he was more at home in cities and was often in the company of kings. Also, whereas Elijah had been more a man of moods, either strongly courageous or despairing to the point of death, Elisha was self-controlled and even-tempered. Elisha never staged dramatic contests nor sulked in a desert. It may be, too, that Elisha was more interested in the needs of people, for many of his miracles were for the purpose of aiding and giving relief to persons in difficulty.

As indicated, the stories from Elisha's life come almost entirely from the reign of Jehoram. No doubt, similar stories could have been included from the reigns of Jehu, Jehoahaz, and Jehoash. Those given are undoubtedly intended to be representative. It is probable, too, that many more could have been included from the reign of Jehoram, and so one may believe that those recorded are very select. An enumeration of them indicates a wide variety of experience.

## 1. Dividing the Jordan (II Kings 2:13, 14)

Elisha's work began immediately after Elijah's homegoing.[6] After receiving Elijah's mantle, he returned to the Jordan River, and there, as his master had done shortly before, he struck the water with the mantle, and it parted. One may believe that, as he crossed through the pathway thus formed, he did so with emotions running high, realizing that his request for Elijah's Spirit, made shortly before, had been granted and that he now was to continue the work of his master. The fifty sons of the prophets, who had witnessed the entire occasion, immediately recognized Elisha's new position as they exclaimed, "The spirit of Elijah doth rest on Elisha."

## 2. Purifying the spring of Jericho (2:19–22)

When Elisha came to Jericho, he found the people complaining of the quality of the water flowing from their spring. He asked them to supply him

[6]See chap. 13, pp. 218–219.

with a new bowl into which he placed salt. Then he cast the salt into the spring and said, "Thus saith the LORD, I have healed these waters; there shall not be from thence any more death or barren land" (2:21). The result was that the waters were made sweet, and the flow from this spring today still provides excellent water for the city of Jericho.

### 3. Cursing young people (2:23, 24)

As Elisha made his way from Jericho to Bethel, an incident occurred which has caused criticism of the great prophet. "Little children" came out of the city of Bethel, met Elisha, and "mocked him and said unto him, Go up, thou bald-head; go up, thou bald-head." Elisha turned and cursed the young mockers "in the name of the LORD," with the result that "there came forth two she-bears out of the wood, and tare forty and two children of them."

The story becomes understandable, however, in view of certain clarifications. For one thing, the word translated "little children" (*ne'arim*) can also mean "young men." Those involved were probably teen-agers. Then it is significant that these boys were from Bethel, the center of calf worship for many years past, where a bitter spirit against God and any true prophet of God could be expected. Likely, news of Elijah's ascension had already reached Bethel and so, as Elisha now came there, these young men came out from the city, parroting thoughts they had heard their parents speak, and urged Elisha to go up in similar fashion as they had heard Elijah did. Elisha probably was naturally bald. This accounts for the particular designation used for him. Elisha's curse of the young men, then, really stood for the curse of God against the anti-God spirit present in Bethel. All Bethel would have soon learned what had happened.

### 4. Supplying water for three kings (3:1–27)

It was probably shortly after this when Elisha was used to provide water for three kings and their armies in the southern part of Moab. The occasion involved the third time when King Jehoshaphat of Judah allied himself with the house of Omri in a way displeasing to God. Jehoram asked Jehoshaphat to go with him against the Moabites to compel the Moabites to continue sending him a large tribute year by year (3:4). Jehoshaphat agreed and the two kings, joined by the king of Edom as they made their journey, found themselves in southern Moab without water. Learning that Elisha was in camp (no doubt because God had instructed him ahead of time to be there to take care of this need), the three kings came to the prophet to let their need be known. Elisha listened and then told them to leave his tent and provide a minstrel to play before him apparently so that he might be brought into a proper attitude to hear from God.[7] This was done and God did grant him a revelation—the kings should have ditches dug in the valley and the valley would then be filled with water. He told this information to the kings, they did as instructed, water did come down from the mountains and fill the ditches, and the army then had water to drink.

An interesting sidelight to this occasion is that Elisha mocked King Jehoram that he had not gone to the Baal prophets for help in getting this water (since Baal was supposed to be the god of storm and rain) but instead had come to Elisha, the prophet of Israel's true God.

### 5. Oil for a widow (4:1–7)

After this Elisha discovered that a widow of one of the students who had been training in his prophet's school was at the point of having to sell her two children to creditors to pay debts she owed. Elisha instructed her to borrow many empty vessels, bring them into her house, and then pour out from the one jar of oil she had into the empty vessels. When she did this, she found that the oil continued to flow until all the vessels were filled. Elisha then told her to sell this oil and use the money to pay the debt she owed. The money proved to be enough, not only to pay the debt, but for her and the children to live on afterwards.

### 6. The Shunammite's son (4:8–37)

Passing through Shunem[8] Elisha made the acquaintance of a "great woman" (great in character) who proposed to her husband that they build a room for the prophet's use in his travels through the land. It was furnished nicely for him, and Elisha appreciated it so much that he foretold to the childless couple that in one year they would have a son. The child was born, but a few years later was suddenly taken ill and died. The woman immediately went to where Elisha was on Mount Carmel and besought his help. Elisha first sent his servant, Gehazi, but Gehazi was unable to restore the young boy. Elisha then came, prayed over the lad, and stretched himself upon the body of the child until life came once again. The mother responded with great rejoicing of heart.

[7]Cf. chap. 3, p. 49.
[8]Shunem was located near the southwest slope of Mount Moreh in the Esdraelon Plain.

## 7. Poisonous food (4:38–41)

A famine now struck the land (cf. 8:1, 2), and food became scarce. Coming to Gilgal, where apparently one of the prophetic schools was located, Elisha asked that food be prepared. One of the sons of the prophets mistakenly brought in poisonous wild gourds. When this became known, Elisha commanded that meal be cast into the pot, and this made the food harmless so that all could eat.

## 8. Multiplying loaves and grain (4:42–44)

It was probably during this same famine that a man came from Baal-shalisha bringing twenty barley loaves and some grain for the young men to eat. The total amount of the food was very small to feed as many as a hundred men, and therefore Elisha's servant objected with the question, "What, should I set this before a hundred men?" (4:43). At Elisha's direction, however, the food was indeed set before the hundred students and it proved to be enough, and some was even left over after all had eaten. This was clearly a miracle of multiplying food, much in the pattern of what Jesus did on two occasions in His day (Matt. 14:15–21; 15:32–38).

## 9. Healing of Naaman (5:1–27)

Elisha now became involved with the commander of a foreign army, Naaman, who may have led the earlier battles of Damascus against Ahab. He had become a leper; and a little servant girl, who had earlier been taken captive from Israel, told him of Elisha and his power. Since there was now peace between Damascus and Israel, Ben-hadad sent Naaman to Jehoram, king of Israel, that he might be healed. This put Jehoram in panic at first, but then Elisha learned of the situation and asked that Naaman be sent to him. Without so much as going out to see Naaman, in spite of Naaman's high position, Elisha gave instructions for him simply to wash seven times in the Jordan River to bring about his healing. At first Naaman was angry and refused to do so, but a wise servant pointed out that he had really nothing to lose. When Naaman did wash, he was healed and immediately returned to express his gratitude to the Israelite prophet.

Elisha refused to take a liberal present that was offered, but later Elisha's servant, Gehazi, ran after Naaman to ask that a present be given after all. The servant wanted this only for himself, and when he returned to Elisha, who had been informed by God miraculously of what Gehazi had done, the prophet rebuked him and told him that as punishment the leprosy of Naaman would now become his. This did happen, and Gehazi was a leper apparently for the rest of his life.

### 10. Saving a lost axe-head (6:1-7)

When the building where one of the prophetic schools met became too small (indicating an apparent increase in number of students), the students asked Elisha for permission to build a larger one. He gave the permission and then went with the students to the Jordan to cut wood for the new building. While occupied in the work, one of the students lost the head of his axe in the water. The young man called to Elisha for help in recovering it, and Elisha threw a stick into the water and immediately the axe-head came to the surface. He told the young man to take it up, much to his relief, for he had borrowed the axe.

### 11. Aiding Jehoram (6:8-12)

It was about this time that Ben-hadad of Damascus made numerous attacks against Jehoram in Israel. Each time he did Elisha aided Jehoram by foretelling where the enemy would strike. This infuriated Ben-hadad, for he thought that one of his own people was betraying him to the Israelite king. But one of his servants informed him that it was not one of his own people but Elisha, prophet in Israel, who was telling the Israelite ruler Ben-hadad's plans.

### 12. Episode at Dothan (6:13-23)

Ben-hadad now determined to seize Elisha and sent an army to capture him at Dothan, where the prophet was residing. Elisha's servant became fearful when he saw an entire army surrounding the city, but Elisha asked God to open his eyes that he might see how much greater God's protecting forces were than the enemy soldiers. Elisha asked God then to strike the enemy with blindness, and Elisha led the entire army the ten miles from Dothan south to the capital, Samaria. When the enemy was allowed to see once again, King Jehoram asked Elisha what he should do with them, and Elisha simply said to feed them and let them return to their master. One can imagine the shock and amazement of Ben-hadad as his troops thus returned to give report of their experience. It is significantly said, "So the bands of Syria came no more into the land of Israel" (6:23).

### 13. Starvation and food in Samaria (6:24—7:20)

In time, however, the army of Damascus did return and laid siege to the capital city of Samaria. Starvation conditions resulted in the capital, so that cannibalism was resorted to by some of the people. Jehoram blamed Elisha and proposed to execute the prophet. In response, Elisha promised that on the following day there would be adequate food for all the people, a promise that was mocked by the king's attendant.

This promise came true as a result of flight by the enemy troops, who imagined that they heard the approaching sounds of an Egyptian army bringing relief to the Israelites. Four lepers went out to the enemy camp, believing they would be no worse off by throwing themselves on the mercy of the Aramaeans than by staying where they were, and they found that the enemy had fled leaving abundant foodstuffs and other material behind. They reported the good news of their discovery in the city, and people hurried out through the gate to get the food. As they did so, the king's attendant, who had scoffed the day before, was killed in the crush of traffic. Elisha had predicted this would happen, and his word again saw fulfillment.

### 14. Return of the Shunammite's property (8:1–6)

It was about this time when the famine, that had started seven years earlier, came to an end. At its beginning, Elisha had advised the Shunammite woman to go down into Philistia and remain there for the duration of the famine, which would last seven years.[9] She did so and when the seven years were over returned to ask the king that her property be restored to her. She arrived before the king just as Gehazi, servant of Elisha, was telling the king about Elisha's raising the Shunammite's son.[10] When the Shunammite appeared, he told the king that this was the woman of whom he spoke, and as a result the king was made sympathetic to the woman's request and her property was duly restored.

[9]Philistia had level, fertile lowlands which apparently produced crops of better quality during these years than did the hilly land of Israel.
[10]That Gehazi was here acting as Elisha's servant may indicate that the earlier story of Naaman, when Gehazi was made a leper, happened after this.

### 15. Elisha and Hazael (8:7–15; cf. I Kings 19:15)

Sometime later, Elisha journeyed north to Damascus to inform Hazael that he would succeed Ben-hadad as the next king of Damascus. This was actually a fulfillment of an instruction God gave to Elijah years before (I Kings 19:15). Ben-hadad, now ill and learning that Elisha had come to Damascus, sent his attendant Hazael to enquire if he would recover from the illness. Elisha's response was that the king might recover from the illness but that he would surely die. Then looking at Hazael the prophet began to weep. Hazael enquired the reason, and Elisha indicated it was because Hazael would become king and would bring terrible destruction upon Israel. Hazael at the time protested, but in later years he did this very thing. When Elisha had departed, Hazael returned to Ben-hadad his master and smothered him so as to insure his own succession as king.

### 16. The anointing of Jehu (9:1–3; cf. I Kings 19:16)

The last action recorded for Elisha in Jehoram's reign concerns the carrying out of another of the orders given to Elijah years before. It was the anointing of Jehu to be successor to Jehoram. At the time, Jehu was a captain in Jehoram's army, and the Israelites had just experienced a defeat at the hands of the Aramaeans of Damascus at Ramoth-gilead. Elisha sent one of his young prophets in training to Ramoth-gilead to anoint Jehu as the next king and instruct him to destroy the family of Jehoram and in fact the whole house of Omri. Jehu did this, with the bloody details set forth in II Kings 9:14–10:28, thus indeed bringing the vengeance God had promised many years before.

### 17. Elisha and Jehoash (13:14–19)

The many years of the combined reigns of Jehu and Jehoahaz elapsed before the next recorded episode from Elisha's life occurred. It came early in the reign of Jehoash, when Elisha was ill and about to die. The king came to see him; Elisha told him to take a bow and arrows in hand, and then Elisha put his own hands on the king's hands. He told the king to shoot an arrow out the window, and when the king did so Elisha said, "The arrow of the LORD's deliverance, and the arrow of deliverance from Syria." Elisha then told the king to smite on the ground with the arrows he had in his hand. The king did this, but only three times; and Elisha showed disappointment. He indicated that now the king would smite the northern enemy only three times. The implication was that had he struck the ground more times he would have defeated the enemy more times.

### 18.  The raising of a dead man (13:20, 21)

The last recorded episode occurred after Elisha's death. As a burial party was in the act of burying another man, they saw an invading company of Moabites coming towards them. In panic they quickly put the body into the grave where Elisha had been buried, and, when his body touched the bones of Elisha, he came back to life and stood to his feet.[11]

In looking back over these miracles, one has to be impressed with their variety and number. Surely God used this prophet in a remarkable way. This fact, however, logically raises a question. Since other prophets equally great did not perform miracles, why did God empower Elisha, and also Elijah before him, to perform them? The answer must be that their day was a very crucial one in Israel's history. Baal worship had been brought in by Jezebel, and the land had few believing people and hardly any God-following prophets. Elijah and Elisha were among the leading prophets of the time, and God wanted them to be especially authenticated so that people could see that indeed they were true and that their message should be believed. These miracles were their credentials.

### B.  THE PERSON

#### 1.  Spiritual status

Several factors show that again a spiritually mature prophet is in view. Witness first the miracles. As indicated, that a prophet did not perform miracles was not necessarily a sign that he was not spiritual, but, on the other hand, the performance of many miracles was certainly a sign that he was. God would not have entrusted such power to a person who was not walking faithfully before Him. Moreover, it was not only the number of miracles that was significant in reference to Elisha, but the variety and kind of miracles. The waters of the Jordan were made to divide, a spring was purified, food

[11]Elisha's tomb was evidently of an open type in which more than one body might be buried.

was multiplied, and even a dead boy was raised to life. Whoever saw such miracles would have been impressed that the one who performed them was a true and remarkable prophet of God.

Elisha was willing to bring rebuke at times, when it would have been easier to speak another kind of message. This is illustrated when the three kings came to him in southern Moab to seek his help in obtaining water. He might have been flattered that the kings were willing to come to him, but his words show a clear rebuke, especially for Jehoram. He even told the kings to leave his presence and send a minstrel to play before him, so that the atmosphere might be made conducive to God's giving a revelation. In other words the kings themselves were contaminating the atmosphere and making it impossible for him to hear from God. Rebuke also was involved in his contact with the young men from Bethel, when he brought curses upon them. As noted, he was really reprimanding the people of the city for their worship at the golden calf center. Elisha did not hesitate to bring rebuke.

Still further, it is significant that God was pleased to respond when Elisha needed revelation. Honor was always involved when God was pleased to give revelation and this was even more true when revelation came in response to a person's request. In the instance just noted regarding the kings' need for water, Elisha waited before God for such revelation. It is true that he did not ask for it in so many words, but he did in his attitude, even having a minstrel come in to set a proper atmosphere for it. God recognized the attitude and did give the revelation in response.

Finally it is noteworthy that God honored Elisha even following his death. This is indicated by the resurrection of a man whose body simply touched the bones of Elisha. The incident, which would have been told far and wide, pointed out the high place God had been giving Elisha all during his life and that He wanted people to continue to recognize this even after Elisha's death.

## 2. Command of respect

Though the scriptural picture of Elisha does not show him to have been an austere person, still when he spoke others listened and gave him respect. This also is demonstrated by the incident in southern Moab when the three kings came to Elisha for water. Jehoram did not retort in anger to Elisha when rebuked for his worship of the Baal prophets, and all three kings seem to have readily left the prophet when he asked that they do so. They also provided the requested minstrel so that the prophet might hear from God.

Jehoram showed respect when on another occasion Elisha warned him regarding the attacks from Ben-hadad to the north. Each time Jehoram took note of the prophet's word and succeeded in thwarting the intention of Ben-hadad. It is also noteworthy that Jehoram was ready to give the Shunammite back her property, simply because of her relationship to Elisha.

One should not miss either the significance of the fact that both Hazael and Jehu, at the times of their anointing, readily accepted the authority of this man. The anointing of Jehu was actually done by a representative of Elisha, but still Jehu, realizing that the word came from Elisha, immediately moved to carry out the instructions given. And finally King Jehoash gave acknowledgment of the aged prophet's authority when he was told to shoot the arrow through the window, and later in accepting Elisha's word that he had done wrong in striking the ground only three times with the arrows.

### 3. Compassion

As one surveys the miracles that Elisha performed, he is struck with the element of compassion for people evidenced in them. It is true that Elisha called down a curse on the young men of Bethel, and one might conclude from this that he was not compassionate. In contrast, however, are the following: the purifying of a spring of water that people might drink; the provision of financial resources that a helpless widow might pay her debts; the request that God grant a son to the Shunammite, when she had first provided an upper room for the prophet's comfort; the removal of poison from food, when a man in ignorance had gathered toxic wild gourds; the multiplying of loaves and grain so that students might have food in a time of famine; the healing of a commander of a foreign army who had leprosy; the restoration of an axe-head for a young man who had borrowed the axe; and the free release of an enemy army from harm, that had come specifically to take his own life, when they were completely in his control. Compassion and interest in others were clearly a prominent characteristic of this likable man of God.

### 4. Indifference to wealth

Most people are overly affected by wealth. Because of a love for money, they act in ways and do things which are not commendable. Elisha was not like this. He readily left his affluent home and followed Elijah when called. To go with Elijah meant leaving all this and submitting to the meager life of a prophet. It is quite possible that Elijah, when he asked Elisha what he could do for him before he was taken home to heaven (II Kings 2:9), had in mind to offer Elisha the privilege of returning to his home. When Elisha responded that he wished a double portion of Elijah's Spirit, he not only indicated that he needed this empowerment, but that he did not wish the material things that others of his family knew.

A clear illustration of this is also given at the time Naaman came to him to be healed. When this man had experienced the remarkable restoration of his health, he actually urged Elisha to receive a large remuneration, consisting of "ten talents of silver, and six thousand pieces of gold, and ten changes of raiment" (II Kings 5:5). Such a gift would have been attractive to any person, but Elisha responded, "As the LORD liveth, before whom I stand, I will receive none. And he urged him to take it; but he refused" (5:16). Then, later, when Elisha's servant Gehazi ran after Naaman and asked for some of the gifts, Elisha rebuked the servant and pronounced that the leprosy which had been on Naaman would now come on him.

### 5. Courage

Though the characteristic of courage does not stand out in Elisha's life, still he clearly was a man who was courageous. When the three kings came to him in southern Moab, he did not hesitate to tell them exactly what the situation was though the message was unpleasant. At another time when Samaria was under terrible siege at the hands of the Aramaeans and Jehoram came to blame Elisha, the prophet did not show fear before the king, but first refused entrance to his messenger and then told Jehoram what he could expect on the morrow. Again he did not quiver before or cater to either the foreign commander Naaman or the foreign king-to-be Hazael. He simply told both the word of God as it had been given to him, without showing fear or favor. The time when he pronounced a curse on the young men at Bethel is also noteworthy. Certainly he knew that this would soon become known in Bethel and elsewhere and could bring ill feeling against him. He did not hesitate in giving the pronouncement, however, knowing it was necessary in order to show God's displeasure at the calf worship of Bethel.

### 6. Stability

Elisha highly respected his master Elijah, but he apparently was quite a different person than Elijah. One matter of difference concerned emotional attitudes. Elijah was a man of variant moods, but Elisha is never seen in extremes. He did not stage elaborate contests nor did he ask for God to take his life. He became neither overexuberant nor despondent. He was a man of stable emotions, able to enjoy remarkable success as well as endure occasions of difficulty without great change of attitude.

## 7. Energy

Still another characteristic is that Elisha was a man of energy. He was active in doing many things and going many places. He was involved not merely in one geographical area but could be found in northern Israel at Mount Carmel, staying at the home of the woman in Shunem, or confronting kings as far south as the southern region of Moab. Several of his miracles involved students in the prophetic schools, as apparently he moved continually from Gilgal to Bethel to Jericho, seeing to it that the schools continued to operate properly and had adequate provisions. Everywhere he went, one may be sure that he gave out God's word, urging people to repent and turn to God. The fact that his dead bones were used of God to give life to a man is probably representative of the work of Elisha all during his ministry. He was a person who was continually giving out life to people around him, as he urged them to do the will of God and thus experience the blessings of true life that only God can give.

# HISTORY CHART III

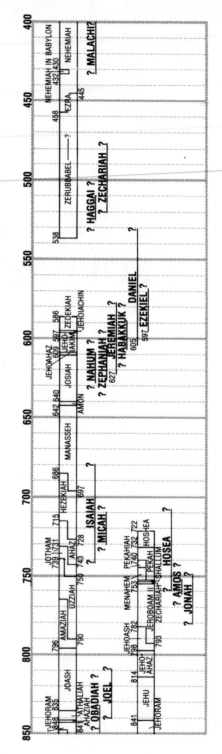

# Section Three

# THE WRITING PROPHETS

| 9th-Century Prophets | Chapter 16 Obadiah Joel |
|---|---|
| 8th-Century Prophets | Chapter 17 Hosea Amos Jonah |
| | Chapter 18 Isaiah Micah |
| 7th-Century Prophets | Chapter 19 Nahum Zephaniah Habakkuk |
| | Chapter 20 Jeremiah |
| Exilic Prophets | Chapter 21 Daniel Ezekiel |
| Postexilic Prophets | Chapter 22 Haggai Zechariah Malachi |

# 16

# Ninth-Century Prophets: Obadiah and Joel

We now come to consider the prophets who are the best known, the writing prophets. These prophets are those whom God used to write books, and their books constitute the prophetic section of the Old Testament. A study of these books is most worthwhile in itself, but there are many volumes that take up this type of enquiry. Our interest remains in the men themselves, the writers of the books, as it has been in the prior chapters.

The structure of the material concerning these men will take on a slightly different form now. One reason is that few of the writing prophets appear in the historical books of the Old Testament to provide information as to their manner of work. Some facts can be deduced from the books they wrote, but one does not often have historical incidents described in which they were involved. Because of this, the character of the men cannot be described in as much detail as has been possible regarding many of the earlier prophets, and sometimes the date of their ministry is left open to question.

A prime interest in this study is to impress on the reader the chronological sequence of the writing prophets. As was indicated in chapter 8, they were not evenly spaced in time but came in groups, and to understand any one prophet we must see him in the time in which he lived and in relation to his group. For this reason the chapters are set up according to the centuries in which the prophets lived, and each chapter shows a chart on its first page indicating the chronological sequence involved.

This first chapter concerns the ninth century, when two writing prophets ministered, Obadiah and Joel. It is true that neither prophet dates himself precisely and there is a difference of opinion among scholars as to their date, but evidence will be shown that favors the ninth century. As was indicated in chapter 14, some overlapping occurs between these two early writing prophets and the last of the monarchy prophets considered in the prior section. It will be observed that the most likely time of Obadiah and Joel was respectively the reigns of Jehoram and Joash, two kings of Judah. It was noted in chapter 14 that the last two prophets considered there ministered in the latter part of Joash's reign and in the time of Amaziah who followed. Then Elisha, considered in chapter 15, served in Israel in the time of Jehoash, which also would have followed the time of Obadiah and Joel. But this raises no problem that calls for discussion. God evidently saw fit to have two writing prophets, who lived in the general time of the last of the earlier group of prophets, record their material in books before all of those earlier prophets had completed their ministry.

## A. OBADIAH

### 1. The date

Some of the writing prophets date their ministries by the reigns of kings in which they served. Obadiah does not do this, and therefore his time must be determined from various things he says in his book. One basic matter concerns a military destruction brought upon Jerusalem shortly before the writing of the book, which was accompanied by a time of mockery of the city by Edomites to the south. The book is written concerning Edom, and Obadiah in verse 11 speaks to the Edomites in this way: "In the day that thou stoodest on the other side, in the day that strangers carried away captive his forces, and foreigners entered into his gates, and cast lots upon Jerusalem, even thou wast as one of them."

There were three times in Judah's history when such a situation occurred. The first came during the reign of Jehoram (853–841 B.C.). Edom revolted against Judah during this time (II Kings 8:20–22; II Chron. 21:8–10), and Arabians and Philistines brought severe devastation on the land (II Chron. 21:16, 17). A second occasion fell in the reign of Ahaz (743–715 B.C.). At this time Edom was involved in an attack against Judah (II Chron. 28:16, 17), and there was an invasion of the land by the Philistines (II Chron. 28:18). A third time came with the fall of Jerusalem to Nebuchadnezzar in 586 B.C. (II Kings 25:1–21; II Chron. 36:15–20). On this occasion, great harm was effected on the city, but there was no direct attack by Edom, though Edom was apparently pleased at Judah's destruction by Babylon (cf. Ps. 137:7).

Of these three times, the one having most to commend it is that involving Jehoram, the first king mentioned. The attack of the Arabians and Philistines was severe and would fit the description in Obadiah 11 very well. It is stated that this combined enemy "came up into Judah, and brake into it, and carried away all the substance that was found in the king's house, and his sons also, and his wives; so that there was never a son left him save Jehoahaz, the youngest of his sons" (II Chron. 21:17). And in respect to Edom, the indication is that "the Edomites revolted from under the hand of Judah unto this day" (v. 10).

Arguing against the time of Ahaz, though Edom is said to have come and brought harm to Judah, the Philistines are spoken of as having invaded only the cities of the low country and of the south of Judah. There is no mention of Jerusalem, which is cited specifically in Obadiah 11.

Arguing against the occasion when the Babylonians came against Jerusalem, Obadiah 11 does not portray a captivity as severe as what was brought upon the city at that time. For instance, Obadiah 11 speaks of strangers carrying captive Judah's "forces," suggesting only military people, while Nebuchadnezzar took away the general populace; and the same verse speaks of foreigners entering into the gates of Jerusalem and casting lots upon the city rather than bringing the full destruction that was effected by the Babylonians. It is sometimes argued that this captivity is referred to in Obadiah 20, where a larger, more general captivity is said to be implied. This, however, does not necessarily follow, because the word for "captivity" there is *galut*, which, as Archer says, may refer merely to the capture of single individuals or limited groups of people.[1] Archer refers to Amos 1:9, where the word is used for certain slaves taken by slave traders of Tyre and delivered over to the Edomites.

Another source of evidence comes from an apparent dependency of later prophets on Obadiah. For instance, Jeremiah 49:7–22 seems to be dependent on Obadiah 1–6. There are two reasons to believe that Jeremiah is here dependent on Obadiah, and not Obadiah on Jeremiah. First, Jeremiah often leans on other earlier prophets in his book; and, second, the passage in Obadiah is both briefer and rougher in style, suggesting that Jeremiah gave it greater expansion and smoothness. Amos, who ministered in the eighth century, also seems to have been dependent on Obadiah; compare Obadiah 4 with Amos 9:2; Obadiah 14 with Amos 1:6, 9; Obadiah 19 with Amos 9:12; and Obadiah 20 with Amos 9:14.

Still a further indication of Obadiah's early date is found in the order in

---

[1]Gleason L. Archer, *A Survey of Old Testament Introduction*, p. 289.

which the book is located in the minor prophets as arranged in the Old
Testament. It falls among the first six of these prophets, all of which date to
either the ninth or eighth centuries, while those that follow come from the
seventh century, the exile, and finally after the exile. This placement would
be strange if Obadiah were written as late as the time of the exile.


## 2. Background history

With the date of Obadiah ascertained, it is possible to place the prophet
in his historical setting. It was a time of great turmoil. Jehoram the king was
the son of Jehoshaphat, a good king, but he had married Jehoram to Athaliah,
daughter of Ahab and Jezebel, probably the result of a formal alliance between Judah and Israel (I Kings 22:44; II Chron. 18:1; 21:6; 22:3, 4, 10). This
marriage worked to the detriment of Jehoram and the land of Judah, much as
the marriage of Ahab to Jezebel had worked to the detriment of Ahab and
Israel. No longer were the pious ways of Jehoshaphat followed; instead,
Jehoram allowed Baal worship in all its degradation to enter the land.

Further, he killed all his brothers to safeguard his throne (II Chron.
21:4), probably as a result of the influence of Athaliah. He was the only king
in either Judah or Israel to take such a drastic step as this. It was in the
pattern of Abimelech back in the days of the judges, who in order to secure
his own throne killed his seventy brothers. Athaliah's influence in this is
strongly suggested by her own action a few years later when she killed all her
own grandchildren in order to seize the throne of Judah for herself (II Chron.
22:10).

Because of the sin that resulted, God withdrew His blessing from the
people and permitted the inroads of the enemies that have already been
noted. Edom had been brought under Judah's control by Jehoshaphat, but
now the country revolted and became independent once again. Then the
invasion of the Arabians and Philistines was devastating. This combined
enemy actually entered the king's own house, carried away the wealth that
was found there, captured both wives and all his sons except Jehoahaz
(Ahaziah). It may be added that this seizure of the royal sons removed them
as possible heirs to the throne. When the remaining son, Ahaziah, was later
killed while visiting in Israel (II Kings 9:27–29), Athaliah, knowing that the
only possible heirs now were her grandchildren, killed them so that she could
seize the throne for herself.

The particular time in Jehoram's reign when Obadiah wrote his book is
perhaps best placed shortly after the destruction brought by the Arabians
and Philistines. This would account for the prominent place Obadiah gives to
this disastrous occasion. It should be realized, however, that his general

ministry would have both preceded and followed the time of this writing. He may well have ministered already in the splendid reign of Jehoshaphat, when God's word was closely followed; if so, this would have made the contrasting activity of Jehoram and Athaliah all the more shocking to him. It is also possible that he continued to minister on into the reign of Athaliah and so knew firsthand of her wicked way. The times indeed were turbulent when God used Obadiah as His prophet.

### 3. Work and person

Very little is known concerning either the work or person of this prophet. The suggestion has been made that he was the Obadiah who was a chief officer under Ahab. This officer appears in the biblical account as a person whom Elijah met on his return to Israel after dwelling in Zarephath (I Kings 18:3–16). The date for the two Obadiahs does make an identification possible, for both men lived about the middle of the ninth century. Two matters, however, make the identification unlikely. One is that the Obadiah of Ahab's reign lived in the northern kingdom, and the Obadiah who wrote the book probably lived in the southern. The other is that the two contrast in character. The Obadiah whom Elijah met did not wish to aid the prophet but showed himself quite unsympathetic to Elijah's interest. The Obadiah of our interest, on the other hand, was used of God to write one of the books of Scripture. If the two were the same, he experienced a radical change of life following the time of his meeting Elijah. This is possible but perhaps not likely.

There is reason to believe that the Obadiah of our interest was a devoted follower of God. The short book he wrote contains passages that show him in this character. As will be observed, the theme of the book concerns a coming punishment of Edom by God, and Obadiah makes clear that the reason for this punishment was Edom's violence against her brother Jacob, God's chosen people. God was going to defend His own honor, to which despite had been done, because His own people had been attacked. God would bring destruction upon Edom as Edom had brought destruction upon Jerusalem (v. 15). In contrast, writes Obadiah, there would be deliverance and holiness for Zion, as the house of Jacob would possess all her possessions (v. 17).

It may be said also that Obadiah was knowledgeable of the world of his day. He knew of Edom, he knew what Edom had done, and he was interested in what God was going to do to this southern neighbor in return. His world was larger than merely Jerusalem and Judah. He evidently had given himself to learning of world affairs whenever this information was available.

It is of interest further that Obadiah, though living during a wicked time in his own land, did not write of the sins being committed at home. He might well have done so, in the spirit of Hosea or Amos a century later, but as inspired of God, he saw fit to direct his statements to Edom in the south. The reason is not apparent why God so guided His servant. One can say only that God saw need for such a book of warning to Edom and chose Obadiah to write it.

One may be sure, however, since the times were so distressing and sin so grievous, that Obadiah was very active in voicing protest in an oral way. He doubtless preached frequently in the gates of the city and contacted specific individuals, urging conformance to God's will. He may have reprimanded Jehoram himself, in spite of the danger from Athaliah. It would be interesting to know details concerning this oral ministry but for some reason the Scriptures do not include them.

## 4. The book

The theme of Obadiah's book has just been indicated. He desired to foretell the coming destruction of Edom (vv. 1–9) due to Edom's attitude towards Judah (vv. 10–14). The book may be outlined as follows:
 I. Edom's destruction predicted (1–9).
 II. Cause of Edom's downfall: malice against Israel (10–14).
 III. The Day of the Lord (15–21).

## B. JOEL

## 1. The date

Joel does not date his ministry either, and evidence must be gained once again from internal factors of his book. The result is that considerable difference of opinion exists, even as with Obadiah. Conservative scholars usually prefer an early date, the time of King Joash of Judah (835–796 B.C.), while liberal scholars favor a later one, usually postexilic.[2] The earlier date is to be preferred as the following argumentation shows.

One of the more significant evidences concerns the enemies of Judah that are listed. These are Tyre and Sidon to the north (3:4), Philistia to the

---

[2]Otto Eissfeldt (*The Old Testament, An Introduction*, p. 394) dates it to the fourth if not the third century B.C.; and Robert Pfeiffer (*Introduction to the Old Testament*, p. 575) dates it to 350 B.C.

west (3:4), Egypt to the southeast (3:19), and Edom to the south (3:19). It should be noted that Assyria, Babylonia, and Persia are not mentioned, and they in order were enemies of Judah continuously after the first contacts of Assyria with the northern nation of Israel in the later half of the ninth century. It is also noteworthy that the Aramaeans of Damascus are not mentioned, and they came strongly against Israel during the time of Jehu and Jehoahaz of Israel and finally forced Joash of Judah to pay heavy tribute in the latter days of his reign (II Kings 12:17, 18; II Chron. 24:23, 24).

The enemies that are mentioned can be nicely accounted for on the basis of the earlier date. As was noted, the Philistines made a severe attack against Jerusalem in the day of Jehoram, and in his time also the Edomites revolted and went out from under the control of Judah. The Egyptians had made their attitude known in the earlier attack of Shishak during the fifth year of Rehoboam (I Kings 14:25, 26). Though no military attacks by Tyre and Sidon are recorded for the time, none are recorded for any of the later periods either, and so their mention does not argue for or against any date.

A second evidence exists in the placement of this book in the sacred canon. It is found among the six earlier minor prophets; this, as noted respecting Obadiah, suggests that all six are to be placed early rather than late. If Joel had been written at a postexilic time, one would expect its location to be in the latter part of this group rather than the early part.

Conservative scholars also refer to an apparent dependence of later prophets on Joel. For instance, Amos 1:2 seems to refer to Joel 3:16, and Amos 9:13 to Joel 3:18. Further, Isaiah 13:6 seems to lean upon Joel 1:15. Admittedly, this evidence is a bit tenuous, for it is difficult to prove that the dependence is in the direction indicated rather than vice versa. That both Amos and Isaiah are early books of the eighth century, however, suggests that, whatever the interdependence, Joel was written early and not in postexilic time.

Liberal scholars find evidence for a late date in the lack of mention of a king anywhere in the book, saying that this implies there was no king—a situation true following the return from exile. However, the lack of mention could also reflect the situation in the time of King Joash. He came on the throne at the early age of seven, so that the ruler in fact was the godly high priest Jehoiada, and the book does make reference to elders and priests in keeping with the idea of this type of leadership being prominent.

Liberal scholars also find evidence in a lack of mention regarding the sin of idolatry, which is stressed so much in books like Hosea and Amos of the eighth century; and they argue that this is in keeping with conditions following the exile, when the people had come back from their time of punishment. This lack, however, is again understandable in terms of the reign of Joash, when the good high priest, Jehoiada, was in control. Athaliah's sinful rule had been brought to an end, and marked reform had been brought into the land, causing idolatrous worship to cease.

Liberal scholars further take evidence from the mention of Greeks in 3:6. It is believed that such a reference could not be expected until after the conquest of Alexander the Great in 333 B.C. This need not follow, however, because this reference to Greeks is in a context implying that they were a far distant people. Actually, after Alexander's conquest, the Greeks, rather than being far distant, were in control of the land, and this reference would then be quite inexplicable. The people of Judah could easily have known of them in an early pre-exilic date, something witnessed by early references to them in Assyrian inscriptions.

An argument for a late date is taken also from a reference in Joel 3:2 to what is believed to be the Babylonian captivity. Since the captivity is implied as past, it is asserted the book must have been written after that time. One must understand, however, that this comes in a definitely eschatological context, in which the regathering of nations in the last days is in view. The captivity mentioned is really the time when Israel has been scattered throughout the world, as is still true in the present day.

These considerations taken together favor the placement of Joel in the reign of Joash, while the good high priest Jehoiada was his advisor. Sufficient years should be allowed for the doing away of influences from Athaliah's wicked reign, though a date in the latter part of Joash's rule cannot be used either, since the Aramaeans of Damascus came then. Perhaps a time around 830–825 B.C. is likely.

## 2. Background history

The background history regarding Joel carries on directly after that noted regarding Obadiah. The two men may well have known each other, and their ministries may have overlapped a few years. Joel, however, was certainly the younger of the two and the center of his ministry is best placed ten to twenty years later. It was noted that Athaliah seized the throne after the death of her son Ahaziah. Jehoram, husband of Athaliah, had died earlier when "the LORD smote him in his bowels with an incurable disease" (II Chron. 21:18, 19). Ahaziah ruled only one year when he was killed on his visit to Israel; and it was then that Athaliah seized control in Judah for herself, killing off her grandchildren so that she would have a clear title to the throne.

One of the grandchildren was saved, however, Joash, who later became king (II Kings 11:1-16; II Chron. 22:10—23:15). He was rescued by

Jehosheba (Jehoshabeath, II Chron. 22:11), sister of Ahaziah, who was able to hide the year-old boy along with his nurse in a bedchamber. He had reached the age of seven when a move was undertaken to make him king. The aged high priest, Jehoiada, who had married the much younger Jehosheba, made the arrangements. He brought together rulers and leaders of the day whom he could trust and disclosed his plan. He divided the group into three sections, giving each a particular task. He declared that above all the young lad of seven years should be kept from harm as the coronation was carried out. When all was ready, the lad was brought forth to the temple and the crown was put on his head. The assembled people clapped their hands and cried, "God save the king."

It was not until this cry that Athaliah became aware of the procedures. She immediately came to the temple and there saw the little king, with the princes and trumpeters rejoicing nearby. Her reaction was to exclaim, "Treason, treason." Immediately Jehoiada commanded officers to seize her, take her out, and slay her. The order was put into effect immediately. Joash thus became the young but official king of the land of Judah.

Joash now began what was for the most part a fine rule though much of the credit must be given to Jehoiada, especially during Joash's early years. For one thing, following the apostate innovations of Athaliah, religious reform was needed, and Joash set about this task. Religious articles imported by Athaliah were destroyed, including the Baal-Melqart temple, its altars, and images. The Baal priest, Mattan, was killed, and the personnel and offerings prescribed in the Mosaic Law were reinstituted. True worship of God was again observed, though some of the high places continued to be used.

Years later, when Joash had come to an age to act for himself, he gave orders for the temple to be repaired of damage done to it by Athaliah's sons (II Chron. 24:7). When priests and Levites were slow in collecting funds for the purpose, Joash, now in his twenty-third year, suggested a new way of raising the money. A box was placed at the side of the altar for people to give when they came with their sacrifices. They did so enthusiastically, and workers were hired and the required repairs made. A high spirit of true worship prevailed in the land.

As long as Jehoiada continued as high priest, Joash remained a true follower of God; when he died the king changed. He then began to listen to new advisors who were more sympathetic to the deposed cult of Baal-Melqart (II Chron. 24:17, 18). This was when the stoning of the good prophet, Zechariah, took place as noticed in an earlier chapter.

One may think of Joel living all through this stormy period of time. He would have known of Athaliah's despicable action in slaying her grandchildren, of her own wicked rule and the Baal worship she imported, and of the great relief experienced when young Joash was made king in her place. As noted, Joel apparently wrote his book a few years after this change had come, when the sinful ways she had instituted were no longer existent.

## 3. Work and person

Though Joel does not mention the grievous sins of Athaliah's time in his book, one may be sure that a man like Joel would have been highly interested and actively opposed in every way possible. Later, he no doubt did all he could to further the reforms instituted by Joash under the leadership of Jehoiada. He probably was still living when Zechariah suffered his shameful death by stoning and no doubt felt great remorse. According to II Chronicles 24:19, prophets were sent at that general time to bring rebuke to the king and his advisors, and it may be that Joel was among this number.

Next to nothing is known of Joel's personal life. His father was named Pethuel, apparently a man of pious character, for the name he gave his son means "Yahweh is God." Nothing is said as to Joel's birthplace or conditions under which he was raised. He must have received a fine education, for his book shows an unusual gift for writing. The style is clear, lucid and powerful, full of figures of speech and dramatic expressions. His early days evidently witnessed one of the terrible scourges known to man, an invasion of locusts,[3] for Joel makes such an invasion the theme of his opening chapter and an illustrative basis for the rest of his book. As God had punished the land by this terrible scourge, so in days to come He would bring a parallel punishment when a nation would come upon the land from the north.

In view of this prediction regarding the future, one may believe that Joel was given to thinking regarding this subject. Warning regarding the future, in fact, constitutes the general theme of the book. One can see a parallel in general approach between Joel and Obadiah. Though Obadiah lived in turbulent times, he did not speak of them in his book but instead of Edom to the south and its impending destruction. Joel, though living in times nearly as turbulent, did not speak of them but of Israel's future punishment.

That Joel was a man of high spiritual status is evidenced by his manner of writing. He speaks of the coming day of judgment because the people had offended God in their grievous sin. God's honor had to be avenged. There was need on the part of the people for prayer, fasting, and repentance in order to avert this divine judgment.

---

[3]This occasion of plague does not help to date Joel's prophecy because such plagues have come across the land of Palestine with some frequency down through the years, the last one being as recent as 1915. See John D. Whiting, "Jerusalem's Locust Plague," *National Geographic* XXVIII (Dec., 1915):511–550.

## 4. The book

As indicated, the principal thrust of the book concerns a coming day of judgment, here called "the day of the LORD." God would bring this day as a punishment for Judah's sin and later would bring deliverance from it. To stress and illustrate this awesome occasion, the locust invasion is described (1:1–20). The people are depicted in repentance as a result of this time of devastation of their land (1:8–20), and Joel then describes the coming day of the Lord itself, saying it will result in weeping by the people (2:1–17).

Because the language used by Joel in describing this day is similar to language used in other passages that predict the time of great tribulation of the future, one may believe that the Spirit of God inspiring the prophet had this time in mind. In 2:1–10, the assembling of a vast Gentile army is described, and this seems to be the army brought together by the Antichrist in the latter days of the great tribulation. Then 2:11 speaks of the destruction of this army, which would correspond to Christ's destruction of Antichrist's army at the climax of that period (see Zech. 14:3, 4; Rev. 19:17–21).

It is true that a partial fulfillment of this description occurred in the Assyrian attack under Sennacherib, which followed a little over a century after the day of Joel, but portions of the language go beyond what happened at that time and so do give evidence for future fulfillment. For instance, 2:2 speaks of this occasion as worse than any that had preceded or any that would follow; this is language like that of Matthew 24:21, which definitely speaks of the great tribulation. Also Joel 2:10 speaks of the heavens trembling and the sun and moon becoming dark with the stars withdrawing their shining, something which did not happen in the time of Sennacherib.

The rest of the book (2:18—3:21) deals primarily with God's intervention in behalf of His people as a result of their repentance. Again there seems to be a twofold fulfillment intended: what God would do for His people whenever they repented, and what He would do for them following the great tribulation. Because Peter quoted 2:28, 29, dealing with the outpouring of the Spirit, as fulfilled at least in part at Pentecost (Acts 2:16–20), one may believe that certain of the matters here in reference were partially fulfilled at Christ's first coming. Because the same reference will find its complete fulfillment only in the millennial day, as the Jewish people are filled as never before by the Holy Spirit, one may believe that the section generally will receive its total fulfillment at that time.

The book may be outlined as follows:

I. A symbolic plague of locusts (1:1–20).
  A. The plague depicted (1:1–7).
  B. Exhortation for repentance and prayer (1:8–20).
II. The day of the Lord symbolized (2:1–32).

A. A great invading army (2:1–10).
B. The army of God (2:11).
C. Resultant repentance (2:12–17).
D. The response of God (2:18–29).
E. Signs preceding the day of the Lord (2:30–32).

III. Judgment of the nations (3:1–16).
A. Restoration of Israel (3:1).
B. The nations judged (3:2, 3).
C. A foreshadowing of judgment on Phoenicia and Philistia (3:4–8).
D. Assembly and destruction of the great army (3:9–16).

IV. Millennial blessings (3:17–21).

| | |
|---|---|
| 9th-Century Prophets | **Chapter 16** Obadiah Joel |
| **8th-Century Prophets** | **Chapter 17** Hosea Amos Jonah |
| | **Chapter 18** Isaiah Micah |
| 7th-Century Prophets | **Chapter 19** Nahum Zephaniah Habakkuk |
| | **Chapter 20** Jeremiah |
| Exilic Prophets | **Chapter 21** Daniel Ezekiel |
| Postexilic Prophets | **Chapter 22** Haggai Zechariah Malachi |

# 17

# Eighth-Century Prophets: Hosea, Amos, and Jonah

We move on now to prophets of the eighth century of whom there were five. In this chapter we consider Hosea, Amos, and Jonah, all prophets either to or from Israel. The next chapter will concern Isaiah and Micah, both prophets of Judah. It is common to speak of only four prophets of the eighth century, omitting Jonah. The reason for this is that Jonah's date is controverted and also his book concerns his mission to Assyria, not Israel. However, because his date as considered herein falls in the general time of Hosea and Amos, he is studied along with them. It should be realized that a number of years elapsed between the two ninth-century prophets considered in the prior chapter and these of the eighth century. Both of them were dated in the third quarter of the ninth century and these will be found to date during and after the middle of the eighth century. This means that something over two-thirds of a century elapsed between the group of two of the ninth century and this group of five of the eighth century.

### A. HOSEA

#### 1. The date

Hosea, unlike Obadiah and Joel, dates himself exactly. He ministered during the reigns of Uzziah, Jotham, Ahaz, and Hezekiah, kings of Judah, and in the days of Jeroboam II, king of Israel (1:1). Since Jeroboam II of Israel died in 753 B.C. and Uzziah of Judah began to reign by himself in 767 B.C., the time of beginning for Hosea's ministry was somewhere between these two dates, perhaps about 760 B.C. Since he continued his ministry at least until the beginning of the sole reign of Hezekiah, which dates at 715 B.C., he had a comparatively long ministry of between forty and fifty years.

An interesting question arises in connection with the rationale of the way in which Hosea dates himself. Though being clearly a prophet to Israel, he dates himself more by the reigns of the kings of Judah than by the kings of Israel, mentioning four of the former and only one of the latter. The probable reason is twofold. First, Hosea along with other prophets recognized the kings of Judah, rather than the kings of Israel, as the true legitimate heirs of David, and therefore desired to date himself by their reigns. Second, the kings who followed Jeroboam II in Israel were short-lived, many suffering assassination, so that numerous names would have had to be included; also, the history represented by them was not of such a nature that any prophet would like to have associated with his name.

## 2. Background history

The historical background for the beginning of Hosea's ministry lies in the strong rule of Jeroboam II (793–753 B.C.). Jeroboam was the third successive descendant of Jehu's dynasty and was one of Israel's most capable rulers. As observed in chapter 15, his predecessor, Jehoash, had begun to remedy Israel's weakness before the Aramaeans of Damascus. Under Jehu and Jehoahaz earlier, this weakness had been obvious, but Jehoash had done much to recover land that Israel had lost to the northern neighbor. Jeroboam II now continued where Jehoash had left off and regained not only all that Israel had lost but added much more. He became the actual leader of all kings along the eastern Mediterranean coast. The Bible does not include a description of the battles Jeroboam fought to accomplish so much, but the end achievement is clear: he established roughly the same boundaries on the east and north that had existed in the empire days of David and Solomon.

It is stated that Jeroboam II placed Israel's northern limit at the "entering of Hamath" (II Kings 14:25), the same phrase used to describe Solomon's northern boundary (I Kings 8:65). It is also stated that "he recovered Damascus and Hamath which had belonged to Judah" (II Kings 14:28). Since he gained control over so much northern territory, it follows that he must have also recovered Transjordan, which Hazael had seized. With these former boundaries restored, Israel became the largest and most influential country along the eastern Mediterranean. The name of Jeroboam II certainly was widely known and respected.

Though Hosea would have been glad to live in a day of prosperity and influence like this, still there was a sobering factor. The day was characterized by wealth and luxurious living that led to sinful conditions. It is not prosperity that normally brings about righteous conduct, but hardship and difficulty. When conditions are good, people tend to be self-confident and self-sufficient, forgetting their dependence on almighty God. It is for this reason that both Hosea and Amos have so much to say concerning the sin they found around themselves. They saw that the land was producing abundantly (II Chron. 26:10) and that many people were enjoying riches. Building activity was flourishing (Hos. 8:14), and this led to a widespread feeling of pride (Isa. 9:10; Amos 3:15; 5:11). Social and moral conditions were developing which were wrong and degrading. Side by side with the wealth, extreme poverty was growing. Through dishonest gain and false balances the strong were taking advantage of the weak (Isa. 5:8; Hos. 12:7; Amos 8:5, 6). Those who had wealth felt quite free to oppress orphans and widows and even to buy and sell the destitute on the public market (Amos 8:4, 8). Justice was at a premium and the courts apparently were doing little to change the situation.

Following the reign of Jeroboam II, Israel suffered another period of weakness, this one due both to the outside power, Assyria, and to internal intrigue as assassinations became commonplace. Zechariah ruled six months and was killed by his successor Shallum. Shallum ruled one month and was killed by Menahem. Menahem ruled longer, a total of ten years (752–742 B.C.), and died a natural death, but his son Pekahiah ruled only two years and was killed by his successor, Pekah. Pekah did rule twenty years (the first twelve probably contemporary with the prior two kings when he ruled only in the Transjordan region), but then was killed by Israel's last king, Hoshea. Hoshea ruled ten years (732–722 B.C.) and saw his country fall to the Assyrians.

It was during the reign of Menahem that the awesome power of Assyria came to be known once more in Israel. During the first half of the eighth century, Assyrian influence had gone into eclipse, but in 745 B.C. the great Tiglath-pileser III came to power and restored all that Assyria had lost. He achieved success first in the east but then turned his attention westward across the Euphrates. His campaign of 743 B.C. reached all the way to Israel and involved Menahem.[1] He was not able to incorporate the country as a province, but he did exact enormous tribute.[2] By making the payment de-

---

[1] The date of this campaign is often given as 738 B.C. but E. R. Thiele (*Mysterious Numbers of the Hebrew Kings*, pp. 94–115) makes a strong case for 743 B.C. based on records of Tiglath-pileser III. See also Merrill F. Unger, *Israel and the Aramaeans of Damascus*, p. 97.

[2] Tilgath-pileser lists several other kings who paid tribute, including Kishtashpi of Hummuh, Rezin of Damascus, Hiram of Tyre, Urikki of Kue, Pisiris of Carchemish, Tarhulara of Gurgum, and Sulumal of Melid. For text, see *Ancient Near Eastern Texts*, ed. James B. Pritchard, p. 283; *Documents from Old Testament Times*, ed. D. Winton Thomas, pp. 54–55.

manded, Menahem was able to "confirm the kingdom in his hand," but in doing so he became another vassal to the Assyrian ruler (II Kings 15:19, 20).

Then in 734 B.C., Pekah's sixth year of sole rule, Tiglath-pileser III returned to the west. He came this time at the request of Ahaz, king of Judah, who was besieged in Jerusalem by Pekah of Israel and Rezin of Damascus (II Chron. 28:5-8; Isa. 7:1f.). Ahaz requested aid from the Assyrian ruler against these two, and Tiglath-pileser complied by conducting the well-known campaign of 734-732 B.C.[3] He first (734 B.C.) moved down the Mediterranean coast as far as Philistia and subdued cities there, apparently to cut off any possible Egyptian assistance to his enemies. Then (probably 733 B.C.) he marched into Israel, destroying cities all across Galilee and taking many people captive (II Kings 15:29). Finally (732 B.C.) he moved against Damascus, likely his prime target from the beginning, devastating the country, capturing the capital city, and executing Rezin the king. All this made for an enormous impact on life in Israel.

The crushing occasion of Israel's final fall to Assyria came soon after this campaign. In 724 B.C., Shalmaneser V marched on Israel (II Kings 17:3-6). Hoshea the king went to meet him, bringing overdue tribute, but this did not satisfy the Assyrian monarch. Hoshea was taken captive and Shalmaneser moved on Samaria, the capital. There was stubborn resistance, even though the king had already been captured, but finally the city fell in 722 B.C., and the days of Israel as a sovereign nation were no more.

### 3. The person and work of Hosea

#### a. THE MARRIAGE OF HOSEA AND GOMER

A significant matter to consider regarding the person of Hosea, son of Beeri, is that God commanded him to marry a woman named Gomer, called by God "a woman of harlotries" (1:2). Because of this command and because of the type of adulterous person Gomer proved to be after Hosea married her, considerable discussion has resulted among scholars concerning the proper understanding of the marriage. Views held may be divided into four principal types.

One view is that the marriage never really happened; the account is to be understood either as a mere vision or else a symbolism of the relation of God and unfaithful Israel. The thinking is that God would not have commanded a prophet to marry an unchaste woman, especially when this had been expressly forbidden to priests (Lev. 21:7, 14). Edward J. Young, an exponent of

---

[3]For inscription, see *Ancient Near Eastern Texts*, pp. 283-284.

this view, adds two other reasons: first, that Hosea's ministry would have been shattered if he had really married an unchaste person; and, second, that the, messages which God gave concerning the names of the three children as each was born to the marriage (1:4, 5; 1:6, 7; 1:9) would have been too far apart in time to be meaningful as related messages in the ministry of the prophet.[4] Evidence against this view exists in the straightforward, narrative-type style of the presentation which gives no indication that symbolism is intended. The story is told in the form of history with numerous details included which would not be expected in a symbolic presentation.[5]

A second view is that the marriage did occur and that Gomer was already an unchaste person, possibly a temple prostitute, at the time. The thinking is that this is the most natural way to understand the story and one is simply avoiding a logical conclusion if he takes the story in any other way. Against this view, however, is the fact that it presents God as directing Hosea to do something intrinsically wrong. Furthermore, the argument of Young that the prophet's ministry would then have been shattered would carry real weight.

A third view, held less widely, is that religious infidelity is intended in the story; Gomer became unchaste in the sense that she became a worshiper of false gods, like Israelites generally of Hosea's day. The principal argument is that this view obviates the ethical difficulty just noted and also that the Scriptures often use the figure of harlotry for spiritual infidelity. One has to wonder, however, if the difficulty of seeing God as commanding a marriage to a woman ethically unchaste is any greater than the difficulty of seeing Him as commanding marriage to a woman religiously unchaste. Also one has to question how Hosea could have effectively used this religious infidelity by his wife for illustrative purposes (as he did) with a people who were taken with the same type of sin.

A fourth view is that the marriage did occur but that Gomer was yet pure at the time of the marriage and became adulterous only later. This view, commonly called the proleptic view, is much to be preferred. Gomer was not a harlot at the time Hosea married her, and, if she was not, then the objections raised to the second view are removed. Such a marriage would have been difficult for Hosea both to contemplate and carry out, knowing his bride would later become unfaithful, but the ethical problem would no longer exist. Besides, this view fits the fact that Hosea clearly loved Gomer, something revealed generally by the story.

[4]*Introduction to the Old Testament*, pp. 245-246.

[5]For instance, Gomer is called the daughter of Diblaim; the third child, Lo-ammi, is said to have been born only after the second was weaned; and the children are said specifically to have been two boys and one girl. None of these matters are made symbolic nor can one find any meaningful symbolism in them.

Also, both of the objections cited by Young can be answered without difficulty. If Gomer was pure at the time of the marriage, there is no reason why Hosea's ministry would have been shattered. People would have felt sympathy for one whose wife had shown herself unfaithful, and they may well have listened more closely to his later messages as a result. That Hosea's messages would have been too far apart, if the story is literal, is not a valid objection either. It is true that Hosea was given a new message each time a child was born, but one need not think that these messages constituted all that Hosea preached, or that he ministered only when a child was born. Perhaps the most convincing evidence in favor of the fourth view is that it supplies an important parallel between Hosea's life and God's relationship with Israel (see 1:2, 6, 7, 9; 2:1-13). The message of the book and the messages Hosea preached to Israel at the time were based on this parallel. God had taken Israel in her pure condition (Jer. 2:2, 3), while knowing very well that she would become unfaithful in due course. Therefore, Hosea was to take Gomer as his wife, when she was still a pure young woman, though he knew at the time that she would become unchaste in the course of the marriage.

Further, it is noteworthy that the phrase "wife of harlotries" is exactly parallel with the phrase "children of harlotries" (1:2). The children in reference are logically understood to be those described in the following verses: Jezreel, Lo-ruhamah, and Lo-ammi. Since these children were born after the marriage, the phrase "children of harlotries" must have been used by God proleptically. And it is only logical to take the phrase "wife of harlotries" in the same way.

b. Person and work proper

In view of Hosea's obedience to God in marrying Gomer, it is clear that he was a man given to following the will of God no matter where it led. Nothing proves the devotion of man to God more than such obedience, and one may be sure that Hosea held a high place in God's evaluation. He was truly a spiritually mature person. The prophet shows this also in his sensitive abhorrence of sin. In a day of abounding sin, Hosea not only was aware of it but spoke strongly against it. He made a parallel between the unfaithful way his wife Gomer had treated him and the way Israel had treated God. He spoke of the calf worship at Bethel and Dan as really a continuing form of Baal worship (2:8; 11:2; 13:1), no doubt because many of the offensive features of Baal worship were still carried on at these centers. Sacred prostitution, for instance, common in the fertility rites of the Baal cult, was yet being practiced (4:10-18). Also, people still built "high places" and set up images and Asherah poles "in every high hill and under every green tree" (II Kings 17:7-12).

Because Hosea makes several references to the kingdom of Judah, some scholars have doubted that he was really a prophet to the kingdom of Israel. That he was, however, is indicated by the fact that the majority of his messages were addressed to the northern people. Besides this, he refers to the ruler in Samaria as "our king" (7:5), and he employs a number of Aramaisms in his writing which might well be due to the influence of the Aramaic-speaking land of Syria immediately north. But the fact that he does refer to Judah several times (e.g., 4:15; 5:5, 10, 12–14; 6:4, 11, etc.) shows that he was interested in and knowledgeable about the country to the south. He was not so provincial that he did not wish the best for the southern neighbor and took occasion to give words of warning and instruction.

Hosea had a sense both of history and of matters pertaining to the future. The former is manifested in the parallel he made basic to his book, that is, the parallel between the way Gomer had acted towards him and the way Israel had acted towards God through prior centuries. The people were still acting in this sinful way in Hosea's time; he makes clear that what they were doing was quite the same as they had been doing in earlier times. His sense of future events is indicated by the several occasions when he brings in reference to better times in days to come for the people of God. For instance, already in 1:10, 11 he speaks of a day when Israel will be "as the sand of the sea" and when "in the place where it was said unto them, Ye are not my people, there it shall be said unto them, Ye are the sons of the living God." Other passages of this kind are 2:14–23; 11:8–11; and 14:2–9.

Hosea should be thought of as a hard-working prophet, fully dedicated to the will of God, ministering faithfully to the sinful people of his day in spite of the great sadness of his own marriage. One may well believe that during the reign of Menahem, when Tiglath-pileser III made his first campaign into the land, Hosea was active in pointing to this attack as a punishment for the people's sin. No doubt, he cried earnestly for their repentance in view of this onslaught. And Hosea would have been active in his ministry during the second great campaign of this Assyrian conqueror, and once more when Shalmaneser V came and brought the final overthrow of the country. How many people may have listened and turned to God there is no way to know. Probably some did, and this would have been pleasing to the prophet, but the numbers evidently were small because God permitted the full punishment to fall. What happened to Hosea himself following the collapse of the country is not indicated. He may have gone down to Judah and spent his last days there until the time of Hezekiah.

In addition to his oral ministry, Hosea found occasion to write the material found in his book. It is not likely that it was all written at one time. Probably the record of Hosea's marriage and the earlier prophecies were recorded prior to the death of Jeroboam II, because in 1:4 Hosea refers to vengeance coming upon "the house of Jehu," and this vengeance came with

the murder of Jeroboam's son Zechariah six months after he began to rule
(II Kings 15:8–12). Other passages refer to assassinations of kings (plural), implying that these events had already happened (e.g., 7:7, 16; 8:4); this
suggests that such portions were written at least after those assassinations
took place, that is, late in the nation's history. Further, there are references to
contact with Assyria (e.g., 5:13; 8:9; 12:1), and these imply that the sections
involved were written no earlier than the time of Menahem, who did
negotiate with Tiglath-pileser III (II Kings 15:19, 20). Finally, in 7:11 mention is made of double-dealing by Israel with Egypt and Assyria, and this
suggests that the passage concerned was written in the days of Hoshea, when
Egypt was pitted by Israel against the eastern power (II Kings 17:4). The
book may have been put together as a unit following the fall of the northern
kingdom, when possibly Hosea had traveled down to Judah.

The principal significance of Hosea as a prophet is that he sounded a
final call to Israel for repentance before the death knell of the country. Other
prophets had given warning earlier, but Israel had not heeded. Sin had continued quite unabated, God now sent Hosea as a final emissary, and the
people would have to heed him or else the crushing punishment would fall.

### 4. The book

One can see five basic themes running through the Book of Hosea. First
and foremost is the fact that God had made a covenant with Israel and Israel
continued to break it by severe sin. This is shown, for instance, in 2:2–13
where Israel is compared to Hosea's unfaithful wife; in 4:1, 2 by an enumeration of Israel's sins; and in 4:5–10 by a setting forth of the sins of the priests.

The second is the broken marriage of Hosea and Gomer and the parallel
made between it and this broken covenant. This is seen, for instance, in 1:2–9
where the marriage of Hosea and Gomer is commanded and children are
born to the union with the symbolism of their names set forth; and in 3:1–3
where Hosea is told to go and love Gomer once again.

The third is God's love and patience with Israel through all this time of
breaking the covenant. One sees this, for instance, in 11:1–4 where God is
depicted as having loved Israel from the time of being a child and as drawing
the people with bands of love; and in 14:1–9 where, speaking of a future day,
God says, "I will heal their backsliding, I will love them freely: for mine
anger is turned away from him."

The fourth is a note of solemn warning of severe punishment upon the
people for breaking God's covenant. This is seen, for instance, in 5:1–15
where general statements regarding this punishment are set forth; in 8:1–14
where, because of the false calf worship, God says, "They have sown the

wind, and they shall reap the whirlwind"; and in 10:5–8 by a direct indication that the people would be carried captive to Assyria.

The fifth is a glory note of future restoration, when Israel would again enjoy gracious benefits at God's hand. This is seen, for instance, in 1:10, 11, a passage noted earlier; in 2:14–23 where abundant produce from the soil is promised; in 3:4, 5 where it is said that Israel would return and seek the Lord their God and fear the Lord and His goodness in the latter days; and in 6:1–3 where the people are depicted in the last days as calling for a return to the Lord who had torn them but now would heal them.

The book may be outlined as follows:

I. Parallel of faithlessness: Gomer and Israel (1:1—3:5).
   A. Hosea's symbolic marriage to Gomer (1:1–9).
   B. Restoration of Israel to God's favor (1:10, 11).
   C. Israel's unfaithfulness condemned (2:1–13).
   D. Indication of Israel's restoration (2:14–23).
   E. Hosea takes Gomer again (3:1–3).
   F. A further indication of Israel's restoration (3:4, 5).
II. Messages to unfaithful Israel (4:1—14:9).
   A. Indictment for sin (4:1—7:16).
      1. A general indictment (4:1–19).
      2. A warning to priests, people, and king (5:1–15).
      3. Words of repentant Israel (6:1–3).
      4. Further general indictment (6:4–11).
      5. Ruinous domestic and foreign policies (7:1–16).
   B. Warning of judgment (8:1—10:15).
      1. Judgment for Israel imminent (8:1–14).
      2. Assyrian captivity designated (9:1—10:15).
   C. Israel's sin and final restoration (11:1—14:9).
      1. God's love and Israel's rebellion (11:1–7).
      2. Israel's restoration in the last days (11:8–11).
      3. The folly of Israel (11:12—12:14).
      4. Israel's fall into sin (13:1–16).
      5. Israel's repentance and God's blessing (14:1–9).

## B. AMOS

### 1. The date

Amos dates his prophetic work much in the way that Hosea does his. He says it occurred during the reigns of Jeroboam II, king of Israel, and Uzziah, king of Judah, two of the kings mentioned by Hosea. This places the time of Amos' ministry about the time when Hosea began his, somewhere between 767 B.C., the beginning date of Uzziah's sole reign, and 753 B.C., the closing date of Jeroboam's reign. The time is thus located in the closing years of Jeroboam's rule, and this is in keeping with Amos 6:2 which implies that the region of Hamath was at the time under the control of Jeroboam. It was pointed out, when we were speaking of Hosea's background history, that Jeroboam made conquest as far north as Hamath sometime during his rule (cf. II Kings 14:25).

Amos also dates his ministry as having been "two years before the earthquake" (1:1), but this is of little help because there is no way to know just when this earthquake occurred. It must have been very severe, however, for it is mentioned also by Zechariah (14:5-7), who lived following the Babylonian exile well over two centuries later. It should be noted that, since Amos mentions this earthquake, he must have written his book after it occurred. This means the oral ministry took place at least two years prior to the recording of the information. It should also be noted that, since Amos does not list other kings of Judah following Uzziah as Hosea does, his ministry apparently did not last nearly as long as that of his contemporary. It probably was confined to years between the two dates noted, 767 and 753 B.C.

## 2. Background history

Like Hosea, Amos carried on his ministry in the northern nation of Israel, but unlike Hosea his home was in Judah to the south. As will be observed more at length presently, he was called by God while he was living in Judah and instructed to go to Israel and there prophesy in the name of the Lord. Background information for his ministry, then, must be seen in terms of Israel's history, while that concerning his home life must be seen in terms of Judah's history.

As to Israel's history, this already has been considered in our discussion of Hosea. Of course, in the case of Amos the history involved had to do solely with the time of Jeroboam II and not the kings following his day. When Amos ministered in Israel, then, it was a day of prosperity and luxury, which led to a life of indulgence and sin.

As to Judah's history, it was the time of Uzziah, one of the strong kings of the southern kingdom. Uzziah, also called Azariah (e.g., II Kings 14:21; 15:1, 6, 8) followed a life pattern approved by God, and God blessed his reign so that a high status in the world was restored to Judah. This improvement in Judah's position came at approximately the same time as Israel's enlargement under the able Jeroboam II. Between the two men, the total land area controlled came to rival even that of the days of David and Solomon.

In the south, Uzziah maintained the control his father Amaziah had gained over Edom and in addition built facilities at Elath on the Gulf of Aqaba for the purpose of trade (II Kings 14:22; II Chron. 26:2). Toward the east he accepted gifts from the Ammonites, indicating a domination imposed upon them. Toward the west, he warred successfully against the Philistines and seized several of their cities including Gath. Uzziah also strengthened fortifications in Judah and he installed ingenious machines for shooting arrows and catapulting large stones from walls. He seems to have reorganized Judah's army, increasing its effectiveness. While Jeroboam II lived he was easily the most influential king along the eastern Mediterranean, and when he died this position was taken by Uzziah.

All this means that the time of Amos' ministry was characterized by national power, both in Israel where he prophesied and in Judah where he lived. Both countries were at a zenith of influence in the world and prosperity reigned.

### 3. Person and work

Amos gives more information concerning himself than do many of the other prophets. For one thing he names his home town as Tekoa (1:1), located about five miles southeast of Bethlehem. He describes his profession as "an herdman, and a gatherer of sycamore fruit" (7:14). The word for "herdman" is *boqer*. The word is best taken in reference to a person who tended cattle, since it is related to the word for cattle—*baqar*. Amos refers to himself as a "herdman" also in 1:1, and here the word is *noqed* (*noqedim*, a participial form). This word refers to one who tended a small variety of sheep called *naqod*. Apparently, he had the care of both cattle and sheep. In addition he cultivated sycamore or wild fig trees (*shiqemim*), which produce a small sweet fruit that was much in demand especially among the poorer classes of people.[6]

Because the term *noqed* is used in II Kings 3:4 (translated "sheepmaster") in reference to Mesha, king of Moab, it is possible that the term connoted the ownership of sheep and not merely the activity of shepherding

---

[6] A task of the people who tended these trees was to make an incision in the fruit when it was about an inch long, a few days before harvesting, to cause the fruit to ripen more quickly. If this was not done, the fig would not ripen properly and on being picked would contain a quantity of watery juice. The value of sycamore figs was sufficient in ancient time for King David to appoint a special overseer for harvesting them (I Chron. 27:28).

them. If so, Amos may have owned the flocks over which he watched and therefore may have been somewhat affluent. That his work involved both cattle and sheep, as well as sycamore trees, lends further credence to this possibility.

Amos differed from Hosea and from most other prophets in that he was not full-time in this work. This is evident from what has just been noted and also from a significant statement made by Amos to Amaziah, priest in Bethel. He told Amaziah, "I was no prophet, neither was I a prophet's son . . . And the LORD took me as I followed the flock, and the LORD said unto me, Go, prophesy unto my people Israel" (7:14, 15). This statement appears in the same context where he talks of himself as being "an herdman, and a gatherer of sycamore fruit," so that his thought in saying he was not a prophet by occupation is unmistakable. Prior to his call to serve as a prophet, then, he had been a layman, as others of the community of Tekoa, and God called him from this life to serve for a time in the ministry of a prophet.

The words of Amos that he was "no prophet" and "not a prophet's son" are understood in different ways. Some believe that he was saying he had not been trained in a school of the prophets. The term *son of the prophets* was used for students in the prophetic schools of the time of Elijah and Elisha, and Amos may have been using that terminology here. It should be realized, however, that Amos lived several decades after the time of Elijah and Elisha, and there is no way of knowing whether those schools still existed. If they did, that Amos is referring to them is possible and perhaps probable; if they did not, then he was merely saying he not only was not a prophet himself but had not been born to a person who was a prophet, thus emphasizing that his profession had indeed not been that of prophecy. Either way it is clear that he was not a prophet by occupation but was called of God from his lay activity to serve for a time in the role of prophetic ministry.

There is no way to know how long Amos continued in this role. God called him from his home in Tekoa to go north into Israel and give warning concerning the sin of the northern people. He was at Bethel when he spoke the words just noted, and he says in the opening statement of his book, "The words of Amos . . . which he saw concerning Israel." Presumably, on being called of God, he went to Israel and stayed long enough to proclaim at least all the messages set forth in his book. This would have been at the time designated, namely, "two years before the earthquake." He evidently returned to his home in Tekoa after this and sometime later, following the earthquake, penned the words that are recorded. Whether he continued in any prophetic ministry after returning to Judah is not indicated, but it is quite possible that God permitted him to return to his former occupation.

As a layman prior to the time of his call, Amos must be thought of as a dedicated person and spiritually mature in the ways of God. Certainly there were full-time prophets of the day whom God might have used to do this work, but God for some reason passed them by and picked a layman. This speaks very highly of the person selected. God saw in him a choice vessel who could do the work in a way which apparently no prophet of the day could.

Amos should also be thought of as energetic and hard-working. This is suggested by his occupation before his call—he tended both cattle and sheep and even took care of a sycamore orchard. It is this kind of person God can use most effectively. Amos further must be seen as a man of considerable courage. God called him to go north to the strong country of Israel, where the great Jeroboam II was ruling, and proclaim a message that could only be unpopular. It would have been enough for layman Amos to be called to preach at all, but here he was called to do it in a powerful foreign country. Amos might easily have objected and refused to go, but he did not. When God called he went, whether the mission was forbidding or not.

It is also noteworthy that Amos was knowledgeable of the world of his day. One could easily think that a person who tended animals in the out-of-the-way locality of Tekoa would have been little aware of what was happening in the world about, but in his book Amos has pungent and appropriate things to say regarding numerous countries that were around Judah and Israel. Included are Damascus (1:3–5), Philistia (1:6–8), Tyre (1:9, 10), Edom (1:11, 12), Ammon (1:13–15), and Moab (2:1–3). More important, Amos had made himself well acquainted with the Old Testament as it existed in his day, something shown by numerous references in his book, especially to the Pentateuch.[7]

Thus, Amos should be thought of as a very unusual and capable layman of his day. He was hard-working, but not so much so that he did not take time to broaden his mind in learning regarding God's revealed will and regarding the world of his day. He evidently took occasion to meet people who could inform him of what was going on around about, and this made him conscious of existing sin that was so displeasing to God. Above all he was fully dedicated to God and ready to serve in whatever way he could. This made him God's appropriate choice to minister in the capacity called for in Israel.

The point is noteworthy that God's call of Amos to go to Israel implies that there are few prophets who lived there. Hosea did, of course, and also Jonah, whom we study next, but apparently God had other places for them to minister. He needed a person to bring His word in the vicinity of Bethel in the extreme south of the land, and for this He summoned Amos from the neighboring country of Judah. It should be realized, however, that the dis-

---

[7]See Gleason L. Archer, *A Survey of Old Testament Introduction*, pp. 307–308.

tance really was not far for Amos to go, even though it involved moving to another country. From Tekoa to Bethel is only about twenty-five miles. Still Israel was a foreign country, and therefore God certainly would have selected a person from Israel to do this work had there been one available and suitable.


### 4. The book

One great value of the Book of Amos is that it provides, along with Hosea, a fruitful source of information regarding conditions in the northern kingdom during the reign of Jeroboam II. As indicated, it was a day of national strength, when trade and commerce flourished and people were prosperous. But it was also a day of moral and religious decay. Bribery of officialdom was common, and it became difficult for ordinary people to receive justice in the courts of the land. The result was that a large gap developed between rich and poor, with the latter often being sold into bondage by their masters for trivial matters (Amos 2:6).

In this situation, Amos' message was that people should leave off their sinful ways and return to seeking God and His will. They should heed the regulations laid down in the Mosaic Law given long before. If they did not, there would be a day of punishment from God. This would be a day of darkness rather than light, one of punishment and sorrow rather than reward and gladness.

The book may be outlined as follows:

  I. Judgment against the nations (1:1—2:16).
    A. Prelude: day of wrath (1:1, 2).
    B. Judgment upon six neighboring nations (1:3—2:3).
    C. Judgment on Judah and Israel (2:4-16).
  II. Sin and punishment of Israel (3:1—6:14).
    A. The certainty of God's punishment (3:1-15).
    B. Past punishments unavailing (4:1-13).
    C. Lamentation for fallen Israel (5:1-27).
    D. Destruction and captivity imminent (6:1-14).
  III. Five visions of the coming judgment (7:1—9:10).
    A. First vision: the plague of locusts (7:1-3).
    B. Second vision: unrestrained fire (7:4-6).
    C. Third vision: the plumbline (7:7-9).
    D. Historical interlude: encounter with Amaziah (7:10-17).
    E. Fourth vision: the basket of summer fruit (8:1-14).
    F. Fifth vision: destruction of the temple (9:1-10).
  IV. Messianic blessing promised (9:11-15).

## C. JONAH

### 1. The date

The general date of Jonah is fixed by a reference to him in II Kings 14:25, which, speaking of Jeroboam II, says, "He restored the coast of Israel from the entering of Hamath unto the sea of the plain, according to the word of the LORD God of Israel, which he spake by the hand of his servant, Jonah, the son of Amittai, the prophet, which was of Gath-hepher." Thus Jonah lived during the reign of Jeroboam II and was active in ministry by a date soon enough to predict to him that he would make conquest of areas to the north of Israel.[8] Since Jeroboam ruled forty-one years, however (II Kings 14:23—793-753 B.C.), and Jonah may have been either an old man or a young man when he made this prediction, the specific time when Jonah lived and visited Nineveh (of which he writes in his book) is still left open to a considerable spread of years. But Assyrian history has been used to identify two points of time as being the most likely.

The one point is about 800 B.C. The Assyrian emperor, Adad-nirari III (810-783 B.C.), is known to have confined his worship to the one god Nebo and so favored a type of monotheism.[9] Since he was the only Assyrian ruler who did this, it may be that he was influenced by the visit of Jonah who proclaimed the worship of one God only, though of course this was the God of Israel, and not Nebo, the god of Assyria. If so, Jonah's visit would have fallen relatively early in Adad-nirari's reign, perhaps even a little before 800 B.C.

The other point is about 760 B.C. At this time there was a psychological condition in Assyria that would have been favorable for Jonah's visit. It was a time of general discouragement in the country and even characterized by panic and fear. For one thing, little remained of Assyria's former great empire due to the ineptness of weak kings. Then a serious plague swept through the land in 765 B.C., taking the lives of many people. And finally a total eclipse of the sun transpired on June 15, 763 B.C., and this is known to have spread general fear. Because such conditions would have measurably contributed to the effectiveness of Jonah's ministry (and it was indeed effective), this latter date becomes a possibility and probably the more likely of the two.

---

[8]Otto Eissfeldt (*The Old Testament, An Introduction*, pp. 404–405) and others doubt that this Jonah and the Jonah of the prophecy are the same. He concludes this, however, on grounds unacceptable to conservative scholars, for he does not accept the historicity of Jonah's book.

[9]His ideas have been compared to the innovations of Amenhotep IV (Akhenaten—1378–1367 B.C.) of Egypt many years earlier.

Jonah no doubt wrote his book after he returned from Nineveh to Israel, when he could look back and assess more objectively the events that had transpired.[10]

## 2. Background history

Regarding background history to Jonah's life in Israel, really nothing more needs to be said. It has been indicated that he lived during the time of Jeroboam II, and this has been described in respect to the prophets Hosea and Amos. It was a time of power for Israel and a period of prosperity and sin for the people. Since Jonah predicted to Jeroboam that he would expand the country as he did, he lived prior to the time when that expansion occurred. Thus, in his early days, he may have known something of the much weaker period that came in the years of Jehoash, but in his later life he certainly knew the position of power that Israel came to enjoy.

Something should be said regarding background history to Jonah's visit to Nineveh. For one thing, it should be realized that, though Nineveh was the largest city of Assyria at this time, it was not the capital city. During most of Assyria's history, the capital had been at Assur well south of Nineveh on the Tigris River, and at the time of Jonah's visit it was at Calah (Nimrud). Calah was much nearer to Nineveh than Assur but still a few miles south. It had been made the capital by Ashur-nasir-pal II (883–859) about one century before the time of Jonah's visit. Though Adad-nirari III made a new palace, he did so yet at this same capital city. Nineveh was first made capital by Sennacherib (705–681 B.C.), more than a half century after Jonah's visit.

Adad-nirari III, the king who held to the worship of the one god Nebo, began to rule at an early age, and his mother, the famous Semiramis, assumed control during his beginning years. One thing he did in respect to biblical history is that he attacked Hazael of Damascus in 804 B.C., and this relieved Israel of Aramaean pressure (II Kings 12:17; II Chron. 24:23f.) and enabled Jehoash to recover numerous towns previously lost to Hazael (II Kings 13:25). Though Adad-nirari ruled twenty-eight years, he was still young when he died. That he died without descendants created some problems over his succession. Internal dissension resulted during the reign of his successor Shalmaneser IV (783–773 B.C.). Matters did not improve but became still worse under his successor Ashurdan III (773–755 B.C.). It was

[10]Liberal scholars generally deny the authorship to Jonah but again on grounds unacceptable to conservative scholars. For discussion, see Archer, *A Survey of Old Testament Introduction*, pp. 297–301; Hobart E. Freeman, *An Introduction to the Old Testament Prophets*, pp. 165–166.

during his reign that the plague and eclipse occurred which spread fear and panic.

## 3. Work and person

Almost nothing is known regarding the work of Jonah as a prophet in Israel. The one reference noted above, II Kings 14:25, indicates that he was active and did predict the expansion of Israel to Jeroboam. What he did besides this is a matter of conjecture. Because he was a prophet and because God called him to the important Nineveh assignment, he must have been used of God in numerous ways. Thus he may be thought of as active in a prophetic ministry around the area of Gath-hepher, both before his visit to Nineveh and probably after.

His work in going to Nineveh is known in some detail, for it is the subject of his book. God called him to go there and cry against the city since its wickedness was great. Jonah rebelled at the call and immediately took a ship for Tarshish in the opposite direction. Enroute the ship became tossed by a raging storm sent by God, and this brought panic to the sailors. Lots were cast (according to their pagan ideas) to see on whose account the storm had been sent, and God used this means to designate Jonah. Jonah admitted that he had sinned against his God, and he told the men to cast him into the sea. This was done and God prepared a great fish to catch and swallow Jonah as he struck the water. Three days later the fish coughed him up onto the shore, and Jonah, now having learned his lesson, headed for Nineveh.

On reaching the great city, Jonah began to preach God's message: "Yet forty days and Nineveh shall be overthrown" (3:4). As he preached, his words took effect and the people in fear came to repent before God and put sackcloth on their bodies. Even the king of Nineveh did this and published a decree that both man and beast should be covered with sackcloth and cry mightily unto God. When God saw this repentance, He turned from bringing destruction on the city. This displeased Jonah, for he felt that he had been made to appear as a false prophet, and he called on God to take his life. God then taught Jonah the lesson—through a gourd that grew in a night and was destroyed in a night—that Jonah should be more interested in the sparing of people's lives than in any possible hurt he thought he had suffered.

It is noteworthy that this is the only occasion when an Israelite prophet was sent to a foreign country. For this reason Jonah has often been called God's foreign missionary of the Old Testament. One must be careful in so designating him, however, in view of the message he brought. It was hardly a message of salvation but rather of warning, as he said, "Yet forty days and

Nineveh shall be overthrown." Jonah was interested in the destruction of Ninevites, not their salvation. Still, that God sent Jonah to Nineveh even with such a message shows God's interest in the great city. The people deserved destruction due to their great wickedness, but God saw fit first to warn them and then to spare them.

One reason for Jonah's remarkable success in preaching at Nineveh has been noted, namely, the psychological conditioning of the people by preceding historical events. There were at least two other reasons. One was a probable effective manner of speaking by Jonah, for he told the people not only of Nineveh's destruction but of God's power to bring it, as demonstrated in his own life by the harrowing experience with the fish so shortly before. His body may still have shown certain effects of that experience. The second and certainly most important of all was God's own power to bring the spirit of repentance demonstrated as the people heard the stirring message. God clearly wanted the people to repent and used Jonah as an instrument to effect this change of heart.

It has been observed that Jonah must have been a true man of God to be called to the important mission to Nineveh. He evidently had proven himself in previous assignments to warrant his selection for this one. That he did not obey God at the time, however, but fled instead for Tarshish shows that he lacked in complete dedication of life. One cannot imagine, for instance, either Hosea or Amos having acted in this way. One has to ask the reason why Jonah did.

One part of the answer no doubt lies in the kind of country Assyria was at the time, a fact that Jonah evidently allowed to prey on his mind too much. Assyria for years had been the great and terrible conqueror of other countries. Fear and terror had spread everywhere as Assyria's armies had made conquest. Assyrian cruelty in these campaigns had become well known. Jonah, no doubt believing that such a country deserved only punishment and not gracious consideration, just did not want to go there.

Another part of the answer is that Jonah was not free from a narrow-mindedness that was characteristic of Jews of the day. Jews had come to think of Gentiles as undeserving of God's blessing. In their thinking the Jews were the chosen people of God, the ones to receive His special attention, and therefore Gentiles were outside of God's pale of grace. This same spirit continued on into New Testament time and caused Peter to hesitate in going to the home of Cornelius with the gospel message (Acts 10:9–21). The same thinking caused the church in Jerusalem to call Peter to account for his action when he did go (Acts 11:1–18). This attitude made a "middle wall of partition" between Jews and Gentiles, which Paul told the Ephesians Jesus had abolished through His death (Eph. 2:14–17). Jonah did not want to go to

Nineveh, then, simply because it was a city of Gentiles, to whom, as it seemed to him, God's message should not be taken.

One can hardly characterize Jonah as lacking in courage, however. One might think this in that he did not want to go to mighty Nineveh, but other factors in the story show differently. For example, he told the sailors in the boat to take him up and cast him into the sea. Anyone who has stood on the deck of a ship and seen angry waves can imagine what this meant. Jonah might have cringed and cried out for mercy, but he did not; he faced up to his guilt and called for the sailors to deal with him appropriately. This took remarkable courage.

Jonah must also have been a gifted speaker. As has been observed, there were other factors that prompted Nineveh's remarkable repentance, but surely one was the powerful preaching of this prophet. Foreigners would not have been new on the streets of Nineveh, and no doubt many attempted to proclaim their own particular messages. When Jonah preached, however, the whole city turned in repentance to God. His manner must have been forceful, his words meaningful, and his poise persuasive. People stopped to listen and they gave heed to what they heard. If Jonah preached this way in Nineveh, he must have done the same in Israel, and it would be interesting to know the results he had there. Of this, however, the Scriptures give no record.

## 4. The book

The Book of Jonah is different from all of the other prophetic books. It contains little prophecy at all but only a history of this one occasion. One could almost have expected it to be included among the historical books of the Old Testament. Because it is so unusual, one has to ask why God wanted Jonah to write it as a part of Sacred Writ. The reasons would seem to include the following:

First, there was a need for people to know that God had a real interest in Gentiles of the day. God had chosen Israel as a special people for Himself centuries earlier and thus had segregated His word for a time, but this was not because of a desire to forget the nations of the world at large. In fact it was to the end of making possible a gospel message that might be extended to all nations in due time. In the Book of Jonah God was showing that He maintained His interest in Gentiles even while He was working with His own people to this end.

Second, there was a need to rebuke the narrow-mindedness of Jews of the day. The experience itself would have done this much for Jonah, but there was need for a record of it if the Jewish people were to be reproved.

Third, Jonah served as a type of Christ. Jesus Himself spoke of Jonah's dwelling in the fish three days and three nights as typical of the time when He would be "three days and three nights in the heart of the earth" (Matt. 12:39–41).

Finally, several lessons were set forth that also were significant for generations to come. One was that God means His call when He gives it; He even provided a special "submarine" ride for Jonah to bring him to respond to His call properly. Second, God's servants should not let selfish interests govern the degree of their obedience when God calls. Third, God's warnings are often conditional; in this story He did not bring about the destruction of Nineveh when the Ninevites repented.[11]

The content of the book simply involves the history of this occasion and may be outlined as follows:

    I. Jonah's assignment and flight (1:1–17).

    II. Jonah's remarkable prayer (2:1–10).

    III. Jonah's assignment renewed and Nineveh's great repentance (3:1–10).

    IV. Jonah's displeasure and God's reproof (4:1–11).

[11]The historicity of Jonah has often been denied. For discussion of the problems involved see Archer, *Survey of Old Testament Introduction*, pp. 297–300; R. K. Harrison, *Introduction to the Old Testament*, pp. 905–911.

| | |
|---|---|
| 9th-Century Prophets | Chapter 16 Obadiah Joel |
| 8th-Century Prophets | Chapter 17 Hosea Amos Jonah |
| | Chapter 18 Isaiah Micah |
| 7th-Century Prophets | Chapter 19 Nahum Zephaniah Habakkuk |
| | Chapter 20 Jeremiah |
| Exilic Prophets | Chapter 21 Daniel Ezekiel |
| Postexilic Prophets | Chapter 22 Haggai Zechariah Malachi |

# 18

# Eighth-Century Prophets: Isaiah and Micah

Our interest now turns south from Israel to Judah, while staying in the same century of time. Isaiah and Micah are the prophets in view. Both were contemporary with Hosea but probably Amos had started and completed his work shortly before either of them began their ministry. Isaiah was one of the major prophets, in contrast to these others who are classified as minor prophets, and is often considered the prince of prophets. Therefore he calls for more detailed consideration than do the others.

## A. ISAIAH

### 1. The date

Isaiah again, like Hosea and Amos, dates his ministry to the reigns of specific kings. They are in fact the same kings of Judah mentioned by Hosea: Uzziah, Jotham, Ahaz, and Hezekiah (Isa. 1:1). He does not mention Jeroboam II, as does Hosea, for Isaiah prophesied to the southern kingdom and not the northern. Moreover, Jeroboam II very likely was dead by the time Isaiah started his work, for it is commonly held that Isaiah began in the late years of Uzziah. It may even have been in the last year of this ruler, in view of a divine call Isaiah received that year, as recorded in Isaiah 6. Isaiah probably lived even following the reign of Hezekiah. Isaiah refers to the death of the Assyrian emperor, Sennacherib, in 37:38 and this did not occur until 681 B.C., five years after Hezekiah's death in 686 B.C. Also II Chronicles 32:32 states that Isaiah wrote a history of Hezekiah and this would not have been possible until Hezekiah had died.

This means that Isaiah lived a few years into the reign of Manasseh, son of Hezekiah. The reason Isaiah does not include the name of Manasseh in his list is perhaps that he was too old to carry on an effective outward ministry by this time. He could still write, but his work of preaching had probably been confined to the time of the earlier four kings. Since Uzziah died in 739 B.C., Isaiah's ministry may be thought of as continuing from about 740 B.C. to 680 B.C., or approximately sixty years. As to a chronological comparison with Hosea, Isaiah began approximately twenty years after this contemporary and continued about thirty years longer. Isaiah's ministry was probably the longest of any of Israel's prophets.

## 2. Background history

The rule of Uzziah, which was discussed in the previous chapter, was coming to an end when Isaiah began his work. Under God's blessing Uzziah had been able to expand the borders of Judah much as Jeroboam II had the borders of Israel. Jotham (750–731 B.C.), his son and successor, was able to continue the power of his father in large part. He was the fourth successive God-approved king of Judah (Joash, Amaziah, Uzziah, Jotham), and accordingly he continued to experience the blessing of God. He won a major military engagement with the Ammonites and received payment of tribute as a result for three years. In Jerusalem he built an important gate of the temple and added to the "wall of Ophel." Elsewhere in the land he enlarged cities and erected forts and towers as a means of defense.

Ahaz (743–715 B.C.) was made co-regent with his father prior to Jotham's death and differed from his father in two major respects. One was that he did not follow the ways of God and the other that he pursued a pro-Assyrian policy in Jerusalem. Because he did, he suffered a siege at the hands of Pekah, king of Israel, and Rezin, king of Damascus (II Kings 16:5-9; II Chron. 28:5-21). They wanted to force Ahaz to unite with them in resisting Assyria, but Ahaz refused, and, in order to rid himself of the siege, he requested Tiglath-pileser III, the great king of Assyria, to come and attack these two northern countries. He sent the Assyrian monarch considerable gold and silver, and Tiglath-pileser did come though he probably did not need such an inducement to do so.

Religiously, Ahaz made images of Baal, observed infant sacrifice in the Valley of Hinnom, and worshiped in the high places. While visiting in Damascus, he saw an altar he admired and had one like it reproduced in Jerusalem, establishing it as his official place of sacrifice at the temple. Besides this, he intentionally damaged several of the sacred vessels of the temple and even closed the temple doors, thus forcing people to worship where and as he desired. Militarily he experienced a revolt by Edom which lost him the important southern trade routes. It was during his time that the Philistines once again invaded Judah and brought severe destruction, even seizing several cities which are listed. It seems he also had to make further payment to Tiglath-pileser after the Assyrian conqueror arrived in the area to make attacks on Damascus and Israel (II Chron. 28:20, 21).

Hezekiah, son and successor of Ahaz (728–686 B.C.), was made co-regent with his father for a few years, probably because of pressure from a growing anti-Assyrian party in Jerusalem who objected to the pro-Assyrian tactics of Ahaz. Hezekiah was definitely anti-Assyrian, and he also was once more a God-pleasing king. In fact Hezekiah proved to be one of Judah's finest kings in the sight of God. The doors of the temple were again opened, and priests and Levites were instructed to remove all foreign cult items. A grand time of sacrificing and celebration marked the return of true Mosaic ceremonies (II Chron. 29:20–36). The land was cleansed of high places, images, Asherah poles, false altars, and even the brazen serpent that Moses had made in the wilderness (Num. 21:5–9). It was a time of needed wide-sweeping reforms.

Militarily, Judah now was the object of Assyrian interest, Israel having fallen in 722 B.C. So long as Israel had existed, this northern neighbor acted as a buffer for Judah, but with Israel gone, Judah was next in line in the Assyrian plan of conquest. For a time Hezekiah avoided an encounter, due especially to his refusal to join a coalition formed against Assyria.[1] A few years later, however, Hezekiah did join one, of which Tyre was the head and to which the Egyptian king, Shabaka, gave promise of support; and now the new Assyrian emperor, Sennacherib, came.[2] Hezekiah made extensive preparations (II Chron. 32:1–8).[3] Sennacherib first came to Tyre, and the king

---

[1]This coalition was led by the city of Ashdod; and Sargon, now the Assyrian ruler, came and crushed it in 711 B.C. Ashdod had been promised help by Egypt but when the Assyrian attack came Egypt did not bring help, and when Ashdod's king fled to Egypt for protection Egypt even handed him back to the Assyrians. For the Assyrian account see *Ancient Near Eastern Texts*, ed. James B. Pritchard, p. 286.

[2]Ibid., p. 287.

[3]He constructed fortifications, made new weapons, reinforced military strength, and built the famous Siloam tunnel, running from the spring of Gihon to a place within the city wall (II Kings 20:20 and II Chron. 32:30).

there fled to Cyprus. Sennacherib then moved south to the region of Judah. The story at this point is told in detail in II Kings 18:13—19:37; II Chronicles 32:9-21; and Isaiah 36-37.

Sennacherib laid siege to Lachish, and Hezekiah sent heavy tribute to him there, showing that he realized the cause of the revolt had already been lost. Sennacherib was not satisfied with this but pursued psychological warfare against Hezekiah and the people. His threats were effective in causing fear in Jerusalem and Hezekiah was prompted to consult with Isaiah to receive a comforting word from God. This was given and God also brought help to His people, first in the form of assistance from Egypt and later by the destruction of no less than 185,000 Assyrian troops in one night. Sennacherib gives no indication of this destruction in his own account of the campaign, but this is to be expected.[4] Definite corroboration is indicated by his immediate withdrawal from the land without attempting to conquer Jerusalem or any more of Judah's cities.

Manasseh (697–642 B.C.) succeeded Hezekiah and served as co-regent prior to his father's death, making him the fifth consecutive Judean prince to begin reigning in this manner. Religiously, Manasseh returned to the wicked ways of Ahaz his grandfather. He restored the offensive cultic objects that Hezekiah had destroyed, placed Baal altars throughout the land, and recognized the Ammonite deity Moloch. Those who protested he killed, thus shedding innocent blood. It may be that Isaiah was among those slain, something to which tradition testifies.

## 3. Work and person

### a. THE WORK

As to the work of Isaiah, a few specific episodes are recorded which are noteworthy. One concerns the call he received in the last year of King Uzziah. In vision Isaiah saw God seated upon a throne high and lifted up in the temple. Around him were six angels called seraphim, having six wings each. They cried to each other, "Holy, holy, holy, is the LORD of hosts; the whole earth is full of his glory" (Isa. 6:3). Isaiah was taken with a strong sense of personal sinfulness, and he cried out, "Woe is me." One of the angels flew to him to place a coal on his mouth and to cleanse it, and then Isaiah heard the voice of God saying, "Whom shall I send, and who will go for us?" Isaiah responded, "Here am I; send me" (6:8). God then spoke a word that must

---

[4]Sennacherib left a record of the campaign on what is called the Taylor Prism, now in the British Museum. For this text, see *Ancient Near Eastern Texts*, pp. 287-288; also *Documents from Old Testament Times*, ed. D. Winton Thomas, pp. 64-68.

have been disquieting for Isaiah—the people would hear him but not understand and they would see but not perceive. In other words, Isaiah should indeed answer God's call, but he should also be aware ahead of time that there would be few results coming from his efforts.

This occasion may have constituted Isaiah's initial call to service or it may have been merely a call to a special aspect of work. If it was the initial call, then Isaiah's ministry did not begin until the closing year of Uzziah's reign. If it was a call to an aspect of work, then he may have begun ministering a few years earlier. Scholars are divided in their thinking and there is no way to know which possibility is the true one.

A second episode is recorded in Isaiah 7 (cf. II Chron. 28:1–15). It took place in the reign of Ahaz and concerned the time of the siege of Pekah and Rezin. The siege was in progress when God told Isaiah to go to Ahaz and encourage him in his difficult situation, and also to instruct him to ask for a sign from the Lord that deliverance would come. Ahaz's response was, "I will not ask, neither will I tempt the LORD" (7:12), thus in false piety refusing to do as God and Isaiah directed. Isaiah gave Ahaz a sign anyway, which was the well-known messianic indication, "Behold, a virgin shall conceive, and bear a son, and shall call his name Immanuel" (7:14). Isaiah went on to say that before this child would know the difference between good and evil, Ahaz would be delivered from the two besieging kings.

But instead of listening to Isaiah's promise or depending on God to bring the deliverance thus indicated, Ahaz in his wickedness sent to Tiglath-pileser III, emperor of Assyria, to come and invade the northern countries so that Pekah and Rezin would have to go home to protect their own interests. In doing this, Ahaz showed his pro-Assyrian leanings and also a lack of recognition that his greatest enemy really was Assyria rather than Israel or Damascus. Isaiah now informed him of this fact in definite terms, though apparently without avail.

Numerous viewpoints exist as to Isaiah's meaning when he gave Ahaz the sign, "A virgin shall conceive, and bear a son, and shall call his name Immanuel."[5] The one that seems to fit the situation best involves a double fulfillment. Certainly the main fulfillment concerned Christ, born many centuries later. He alone would be born of a virgin, and He alone could be called Immanuel ("God with us"). There was reason for Isaiah to refer to Christ in this context in view of the dark day Judah was experiencing. Isaiah was saying that, in contrast, a bright day was coming when the great Deliverer of God would arrive and bring relief from all such dark days for God's people. At the same time, Isaiah must have had a preliminary fulfillment in

[5]For enumeration of viewpoints, see Hobart E. Freeman, *An Introduction to the Old Testament Prophets*, pp. 203–207.

mind, one that would be meaningful for Ahaz in his dire situation in that day. He was being besieged and desperately wanted deliverance. Thus, Isaiah must have intended to say also that before a child soon to be born at that time would be old enough to know good and evil, this deliverance would come. Just what child was in mind is not clear, though it may have been Maher-shalal-hash-baz, Isaiah's son (Isa. 8:1-4).

The third episode is recorded in Isaiah 36 and 37 (cf. II Kings 18:13—19:37) and concerns Isaiah's contacts with King Hezekiah in the time of the invasion by Sennacherib of Assyria. Isaiah was involved two times. The first came following the visit to Jerusalem by three emissaries of Sennacherib, who brought great fear to the entire city. As a result, Hezekiah sent a messenger to Isaiah to inform him of what had happened and to urge him to beseech God for help. Isaiah sent a word of response that Hezekiah should not fear, for God would so work that Sennacherib would return to his own land without harming Jerusalem.

The second contact came after Hezekiah received a letter from Sennacherib, written apparently from Lachish when Sennacherib realized he had to meet a challenge from the king of Egypt. Hezekiah prayed for help unto God and God sent a message of wonderful encouragement through Isaiah. The message was of some length but had one main point: the king of Assyria would not come near Jerusalem but would be made to return to his own city. The prophet's words were, "He shall not come into this city, nor shoot an arrow there, nor come before it with shields, nor cast a bank against it. By the way that he came, by the same shall he return, and shall not come into this city, saith the LORD" (37:33, 34).

An important role played by Isaiah in the day of Hezekiah had been that of warning the king and all Judah against depending upon Egypt or any foreign alliance to help withstand an attack by Assyria (e.g., Isa. 30:1-7; 31:1-3). In this he had been opposed by false prophets (30:8-11). Isaiah's warning was heeded by Hezekiah in respect to the alliance of 711 B.C., when Sargon, father of Sennacherib, came and destroyed Ashdod. But apparently greater pressure was brought on the king in respect to the alliance of 701 B.C. when Sennacherib came, for Hezekiah did join then as has been seen.

It is obvious that the episodes that have been noted concern only a small part of Isaiah's total ministry. What can be said of his life's work in general? In view of his great character and the remarkable book he wrote, one may be sure that this man was active all during the reigns of the kings designated. Beginning with the close of Uzziah's reign and continuing through the days of Jotham, Ahaz, and Hezekiah, Isaiah was the leading prophet of the time, active wherever he could be in carrying out God's assignments. Since he had contacts with kings that have been recorded, it is likely that he also had contacts that have not been recorded. He may well have opposed the ascendancy of Ahaz as co-ruler with Jotham in view of the pro-Assyrian policy of Ahaz. In the same vein, he probably had something to do with the accession of Hezekiah as co-ruler with Ahaz, when the thinking of the day turned against this pro-Assyrian program. And one has to believe that Isaiah was involved in promoting the reforms that Hezekiah instituted.

Besides this, Isaiah would have been active in preaching to people on street corners, at the gates of the city, or wherever they might be assembled. Since he was knowledgeable of the world of his day (as his book shows), he would have kept close contact with activities of Israel to the north. Devastations brought there by Tiglath-pileser would have provided a forceful illustration of what could happen to Judah if the people persisted in their wicked ways. Then the final overthrow of the northern neighbor would have provided a still more forceful occasion to stress this warning.

The outstanding significance of Isaiah is probably to be found in this warning to Judah in view of Israel's destruction. Certainly God wanted Judah to take notice of the punishment Israel experienced, in order that Judah might profit and turn in repentance to God. But if she was to have the forceful lesson driven home, there needed to be a great prophet like Isaiah—and also Micah whom we consider next—to do this. God therefore had an Isaiah and a Micah available for the purpose.

b. THE PERSON

Coming now to speak of Isaiah as a person, Isaiah states that he was the son of Amoz (not Amos, the contemporary prophet), that he was married to a "prophetess" (8:3), and that he had two sons, Shear-jashub (7:3) and Maher-shalal-hash-baz (8:1–4). Many fine characteristics of this great man are implied and illustrated in the materials he recorded in his book.

*1) Prince of prophets.* Isaiah is often called the prince of prophets. The designation is probably appropriate and for two reasons. The first is the ability of Isaiah. As will be noted, he was a man of unusual ability, showing excellent training and widespread knowledge of the world as well as a capacity for work. Few prophets and perhaps few people in the land could have matched him. The second concerns the amount of messianic prophecy God was pleased to reveal through him. It seems fair to say that God told him more regarding the Messiah than He did to any other man of the Old Testament. This was certainly a great honor and privilege.

*2) Spiritual status.* That Isaiah was spiritually mature in his walk with God is beyond question. Evidence may be noted already from the call to service he received. When he saw God high and lifted up, his first reaction was to think of his own sinfulness. His life otherwise was certainly righteous when compared with others, but he recognized that in comparison with God he was most unworthy. This in itself was a mark of high spirituality. Another such mark was his willingness to respond affirmatively to God's call when God told him plainly that his ministry would have little effect. Certainly this was a discouraging word with which to begin, but Isaiah did not hesitate. He still went ahead, obedient to the call God had given.

Another indication comes from Isaiah's manner of contact with kings. To Ahaz he came with a word of rebuke. Though Ahaz was king, holding supreme power in the land, Isaiah did not fear to bring God's message of reprimand for the king's action in sending to Tiglath-pileser for assistance. This required a true sense of obedience, commitment, and dedication. Then Isaiah was the man of whom Hezekiah thought first in his time of great danger before Sennacherib. There were certainly other prophets in the land, but it was to Isaiah that Hezekiah sent, and again it was through Isaiah that God responded to Hezekiah when he received the letter from the Assyrian conqueror. Hezekiah clearly recognized Isaiah as the leading prophet of the day, the one through whom God would likely reveal in this time of trouble for the country.

Still another indication comes from the book Isaiah wrote. In it he exalts God in the highest terms. Especially he stresses the theme of God's holiness. His early vision of God high and lifted up in the temple, when the angels cried out before God, "Holy, holy, holy," seems to have set the tone for his life and for all of his book. A recurrent phrase in his writing is, "The holy One of Israel."

*3) Ease at the royal court.* Probably none of the prophets exhibited greater ease than did Isaiah in visiting the royal court. He came to Ahaz and not only had courage to bring rebuke, but spoke at considerable length in enlarging on the danger Ahaz faced from Assyria. Later it was to Isaiah that Hezekiah sent for help, when Sennacherib was in the country. This showed Hezekiah's high respect for Isaiah as a prophet and friend. Soon after, God sent Isaiah to tell the ailing Hezekiah that God would make him well and also extend his life for fifteen years (Isa. 38:5). Though no indications are given of similar visits to the court of Jotham earlier, one can believe they occurred, especially since Jotham also was one of Israel's good kings.

This ease of royal contact may have been due to a blood relationship Isaiah held to the royal line. Jewish tradition says that Isaiah's father, Amoz, was a brother of King Amaziah, the father of Uzziah, thus making Isaiah a cousin of King Uzziah. Ease of contact was probably due also to Isaiah's own knowledge and ability, which were apparent in his day. Kings liked to have people of Isaiah's caliber on whom they could call, and they gave them respect and honor accordingly.

*4) Intellectual ability.*   Isaiah clearly was one of the intellectuals of his day. He was a man of broad knowledge of the world. No less than eleven chapters of his book (13–23) are devoted to prophecies of judgment that God would bring on surrounding nations. These nations were not only those near to Judah but included Babylonia and Assyria far to the east and Egypt and Ethiopia far to the southwest. To write in as much detail as he does shows that he was informed regarding these lands. He must have read widely and also made a point to speak with caravan travelers and visiting foreigners.

Then his literary ability shows an excellence unsurpassed elsewhere in the Old Testament and seldom matched in any literature. Much of his material is in poetry and it is truly superb in form. Many sections constitute literary masterpieces. He excelled in the use of figures of speech. He personified cities (47:1f.; 51:17), nature (44:23; 49:13), the points of the compass (43:6), God's arm (40:10; 51:9), God's word (55:11). He represented Zion as a wife (49:18; 54:5) who was barren (54:1), and as a mother (49:17; 51:18–20) who was bereaved of her children (49:21; 51:20). Isaiah's use of such figures gives an imagery to his book that makes it live and strike home with force to the reader. He must have been trained in the finest schools of the land.

*5) Courage.*   One must also see Isaiah as a prophet of outstanding courage. The evidence is clear. It took courage to go to Ahaz with words of denouncement and rebuke. Ahaz was the king and might retaliate with severe punishment, but this apparently made no difference to Isaiah. It took courage to speak as he did in the day of Hezekiah. He warned repeatedly concerning the danger of foreign alliance and especially dependence upon Egypt. This was an unpopular message, for people were interested in any measure that would be anti-Assyrian. Isaiah was not in favor of Assyria either, but he knew the folly of trusting in Egypt and local alliances. He therefore gave the warning whether popular or not.

## 4. The book

The Book of Isaiah is considered one of the most significant of the Old Testament. This is indicated for one thing by the frequency of its quotations in the New Testament: by name no less than twenty-one times, and numerous illusions and references to it besides. Its theme is similar to the meaning of Isaiah's name: "Yahweh [Jehovah] is salvation." The purpose is to teach that God's salvation for His people is by grace alone. This theme is presented under two main divisions. In chapters 1–39 the prophet depicts Judah's sin and warns the people of sure punishment to come if this sin is continued. Intermixed are warnings to other nations as well. The time in view is the day in which Isaiah himself lived.

In chapters 40–66, Isaiah brings a word of comfort and also messianic prediction. Here for the most part the time in view is future to Isaiah's day, as the prophet projects himself ahead and sees Judah's punishment as already having taken place. He gives comfort to the people that there will be deliverance from it. He enlarges on this comfort by saying that eventually the Messiah Himself will come and bring deliverance from the cause of this punishment, the sinfulness of the people. Still further he tells of the glorious millennial day when Israel as a nation will rule in the world and be the supreme people.

The question of the unity of the Book of Isaiah has been cause for extensive discussion. Conservative scholars believe that Isaiah wrote the entire book, while liberal scholars believe that it was written by at least two if not three or more authors.[6] Because this is so there is reason to note at least briefly some principal evidences for a sole authorship.

First and foremost is the certain witness of the New Testament. As noted, the book is quoted no less than twenty-one times in the New Testament with these quotations coming from all parts of the book and the only author of them named is Isaiah. For instance, Isaiah 53:1 is quoted in John 12:38, with the indication, "That the saying of Esaias the prophet might be fulfilled."

Another evidence is that the book is assigned to Isaiah in 1:1 and in no place is another author named. The implication is that the entire book comes from this one man. Certainly if another person had written, for example, chapters 40–66, which are so outstanding for their literary value, he would have designated his name, but none is given.

A third indication is that a belief in Isaiah's authorship for all the book can be traced back to a time well before the birth of Christ. For instance, Ben Sirach, who wrote the apochryphal book Ecclesiasticus about the year 180 B.C., so believed. He stated, "He [Isaiah] comforted them that mourn in Zion. He showed the things that should be till the end of time, and the hidden things or ever they came" (48:24, 25). He clearly was referring to the most controverted section of Isaiah, chapters 40–66, and still he assigned it to Isaiah, with no intimation of any other author. Then the Septuagint was translated about the time that Ben Sirach lived, and it gives no hint either of

---

[6]For a review of positions both conservative and liberal, see R. K. Harrison, *Introduction to the Old Testament*, pp. 765–774.

another author for any part of the book. And further, the testimony of the Dead Sea scroll of Isaiah is most significant. Not only does it give no implication of another author writing any part of the book, including chapters 40–66, but it shows chapter 40 beginning on the last line of the column which contains 38:8 to 40:2. This is strange indeed if the copier of the day believed that another author wrote the closing section.

Again the author of Isaiah 40–66 shows greater familiarity with Palestine than Babylon. This would not be true if the author lived in Babylon, as the liberal critics contend. Actually, little is said regarding Babylon but considerable regarding Palestine. The author speaks of Jerusalem and the mountains of Palestine; he mentions some of the trees that were native there, as, for instance, the cedars, the cypress, and the oak (41:19; 44:14). Also in 40:9, the cities of Judah are spoken of as still in existence, and in 62:6 the walls of Jerusalem are seen to be standing, neither of which would have been true at the time of an alleged later writer living after the destruction of Judah and Jerusalem.

Further, suitable response is possible to a principal argument used by liberal critics concerning style differences between chapters 1–39 and 40–66. It is true that there are style differences, but there are also style similarities. For instance, the phrase, "Holy One of Israel," as a designation for God is used twelve times in chapters 1–39 and fourteen times in chapters 40–66. It is used elsewhere in the Old Testament only five times. Other concepts run all the way through the book, such as "highway," "remnant," and "Zion." The differences in style that exist can well be attributed to certain portions of the book having been written at different times in Isaiah's life and also to a variety in subject matter.

And lastly two matters that constitute problems for the liberal critic present no difficulty for the conservative scholar. One is the existence of precise predictive prophecy, as for instance a reference to Cyrus by name in Isaiah 44:28 and 45:1. For those who deny the possibility of supernatural prediction, Isaiah could not have written this for he lived a century and a half too early. Conservative scholars, however, believe the name was revealed by God. The other is a difference in stress as to theological concept between 1–39 and 40–66. The majesty of God is made more prominent in the earlier part and the uniqueness and infinitude of God in the latter. The conservative scholar, once more, has no difficulty accounting for this difference, doing so again in terms of subject matter. It is God's majesty that is to be stressed when the sin of people is the primary subject, and it is His uniqueness and infinitude that are important when one speaks of God's mighty deliverance from the Babylonian captivity and man's captivity to sin.

The book may be outlined as follows:

I. Prophecies from the standpoint of Isaiah's day (1:1—35:10).

A. Prophecies regarding Judah and Jerusalem (1:1—12:6).
   1. Judah's sin condemned (1:1-31).
   2. Millennial blessing following cleansing (2:1—4:6).
   3. Punishment for Judah's sin (5:1-30).
   4. Isaiah's vision and call (6:1-13).
   5. Prediction of Immanuel (7:1-25).
   6. Prediction of Assyrian invasion (8:1-22).
   7. Messianic prediction and warning (9:1-21).
   8. Assyrian pride and punishment (10:1-34).
   9. Christ's millennial reign (11:1-16).
   10. Millennial worship (12:1-6).
B. Prophecies against nations (13:1—23:18).
   1. Babylon (13:1—14:23).
   2. Assyria (14:24-27).
   3. Philistia (14:28-32).
   4. Moab (15:1-16:14).
   5. Damascus (17:1-14).
   6. Ethiopia (18:1-7).
   7. Egypt (19:1—20:6).
   8. Babylon, Edom, Arabia (21:1-17).
   9. Jerusalem (22:1-25).
   10. Tyre (23:1-18).
C. Prediction of destruction and deliverance (24:1—27:13).
   1. Destruction of the land (24:1-15).
   2. The great tribulation (24:16-23).
   3. Worship and testimony of restored Israel (25:1—27:13).
D. Prediction of punishment by Assyria (28:1—31:9).
   1. Fall of Samaria predicted (28:1-13).
   2. Warning to Judah (28:14-29).
   3. Attack on Judah (29:1-16).
   4. Promise of deliverance (29:17-24).
   5. Warning against an Egyptian alliance (30:1—31:9).
E. Predictions of the far future (32:1—35:10).
   1. Future deliverance by the Messiah (32:1—33:24).
   2. The day of the Lord (34:1-17).
   3. Millennial blessings (35:1-10).
II. A historical section (36:1—39:8).
A. Invasion of Sennacherib (36:1—37:38).
B. Hezekiah's illness and recovery (38:1-22).
C. Prediction of the Babylonian captivity (39:1-8).
III. Prophecies from a standpoint future to Isaiah (40:1—66:24).
A. Comfort in view of promised restoration (40:1—48:22).

## B. MICAH

### 1. The date

Micah was a contemporary of Isaiah, possibly a few years younger. He dates his ministry to the reigns of Jotham, Ahaz, and Hezekiah (1:1). Because he does not mention Uzziah as Isaiah does, he evidently started his ministry a little later than Isaiah, and because he mentions nothing concerning the invasion of Sennacherib in the day of Hezekiah he probably ceased earlier. Perhaps the years 735–710 B.C. are likely for his time.

Some scholars have challenged these dates of Micah, but still further evidence can be cited to show that they are correct. That he ministered during the time of Hezekiah is indicated directly by Jeremiah: in 26:18, 19 this prophet refers to Micah as prophesying in Hezekiah's day and quotes Micah 3:12. Then that he prophesied prior to 722 B.C., the date of Samaria's fall—during the reign of Ahaz—is indicated by Micah's direct prediction of that fall in 1:2–6. And further, that he was active in the time of Jotham is implied by his reference to the horses and chariots of Judah in 5:10, a suggestion of prosperity in the land. This would have been true especially in Jotham's time following the great days of Uzziah.

## 2. Background history

Really nothing more needs to be said regarding background history than what was said in respect to Isaiah, who began earlier and ministered longer than Micah. It need only be made clear that the invasion of Sennacherib apparently did not involve Micah, who may have died before that occasion. He would have lived through the stirring days of Assyrian attacks against Israel, however, and the final fall of that country to the eastern enemy, and this would have affected his ministry just as it did that of Isaiah.

## 3. Work and person

Micah gives a few clues in his book as to his work and person, but he does not include any historical episodes as does Isaiah nor is he mentioned in any of the historical books of the Old Testament. He identifies his home town as Moresheth (1:1), which is no doubt to be identified with Moresheth-gath (1:14), located in the western lowlands of Judah about twenty miles southwest of Jerusalem. Since Moresheth was a small rural city, Micah from the first had contact with rural people, who were for the most part poor people, and his book reflects a grave concern for the poor of his day. The city also was located near the international highway leading north and south for caravan travel, and this may account for his acquaintance with international affairs. He shows particular interest in and knowledge of Israel to the north. In this interest, he may have been influenced by Amos who had ministered at Bethel only about twenty-five years earlier. He may also have been influenced by Amos' writing, as indicated by a comparison of Micah 2:6 with Amos 2:12 and 7:10–16. It should be realized that Tekoa, the home town of Amos, was only twenty miles east of Moresheth. There could well have been contact between the two.

That Micah did move about and not stay merely in the area of Moresheth is indicated by implied contacts with Jerusalem and people there. For instance, he was familiar with false prophets, whose center was especially the capital city, saying that they made God's people err (3:5-7). That Micah was well known is implied in that Jeremiah makes mention of him, as noted above (Jer. 26:18). Since the prophets did not ordinarily mention each other and especially since Jeremiah lived a century after Micah, this reference to Micah is very unusual. It implies that Micah made a strong impression in his day, and this indicates in turn that he must have ministered frequently in and around Jerusalem, the place where a lasting impression would have been made. Furthermore, the manner of reference of Jeremiah is significant for it shows that Hezekiah, king during Micah's later ministry, not only knew Micah but held him in high respect. There is insufficient reason to believe that Micah had as much contact with kings as did Isaiah, but then few prophets did. Isaiah doubtless had more than anyone else, but Micah at least had some and should not be unduly minimized in importance. One should not regard him as a mere shadow of the great Isaiah.

In summary, one should think of Micah as a worthy contemporary of Isaiah, no doubt greatly influenced by him. Micah may have had a greater interest than Isaiah in the poor and downtrodden of the day, and God may have used him in this area of ministry especially. The main stress of both was to speak of sin and warn of certain punishment if no repentance was shown. Both prophets were fully aware of what was happening to Israel in the north, where destruction was already being experienced, and they used that illustration to impress Judah that the same could well happen to her.

## 4. The book

The Book of Micah is made up of three sections, each beginning with the imperative "Hear" (1:2; 3:1; 6:1). Some expositors have thought of these sections as three unit messages, but it is more likely that they are compilations of thoughts, spoken at various times in Micah's public ministry. In bringing together a variety of thoughts in this way, taken from different times of ministry, Micah shows a parallel with Isaiah, for Isaiah does the same thing. Micah also shows similarity to Isaiah in many of the thoughts he brings and the way he brings them, even including at one time a passage which is nearly identical with one in Isaiah (Mic. 4:1-3; cf. Isa. 2:2-4). Scholars have sought to account for this in a variety of ways, including Isaiah's dependency on Micah, Micah's dependency on Isaiah, or the dependency of both on a common source. There seems to be no way to be sure regarding the matter.

Because the Book of Micah treats numerous subjects, passing rather quickly from one to another, many liberal scholars have held that the book is not a unity but came from more than one author. However, Isaiah also treats subjects in a similar way, and it has already been seen that there is insufficient reason for believing in a multiple authorship for Isaiah. One need not conclude this regarding Micah either. Liberals refer also to ideas of salvation and future glory days for Israel in the book; and this is said to indicate a later author for the passages involved, since these ideas were not current in Micah's day. But conservative scholars believe otherwise and point out that the same ideas are presented also by Isaiah and other early prophets.[7]

Some matters to note from the content of the book are the following: a definite reference to the fall of Samaria (1:5-7); exhortation regarding the oppression of the poor (2:1—3:4); and prediction of the Messiah both as to His first and second advents (4:1-8; 5:2-8; 7:7-20).

The book may be outlined as follows:

I. Coming punishment on Israel and Judah (1:1—2:13).
   A. Both Israel and Judah to be punished (1:1-16).
   B. This punishment the result of sin (2:1-13).
II. The future messianic kingdom (3:1—5:15).
   A. Preparatory punishment of wicked leaders (3:1-12).
   B. The glorious kingdom (4:1-13).
   C. The glorious King and His work (5:1-15).
III. Punishment of the people and final mercy (6:1—7:20).
   A. God's controversy with the people (6.1-16).
   B. Reproof and promise (7:1-20).

[7]For a survey of positions and arguments see Harrison, *Introduction to the Old Testament*, pp. 922-925.

| | |
|---|---|
| 9th-Century Prophets | **Chapter 16** Obadiah Joel |
| 8th-Century Prophets | **Chapter 17** Hosea Amos Jonah |
| | **Chapter 18** Isaiah Micah |
| 7th-Century Prophets | **Chapter 19** Nahum Zephaniah Habakkuk |
| | **Chapter 20** Jeremiah |
| Exilic Prophets | **Chapter 21** Daniel Ezekiel |
| Postexilic Prophets | **Chapter 22** Haggai Zechariah Malachi |

# 19

# Seventh-Century Prophets: Nahum, Zephaniah, and Habakkuk

We now move on from the eighth-century prophets to those of the seventh century, and like those of the eighth century, these also came in a group. It was noted that the eighth-century prophets ministered between 760 and shortly after 700 B.C., whether they prophesied in Israel or Judah. The time of the seventh-century prophets is even more confined, beginning probably not before 630 B.C. and running again shortly after the turn of the following century. No writing prophets ministered during the first two-thirds of the seventh century except for Isaiah, who lived perhaps the first twenty years of that time. This does not mean that there were no prophets ministering at all, for, as was noted in chapter 8, there probably was not a time in Israel's history when there were no prophets available for service. None of the writing prophets, however, who no doubt were the more influential prophets, lived and ministered during those intervening years.

There were four writing prophets who ministered during this last part of the seventh century: Nahum, Zephaniah, Habakkuk, and Jeremiah. Because the first three were minor prophets, much less is known about them, and they can all be treated in this chapter. More is known regarding Jeremiah, and he will be considered in the following chapter.

## A. NAHUM

### 1. The date

Nahum does not date his ministry to the reign of one or more kings, as do the eighth-century prophets, so his time must be determined by internal evidence from his book. Two matters in particular give help. One is a reference to the destruction of the city of No in Egypt. The city in mind was No-Amon (Thebes), which was destroyed in 663 B.C. by the Assyrian Ashurbanipal. The event is spoken of as past, and therefore Nahum must have prophesied after it happened (3:8-10). The other clue is that the fall of Nineveh is indicated as still future. In fact the theme of the book concerns the predicted destruction of this great Assyrian city. This destruction came in 612 B.C., and therefore Nahum's ministry lay somewhere between these dates. A precise date is impossible to designate, but since Zephaniah, who dates his ministry more precisely as transpiring in the rule of Josiah, also foretells the fall of Nineveh (2:13), it may be that Nahum made his prediction about the same time. The rationale for grouping the seventh-century prophets closely together (something to be discussed later) gives further cause to believe Nahum came roughly at the time of Zephaniah. Thus it may be that the beginning of his ministry fell about 630 B.C., and it is quite possible that he continued to serve during most of Josiah's reign.

### 2. Background history

Though Nahum is best located in the good reign of Josiah, his prophecy and that of the other seventh-century prophets cannot be appreciated or understood apart from some notice of the preceding wicked reigns of Manasseh and Amon. Manasseh (697–642 B.C.) was the son and successor of good king Hezekiah. He ruled fifty-five years, the longest of any king in either Judah or Israel. Manasseh did not follow the pattern of his godly father but pursued the way of wicked Ahaz, his grandfather. He restored the offensive cultic objects that Hezekiah had destroyed, placed altars of Baal throughout the land and even in the temple, and recognized the Ammonite deity, Moloch, by sacrificing his children in the Valley of Hinnom. He approved various forms of pagan divination and erected an image of the Canaanite goddess Asherah in the temple. Those who protested he killed. Manasseh is said to have caused the people to do more evil than did the nations whom God had dispossessed from the land centuries before (II Kings 21:9).

Accordingly he experienced punishment from God by being taken captive to Babylon (II Chron. 33:11). Little is known regarding the captivity, but it was effected either by Sennacherib's son Esarhaddon (681–669 B.C.), or grandson Ashurbanipal (669–633 B.C.), in whose successive reigns Assyria reached a zenith of power. Both rulers made campaigns as far south as Egypt and both recorded references to the region of Palestine, which could imply such a captivity. Manasseh was permitted eventually to return to Judah, when he repented before God, and then he commendably sought to make amends for his earlier wickedness. There is no indication of how many years of his rule remained in which he could carry out this reformation activity.

The son and successor of Manasseh was Amon (642–640 B.C.). He reverted to wicked practices again, apparently not being impressed by the reforms of the closing years of his father. Perhaps his own servants came to be repulsed by his sinful actions, for some of them banded together in a conspiracy and killed him in his own house after two years of rule. Since he reigned only this short period, his influence was not nearly that of his father.

Because Amon died early, his son and successor, Josiah (640–609 B.C.), began to rule at the young age of eight years. Though starting young, Josiah proved to be one of the finest rulers in Judah's history, and the three decades of his reign were among the happiest in Judah's experience. They were characterized by peace, prosperity, and reform. Assyria, the great enemy until his time, was no longer strong. Ashurbanipal's closing years witnessed little military activity, and only weak leaders followed until Nineveh's fall in 612 B.C. Babylon, the next great enemy power of the Middle East, did not take over leadership until 605 B.C., leaving smaller kingdoms of the area free to rule themselves. The Aramaeans of Damascus were no longer a menace either, having been brought to complete submission by the Assyrian power some years before.

Josiah as a lad had God-fearing advisors who offset the influences of his father, for Josiah followed the ways of God from the first. Already at the age of sixteen he began "to seek after the God of David his father" (II Chron. 34:3). At the age of twenty he began to cleanse Jerusalem and Judah of the idolatrous objects his father and grandfather had brought into the land (II Chron. 34:3–7).

At the age of twenty-six (622 B.C.), Josiah proceeded with still more concentrated efforts in reformation. This special endeavor was prompted in part by the discovery[1] of "a book of the law of the LORD given by Moses" (II Chron. 34:14).[2] Josiah was disturbed at the deviation he recognized between

[1]Manasseh may have destroyed all copies of the Law that he could find. This copy may then have been hidden so that it became lost to knowledge. It is possible, too, that this copy had been placed in the cornerstone of the temple by Solomon, a practice not uncommon for the day.

[2]Probably a copy of the five books of Moses. That Josiah kept a remarkably detailed Passover at the time requires that this book was more than merely Deuteronomy, as many hold (see G. Ernest Wright, *Interpreter's Bible*, ed. George A. Buttrick et al., II, pp. 311–330). It

the requirements set forth in the book and actual practices in the land. The counsel of a prophetess, Huldah, was sought, and she warned that punishment was inevitable in view of this deviation. She indicated that this punishment would not come in Josiah's day, however, due to his commendable attitude, and Josiah then inaugurated the reforms the book called for. All foreign cult objects were removed, the idolatrous priests were driven from the land, and houses of religious prostitution were destroyed. Child sacrifice in the Valley of Hinnom was abolished, horses dedicated to the sun were removed from the entrance to the temple, and their chariots were burned with fire (II Kings 23:4–14).

Not being content to effect these reforms in Judah only, Josiah extended them also to the region north, former Israel, taking advantage of Assyria's general period of weakness. A particular place of interest was Bethel, long the center of golden calf worship. According to a promise given over three hundred years before,[3] Josiah burned the bones of former false priests on the altar that Jeroboam I had erected and then destroyed the altar and its high place (II Kings 23:15, 16).

### 3. Work and person

Little is known regarding the work and person of this prophet, because he gives no historical notices regarding himself in his book and he is not mentioned elsewhere in the Old Testament. The one item he does mention is that he was an Elkoshite, which is generally taken to mean that he was from a city named Elkosh. Four possible locations have been proposed for this site, though none is certain. One is a location in Mesopotamia north of Mosul near the Tigris River. The place was first suggested by Nestorius, and there is still today "a tomb of Nahum" found at a town called Elqush. Arguing strongly against this suggestion is the lack of any reason for Nahum's having lived or died as far away as Mesopotamia. He did not live early enough to be taken in the captivity of the northern tribes in 722 B.C., nor long enough to be taken there in the Babylonian captivity after 605 B.C. A second site is located in Galilee, called Elkesi or El Kauze. This place was first suggested by Jerome but really has nothing to commend it except the similarity of the name. The third site, Capernaum, also in Galilee, has more in its favor, for the name means "village of Nahum." The thinking is that the city, originally called El Kauze, was renamed following the death of its most celebrated citizen in

---

should be observed further that nothing in the biblical story suggests that this book had recently been written, as liberal scholars have long believed.

[3]See chap. 11, p. 185.

honor of him. The fourth site is probably the most likely, however, if indeed any are correct. It is a place called Bir el-kaus near Beit-jibrin in the territory of Judah, the likely home-country of Nahum.

Because the Book of Nahum is concerned entirely with the destruction of the great city Nineveh, the prophet must have been knowledgeable of the world around him and particularly the Assyrian Empire and its capital of the day, Nineveh. Though Nahum was probably born in a rural area as was Micah, he too must have had considerable contact with larger cities where such information would have been available. Writing as he did concerning the foreign power, he must have been conversant with its past history. He would have known, for instance, of the fall of Israel to the Assyrians in 722 B.C. and the great danger this portended for Judah. He would have been familiar with the campaign of Sennacherib in the day of Hezekiah and the extensive ruin he brought upon the country. And he would have been very familiar with the powerful reign of Ashurbanipal (669–633 B.C.), grandson of Sennacherib, who died about the time he began his ministry. Ashurbanipal's reign had been a glory period for Assyria, when the empire reached its highest point of power, and this fact would have dominated Nahum's thinking as he wrote of the destruction of the great capital city.

Though Nahum did his writing only regarding Nineveh, one should not think that he was silent to his own people in oral ministry. He may be likened in this respect to Obadiah, who wrote only of Edom but surely was active in preaching to his countrymen. Being thus knowledgeable of Assyria, Nahum would have known of Manasseh's captivity there and doubtless used this fact as a word of warning to people generally. Knowing also of the destruction of Thebes in Egypt (3:8–10), he may have warned against any dependence on Egypt, in the vein of Isaiah a century earlier. Being thus aware of the world at large, he certainly had contact with the king of his own country, Josiah, and no doubt along with Zephaniah and Jeremiah had much to do with encouraging the king in making his reform.

A logical question arises as to the relationship between Nahum and Jonah. Jonah's book also concerns Nineveh and in particular the repentance of the great city when Jonah went there to preach regarding its destruction. At the time God did not destroy the city because of this repentance, and therefore one must ask why Nahum was directed of God to speak once more of such destruction. The answer lies in the chronological relationship of the two prophets. Approximately a century and a half had elapsed and Jonah had no doubt long been forgotten by the time of Nahum. Sin again abounded with punishment much in order, and Nahum predicted that it would come. Nineveh did fall in 612 B.C., as the city was overrun by a combined force of Babylonians, Medes, and probably Scythians.

## 4. The book

In the first chapter Nahum begins with a psalm of triumph, in which he praises God and announces God's punishment on the wicked and bestowal of goodness on those who trust Him. In chapter 2 he predicts actual scenes from Nineveh's destruction, using forceful and vivid language. In 2:6, for instance, he speaks of "the gates of the rivers" being opened, which is quite clearly a reference to a part of Nineveh's walls being carried away by a flood. This actually happened, and the opening in the walls thus made was used by the besieging enemy of 612 B.C. to take the city. Then in chapter 3, using vivid language still, Nahum sets forth the reasons that called for this destruction. The book has the form of a unit production, and there is no reason for thinking of any author other than Nahum himself. Attempts at finding evidences for a multiple authorship have been made but not with agreement or success. They must be rejected.

The book may be outlined as follows:

I. A psalm of God's majesty (1:1–15).

II. Description of Nineveh's destruction (2:1–13).

III. Reasons for Nineveh's destruction (3:1–19).

## B. ZEPHANIAH

### 1. The date

Zephaniah (1:1) dates his ministry more definitely: the reign of King Josiah (640–609 B.C.). He evidently wrote his book before 621 B.C., the time when Josiah inaugurated his major reforms, for he speaks against idolatrous practices that were abolished by the king at that time, and in 3:1–7 of serious sinful conditions that also were changed. The fact that he speaks of Nineveh's destruction as still future (2:13) is an indication that he wrote his book before 612 B.C. He may well have ministered some years after writing his book, though perhaps not after the time of Josiah's death in 609 B.C. Nahum and Zephaniah were probably contemporary for much of their time of service.

### 2. Background history

Nothing further really needs to be said regarding background history for Zephaniah, since the world of Zephaniah was the same as the world of Nahum.

It is appropriate, however, to speak here of the rationale for the coming of Zephaniah and the three other seventh-century prophets in a group. That rationale is that together they were to sound a forceful eleventh-hour warning to Judah. It was noted earlier that Hosea and Amos had sounded such a final message to Israel just prior to her fall to Assyria, and now these four, Nahum, Zephaniah, Habakkuk, and Jeremiah, were to do the same in respect to Judah's fall. The wicked rules of Manasseh and Amon had taken away the effect of the previous warnings of Isaiah and Micah, and now there was need for the serious messages of these four a century later. At first the warnings had a good result, as Josiah instituted excellent reforms, something quite parallel to the day of Isaiah and Micah and the reforms made by Hezekiah. But Josiah's good actions were once more offset by wicked reigns, those of Jehoiakim and Zedekiah (corresponding with those of Manasseh and Amon earlier). Punishment thus was sent on Judah in the form of captivity in Babylon, which followed the pattern of Israel's earlier captivity in Assyria.

## 3. Work and person

Zephaniah is unusual in tracing his lineage over four generations. Since he is the only prophet that does this, there must be a reason, and that reason apparently lies in the identity of the fourth person mentioned. The name given is Hizkiah. The significance of this may well be that King Hezekiah is in mind. The length of time since King Hezekiah lived also fits this identification. If this is correct, Zephaniah was a descendant of the royal line. The lineage he gives is Hezekiah, Amariah, Gedaliah, Cushi, and Zephaniah. Comparing this with the line of Judah's kings, the following results: King Manasseh and Amariah were brothers, King Amon and Gedaliah were first cousins, King Josiah and Cushi were second cousins, and the three sons of Josiah, all of whom ruled (Jehoahaz, Jehoiakim, and Zedekiah), were third cousins of Zephaniah. If this relationship did exist, Zephaniah had an access into the royal court not available to other prophets. He may have been able to contact and have influence with Josiah to a greater degree than either Nahum or Jeremiah.

It is also noteworthy that Zephaniah was knowledgeable of the world much as some others before him. In 2:4–15 of his book, he speaks of God's judgment upon four areas surrounding Judah—Philistia to the west, Moab and Ammon to the east, Ethiopia to the southwest, and Assyria to the northeast. He writes in the vein of Isaiah before him in this respect, though Isaiah referred to still more countries.

In general, one may think of Zephaniah beginning to minister somewhere around 630 B.C. like Nahum and continuing on for the better part of

Josiah's time. In the early part of his ministry, using the probably easy access to the royal court noted, he no doubt visited Josiah numerous times and urged the institution of reforms. Sometime during those years he wrote his book.

### 4. The book

The Book of Zephaniah sets forth first a theme of warning and then of promise. The warning pertains to the coming day of the Lord. A double fulfillment seems to be in reference. The first is that of the captivity to Babylon that was to come within a few years of Zephaniah's time. This was truly to be a day of severe punishment at the hand of God. The second is that of the great tribulation of the last days. This aspect of the fulfillment is evidenced both by the description of the day of the Lord and by a reference in the last of the book to the coming millennial day which will follow the great tribulation. If such an eschatological theme is treated in the latter part of the book, there should be a corresponding theme set forth in the first part. And there this theme of punishment is discussed in respect to both Judah and the surrounding nations.

The theme of promise is presented in the last two-thirds of chapter 3 and concerns the future day of millennial blessing that Israel will experience. It will be a day when "the King of Israel, even the LORD," will be in the midst of Israel and the people will not see evil any more (3:15).

Though some attempts have been made to find evidence of multiple authorship in this small prophecy, these have been based on presuppositions contrary to conservative theology, and there is actually little agreement among those who make them. We need not take occasion to note them.

The book may be outlined as follows:

I. The day of the Lord prefigured (1:1—3:7).
    A. Judgment on Judah and Jerusalem (1:1—2:3).
    B. Judgment upon neighboring nations (2:4-15).
    C. Threatened punishment of Jerusalem (3:1-7).
II. Prediction of the millennial kingdom (3:8-20).

## C. HABAKKUK

### 1. The date

Once again with Habakkuk the time of the prophet's ministry must be established upon the basis of internal evidence from the book he wrote.

Habakkuk does not mention the reign of any king. Evidence available points to the rule of Jehoiakim (609–598 B.C.) as the period during which he penned his book, perhaps more particularly to the approximate time of Nebuchadnezzar's first invasion of Jerusalem in 605 B.C. First, in 1:6–10, the invasion of the Babylonians is predicted, and this is made in a context which suggests that the invasion was relatively near at hand. (It actually occurred in three attacks in 605, 597, and 586 B.C.) Second, no reference is made to Assyria as either an enemy or an object of portended destruction as in Nahum and Zephaniah, and this suggests that Nineveh had already been destroyed, an event which happened in 612 B.C. Third, 1:2–4 implies that severe sin existed at the time in Judah, and the strong language used is not in keeping with the reforms Josiah had instituted, but, rather, is in keeping with the wicked ways of Jehoiakim. Fourth, that the time likely preceded the first invasion by Nebuchadnezzar follows from the manner in which reference to the invasion is made. Habakkuk asks God how long it will be before God does something to bring punishment on Judah for her sin, and God responds that during Habakkuk's days (1:5) He will act by bringing the Babylonians. Such language means of course that He had not done so yet.

Some scholars (for instance Keil) favor a time in the closing days of Manasseh's rule. Evidence is taken from II Kings 21:10–16 where it is asserted that prophets in Manasseh's day predicted the type of severe destruction that the Babylonians did bring in due time. Habakkuk is thought to have been one of these prophets. In further support it is noted that Manasseh's day was one of great wickedness, which could account for the concern of Habakkuk just noted. However, the later time of Jehoiakim remains more likely, both because of any lack of mention regarding Assyria and because of the implication that the Babylonian invasion was near at hand.

The view of Duhm, Sellin, and Torrey that Habakkuk's prophecy was directed against Alexander the Great must be rejected. To hold the view, these men alter the word for "Chaldeans" (*kasdim*) in 1:6 to read "Cypriots" (*kittim*), but this has no textual support and, most significantly, this variant is not found in the Dead Sea Scrolls.

## 2. Background history

Historical background for the seventh-century prophets has been reviewed up to and including the reforms of Josiah. It needs to be continued now until the first invasions of Babylonia.

Josiah was an able king. The sweeping reforms he instituted could hardly have been brought about by a ruler of mediocre qualities. He made his authority felt even in the erstwhile provinces of Israel, thus enlarging Judah's sphere of influence. When he attempted to interfere in world developments, however, he exceeded himself and brought about his death.

The occasion involved an attempt to stop a northward march by Pharaoh Necho II of Egypt in 609 B.C. Necho was moving north in an effort to stop Babylonia from becoming the new world leader, following the recent fall of the Assyrians. Assyria's two main cities, Assur and Nineveh, had been taken in 614 and 612 respectively, with the Babylonians being the principal invader. At the time, the remnants of Assyria's army under Ashuruballit II had fled westward to Haran. In 610 B.C. Haran had finally fallen to Nabopolassar, king of Babylon, and this all but finished the Assyrians. Now in 609 B.C., Necho, who evidently wanted to regain world prominence for Egypt, was marching north to counter the efforts of Babylonia. Josiah, perhaps in an indication of favor toward Babylonia, attempted to stop the Egyptians at strategic Megiddo, and was killed in the effort. His body was returned to Jerusalem for burial.

On his death, the second son of Josiah, Jehoahaz, was put on the throne, the people by-passing his eldest son, Eliakim. Jehoahaz had reigned only three months, however, when Pharaoh Necho, now in authority over Judah since the defeat of Josiah, ordered his replacement by the older brother, whose name was now changed to Jehoiakim.[4] It may be that Necho believed Jehoahaz would not cooperate with him and thought the older son would do so in greater degree. He took Jehoahaz prisoner to Egypt where the man died as predicted by Jeremiah (22:11, 12).

Jehoiakim was twenty-five—two years older than his deposed brother—when placed on the throne. Jehoiakim was an evil king in God's sight and also was incapable of efficient rule. It may be that the people had by-passed him earlier because they recognized the second son had more ability than the first. At one time Jehoiakim squandered state funds in the building of a new palace, and because of it the great prophet Jeremiah showed disdain for him and declared that he would be "buried with the burial of an ass" (22:13-19). The king also foolishly cut up and burned Jeremiah's book at another time, apparently thinking that in this way he could offset its dire warning (36:23).

It was in 605 B.C. that Babylon achieved clear supremacy in Middle Eastern power. At the famous battle of Carchemish, a final and complete victory was won over the Egyptians, and then Nebuchadnezzar (conqueror in the battle, crown prince at the time, and soon to be king of Babylon) began to let his new authority be known in Middle Eastern cities; he came that same year in his first invasion against Jerusalem. As the great conqueror moved

---

[4]Eliakim means "God has established," and Jehoiakim, "Yahweh has established." Since the meaning is basically the same, Necho, who seems to have ordered the name change, must have wanted only to show his authority to do so.

from one city to another in this way, he apparently wanted not only the submission of each but also the procurement of able young men whom he might relocate in Babylon as prospective government personnel. At least from Jerusalem he received such, including Daniel and his three friends, Hananiah, Mishael, and Azariah. While engaged in this activity, Nebuchadnezzar was suddenly interrupted by the death of his ailing father, Nabopolassar, in August of the same year, and he quickly returned to Babylon to receive the crown as Nebuchadnezzar II.

All this means that Habakkuk's time of ministry, if indeed it fell in the time of Jehoiakim as indicated above, was a period of anxiety and distress. The days of peace, prosperity, and reform of Josiah were gone, and a period of stress and wickedness was present.

### 3. Work and person

Habakkuk gives no history regarding himself nor is he mentioned in other places of Scripture. In view of the historical background just seen, however, one may conjecture certain matters regarding him. He would have been active in attempting to counteract the wicked practices of Jehoiakim. He would have known of the earlier contrasting ways of Josiah and longed that these could still continue. He certainly would have known of the influence that Nahum and Zephaniah had been able to bring on Josiah in effecting reforms, and he would have desired to do all he could in his day to the same end. Though Nahum and Zephaniah were likely now dead, Jeremiah still continued, and it may well be that Habakkuk teamed up with Jeremiah to bring about the best conditions possible.

As to the person of Habakkuk, he tells us next to nothing regarding himself, not even naming his father. Certain legendary stories have arisen regarding him, but they seem to be only stories. One is that he was the Shunammite's son whom Elisha first promised to the woman and then raised from the dead (II Kings 4:8-37), but this is impossible because of a difference in dates of two centuries. Another makes Habakkuk the watchman placed by Isaiah to watch for the fall of Babylon (Isa. 21:6). And in Bel and the Dragon, an apocryphal book, Habakkuk is said to have carried pottage and bread to Daniel in the lions' den, having been carried there for the purpose by an angel.[5]

Apart from these fanciful tales, however, one may know on the basis of Habakkuk's writing that he was a true man of God. In fact, the major thrust of his book is that the holiness of God be properly recognized in his day. It

[5]For discussion of such stories see R. K. Harrison, *Introduction to the Old Testament*, p. 931.

seemed to him that God should do more about guarding His own holiness, in view of the widespread sin of the time. Habakkuk's prayer, recorded in his third chapter, indicates further a heart fully devoted to the interest and will of God. It would be interesting to know how much contact there was between the great Jeremiah and this godly man, but one has to believe they often saw each other, perhaps met for fellowship, and frequently prayed together.

One matter is worth at least passing notice. It is that Habakkuk may have been a Levitic singer in the temple. This possibility is based on the closing statement of his book, "To the chief singer on my stringed instruments" (3:19). This implies that he was a singer and that he could play one or more stringed instruments. Also, the apocryphal book mentioned above, Bel and the Dragon, supports the idea in stating, "Habakkuk, the son of Joshua of the tribe of Levi." There is nothing remarkable about the matter, whether he was a Levitic singer or not, for several of the prophets were Levites. They simply doubled in their avenues of ministry.

## 4. The book

The Book of Habakkuk is quite unique in form among the other prophetical books. Rather than setting forth a series of prophetic statements or addresses warning people of sin and punishment, Habakkuk presents his first two chapters in the form of a dialogue between God and himself. The prophet first shows his concern that sin in the land seemed to go unchecked on the part of God. He then tells of God's response that there will be punishment for it and that this punishment will come in the form of an invasion by the Babylonians.

This quickly raises a question in the prophet's mind, for he wonders how God can use a nation that is still more wicked than the people of Judah to punish God's people. He says, for instance, "Thou art of purer eyes than to behold evil, and canst not look on iniquity: wherefore lookest thou upon them that deal treacherously, and holdest thy tongue when the wicked devour the man that is more righteous than he?" (1:13). God answers, "Behold, his soul which is lifted up is not upright in him: but the just shall live by his faith" (2:4). The thought is that those who are proud, meaning the Babylonians, have no faith and therefore will in the end stand condemned before God. Those who will live at that time are those who have faith and who live by this faith. In other words, the punishment God will bring by means of the Babylonians will give the Babylonians ascendancy only for a time, just long enough to bring the punishment. But eventually they will experience their own deserved punishment and it will be far more severe than that of Judah.

Then the third chapter of Habakkuk is different in that it is a prayer offered by Habakkuk. It shows his settled faith in God and unshakable trust that all is well when God is in charge.

Though liberal scholars have raised some questions relative to the authorship of chapters 1 and 2, suggesting certain additions or rearrangements of material, the principal criticism concerns chapter 3. Because this chapter is a psalm rather than a prophetic message, because it mentions allegedly late musical terms in its first and last verses, and because it is not included in the Habakkuk commentary of the Dead Sea Scrolls, it is held that the chapter was added by a later hand.[6] In response, the following may be asserted: first, there is no intrinsic reason why an author could not close his book with a psalm, and as a matter of fact certain thoughts in the psalm logically tie back to the earlier part of the book; second, musical terms are not themselves an indication of a late date of authorship but were much in use already in David's day in the psalms he wrote; third, that the third chapter was not treated in the Habakkuk commentary is only an argument from silence and it is quite possible that the commentary was never finished so as to include comments on this part of the book. It is noteworthy that the Septuagint translation, which dates approximately to the same time as the Habakkuk commentary, does have the third chapter in it.

The book may be outlined as follows:

I. A divine-human dialogue (1:1—2:20).
  A. First question: Israel's sin and God's silence (1:1-4).
  B. God's response: the Babylonian invasion (1:5-11).
  C. Second question: Babylonian cruelty and God's silence (1:12—2:1).
  D. God's response: eventual destruction of the Babylonians (2:2-20).
II. Habakkuk's prayer of faith (3:1-19).

---

[6]See Robert Pfeiffer, *Introduction to the Old Testament*, p. 598.

| | |
|---|---|
| 9th-Century Prophets | **Chapter 16** Obadiah Joel |
| 8th-Century Prophets | **Chapter 17** Hosea Amos Jonah |
| | **Chapter 18** Isaiah Micah |
| 7th-Century Prophets | **Chapter 19** Nahum Zephaniah Habakkuk |
| | **Chapter 20** Jeremiah |
| Exilic Prophets | **Chapter 21** Daniel Ezekiel |
| Postexilic Prophets | **Chapter 22** Haggai Zechariah Malachi |

# 20

# Seventh-Century Prophets: Jeremiah

The fourth prophet of the seventh century was Jeremiah. Because he was a major prophet and more is known regarding him, a complete chapter is appropriately designated to him. Like Isaiah of the preceding century, Jeremiah stands as a towering giant in his century. He was a great prophet, a mighty power for God, one whom God significantly used to minister His word. Because he was contemporary with the three prophets noted in the prior chapter and because all four served in Judah, it is apparent that in these four men a greater concentration of writing prophets existed than at any other time in biblical history.

## A. THE DATE

Jeremiah dates his ministry to the reigns of specific kings. In 1:2, 3 (cf. 25:3), he says, "The Word of the LORD came [to him] in the days of Josiah . . . in the thirteenth year of his reign," and "it came also in the days of Jehoiakim . . . and unto the end of the eleventh year of Zedekiah," this "eleventh year" being the year when Jerusalem was taken captive. Thus Jeremiah first received revelation in the thirteenth year of Josiah, 627 B.C., and continued until the captivity of the people in Babylon. The short reigns of Jehoahaz and Jehoiachin are not mentioned, probably because of their brevity.

It should be observed that in this opening chronological reference

Jeremiah does not speak of a ministry during the captivity, but in chapters 40–44 he makes clear that he continued to serve for a while also then. A part of this service was in Judah, while governor Gedaliah lived, and part in Egypt after Jeremiah was taken there by fearful Jews who disobeyed God in going to Egypt. The time of Jeremiah's death is not given, but perhaps a date near 580 B.C. is as likely as any. Since his ministry began in 627 B.C., this means his total ministry lasted approximately forty-seven years. It is likely only Isaiah exceeded him in length of prophetic service.

## B.  BACKGROUND HISTORY

Background history was traced for the seventh-century prophets in the prior chapter as far as the first attack of Nebuchadnezzar on Jerusalem in 605 B.C. Because Jeremiah ministered longer than the others, it is necessary now to continue that history for the remainder of his life.

Following the attack on Jerusalem in 605 B.C., Nebuchadnezzar was called back to Babylon to be crowned king in August of that year. He stayed in Babylon for a few weeks but then returned to the westland to force other cities to recognize his supremacy. He continued in this effort until all the Mediterranean coastland acknowledged him and only then was content to remain at home. He did so until 601 B.C. but then moved out again, this time against Egypt where he was met by Pharaoh Necho at the Egyptian border. Both sides lost heavily in the ensuing engagement, and neither could claim victory. Nebuchadnezzar was at least repulsed and had to return to Babylon. But he did not stay home long, for in 597 B.C. he made a second attack on Judah. The cause was a rebellion on the part of Jehoiakim, who now looked once again to Egypt for support (II Kings 24:1). At first the Babylonian ruler sent only contingents of his army against the area, reinforced by bands of Aramaean, Moabite, and Ammonite troops (II Kings 24:2; Jer. 35:11), but finally he saw the need of a major campaign and came himself.

He left Babylon in December, 598 B.C., and in the same month Jehoiakim died in Jerusalem.[1] Jeremiah's scathing predictions regarding Jehoiakim's death and burial (Jer. 22:18, 19; 36:27–32) suggest that the king was killed in battle with one of the marauding bands in conditions that prevented a normal burial. Jehoiachin, the eighteen-year-old son of Jehoiakim, now became king and received the blow of the Babylonian attack the following March, 597 B.C. As was frequently the case, Egyptian support

---

[1] The exact time is established by comparing the Babylonian Chronicle with II Kings 24:6, 8.

did not materialize and Jehoiachin was taken captive to Babylon along with the queen mother, his wives, servants, and booty. Ezekiel the prophet was also taken, and with him ten thousand leading citizens (II Kings 24:11–16).

Nebuchadnezzar now installed Mattaniah, the third son of Josiah and uncle of Jehoiachin, on the throne. He was twenty-one at the time, fifteen years younger than Jehoiakim, the oldest of the three sons. The Babylonian ruler changed his name to Zedekiah. Zedekiah seems never to have been really accepted by the people, possibly because of having been appointed by the Babylonian king, and as a result his rule was beset by continual agitation and unrest. During his time a strong anti-Babylonian party developed in Jerusalem and brought pressure for revolt, urging Zedekiah to look again to Egypt for help. A new coalition was being formed in the area, consisting of Edom, Moab, Ammon, and Phoenicia (Jer. 27:1–3), and Zedekiah was urged to join. False prophets added their influence, declaring that God had already broken the power of Babylon so that within two years the captives from Judah would return home to Jerusalem (Jer. 28:2–4).

Jeremiah attempted to counteract this "prophecy" by declaring it false and urging continued acceptance of Babylonian control (Jer. 27:1–22). For a time Zedekiah listened to Jeremiah, but finally he chose to revolt and did look to Egypt for support. As a result, early in 586 B.C. Nebuchadnezzar once more marched into the west, and his army laid siege to Jerusalem.[2] The siege was lifted temporarily when the Egyptians this time sought to honor their alliance with troops, but apparently the Babylonians had little difficulty in meeting and inflicting defeat on them. Nebuchadnezzar's army soon returned to the walls of Jerusalem.

The result was that the city fell to the Babylonians in July, 586 B.C.[3] Zedekiah tried to flee but was captured near Jericho and brought to Nebuchadnezzar's headquarters at Riblah. There his sons were slain as he watched, and his own eyes were put out. He along with many others was taken captive to Babylon while Jerusalem suffered severe damage at the hands of Nebuzaradan, an officer of Nebuchadnezzar. Included was the complete destruction of Solomon's temple, which had stood for four centuries.

Judah now existed only as a province of Babylon and accordingly a governor was appointed by the foreign authority. The first governor was Gedaliah, and he established his capital at Mizpah, eight miles north of

---

[2]He established headquarters at Riblah on the Orontes River, north of Palestine. He may have sent army contingents in various directions from there, for he besieged the city of Tyre from the years 587 to 574 B.C., and the Lachish Letters indicate devastation all through Judean cities at the time; cf. *Documents from Old Testament Times*, ed. D. Winton Thomas, pp. 212–217.

[3]The Babylonian siege began in the tenth month of Zedekiah's ninth year and continued until the fourth month of his eleventh year (July, 586 B.C.), a total of eighteen months.

Jerusalem.[4] The people he governed were "the poor of the land," those who had been left by the Babylonians to cultivate the soil (II Kings 25:12). Their number was not great. Many of Judah's citizens had died in the war of 597 B.C., and ten thousand captives (II Kings 24:14) had been deported at that time; then many more had perished during the long siege, after which again a large number had been taken captive.

Gedaliah had been governor only two months when he was treacherously murdered by Ishmael, who had fled from Judah at the first approach of the Babylonians and taken residence in Ammon. Ishmael along with others returned to Judah and killed the governor and a small garrison of Babylonians at Mizpah. The deed was done with secrecy so that it was unknown outside the governor's house at the time. On the second day following, however, Ishmael and his men found it necessary to kill a group of visitors and then they fled in haste for Ammon, fearing that news of their action would now leak out. Ishmael took a number of hostages whom for some reason he had not killed. At this point Johanan, a military leader under the slain Gedaliah, became aware of the atrocity and pursued Ishmael and his men. He caught them at Gibeon where he succeeded in liberating the hostages, but Ishmael and eight of his men made good their escape to Ammon.

The result for the people of the land was that they were made fearful lest the Babylonians return and bring reprisal for this assassination of the appointed governor. Jeremiah, who had taken up residence at Mizpah, was consulted by Johanan and his companions who needed advice as to what to do. They asked Jeremiah to seek a word from God, promising to do whatever God said. Ten days later Jeremiah received a message from God and it was that the people should stay in the land and not flee to Egypt as they were thinking of doing. Jeremiah communicated this information to them, but the people now broke their promise and in disobedience made plans to go to Egypt anyway.

The number who made the journey was large, composed as it was of those who had been placed under Gedaliah's charge besides others who had returned from surrounding countries where they had earlier fled (Jer. 43:5, 6). Jeremiah went as well, certainly against his will, but likely in an effort to keep God's word before the people as best he could. The land of Judah must have been quite depopulated when the group left. The migrators came to Tahpanhes[5] in the eastern delta of Egypt where apparently all took up residence for a time.

<hr />

[4]Identified with present Tell En-Nasbeh.

[5]Identified as Tell Defenneh, located twenty-seven miles southwest of Port Said. The same consonantal spelling, *Thpnhs*, has been found in a Phoenician letter from sixth-century Egypt (cf. A. Dupont-Sommer, *Palestine Exploration Quarterly*, 81 [1949]:52, 57).

## C. WORK AND PERSON

### 1. Work

More is known regarding the life and work of Jeremiah than of any other of the writing prophets, for Jeremiah makes many historical references involving himself. He grew up as a boy in the priestly city of Anathoth,[6] a son of the priest, Hilkiah. While still a young man of perhaps twenty years, he was called of God to be a prophet and told that even before he had been formed in the womb of his mother God had ordained him to this ministry (Jer. 1:5-10). This occasion of his call is quite clearly the time Jeremiah had in mind when he later wrote that the word of the Lord had come unto him first in the thirteenth year of Josiah's reign (1:2; cf. 25:3). His life divides itself into three periods.

The first may be characterized as the pleasant period of his life, when he experienced little opposition and suffering. This was when Josiah was king, and righteousness prevailed in the land. It was the time also when Nahum and Zephaniah lived, and all three prophets likely brought influence on the king for instituting his reforms. The Book of the Law was found in Josiah's eighteenth year, five years after Jeremiah's call, and this further brought a good effect.

Though probably living still in Anathoth at the time of his call, Jeremiah certainly visited Jerusalem many times in his early years and likely came there to live soon after his call. In view of 11:18-23, he did experience some rather serious opposition during the early years, especially from his home town of Anathoth. It may be that certain ones there were jealous of the prominent young man and therefore sought to take his life (11:21). As a result God said He would bring "evil upon the men of Anathoth" in punishment. For the most part, however, one may be sure that Jeremiah's years while Josiah lived were pleasant. Though God had told him at the time of his call that people would "fight against" him (1:19), the days when this would be true were primarily still future. Jeremiah, no doubt, held a close relationship with Josiah and one need not be surprised at the chronicler's indication that, when the king died, "Jeremiah lamented" for him (II Chron. 35:25).

The second period was in marked contrast; it was characterized by severe opposition and suffering. It was the time when the three last kings of Judah ruled, all of them wicked, Jehoiakim, Jehoiachin, and Zedekiah. These were the years when the three attacks of Babylon were made against the land

---

[6]Modern Anata, just northeast of present-day Jerusalem.

and when Jeremiah was told by God to preach the unpopular message of submission to the foreign power. Just to have preached such a message under the trying circumstances then existent would have been difficult enough, but in addition direct opposition developed and Jeremiah was made to suffer.

At one time, probably during the reign of Jehoiakim, Pashur, "chief governor in the house of the LORD" (20:1), struck Jeremiah and "put him in the stocks that were in the high gate of Benjamin, which was by the house of the LORD" (20:2). He did this because Jeremiah had proclaimed in the temple court that God would indeed bring evil upon the city due to the sin of the people. At another time, still in the reign of Jehoiakim and again when Jeremiah had preached a similar message, priests and false prophets put forth an effort to have Jeremiah put to death (26:11), though in this they were unsuccessful. But another prophet of the time, Urijah, unknown otherwise, did suffer this fate for preaching a similar message (26:20–24).

It was in Jehoiakim's fourth year that God told Jeremiah to write down words that had been given him, and Jeremiah did so using Baruch as his secretary (36:1–4). The book was read to the people, and news of it soon came to King Jehoiakim. He ordered it brought and read before him; and when this was done, he cut the pages and threw them into a fire, apparently thinking that this would somehow do away with the message they contained. Undaunted, Jeremiah dictated the information to Baruch again and this time added to it (36:27–32).

Jeremiah apparently had little or no contact with Jehoiachin (also called Coniah), who reigned only three months before he was taken captive to Babylon. Jeremiah did predict that this would happen (22:24–30), however. As noted, Nebuchadnezzar then placed Zedekiah on Judah's throne and it was during his time that Jeremiah suffered the most. He continued to preach that the people should submit to Babylonia, saying, "Bring your necks under the yoke of the king of Babylon, and serve him and his people, and live" (27:12). Zedekiah did not give heed, however, but joined the coalition against the eastern ruler noted earlier, and therefore a third attack was brought against the city. In Zedekiah's tenth year, at a time when Jeremiah sought to leave Jerusalem to go out to Anathoth to claim a portion of land he had recently purchased, he was stopped and arrested on a charge of treason (32:1–15; 37:11–16). He remained in prison for several days, and then Zedekiah sent for him to ask him secretly, "Is there any word from the LORD?" (37:17). The prophet answered that there was and then told him again the message that he had been preaching all along. At this, Zedekiah released Jeremiah to the somewhat greater freedom of the prison court, but enemies learned of this and demanded the life of the prophet. They took Jeremiah and cast him into a slimy dungeon which seems to have been an unused cistern, and there he "sunk in the mire" (38:6). From here he was rescued with the king's permission by one named Ebed-melech, an Ethiopian who apparently was sympathetic to Jeremiah (38:7–13). It was probably soon after this that the city fell and Zedekiah went through the experience described above.

The third period was the time following the fall of Jerusalem until the day of Jeremiah's death. At first things must have been quite pleasant for Jeremiah, for his predictions regarding the city had proven true, and false prophets and priests who had earlier opposed him had been put to silence. So long as Gedaliah lived, Jeremiah was his helper and very likely the two enjoyed a happy relationship. The response of the people in not believing the word God gave to Jeremiah would have constituted an unhappy experience, and certainly the trip down into Egypt was not one that Jeremiah enjoyed. No indication is given, however, that he was made to suffer imprisonment during this time. On arrival in Egypt, Jeremiah continued his ministry and probably was appropriately respected. His closing years may have been reasonably pleasant, though spent in the foreign land.

The significance of Jeremiah's ministry was the same as that of the other seventh-century prophets. He was one more eleventh-hour prophet, warning the people in respect to their sin and telling them that punishment would come if they did not repent. His significance following the fall of Jerusalem was that he served as a shepherd to the people who were left in the land. Being their shepherd, even though they sinned in going to Egypt, he stayed with them to care for them there.

## 2. Person

### a. SPIRITUAL MATURITY

That Jeremiah was a spiritually mature person is beyond question. He was dedicated and committed to all that God wanted of him. This is evidenced by the fact that God used him so long in His service. Certainly Nahum, Zephaniah, and Habakkuk were godly men also, but their periods of ministry were quite brief in comparison with that of Jeremiah. If God saw fit to use Jeremiah for so many years, it must be that God saw special qualities in him.

Then there is the fact that Jeremiah preached an unpopular message even though he knew people would not like it. It is never easy to do this and it takes a person of true dedication. He dared to bring this message even to the king, though it included the prediction that the king and his advisors would suffer greatly. It was a day when prophets generally were telling the king what he wanted to hear, but Jeremiah told him that Jerusalem would fall and he as king would be seized.

Besides this, Jeremiah's book abounds with the highest exaltations of God. He knew God, held the warmest devotion for God, and was fully committed to the call that God had given him.

### b. COURAGE

These same considerations prove that Jeremiah was a man of great courage. One might think otherwise in view of times of occasional despondency and discouragement (15:10; 20:14-18), but those times came only in reaction to the severe opposition he faced. He was only human after all, and when one encounters almost continual conflict he can hardly help but break occasionally.

But overall Jeremiah demonstrated remarkable courage. He stood up day after day and proclaimed a message that others believed to be not only wrong but traitorous. His message was one of capitulation when others spoke of victory. Jeremiah by nature certainly wanted victory too, but God had given him this contrary message, and he was willing to stand and proclaim it before people and king alike.

### c. DEEP EMOTION

Jeremiah gives evidence of being deeply emotional in temperament. He may have seemed hardhearted to people as he preached his message regarding the coming defeat at the hands of the Babylonians, but in his own heart he cried out with anguish. For instance in 9:1 he writes, "Oh that my head were waters, and mine eyes a fountain of tears, that I might weep day and night for the slain of the daughter of my people!" Again in 13:17 he says, "But if ye will not hear it, my soul shall weep in secret places for your pride; and mine eye shall weep sore, and run down with tears, because the LORD's flock is carried away captive." Still again in 14:17 he states, "Therefore thou shalt say this word unto them; Let mine eyes run down with tears night and day, and let them not cease: for the virgin daughter of my people is broken with a great breach, with a very grievous blow." Thus he was a man to whom tears were not strange, as he contemplated the fate of his people.

At the same time Jeremiah could rise to heights of exaltation as he expressed joy and confidence that God was with him to provide in all ways. For instance, he writes of his joy in 15:16, "Thy words were found, and I did eat them; and thy word was unto me the joy and rejoicing of mine heart: for I am called by thy name, O LORD God of hosts." And he writes of confidence in 20:11, "But the LORD is with me as a mighty terrible one: therefore my persecutors shall stumble, and they shall not prevail; they shall be greatly ashamed; for they shall not prosper: their everlasting confusion shall never be forgotten."

This tendency to deep emotionalism no doubt contributed to a tension within Jeremiah which is manifested occasionally in his book. On the one hand, as noted, there are passages that indicate a spirit of despondency and a readiness to quit God's work, and, on the other, there are passages that show an even deeper sense of dedication and compulsion to carry on all that God assigned. God evidently saw that this second part to the tension needed bolstering, for we read Him telling the prophet, "I will make my words in thy mouth fire, and this people wood, and it shall devour them" (5:14); and again, "Is not my word like as a fire? saith the LORD; and like a hammer that breaketh the rock in pieces?" (23:29).

### d. COMPASSION

In keeping with this emotional temperament, Jeremiah was a man of compassion for people around him. He saw the extreme sin of the day, and knew of certain punishment to come, and his heart went out to those involved. He said to them, "As for me, I have not hastened from being a pastor to follow thee: neither have I desired the woeful day" (17:16). At another time, addressing God in reference to the people, he stated, "Remember that I stood before thee to speak good for them, and to turn away thy wrath from them" (18:20). At the same time, Jeremiah could speak very strongly, rebuking the people for their sin. For instance, he said, "But, O LORD of hosts, that judgest righteously, that triest the reins and the heart, let me see thy vengeance on them: for unto thee have I revealed my cause" (11:20). Again he stated, "O LORD, thou knowest: remember me, and visit me, and revenge me of my persecutors" (15:15). Jeremiah despised the sin being committed, but he had great love for the people and wanted them to cease the sin so that their punishment might be lessened.

### e. A MAN OF INTEGRITY

Jeremiah was a man of the highest integrity. His word was his bond, his commitment was unchangeable. God gave him a very difficult assignment at his call, and Jeremiah carried it out. People did not like his message, but the message was not altered. Leaders of the day warned him that he would suffer, but he kept on. He was put in stocks and later in prison, but this did not make him change. He did not vary the message even when he was cast into the terrible slimy dungeon where he spent many hours and possibly even a few days. An experience of this kind would have been horrible, but still Jeremiah remained true to the commitment he had made to God.

## D. THE BOOK

The book that Jeremiah wrote is one of the great prophetic documents of the Old Testament, ranking probably second only to Isaiah in its force and significance. Like other prophetic books, it is composed of numerous messages by the prophet that were written at different periods of his life. Part of it is in poetry and part in prose, both exhibiting a wide range of literary figures and types. Though it does not show quite the literary excellence of Isaiah, it displays a splendid style which rates high among the other prophetical books. One matter that is particularly noteworthy is that the book contains so much historical material, a great portion of which is autobiographical in that various episodes and situations from the life of Jeremiah are set forth.

A natural question concerns the relation of this book with the material Jeremiah dictated to Baruch. It has been observed that in the time of Jehoiakim God came to Jeremiah and told him to record in a book all the things that God had revealed to him, and Jeremiah did so (36:1, 2). Later, after this book had been burned by the foolish king, Jeremiah rewrote it and added to it (36:27-32). The present book of Jeremiah, however, could not be that work because much of what is recorded concerns history and revelation following that time. Possibly Jeremiah continued to add to what he wrote then, or it may be that the final work was a new one based on the earlier one as far as that went historically.

It may be there were two editions of the final work, since the Septuagint version is shorter than the Masoretic text. It is in fact one-eighth shorter and has a somewhat different arrangement of chapters.[7] Gleason Archer suggests that Jeremiah himself made the first edition while he yet lived and that Baruch, his secretary, made a more comprehensive collection of materials later.[8] Edward J. Young suggests that the Septuagint translators, being Alexandrian Jews and possibly influenced by Greek philosophy, sought to give what they thought was a still more logical arrangement to the material than Jeremiah had.[9] Evidence is insufficient for giving a certain answer to the question.

---

[7]Chapters 46-51 of the Masoretic text are placed after chapter 25 in the Septuagint, and they are given a slightly different sequential arrangement. Also Jeremiah 33:14-26 of the Masoretic text is missing in the Septuagint.

[8]*A Survey of Old Testament Introduction*, pp. 349-350.

[9]*Introduction to the Old Testament*, p. 232.

Another question relates to the arrangement of material in the book as we now have it. In view of the numerous historical notices the book contains, one would expect the material to have been arranged chronologically, but this is not always so. Portions, for instance, from the time of Zedekiah are intermixed with portions from Jehoiakim, and vice versa. Though it is difficult to be sure regarding every passage as to when it was first uttered, the following arrangement as suggested by Young has much to commend it:[10]

 a. From Josiah's reign: chapters 1–20.
 b. From Jehoahaz' reign: nothing.
 c. From Jehoiakim's reign: chapters 25–27, 35, 36, 45, and possibly 46–49.
 d. From Jehoiachin's reign: nothing, though 22:24–30 mentions this king.
 e. From Zedekiah's reign: chapters 21–24, 28–34, 37–39.
 f. From Gedaliah's reign: chapters 40–42.
 g. From Jeremiah's time in Egypt: chapters 43, 44, 50, 51 (chapters 50 and 51 may possibly come from Zedekiah's reign).
 h. Historical appendix: chapter 52.

The rationale for this arrangement lies basically in logical relationship. Chapters 1–25 form a unit and contain prophecies of both warning and comfort for the people of Judah. Chapters 26–45 concern the personal life of Jeremiah. Chapters 46–51 present prophecies against foreign nations around the land of Judah, and finally chapter 52 is a historical appendix bringing the book to a close.

It may be surmised that liberal critics present quite a different view. They posit a multiple authorship, but significantly, there is considerable variation among them as to how the book should be divided. From the conservative point of view there is no reason to think seriously in terms of a multiple authorship.[11]

The book may be outlined as follows:
 I. Prophecies concerning Judah and Jerusalem (1:1—25:38).
  A. Jeremiah's call (1:1–19).
  B. Unparalleled sin of Judah (2:1—3:5).
  C. Prediction of invasion from the north (3:6—6:30).
  D. Warning of Babylonian captivity (7:1—10:25).
  E. The broken covenant and the sign of the girdle (11:1—13:27).
  F. A message concerning drouth (14:1—15:21).
  G. Sign of the unmarried prophet and a warning concerning the Sabbath (16:1—17:27).

[10]Ibid., pp. 225–229.
[11]For various views see R. K. Harrison, *Introduction to the Old Testament*, pp. 809–817.

    H. The sign of the potter's house (18:1—20:18).
    I. Babylonian punishment of Zedekiah and the people (21:1—25:38).
  II. Episodes concerning Jeremiah (26:1—45:5).
    A. A temple sermon and Jeremiah's arrest (26:1-24).
    B. Symbolic act depicting the yoke of Babylon (17:1—28:17).
    C. Jeremiah's letter to the exiles (29:1-32).
    D. Jeremiah's message concerning the messianic kingdom (30:1—31:40).
    E. Land restoration symbolized by Jeremiah's field (32:1-44).
    F. Further message concerning the messianic kingdom (33:1-26).
    G. Zedekiah's sin and the loyalty of the Rechabites (34:1—35:19).
    H. Jeremiah's scroll written and destroyed (36:1-32).
    I. Jeremiah's suffering during the siege (37:1—39:18).
    J. Jeremiah and the remnant in Judah (40:1—42:22).
    K. Jeremiah and the fugitives in Egypt (43:1—44:30).
    L. Jeremiah's message to Baruch (45:1-5).
  III. Prophecies against nations (46:1—51:64).
    A. Against Egypt (46:1-28).
    B. Against Philistia (47:1-7).
    C. Against Moab (48:1-47).
    D. Against Ammon, Edom, Damascus, Arabia, Elam (49:1-39).
    E. Against Babylon (50:1—51:64).
  IV. Historical appendix (52:1-34).

| | |
|---|---|
| 9th-Century Prophets | Chapter 16<br>Obadiah<br>Joel |
| 8th-Century Prophets | Chapter 17<br>Hosea<br>Amos<br>Jonah |
| | Chapter 18<br>Isaiah<br>Micah |
| 7th-Century Prophets | Chapter 19<br>Nahum<br>Zephaniah<br>Habakkuk |
| | Chapter 20<br>Jeremiah |
| Exilic Prophets | Chapter 21<br>Daniel<br>Ezekiel |
| Postexilic Prophets | Chapter 22<br>Haggai<br>Zechariah<br>Malachi |

# 21

# Exilic Prophets: Daniel and Ezekiel

We now come to the exilic prophets, of whom there were two. Actually little time elapsed between the seventh-century prophets just studied and these exilic prophets. In fact, Jeremiah continued to live during the earlier years of their captivity, and even Habakkuk may well have been living when both were first taken captive. The reason for considering these prophets separately is not so much chronological as it is logical. The seventh-century prophets all ministered in Jerusalem, warning of its portended destruction, while the two exilic prophets were taken captive and conducted their ministry in Babylon.

The first exilic prophet was Daniel, who was taken in the first aspect of the captivity, 605 B.C., which would have been about the time Habakkuk wrote his prophecy. The second was Ezekiel, who was taken in the second aspect of the captivity, 597 B.C., when Habakkuk may have still been alive, and Jeremiah was continuing his vigorous ministry. Of these two, Daniel was not a prophet in the sense of an occupation. His work in Babylon was as an administrator in the palace rather than a preacher among the people. He is classed as a prophet, however, because of the remarkable predictions God gave him in visions, and because of the prophetic book he wrote. Ezekiel, on the other hand, was very much a prophet and did preach among the people, serving especially as a shepherd to the captives in the foreign land.

## A. DANIEL

### 1. The date

Daniel gives a definite date to his time of service. He says that he and three of his friends (1:6) were taken captive when Nebuchadnezzar came against Jerusalem "in the third year of the reign of Jehoiakim, king of Judah" (1:1). This third year extended to the month Tisri (October), 605 B.C., meaning that this aspect of the captivity took place some time before that month.[1] There is reason to believe that Daniel's captivity occurred in the six months preceding Tisri, 605 B.C., since Jeremiah 46:2 dates the event to Jehoiakim's fourth year. Jeremiah apparently was figuring on the basis of what is called "Nisan reckoning," which ended each year in the spring at the month Nisan, rather than in the fall at the month Tisri (these two months came exactly six months apart). The only period that would qualify as included in both the third and fourth years of Jehoiakim when figuring on these two respective bases would be the six months between these two termini.

Relating these facts to the history outlined in the prior chapter, we conclude that the captivity of Daniel and his friends took place shortly after the victory Nebuchadnezzar won over the Egyptians at the battle of Carchemish in the early summer of 605 B.C. Nebuchadnezzar must have followed up that victory with an immediate march southward into the land of Palestine and with the attack on Jerusalem indicated by Daniel. It is not likely, however, that Daniel and the other captives were taken back to Babylon that same summer, because Nebuchadnezzar had to return there in a considerable hurry to be made king. They probably were transported a few months later, after the newly-crowned king had returned to the westland to continue the occupying activities that had been interrupted.

The duration of Daniel's activity in Babylon can also be indicated within close limits. In 10:1, Daniel says that his fourth vision came to him in the third year of Cyrus. That means the third year after Cyrus captured Babylon, which occurred in the fall of 539 B.C. Thus Daniel was still alive and ministering as late as 536 B.C., which means at least sixty-nine years following the time of his captivity. Therefore, his years of service lasted longer than those of Isaiah, though as noted he was not a prophet by occupation as was this great predecessor.

---

[1]Jehoiakim began to rule in the fall of 609 B.C. (following the three-month rule of Jehoahaz, who had immediately succeeded Josiah when he was killed by Pharaoh Necho at Megiddo, July, 609). This means his accession year ended in the month Tisri, 608 B.C. His first year thus ended in Tisri, 607 B.C., and his third year in Tisri, 605 B.C.

## 2. Background history

Background history in respect to Daniel's captivity has for the most part been studied already in connection with the seventh-century prophets. The same historical situation existed for Daniel as for them. As was indicated, Nebuchadnezzar following his great victory at Carchemish came south into the Palestine area to assert his control over cities of the eastern Mediterranean seaboard. Jerusalem apparently was one of the first contacted, and Nebuchadnezzar wanted two things from the city. One was booty and this proved to consist especially of the valuable objects of the temple. The other was captives including especially choice young men whom Nebuchadnezzar might train, and from whom he might later make selection for staffing offices in his kingdom. Those selected had to measure up to high qualifications as indicated in 1:4, but apparently having been so selected they had no option as to whether or not they would go. It is likely that similar demands were made in other cities where Nebuchadnezzar went, so that the total number of choice young men who finally were brought to Babylon was rather sizable.

## 3. Work and person

### a. WORK

Because about one-half of the Book of Daniel is concerned with historical events, most of which involved Daniel directly, information regarding him is relatively extensive. It can be divided into general and specific matters.

*1) General matters.* There were three general areas of work that God accomplished through Daniel, situated as he was in a prominent position of influence in the palace of Babylon. One was serving as an instrument through whom God could maintain His honor in a foreign land that otherwise was not given to honoring Him. When the captivity of Judah had been accomplished by the Babylonian power, the Babylonians would have thought their gods were greater than the God of the people they had been able to capture. A criterion used at the time regarding the relative strength of gods of various countries concerned the strength of the armies involved and victories won, as well as the relative prosperity of the lands.

God did not want this evaluation to stand, however, and worked through Daniel to change it. Accordingly two dreams were given to Nebuchadnezzar that only Daniel could interpret (chaps. 2 and 4); also, the three friends of Daniel were delivered from Nebuchadnezzar's fiery furnace (chap. 3). Further, Belshazzar was amazed at the miraculous handwriting on his palace wall, and again it was Daniel alone who could read it and give its interpretation (chap. 5). Later, Daniel was miraculously delivered from the den of lions into which he had been cast by Darius, the new Persian ruler of Babylon (chap. 6). It is significant that when each of these occasions transpired, the record says the king concerned gave remarkable acknowledgment of the greatness of Daniel's God as over against the gods of Babylon. For instance, following the deliverance of Daniel's three friends from the fiery furnace, Nebuchadnezzar said, "Therefore, I make a decree, That every people, nation, and language, which speak anything amiss against the God of Shadrach, Meshach, and Abednego, shall be cut in pieces, and their houses shall be made a dunghill: because there is no other god that can deliver after this sort" (3:29).

A second general work concerned the welfare of the captive people of Judah. Because Daniel was taken in the first aspect of the captivity, with the great bulk of the captives coming a few years later, Daniel was in Babylon in time to achieve a high place in the kingdom and bring influence to bear to make their situation the best possible. The result was that the conditions for the captives proved to be remarkably good. The people were able to keep their own institutions of prophets and priests (Jer. 29:1). Also, the captives enjoyed freedom in their living conditions: Ezekiel had his own house (Ezek. 8:1) where elders came to visit him. The people were given correspondence privileges with their friends and relatives back in Judah; Jeremiah speaks of such letters (29:25) and he also wrote to the captives in Babylon himself (29:1). Further, the people seem to have had good employment opportunities. Many business tablets were discovered at Nippur and these contain Jewish names in a context showing that they were active in businesses of the day. Though the tablets date from the fifth century, and so represent the situation after the exiles had been in Babylonia for more than a hundred years, they imply that similar conditions had existed for some time. And finally, the captives were permitted to live on fine, fertile land. Many apparently resided near the river Chebar (Ezek. 1:1, 3; 3:15, 23), which is likely the canal Kabari known from certain of the texts just mentioned. The city, Tel-abib, where Ezekiel at one time remained with resident captives for seven days (Ezek. 3:15), was on this canal. The canal supplied irrigation for rich farming, which means that Jews were favored with a fertile land area, whether working for themselves or for others. Advantages of this kind would hardly have come to them had there not been someone bringing influence on the king.

Then Daniel may also have had much to do with effecting the return of the captives to Judah in due time. He still lived at the time of their return (538–537 B.C.), and he then actually held the highest governmental post of his life (6:2, 3). That he did was most remarkable, especially since a complete change in government had occurred when Babylon had been conquered by the Persians, and also Daniel was more than eighty years of age. God's hand is unmistakable in all this, suggesting that He still had work for Daniel to do. This work could well have been to bring influence on King Cyrus to issue the decree that permitted the Jews to return to their own land.

A third area of work was the recording of revelation that God gave to Daniel regarding the future. The Book of Daniel has well been compared with the Book of Revelation in the New Testament for its remarkable predictions relative to the last days. One could easily think that God would have selected a full-time prophet to receive such important information, but in His own good pleasure He chose the palace administrator, Daniel. This is a significant commentary on the high standing Daniel held in God's sight, and at the same time it identifies a further work God had for him to do.

*2) Specific work.* Several episodes are presented regarding Daniel's life in Babylon which indicate specific aspects of work God had in mind for him. These do not begin to present all that Daniel did, but they are representative events out of his busy and significant life. The initial episode concerned a test Daniel and his three friends faced on first arriving in Babylon. The order of the king was that they were to eat the same food that the king ate, which would have been tasty, tempting food. But it was also food which would have first been sacrificed to the Babylonian gods, and which might contain meat that was unclean according to Jewish law and unsuitable for Jews to eat. The young men commendably asked for a substitute menu, in spite of great attractions to do otherwise, and this was granted. God was pleased with their decision, and the result was that the four were eventually graduated from their years of training with higher honors than were any of the other young men.

The second occasion involved a dream God gave to Nebuchadnezzar and the inability of Nebuchadnezzar's own wise men to interpret it. God worked matters out so that Daniel was called to give the interpretation. The result was that Nebuchadnezzar rendered great honor to the God of Daniel and also gave Daniel two high positions in his government.

The third concerned Daniel's three friends as they had the choice of whether or not to bow to Nebuchadnezzar's gold image in the plain of Dura. They chose not to do so, suffered the humiliation of being thrown into a fiery furnace, but then experienced the joy of deliverance from it much to the consternation of Nebuchadnezzar and his officers. As a result, Nebuchadnezzar again gave high honor to the God of these Jews.

The fourth concerned a second dream of Nebuchadnezzar, which once more Daniel interpreted. It concerned a severe punishment to come on the great king. Nebuchadnezzar as a result experienced a period of insanity for seven years, apparently at the close of his life, and when he was restored to his kingship he once more gave due honor to the God of heaven.

The fifth came many years later at the time of the fall of Babylon to the Persians. Belshazzar was now king, and at a great feast he gave for his officers God made handwriting appear on a wall which neither the king nor the wise men could read. Once more Daniel was brought in; he read it and gave the interpretation that the kingdom was soon to fall to the Persians, and it did that very night.

The sixth concerned the new kingdom of Persia and especially King Darius, who was appointed over Babylon by Cyrus. It was an occasion when other officers became jealous of Daniel and through a plot were able to force the king to cast Daniel into a den of lions. This was contrary to the king's own wishes, and he himself went early the next morning to the den to see if Daniel still lived. The king greatly rejoiced that Daniel was still alive, and then he ordered that all the officers who had plotted Daniel's death be cast into the den where they were immediately consumed.

Along with these historical episodes, God gave Daniel four occasions of revelation relating to times future to himself and even on to the last days. The first revelation is recorded in chapter 7, the second in chapter 8, the third in chapter 9, and the fourth in chapters 10, 11, and 12.

It must be realized that time moves quickly in the Book of Daniel. Daniel was probably only in his middle teens in the first chapter, when taken captive with his three friends. But as noted, by the time of his final vision in the third year of Cyrus, no less than sixty-nine years had elapsed. Since the well-known occasion involving the den of lions came following the fall of Babylon to the Persians, a great deal of time had elapsed already by then—Daniel was probably in his mid-eighties.

## b. PERSON

Daniel stands as one of God's most admirable servants. His parents are not named, but he was clearly of either royal or noble descent (Dan. 1:3),[2] and his parents must have been devoted people to account for his own remarkable dedication to God. He spent most of his life as a captive in foreign Babylon, though in a very honored position of high administration in the palace.

*1) Spiritual status.* Marks of spiritual maturity on the part of Daniel are probably as numerous as of any person in the Old Testament. One mark is

---

[2]Josephus (*Antiquities* X.10.1) says that Daniel and his three friends were all kinsmen of King Zedekiah.

that God revealed through him the four visions. As has been noted, such revelation was a great honor for anyone to receive, and God selected layman Daniel in the palace for the honor rather than a full-time prophet. Certainly this says much regarding the character of this man.

Then Daniel was not backward about giving rebuke and divine communications even to kings in foreign Babylon. Nebuchadnezzar's second dream involved a very unpleasant message to the effect that he as king would become insane for seven years. It may be that his own wise men hesitated to give their interpretation of the dream because they also realized that it portended something most unfavorable for the monarch.[3] Daniel, however, did not hesitate but told the king directly God's intended message. The same is true regarding the handwriting on the wall that Belshazzar saw. This too spelled a message of fatal content for the king, but Daniel did not hesitate to give the interpretation. Not only did he state it, but he gave the king additional warning that he should humble himself before God and not act as his father Nebuchadnezzar had done.

Another indication comes from the evident God-centeredness of Daniel's thinking when he interpreted Nebuchadnezzar's dream in chapter 2. He might have claimed credit for himself at the time, but he went out of his way to tell the king that the interpretation was not of himself but was totally of God (2:27–30).

A further indication of Daniel's spiritual maturity comes from the remarkable faith he demonstrated. In respect to the same first dream of Nebuchadnezzar, when Daniel would have been only about seventeen years of age,[4] Daniel had faith to believe that God would reveal to him what the king had dreamed when at the time Daniel had no idea what it was. An order had gone forth from the king that all wise men, including the young men in training, should be killed because of their inability to interpret the king's dream. Daniel found out through the chief executioner the reason for the order; and when told, he forthrightly stated to the king that if he were given time he would tell what the dream had been. When he returned to his three friends and told them what he had promised, they must have been amazed. It shows the great faith of all four that they then went to God in prayer to make request that they be told the information. The joy and delight of Daniel on receiving it must have been beyond words, for God did honor his faith by telling him the dream that very night.

---

[3]These wise men could give their own interpretations of dreams because they had books and manuals to indicate the significance of almost anything that might occur. Such interpretations would not have been correct, but a dream such as Nebuchadnezzar had concerning the cutting down of the great tree could have portended only some type of disaster for the king.

[4]It was the second year of Nebuchadnezzar, so Daniel was seventeen if he had been fifteen when taken captive (2:1).

Still another indication is the high degree of obedience of Daniel. In chapter 6 when the other officers of the day conspired against him, Daniel did not alter his manner of life in order to escape their trap, though he certainly recognized what they were doing. They told the king that if anyone prayed to any god or man other than the king for thirty days, that man should be cast into the den of lions. All Daniel had to do to escape the terrible fate was simply to cease praying or even to pray quietly in a closet for thirty days, and they would not have been able to carry out their plan. But Daniel still went to his open window where all could see him and prayed according to his custom three times a day. The reason he did, no doubt, was that his testimony might remain true, and that everyone might know that he was not changing his manner of life simply to escape a den of lions. This was obedience of the highest order.

*2) Righteousness.*   Closely related to Daniel's spiritual maturity was the righteousness he demonstrated at all times. Remarkable righteousness was evidenced, for instance, already in the first episode regarding him. There were real attractions for Daniel and his friends to accept the menu the king laid down. For one thing it came in the form of an order from the king, and not merely an opportunity presented. For another, there could be severe punishment if the order was not observed. Again, it must have seemed that to turn the menu down would be to forsake all possibility of getting ahead in the training program so as to gain a fine position at the close. And finally the food would have been very attractive, and the alternative diet of pulse[5] and water (see 1:12) would not have been pleasant to contemplate. Yet, in spite of these attractions, Daniel and his friends did request that the menu be changed because they knew this was the right thing to do.

Again, in chapter 6, the conspirators against Daniel first attempted to find something wrong with his work. They investigated him thoroughly and one may be sure they also combed the department over which he was head with its many employees, but they found nothing wrong either in workmanship or integrity. Daniel's propriety in conduct thus was made unmistakably apparent.

*3) Courage.*   Daniel was also a person of remarkable courage, something that appears again and again in the stories regarding him. In the first story, for instance, in taking a stand along with his friends to refuse the menu prescribed by the king, Daniel made his decision in spite of the danger entailed and the attractions to do otherwise. He made request of the proper

---

[5]The original word comes from the basic root "to seed" (*zara'*), meaning food that grows from seed, especially vegetables.

official that he and his friends be permitted to have a substitute menu. The placing of this request would have taken courage in itself. Daniel might have reasoned that a high official in the country would simply not listen to a newcomer, especially one who was a captive. Quite clearly he did not hesitate, however, but made an appointment with the man and voiced the petition.

In chapter 2, Daniel showed courage in the way he encountered the executioner of the king, Arioch. Many would have reacted in fright and pleaded for mercy, but Daniel simply asked the man why it was that the order had gone forth from the king to kill all wise men. He then even arranged through this man to see the great Nebuchadnezzar himself. This took unusual courage on the part of a seventeen-year-old who was just a captive in the country. And still further, it took courage to promise the king to tell him what he had dreamed, when at the time Daniel had no idea what it had been.

In chapter 4 Daniel showed courage in telling the king the shocking and unpleasant news that the great monarch would become insane. One can hardly think of a more unpleasant message to convey, but Daniel did so.

The same was again true in chapter 5 when he gave the interpretation of the writing on the wall to King Belshazzar. This also was unpleasant news concerning the fall of the kingdom, but Daniel brought it and even gave reprimand and advice to the king in doing so. Certainly the greatest of courage was called for on his part.

*4) Capability.*    Daniel gives evidence of being a highly capable person already as a student in the three years of training in the Babylonian palace. Daniel and his three friends began the period in what would have to be called a disadvantageous situation. They asked for a special menu to be given to them, and when one asks for special treatment he normally brings himself into a position of suspicion if not actual disfavor. But by the time the three years of training were over, the situation was totally different. Due no doubt to diligent effort and study (under God's blessing, of course) the four were found to be "ten times better" than the others (1:20). This means that they were the leading students of all who graduated at the time, and it may be remembered that all of the group were first-rate.

After graduation, Daniel and his three friends were given high positions of honor as a result of their good work (2:48, 49). Daniel was actually assigned two demanding responsibilities, the more important of which was chief of the wise men. It is one thing to receive such an important position and another to keep it, for one has to produce to do so, especially when the king is a man of high ability as was Nebuchadnezzar. Daniel apparently did not have trouble keeping this position, for Nebuchadnezzar toward the close of his rule referred to Daniel with the words, "Oh Belteshazzar, master of the magicians" (4:9). This means that Daniel must have been capable both as an administrator and as a speaker. Being head of the magicians he would have had administrative work to do, and he would have had to speak many times before the king and show demonstration of being articulate in forming ideas and expressing them.

Still another indication comes from Daniel's remarkable situation when Darius became king of Babylon following the change-over of government. In chapter 6 Daniel was then made one of three leading administrators over 120 princes. Not only this, but the king was actually planning to make him the head of these three. The granting of such a high position would not have come except for demonstrated ability in years past of which Darius had become knowledgeable.

*5) Thoughtfulness of others.*    A last matter to notice is that Daniel was thoughtful of others. In the last of chapter 2, after Daniel had given the interpretation of Nebuchadnezzar's dream and the king had bestowed two high positions on Daniel, Daniel immediately thought of his three friends who did not have such positions. Accordingly, the last verse of the chapter reads, "Then Daniel requested of the king, and he set Shadrach, Meshach, and Abednego over the affairs of the province of Babylon." Sometimes people forget their friends when they themselves have been honored, but not Daniel. He wanted Shadrach, Meshach, and Abednego to receive high positions along with himself.

At a later time he showed thoughtfulness regarding Nebuchadnezzar. The occasion is related in chapter 4, which tells of Nebuchadnezzar and his dream of the tree that was cut down. When the king told Daniel the dream, Daniel at first did not respond. The king wondered at this reaction, fearing lest somehow Daniel could not interpret the dream this time, but Daniel quickly answered him with the words, "My lord, the dream be to them that hate thee, and the interpretation thereof to thine enemies" (4:19). In other words, Daniel was not happy that Nebuchadnezzar was to experience the form of punishment the dream portended. Apparently he had come to admire Nebuchadnezzar for his ability as a king, and, even though the king was proud and had his deficiencies, Daniel was thoughtful of him and personally desired that this punishment not be inflicted on him.

### 4. The book

The Book of Daniel divides itself into two parts that are of equal length. The first part is constituted of the first six chapters, which are primarily historical. These chapters present the events that have been considered in the preceding discussion. The second division is comprised of the last six chapters, and these tell of the four visions God gave to His prophet.

Chapter 7 presents the first vision as it sets forth four great beasts that appeared before Daniel, representing four empires that either had already arisen (Babylonia) or were to arise in the future (Medo-Persia, Greece, Rome). The vision also carries reference to events of the last days. A little horn is described as arising among ten prior horns of the fourth beast, and this little horn represents the Antichrist, who will rule over a reestablished Roman confederacy in the last days during the great tribulation period.

Chapter 8 presents the second vision, and this sets forth two other beasts. These are said to symbolize the Medo-Persian and Grecian empires (vv. 20, 21). A goat with one horn comes and destroys a ram with two horns, symbolizing the time when Alexander the Great took over the vast Persian Empire from the Persian kings. This vision also presents a little horn, but this time the person symbolized is Antiochus Epiphanes, who ruled over Syria after 175 B.C. and brought enormous suffering on the Jewish people. He is called "little horn," as is the Antichrist in chapter 7, because he was typical of the Antichrist in what he did in intertestamental times.

Chapter 9 gives the third vision, and this is the well-known vision of the seventy weeks. These are weeks of years rather than weeks of days, meaning that they represent 490 years total. The seventieth week or final period of seven years represents the great tribulation period of the future.

Chapters 10, 11, and 12 give the fourth vision. Chapter 10 tells of the glorious heavenly messenger who brought the vision to Daniel, and chapters 11 and 12 present the vision proper. It concerns especially Antiochus Epiphanes and the one he typified, the Antichrist. Chapter 12 is concerned particularly with the great tribulation period when the Antichrist will be the ruler of the restored Roman confederacy.

The Book of Daniel is written in two languages: Aramaic, extending from 2:4 to 7:28, and Hebrew, covering the other parts of the book. The reason for the use of the two languages is best seen in terms of the subject matter involved. The Aramaic sets forth matters pertaining to the Gentile world, with little notice of God's people the Jews; and, apparently, God saw that Aramaic, the language of the Gentile world, was more suitable to record those matters than was Hebrew, which was distinctly Jewish. The Hebrew, on the other hand, concerns Jewish matters. The first chapter of the book presents itself in the Jewish category, because four young Jews are there taken captive and placed in a position where they must decide whether to remain faithful to their God or not. The eighth chapter is again of this category, for it concerns oppression of the Jews by the Syrian ruler, Antiochus Epiphanes, and this oppression is typical of similar actions to be brought by the Antichrist in the last days. The ninth chapter belongs to this group because it concerns seventy weeks of years in the history of the Jews. And chapters 10-12 must be so classified because they set forth oppressions of the Jews effected first by Antiochus Epiphanes and then by the Antichrist.

The intervening six chapters, however, place matters pertaining to Gentile history in the forefront. The second and seventh chapters are parallel in content, setting forth the overall scope of Gentile history following the time of Daniel. The second chapter does this through the symbolism of the image of Nebuchadnezzar's dream, and the seventh chapter through the symbolism of the four successive beasts noted above. Between these two chapters are four chapters which picture Gentile power in action, with its definite limitations before almighty God.

These four chapters (3-6) fall into two pairs. The third and sixth chapters set forth Gentile power as it brings persecution on the people of God—the former telling of King Nebuchadnezzar's order to Daniel's friends to bow to his image, and the latter describing how officials under King Darius sought to take the life of Daniel by subterfuge. The fourth and fifth chapters tell of supernatural revelations given to Gentile kings, and the need in each instance for a man of God to give the interpretations. The former concerns Nebuchadnezzar's second dream which remained an enigma for him until Daniel came to give the meaning, and the latter the miraculous handwriting on the palace wall of Belshazzar which again called for interpretation by Daniel. The first pair of chapters illustrates the fact that the world has long brought persecution on the people of God and that God has granted gracious protection for those faithful to Him. The second pair pictures the dependence of the world upon God, and the need for the children of God to tell the people of the world about God's truth.

The author of the book clearly was Daniel himself, who speaks frequently in the first person and also shows intimate knowledge of the Babylonian and early Persian history when he lived. Liberal critics have long disclaimed the authorship by Daniel, principally because of the predictive history the book contains. This is no problem, however, for conservative scholars, who believe that God could and did supernaturally reveal such information to those who wrote the Scripture.[6]

The book may be outlined as follows:

I. Section of historical events (1:1—6:28).

    A. Captivity and testing of the four friends (1:1-21).

    B. Nebuchadnezzar's dream of the image and its interpretation (2:1-49).

---

[6]For a discussion of the liberal viewpoint and evidence presented, see R. K. Harrison, *Introduction to the Old Testament*, pp. 1110-1127; Gleason L. Archer, *A Survey of Old Testament Introduction*, pp. 367-388; or see my *Commentary on Daniel*, pp. 19-23.

## B. EZEKIEL

### 1. The date

Ezekiel dates his ministry precisely. He was taken captive in the second aspect of the captivity, 597 B.C. This is evident from Ezekiel 33:21 where the prophet speaks of his captivity as occurring in the twelfth year before the time when the city of Jerusalem was destroyed, which came in 586 B.C. Again in 40:1 he speaks of an event that occurred in the twenty-fifth year of his captivity, which he says was in the "fourteenth year after that the city was smitten." The captivity of 597 B.C. was the time when King Jehoiachin was taken, along with ten thousand captives (II Kings 24:11–16). Ezekiel indicates that his call to the prophetic ministry came in "the fifth year of King Jehoiachin's captivity" (1:2), which would have been 592 B.C. He continued in service at least until the twenty-seventh year of his captivity (29:17), which would have been 571 B.C., thus making at least a twenty-two year span of prophetic service. He may have continued still longer, but this is the last reported date in his book.

### 2. Background history

Once again the basic historical background here involved has already been given in respect to the seventh-century prophets. Judah's king, Jehoiakim, who had managed to remain on Judah's throne at the time of Nebuchadnezzar's first attack in 605 B.C. when Daniel was taken captive, now rebelled against the Babylonian monarch. Nebuchadnezzar came again into the westland to take appropriate measures. As was indicated, for a time Nebuchadnezzar sent only contingents of his army, reinforced by Aramaean, Moabite, and Ammonite troops (II Kings 24:2), to keep the revolt in check. But finally, he saw the need of a major campaign and came himself. He left Babylon in December, 598 B.C., which was the same month that Jehoiakim died in Jerusalem. This means that Jehoiachin, the son and successor of Jehoiakim, was just on the throne when the Babylonian monarch arrived at Jerusalem. The attack was launched in March, 597 B.C., and the city fell with comparative ease. Jehoiachin was taken captive along with the queen mother, his wives, and servants. That Nebuchadnezzar also took ten thousand leading citizens who were mainly craftsmen suggests that he wanted these to bolster his own working force in Babylonia. Of course, the measure had the secondary effect of depriving Jerusalem of its leading citizenry.

### 3. Work and person

#### a. WORK

In understanding the work Ezekiel performed, it is well first to see him in relation to Daniel both chronologically and socially. As indicated, Daniel had been taken captive eight years earlier than Ezekiel. By the time of his arrival, then, Daniel's three years of training were over and he had already experienced five years in his work as head of the wise men.[7]

The relative ages of Ezekiel and Daniel can be conjectured, resting mainly on Ezekiel's indication that it was "in the thirtieth year" (1:1) when he received his call. He does not specify "the thirtieth year" of what, but the implication is that it was the thirtieth year of his own life. In other words he was thirty years old at the time.[8] If now Ezekiel was thirty at his call and this was five years after he was taken captive, he was twenty-five years old at that time. Daniel was then about twenty-three, for he had been in the land eight years and had come to the land, as indicated, when he was about fifteen. This means that the two were roughly two years apart, Ezekiel being that much older than Daniel.

In terms of social position, there was great contrast between them at the

---

[7]Daniel had also been assigned the governorship of the province of Babylon (Dan. 2:48). This would have been a very important task also, but probably the primary work was turned over to Shadrach, Meshach, and Abednego, who apparently were appointed as his assistants (Dan. 2:49). Daniel's work as head of the wise men no doubt occupied his time rather fully.

[8]Other meanings suggested involve too many difficulties to take them seriously. For these views see Hobart E. Freeman, *An Introduction to the Old Testament Prophets*, pp. 301–302.

time Ezekiel entered the land. By this time, Daniel had been head of the wise men for five years, meaning that he was very prominent in the land. Ezekiel, on the other hand, was simply a newly arriving captive. One may believe that on arrival he would have soon taken steps to learn about his fellow countrymen who were high up in the Babylonian court. Doing so and being the kind of capable person he was in his own right, he would have then made careful enquiry regarding such a young man. He would have wanted to know what sort of a person Daniel was and what events had transpired that resulted in his attaining his high position. An actual meeting between the two probably occurred before long, and a close friendship may have been established in spite of their different stations in life.

Ezekiel by birth was a priest, a son of Buzi (1:3). He probably served as a priest in whatever ways priests were able to carry on their work in the foreign land, until the time God called him. In the fifth year of his captivity, however, God did commission him as a prophet, and then he took up this new form of work. There may have been others among the ten thousand captives who were also prophets, but in that God especially called Ezekiel to serve one may be sure that he was God's primary servant to minister in this capacity. One may think of him, then, from this time on pursuing a prophetic ministry: preaching to the people, urging conformance to the will of God, and conducting pastoral work as he counseled and extended comfort. He lived by the river Chebar, probably the great canal which flowed near Babylon, as noted. This canal, called *Naru Kabari* in the cuneiform inscriptions, ran out of the Euphrates River just north of Babylon, flowed sixty miles in a southeasterly direction to Nippur, and rejoined the Euphrates below Ur. It was an important part of the irrigation system of Babylonia. Ezekiel's home was located somewhere near the city Tel-abib, which he visited at least one time. He and other Jews were able to move about freely, for he received elders of the Jews in his home apparently for the purposes of fellowship and consultation (8:1; 20:1). Ezekiel was married but his wife died in the ninth year of his captivity (24:1, 15–18). Ezekiel continued his prophetic ministry at least until the twenty-seventh year of captivity or until an age of fifty-two years.

There was a marked difference between the respective ministries of Daniel and Ezekiel. Daniel served in the palace court in an administrative capacity. Here he had the important tasks of maintaining the honor of God and of watching out for the welfare of the Jewish people. He was not occupied in going about the land in a preaching or pastoral-type ministry. Ezekiel, on the other hand, did have this kind of work. His time was spent in proclaiming God's word, visiting people, and doing the work of a prophet. He was not connected with the palace, nor did he have any administrative position. Both men were important in their own place. The tasks of both were crucial to God's overall program for the captivity period.

Another difference pertained to length of life. Daniel lived on into the time of the Persian takeover of the kingdom, while Ezekiel probably died even before the close of Nebuchadnezzar's rule. How God may have provided for prophetic work among the captive people following Ezekiel's death is not indicated. Probably other prophets were available, but their names are not recorded.

### b. PERSON

*1) Spiritual status.* Ezekiel's spiritual maturity is evidenced in fewer ways than that of Daniel, but one may be sure that Ezekiel did possess this important virtue. For one thing, he was selected by God to be a prophet when he had been born a priest. Quite clearly he had not planned to be a prophet nor had he especially prepared himself for the task, but God saw him as qualified for it. That he was first a priest was no doubt pleasing to God, but evidently a larger ministry lay before him in being a prophet, and one must believe that he was truly a God-fearing person to be called of God to this office.

Moreover, as noted in chapter 6, Ezekiel was unusually controlled by and conscious of the Holy Spirit. For instance, no less than seven times Ezekiel speaks of the Spirit's transporting him some place (3:12, 14; 8:3; 11:1, 24; 37:1; 43:5). He appears to have been taken to Tel-abib, where he stayed for a period of seven days (3:15), and was transported even to Jerusalem, though this no doubt was only in the manner of a vision (8:3). In addition, Ezekiel speaks of the Holy Spirit eight other times (1:12, 20, 21; 10:17; 36:26, 27; 37:14; 39:29). For instance, in chapter 1 the Spirit is presented as controlling a vision that was given to Ezekiel. In chapter 10 the Spirit is seen in command of matters involving a vision of a similar nature. And in chapter 36 God promises to put His Spirit within His people in a day yet future when they will have a new heart and attitude towards Him. Spirit-awareness of this kind is a clear indication that the person concerned was fully committed to knowing and doing the will of God.

*2) Priestly characteristics.* Ezekiel gives evidence that along with conducting his prophetic work, he continued his interest in priestly matters. For instance, while in 22:25 he speaks of false prophets and their devious ways, in 22:26 he speaks also of priests who had violated God's Law and profaned His holy things, putting no difference between the holy and profane. Then, very clear evidence of his priestly interests comes from his extensive treatment of the future temple of Israel (40–48). Though differences of opinion exist among expositors as to the interpretation of these chapters,[9] the only exegeti-

---

[9] For discussion see Archer, *A Survey of Old Testament Introduction*, pp. 361–364.

cally sound explanation is that they present a view of the millennial temple. That God would see fit to inspire Ezekiel to write regarding this temple at all indicates His recognition of the natural bent of Ezekiel's mind. The way in which the prophet writes regarding it shows his own interest in and familiarity with the many sacrifices and offerings that had been presented in the temple down through the years (42:13; 43:27; 44:29–31; 45:17; 46:20).

*3) Magnanimity.* That Ezekiel was a magnanimous person is indicated in a general way by his unselfish manner in giving himself for ministry among his captive people. It is indicated also in a remarkable passage of his book (14:14–20) which speaks of Daniel. In recognizing the significance of the passage, one must remember the relationship between Daniel and Ezekiel. Daniel had been in Babylon eight years and was already high up in the palace when Ezekiel arrived as a mere captive. Ezekiel would have investigated what kind of person Daniel was and probably at first might have thought unkind things regarding him—only a person who had catered to Babylonian ways could possibly have arisen so far so soon. It would have been natural, too, for Ezekiel to have felt a little jealous.

In this passage, however, Ezekiel shows that he was not jealous at all. In fact, he had come to admire Daniel very highly. The passage talks of the great sin of Jerusalem and says, "Though these three men, Noah, Daniel, and Job were in it [Jerusalem], they should deliver but their own souls by their righteousness, saith the LORD God" (14:14). Ezekiel thus picked out three very righteous men and said that, even though these were living in Jerusalem at the time, the sin of Jerusalem was so great that their righteousness could not deliver the city from destruction. One can readily see why he would have picked out Noah and Job, because Noah is described as "a just man and perfect in his generations" (Gen. 6:9), and Job as "perfect and upright, and one that feared God, and eschewed evil" (Job 1:1). But it is most remarkable that the third man was Daniel.[10] Ezekiel thus passed over others who might have been included, such as Abraham, Samuel, or David, or one of the other great prophets, and came to his contemporary, a man who was even younger than himself. Ezekiel had not let any possible jealousy or other emotional attitude blur his thinking in respect to this remarkable young man. He had found him truly righteous as a court official, and he was ready to give him that honor. This speaks highly of Ezekiel's magnanimity.

It should not be missed in passing that this speaks also of the outstanding righteousness Daniel had achieved. Certainly Ezekiel had considered Daniel

---

[10]Some believe this to be the Daniel of the Ras Shamra texts (see Charles Virolleaud, *La légende phénicienne de Danel*), but it seems strange that Ezekiel would have made that Daniel parallel with Noah and Job of biblical history. Certainly he was referring to his friend Daniel, the head of the wise men. For further discussion see Edward J. Young, *The Prophecy of Daniel*, pp. 274–275.

in every way possible and from the most critical standpoint, coming to Babylon as he had after Daniel had achieved his high position. Still it is clear that Ezekiel had found nothing to criticize but only to admire. Daniel had not compromised his position nor done anything wrong to achieve the high place he enjoyed. A more significant indication of the righteous life of a person is hard to imagine.

*4) Knowledge of the world.* Like several of the other prophets, Ezekiel was knowledgeable of the world in which he lived. One of the reasons why liberal scholars have been impressed by the Hebrew prophets generally is their world-wide knowledge. Normally people of the day were concerned with their own affairs, and their world was about as large as the local community in which they lived. Several of the prophets, however, as has already been noticed, knew of countries around them and wrote regarding them. Ezekiel was of this group. He devotes one whole portion of his book to speaking regarding Ammon, Moab, Edom, Philistia, Tyre and Sidon, and Egypt. All these were near to the land of Israel and Judah. It would not be so remarkable that Ezekiel knew of them if he had lived in Israel or Judah, but he was living in the land of Babylon. He, of course, may have learned something about them before being taken captive at the age of twenty-five, but certainly his book was written much later than this, and he shows that his knowledge of and interest in these countries had not diminished but probably grown. Somehow he had found ways of availing himself of information regarding these countries and made use of it.

## 4. The book

The Book of Ezekiel divides itself into three parts: first, there is the announcement of the approaching fall of Jerusalem, written between the time of Ezekiel's call and the time when Jerusalem proper fell in 586 B.C.; second, there are prophecies against foreign nations as just indicated; and third, there are prophecies of Israel's future restoration.

Liberal scholars have sometimes spoken of Ezekiel as a prophet who was mentally unbalanced, this particularly because of the manner of his frequent references to the Holy Spirit and his description of the millennial temple. When one examines Ezekiel's book properly, however, he finds no indication of a mind that was unbalanced. The book actually carries a very orderly arrangement, and Ezekiel even dates many of his prophecies in careful chronological sequence. The basis for this dating is a reference always to the captivity of Jehoiachin. For instance, in 1:2 he states that his own call to the prophetic ministry came in the "fifth year of king Jehoiachin's captivity."

In the first section of his book, written prior to Jerusalem's destruction in 586 B.C., Ezekiel speaks strongly against the sin of the people, whether of those still living in Judah or those already in captivity. The sins mentioned are largely the same as those referred to by Jeremiah, for Jeremiah was writing from Jerusalem at the same time that Ezekiel was writing from Babylon. Ezekiel vigorously denounced false prophets of the time, who were leading the people on in false hopes of peace. He saw the people of Jerusalem as a worthless vine, suitable only as fuel for fire, and the people among whom he lived as a "rebellious house," "briars and thorns," and "scorpions." All were continuing in the ways of their fathers, seeking sin and enjoying their rebellious actions.

In the last division, however, the prophet brings a message of hope and anticipation of a glorious future. The people now captive could look forward to a day of deliverance when their disgrace and suffering would be over and the long separated kingdoms of Judah and Israel would be united. Their enemies would all be defeated, and a grand new temple and manner of worship would be restored in the land.

The author of the book in its entirety was Ezekiel. This fact was not challenged seriously even by liberal critics until a comparatively recent time. As late as 1924, in fact, Gustav Hölscher asserted that the critical knife had been laid on practically all the prophetical books except Ezekiel.[11] He then proceeded to use that critical knife himself, and when he was through he left with Ezekiel only 170 of a total 1,273 verses. Since his time, others have followed his lead, and numerous suggestions have been made either more or less radical than Hölscher as to multiple authorship, all of which must be rejected.[12]

The book may be outlined as follows:

I. Prophecies against Judah prior to Jerusalem's fall (1:1—24:27).
   A. Ezekiel's call and commission (1:1—3:27).
   B. Prediction of Jerusalem's destruction (4:1—7:27).
   C. Vision of Jerusalem's sin and coming punishment (8:1—11:25).
   D. Certainty of punishment due to sin (12:1—19:14).
   E. Final warnings before Jerusalem's fall (20:1—24:27).
II. Prophecies against foreign nations (25:1—32:32).
   A. Against Ammon, Moab, Edom, and Philistia (25:1-17).
   B. Against Tyre and Sidon (26:1—28:26).
   C. Against Egypt (29:1—32:32).
III. Prophecies of Israel's future restoration (33:1—48:35).
   A. Events transpiring prior to the millennium (33:1—39:29).

[11]*Hesekial, der Dichter und das Buch*, p. 1.
[12]For discussion see Harrison, *Introduction to the Old Testament*, pp. 823-832.

   1. Parable of the watchman (33:1–33).
   2. False shepherds and the true shepherd (34:1–31).
   3. The land of Israel to be restored (35:1—36:38).
   4. Visions of the dry bones and the two sticks (37:1–28).
   5. Godless nations (Gog and others) to be destroyed (38:1—39:29).
B. Worship in the millennial kingdom (40:1—48:35).
   1. The millennial temple (40:1—43:27).
   2. The millennial worship (44:1—46:24).
   3. The millennial land (47:1—48:35).

| | |
|---|---|
| 9th-Century Prophets | Chapter 16<br>Obadiah<br>Joel |
| 8th-Century Prophets | Chapter 17<br>Hosea<br>Amos<br>Jonah |
| | Chapter 18<br>Isaiah<br>Micah |
| 7th-Century Prophets | Chapter 19<br>Nahum<br>Zephaniah<br>Habakkuk |
| | Chapter 20<br>Jeremiah |
| Exilic Prophets | Chapter 21<br>Daniel<br>Ezekiel |
| Postexilic Prophets | Chapter 22<br>Haggai<br>Zechariah<br>Malachi |

# 22

# Postexilic Prophets: Haggai, Zechariah, and Malachi

We now come to study the postexilic prophets. These are the prophets who ministered in Judah after the return from captivity. There are three of them, Haggai, Zechariah, and Malachi. The first two prophesied contemporaneously and the last one several decades later. At the time these three ministered, there were still many Jewish people living in the east, but these three lived and conducted their work in Judah.

## A. HAGGAI

### 1. The date

Haggai, like Ezekiel, dates the time of his prophecy precisely. He says that the word of the Lord came to him for the first time in the second year of Darius (520 B.C.) in the sixth month (approximately September) on the first day of the month (Hag. 1:1). He gives similar precise dating for three other times of revelation, all falling still in Darius' second year. The material Haggai records in his book all came to him from God within a space of four months in the year 520 B.C. One should realize that he no doubt had been active as a prophet for some time before this and continued for a few years following. The period when his ministry was the most significant, however, was probably the time indicated in his book. As was seen, Daniel continued to live in Babylon until about 535 B.C.; the ministry of Haggai took place roughly fifteen years later, though in Judah. There were more years that had intervened since the time of Ezekiel for Ezekiel died several years prior to Daniel.

## 2. Background history

Somewhat parallel to the fact that there were three times when people of Judah were taken captive, there were also three times when people who had been in captivity returned to Jerusalem and Judah. The first came shortly after the Persian conquest of Babylon, in 538/537 B.C. (Ezra 1:1), led by Sheshbazzar. The second came eighty years later in the seventh year of Artaxerxes Longimanus, 458 B.C. (Ezra 7:7), led by Ezra. And the third came thirteen years after this in the twentieth year of Artaxerxes Longimanus, 445 B.C. (Neh. 2:1), led by Nehemiah. All three returns need to be kept in mind in respect to the historical backgrounds of the three prophets here concerned, but only the first one in respect to Haggai and Zechariah.

The great conqueror, Cyrus, king of Persia, gave permission to the Jews to return to Judah in the first year of his reign following the fall of Babylon. The edict he issued in permitting this return was unusual and is recorded twice in Scripture: Ezra 1:2–4 and 6:3–5.[1] The edict was remarkable in that it gave orders that the Jerusalem temple be rebuilt and that the cost should be defrayed from Cyrus' own treasury. One has to wonder if Daniel did not have something to do with its origin and possibly its very writing.

The people who came back at this time are listed in Ezra 2, and their number is indicated as 42,360 besides 7,337 servants (Ezra 2:64, 65). This is a substantial number, but it did not include all the Jews who lived in the east. In fact it probably did not include even the majority, for just over a half-century later, in the time of Esther, enough Jews yet lived there to kill as many as 75,000 enemy neighbors in two days of fighting (Esther 9:16). As was noted, Jews had achieved surprisingly pleasant conditions in the east and quite clearly many did not want to leave when given the opportunity.

Those who did return properly recognized that a first order of business concerned the rebuilding of the Jerusalem temple. Construction began soon after arrival in the land. The first act was to build an altar and reinstate prescribed sacrifices, which was done in the seventh month of the first year

---

[1]The first is written in Hebrew and has the form of a royal proclamation. The second is written in Aramaic and has the form of a *dikroma*, which is a memorandum of an oral royal decision. For discussion see E. J. Bickerman, "The Edict of Cyrus in Ezra One," *Journal of Biblical Literature*, 65 (1946):244–275.

of return. In the second month of the second year, the work on the temple proper began. The first step was to lay the foundation, which seems to have been accomplished rather quickly. When it was completed the people celebrated. At this point, however, trouble began. Opposition was experienced from Samaritans to the north (Ezra 4:1–5), and the Jews themselves working on the temple began to use more of their time for building their own houses and farming their own lands (Hag. 1:3–11). Tragically, it was not long before all work ceased, with the result that the temple remained little more than a foundation until the second year of Darius, the time of Haggai's prophecy, a total period of about sixteen years. It was the need for the restarting of this building activity that called for the ministries of Haggai and Zechariah.

### 3. Work and person

Accordingly the work of Haggai, as reported in his book, revolved around his efforts to this end. The need for construction to be started again was pressing. As long as the Jerusalem temple was not functioning, there was no temple in all the world where God was being worshiped. It had been serious enough to have the temple in a destroyed condition during the captivity proper, but this captivity had been necessary in order that God's people be punished for their sin. When the captivity was over, however, the temple could be rebuilt and one may be sure that God desired this to be done as quickly as possible. The act of starting to rebuild was good, but the cessation of this work was very wrong in the sight of God.

In fact, the situation of the temple lying in a destroyed condition after the people had returned from captivity was more serious than while they had still been away. As long as the captive condition had continued, peoples around Judah had reason to know why the temple remained destroyed. But when the Jews had returned to their land, there was no longer any excuse for the destroyed condition to continue. Accordingly, when only a start was made and the temple then was left as merely a foundation, peoples round about could only have thought that the Jews held their God in low esteem. It should be recognized that peoples of the day measured how much another people thought of their god by how fine a temple they erected to him. As long as this condition existed the testimony of the Jews was only negative. There was no reason to tell others that they loved their God so long as the temple remained in this unfinished condition. Thus it was vitally important that work be started again, and God called Haggai as well as Zechariah to instigate action on the part of the people.

In that God saw fit to use Haggai in this way, it may well be that the prophet had already been personally concerned about this condition prior to his call. God often calls those to a work who are already burdened concerning that work. It was in the sixth month of 520 B.C., however, that God definitely spoke to him about it and told him to take up the ministry of urging people to get busy. Three times during the fall of this year, God gave further revelations to the prophet, with the result that Haggai did preach and the people did begin to rebuild. Though Haggai gives no indication concerning the work he performed while the building was going on, one may believe that he voiced repeated urgings that the people continue.

Haggai gives no information regarding his personal life. He does not even mention the name of his father or the city from which he came. It is generally considered that he was older than Zechariah since his name always comes first when the two are mentioned together. Because in 2:3 he asks the question, "Who is left among you that saw this house in its first glory?" it is sometimes suggested that Haggai saw the first house before it was destroyed. If so, he lived before 586 B.C. This means that he was now at least seventy years old. This is possible but perhaps not likely. Because God used him in this service, along with Zechariah, God must have seen him as a devoted person, one who longed to see the temple rebuilt and its sacrificial system restored. God also must have judged him as one who could receive revelations from God and still remain humble. And God must have equipped him to be a capable speaker, because he would have needed to inspire people to action. It is one thing to have a message and it is another to deliver it in a way that compels people to get busy. The need was that people not only learn what they should do but be impelled to do it. Haggai may be thought of as an articulate person who could speak with force and persuasion.

### 4. The book

Because the Book of Haggai concerns only the four revelations given to the prophet in the fall of 520 B.C., it is likely that he wrote the book shortly after this, perhaps about the time that the rebuilding of the temple actually got under way. It is second only to Obadiah for brevity, comprised of merely two chapters, a total of thirty-eight verses. Though it is brief, however, it still contains four divisions corresponding to the four messages God revealed. The first was given on the first day of the sixth month, 520 B.C., and concerns a general urging of the people to get busy and rebuild the temple. The people were reminded that since they had ceased building sixteen years before, they had not been as prosperous as they had thought they would be. They had sown crops but had not enough to eat, and prices were high because food was scarce. The reason was that God's blessing had been withheld, since they had not been doing His will. The solution to the problem was that they should go to the mountain, bring wood, and start building the temple again; then God would send rain from heaven so that crops would grow and the people would once more prosper. When Haggai had brought this message, the people obeyed and on the twenty-fourth of the month did begin to work as he urged.

The second message came on the twenty-first day of the seventh month of this year. Its thrust was to give encouragement to Zerubbabel the civil leader, Joshua the religious leader, and the people in general to move along with the work. The people were to be strong and believe that God would enable them to accomplish what seemed to be a very large task. They were not to fear since God was in control of all the world, owning the silver and the gold and all the materials necessary for the building, and had promised that He would indeed fill the house with His glory when it was completed.

The third message came on the twenty-fourth day of the ninth month. Its intent was to warn the people that God wanted more than merely the building of a temple or even the offering of sacrifices. He wanted the people to be in a right relation to Himself in their hearts. God did want the temple rebuilt, but He wanted even more an obedient people who were dedicated to doing His will.

The fourth message came on the same day as the third one. It was different from the others for it spoke of a day still future when God would overthrow the kingdoms of the world and establish His own glorious kingdom.

The book may be outlined as follows:

I.  Neglect of the temple the cause of economic depression (1:1-15).

II.  A message of encouragement (2:1-9).

III.  Obedience more important than sacrifice (2:10-19).

IV.  The overthrow of world kingdoms (2:20-23).

## B. ZECHARIAH

### 1. The date

As has been indicated Zechariah was contemporary with Haggai. He dates three of the occasions of revelation he received just as precisely. The first came in the eighth month of Darius' second year, 520 B.C. (1:1); the second three months later in the eleventh month of Darius' second year, 520 B.C. (1:7); and the third about two years later in the ninth month of Darius' fourth year, 518 B.C. (7:1). A fourth message begins at 9:1 but is undated. It is commonly placed several years later, even after 480 B.C., because it contains a reference to Greece (9:13), and Greece became much more prominent after that time. As will be noted, Zechariah was probably a much younger man than Haggai and could have lived until after 480 B.C., while his older contemporary may have died soon after his ministry in 520 B.C. In keeping with this, Zechariah's ministry probably did not begin very long before the date of 520 B.C.; thus the two overlapped in their service at this time.

## 2. Background history

Because Zechariah and Haggai were contemporary, the same background history applies to each. The work on the temple that had ceased approximately sixteen years earlier needed to be started again. God saw the need urgent enough to use two men in a special way to inspire people to become occupied in the task. He spoke to Haggai in the sixth month and two months later to Zechariah.

Since it is likely that Zechariah did live many years after 520 B.C., it is appropriate to say something regarding this later history. As was noted, the people began to rebuild the temple in 520 B.C. as a result of the preaching of these two prophets; and the structure was completed in the sixth year of Darius, March, 515 B.C. (Ezra 6:15). Darius continued to rule over Persia until 486 B.C., when he was followed by Xerxes I until 465 B.C. It was during the rule of Xerxes that the history of Esther transpired, and, if Zechariah still lived then, he may well have become familiar with it. Politically during these years, Judah was a part of the large Persian satrapy of Abarnahara, which included all land southwest of the Euphrates to the border of Egypt, principally Syria and Palestine. In this large unit, Judah constituted one province over which normally a governor, *Tirshatha*, meaning "He who is to be feared" (Ezra 2:63; Neh. 8:9; 10:1), ruled.[2] It may be that at times Judah did not have its own governor and was ruled directly by the district satrap.

Little information is known regarding life in Judah during these years, but three clues give some help. From Haggai's indictment against the people in his first message (1:3–11), it is clear that they were rebuilding comfortable houses and farming their land. From the fact that Nehemiah found it necessary much later (445 B.C.) to come from Persia and build Jerusalem's walls, it is evident that little was being done in reconstructing the capital city apart from erecting private homes. And from Ezra's confession of the people's sin regarding intermarriage with surrounding pagans (Ezra 9:1–15), it is apparent that Jews were interacting improperly with neighboring peoples, which no doubt led to wrong religious practices.

---

[2]For discussion see Michael Avi-Yonah, *The Holy Land*, p. 12.

## 3. Work and person

In substantial part, the work of Zechariah was parallel to that of Haggai. The temple needed to be rebuilt and both prophets were called for the purpose of instilling a desire in the people to get busy at the task. However, it appears that the approach God wished each to take in doing this varied. Haggai's assignment basically was to impel action. The people were simply to get busy and do what they should have done long before. But Zechariah's messages were directed more to the manner and attitude of the people as they worked. His interest was that the people have right attitudes of heart, showing true dependence on God for His blessing. To this end he was given a series of eight visions, recorded in chapters 1–6, and these centered in symbolism around this factor of approach and attitude.

Because Zechariah continued his ministry following the beginning of the rebuilding activity, it follows that God had other work for him to do as well. On the basis of what is included in his book, this seems to have been especially in two areas. First was the area of answering practical questions on the minds of people, one of which was whether or not God wanted them to fast. Zechariah's reply was that God desired obedience more than merely outward fasting (8:19). The second area pertained to the future. Evidently the people were wondering what the future held, now that they were back in the land with their temple rebuilt. God's answer to them through the prophet concerned the far future and was to the effect that a glorious time of a messianic kingdom awaited them.

Besides these matters, one may conjecture that Zechariah, being yet young at the time of the rebuilding of the temple, engaged himself in an energetic ministry urging proper observances of the Mosaic sacrificial system. If the temple had now been rebuilt, the people should visit it regularly and carry out all that God wanted in respect to it. Also, Zechariah would have spoken vigorously against sin that continued to exist. A tendency to intermarry with people around about, against which Ezra would take such strong steps later in 458 B.C., had perhaps already started, and Zechariah may well have had much to do with keeping this from developing more rapidly than it did.

As to his person, Zechariah indicates that his father was named Berechiah and his grandfather, Iddo (1:1). Zechariah was a priest, being so listed in Nehemiah 12:16. Here he is called the son of Iddo (cf. Ezra 5:1; 6:14). It may be that his own father Berechiah had died young, or it is possible that Iddo simply was a more prominent ancestor. In Zechariah 2:4, the prophet is spoken of as a "young man" (na'ar), which is in keeping with the theory that he was young at the time of his ministry in 520 B.C.

That Zechariah was spiritually mature is attested especially in two ways. One is that he was selected by God, along with Haggai, to rekindle a desire of rebuilding the temple on the part of the people. As noted, this rebuilding was very important in God's sight and therefore those selected to lead in it would have been choice servants. One should think of Haggai as having been selected for this purpose at the close of his life and Zechariah at the beginning of his, thus complementing each other as a team. Haggai would have had more appeal to older folk to encourage their participation and Zechariah to younger people.

The other factor is that God gave revelations to Zechariah, including the eight visions mentioned. Frequently an angel served as a sort of host to Zechariah in these visions, and certainly one to whom this kind of revelation was given would have to be a man who stood high in the evaluation of God.

As was indicated regarding Haggai also, likely Zechariah was a forceful speaker. God would have wanted a prophet who could impel action and be forceful in his presentation in order that the work on the temple might be started and done properly. Further, one may think of this person as naturally given to reflecting on the future. At least it was through him that God gave some of the more specific information in the Old Testament regarding the last days. The closing chapters of his book are referred to frequently in prophetic sermons preached today.

## 4. The book

Zechariah's book divides itself into four sections, based on both logical and chronological considerations. The first division constitutes a general call to the people to repent before God. It was given in the eighth month of 520 B.C. The second records the eight visions that have been mentioned, which have as their central message instructions regarding the rebuilding of the temple, though they also contain overtones of eschatological significance. They were given in the eleventh month of 520 B.C. The third section (7:1—8:23) was a message given in the ninth month of 518 B.C. and considers two matters. One concerns whether or not God desired the people to fast, and the other the fact that God held in store a grand day of blessing for His people in the far future. The fourth section (9:1—14:21) is undated and likely was given much later. It also divides itself into two parts, each beginning with the phrase, "The burden of the word of the LORD." The two parts deal with the same subject matter, however: the overthrow of world powers and the final supremacy of the nation of Israel. The first part is more general in its presentation and stresses the overthrow of the powers; the second is more specific and stresses Israel's final purification and supremacy.

As to authorship, though almost all scholars agree that the first eight chapters were written by Zechariah, many liberal scholars believe that chapters 9-14 came from other hands. The reason is basically the difference in subject material. The first eight chapters concern matters that pertain largely to the time of Zechariah, but the last chapters are mainly eschatological. It is believed that the same man would not have written two such different types of material.[3] This poses no problem for the conservative scholar, however.

The book may be outlined as follows:

I. Messages during the building of the temple (1:1—8:23).
   A. First message: a call to repentance (1:1-6).
   B. Second message: eight night visions (1:7—6:15).
      1. The horseman among the myrtles (1:7-17).
      2. The four horns and smiths (1:18-21).
      3. The man with the measuring rod (2:1-13).
      4. The cleansing of Joshua the high priest (3:1-10).
      5. The golden lampstand (4:1-14).
      6. The flying scroll of divine judgment (5:1-4).
      7. The woman in the ephah (5:5-11).
      8. The four chariots of divine judgment (6:1-8); the symbolical crowning of Joshua after the visions (6:9-15).
   C. Third message: fasts and the far future (7:1—8:23).
II. Message after the building of the temple (9:1—14:21).
   A. The first prophecy (9:1—11:17).
      1. Overthrow of world kingdoms and Israel's deliverance (9:1—10:12).
      2. Rejection of the true shepherd and rule of the false shepherd (11:1-17).
   B. The second prophecy (12:1—14:21).
      1. Israel's victory over world kingdoms (12:1—13:6).
      2. Final victories of the Messiah-King (13:7—14:21).

## C. MALACHI

### 1. The date

Malachi, the last of the Hebrew prophets, does not date his ministry. Clues as to his time must be found in his book, but there are several that help. First, a Persian governor (*pehah*) was in authority (1:8), which locates the time as following the return from captivity when Judah was under Persian gover-

---

[3]For a detailed discussion of various viewpoints held see R. K. Harrison, *Introduction to the Old Testament*, pp. 950-956.

nors. Second, religious ceremonies, evidently conducted at the temple, were in evidence (1:7–10; 3:8), placing the date after 515 B.C., when the temple was finally brought to completion. Third, the sins of the people to which Malachi gives attention are not those condemned by Haggai and Zechariah, who were interested especially in laxity and improprieties in respect to rebuilding the temple, but are similar to those mentioned by Ezra and Nehemiah at the middle of the following century. Affinities on this count are particularly evident with Nehemiah, since both speak of laxity among the priests in temple ceremonies (Mal. 1:6–14; Neh. 13:4–9), failure to pay tithes (Mal. 3:8–10; Neh. 13:10–13), and intermarriage with foreign women (Mal. 2:10–12; Neh. 13:23–28). Fourth, since neither Ezra nor Nehemiah mentions Malachi, it is not likely that he ministered at the time they wrote or even a few years previously. Nehemiah, who came after Ezra, wrote his book around 430 B.C., following his return to Jerusalem after having gone back to Babylon for a few years. A date shortly after this return seems as likely as any for the time Malachi wrote. It should be realized, of course, that Malachi could have ministered several years prior to this writing and probably continued to do so following. It is perhaps best simply to say that Malachi served sometime during the last half of the fifth century B.C.

## 2. Background history

As indicated, there were three returns from the Babylonian captivity. The first occurred in 538/537 B.C., and we have already noted matters concerned with it. The second came eighty years later, in the seventh year of Artaxerxes Longimanus, 458 B.C., and was led by Ezra.[4] Ezra was known to Artaxerxes, for he had attained a position of some standing at the court. He may have held an office something like a minister of Jewish affairs. In some undisclosed manner he was able to persuade the king to permit him to travel to Judah for the purpose of effecting needed reforms.

As was true regarding the first return, Ezra also received notable privileges from the Persian monarch. These privileges included authority to take with him as many of his countrymen as desired to go, to receive financial support from the Persian court as well as from Jews of the east for the Jerusalem temple, to draw upon the treasury of the satrapy of Abarnahara for needs that might arise, to exempt temple personnel from Persian taxation, and to appoint civil leaders in the land of Judah to enforce the laws.

---

[4]Some scholars date Ezra at the seventh year of Artaxerxes II (398 B.C.), and others at the thirty-seventh year of Artaxerxes I (428 B.C.). Both dates must be rejected. For discussion, see H. H. Rowley, "The Chronological Order of Ezra and Nehemiah," *The Servant of the Lord and Other Essays on the Old Testament*, pp. 131–159.

The principal problem that Ezra encountered on reaching Jerusalem concerned intermarriage of many Jews with surrounding peoples. Ezra was told of this defection from the Law soon after he arrived in Jerusalem, and he reacted with extreme remorse. He tore his clothing, pulled hair from his head, and sat confused until evening on the day that he learned of it. Then he offered a prayer of confession, and, when he finished, those standing by expressed their conviction that the marriages should be dissolved. Ezra agreed and details were worked out for bringing this about.

The third return came in the twentieth year of Artaxerxes, 445 B.C., led by Nehemiah (Neh. 1:1). Nehemiah was also known and favored by the Persian ruler, with the result that when he made this trip "captains of the army and horsemen" (Neh. 2:9) were given him to serve as guards along the way. Nehemiah's main purpose in coming was to rebuild Jerusalem's walls; strange to say, the walls of the city had not been rebuilt before this, though the people had been back in the land nearly a century. Accordingly, within three days after arrival in Jerusalem, Nehemiah made an inspection of the walls to determine their condition. With facts assembled, he gathered the Jerusalem leaders and presented his ideas for the rebuilding. He evidently made a forceful presentation, for response was forthcoming and a decision made to move ahead with the project. Workers were recruited both from Jerusalem and outlying cities, and all were assigned particular sections of the wall on which to labor.

The work progressed with surprising rapidity in spite of opposition from people on the outside. Nehemiah held full authority from the king for the task, but enemies still did their best to hinder him. Apparently neighboring provinces, especially Samaria, had benefited from Judah's weakness until this time, and did not wish to lose this advantage. At first adversaries were content merely to make mockery (Neh. 2:19, 20; 4:1-3), but later plans were formulated actually to attack Jerusalem and force a cessation of the work. News of this terrorized the Jews, but Nehemiah responded by dividing his workmen into two groups, one to continue building and the other to bear arms. In this way the work still progressed, though more slowly. Even so the full work was completed in the remarkably short time of fifty-two days, all much to the consternation and displeasure of the enemies.

Following the completion of the wall, Nehemiah continued as governor of Judah. One of his first actions in this capacity was to remit debts of poor people. The province of Judah was in serious economic straits as a result of high Persian taxes and successive poor crops. In this situation some of those who were more wealthy had taken advantage of the poor and had laid high interest on them for loans granted. Nehemiah asked that this practice be stopped and that restoration be made. Nehemiah again was persuasive in his efforts. Other measures he took involved matters of security for the city

(Neh. 7:1–4; 11:1–36), the reading of God's Law (Neh. 8), and the dedication of the newly-made walls (Neh. 12:27–47).

Nehemiah lived in Jerusalem during two periods of time. He was there the first time for twelve years, from the twentieth to the thirty-second years of Artaxerxes, 445–433 B.C. (Neh. 1:1; 13:6). He went back to his former position in the Persian court for a short time, but then was permitted to return to Jerusalem to continue his work. Upon arrival the second time, Nehemiah was grieved at the increased laxity towards God's Law. Most shocking was the fact that Eliashib, the high priest, had allowed Nehemiah's old enemy Tobiah, the Ammonite, actually to live in a room of the temple. Nehemiah quickly ordered the room cleared of the man's effects and restored it to its original purpose as a storage area for tithes of the people (Neh. 13:4–9).

Nehemiah's reforms also concerned mixed marriages again (Neh. 13:23–28). In spite of Ezra's earlier efforts in 458 B.C., this sin once more existed. Nehemiah found children who could not even speak Hebrew, because Jews had married foreign partners, especially from Ashdod, Ammon, and Moab. Nehemiah ordered the people to promise that no more marriages of this kind would be contracted.

### 3. Work and person

Malachi makes no references to his personal life or work, and he is not mentioned elsewhere in the Old Testament. Accordingly the nature of his work must be deduced from material he wrote. This shows him to have been a dedicated prophet, used effectively to warn people of sin and urge them to conduct their lives in a manner pleasing to God. The main sins with which he was concerned have been enumerated: intermarriage with foreign people, failure to pay tithes, and offering of blemished sacrifices. Probably the most outstanding matter regarding him was that God granted him the privilege of bringing the illustrious line of writing prophets to a close. He was the last.

As to his person, Malachi gives no information, not even the name of his father or of the city in which he was born. His name means "my angel" or "my messenger," and some have suggested that it should be understood as merely a designation of an office rather than a proper name. Evidence is taken from the Septuagint translation of 1:1, where instead of "by Malachi" one reads "by the hand of his messenger."[5] Since this suggestion would leave the book as the only prophecy without the author's name, it is best to reject it.

---

[5]For other evidences and general discussion, see Hobart E. Freeman, *An Introduction to the Old Testament Prophets*, pp. 350–351.

Because this man was selected to be the leading prophet in the closing days of the Old Testament, one may believe that God saw him as a spiritually mature person. No doubt, there were other prophets living, but he was chosen to write the prophetic book of the time. That he spoke plainly concerning sin and urged people to put their sin away indicates further that he was a man conscious of sin and sensitive to its seriousness. If the date suggested for him is correct, one may think of him working in this way side by side with Nehemiah, after Nehemiah returned from the Persian capital. How long each lived or which one lived longer, there is no way to know. One may expect, however, that they knew each other well and labored together in furthering God's work.

### 4. The book

The Book of Malachi is composed of four divisions. First is a statement of God's great love for His people Israel. This is followed by a rebuke of the sins of priests, as they were negligent in carrying out the Mosaic ceremonies. Then comes a rebuke for the sins of people generally, among which were the intermarriages with foreigners, the neglect of paying tithes, and the deficiency in offering sacrifices. Finally there are concluding admonitions to keep God's Law and wait for the return of Christ.

The book may be outlined as follows:

I. God's love for Israel (1:1-5).
II. Rebuke of priests (1:6—2:9).
III. Rebuke of the people (2:10—4:3).
IV. Admonition to keep the Law and wait for Christ's coming (4:4-6).

# Bibliography

Aharoni, Yohanan, and Avi-Yonah, Michael, eds. *The Macmillan Bible Atlas*. New York: Macmillan, 1968.

Albright, William F. *Archaeology and the Religion of Israel*. 3rd ed. Baltimore: Johns Hopkins Press, 1953.

_____. *From the Stone Age to Christianity*. 2nd ed. New York: Doubleday Anchor Books, 1957.

_____. "The Old Testament World." In *The Interpreter's Bible*, edited by George A. Buttrick et al., vol. I, pp. 233–271. New York: Abingdon Press, 1952.

_____. "Recent Progress in North Canaanite Research." *Bulletin of the American Schools of Oriental Research* 70 (1938).

_____. "Some Important Recent Discoveries: Alphabetic Origins and the Idrimi Statue." *Bulletin of the American Schools of Oriental Research* 118 (1950):11–20.

Alexander, Joseph A. *Commentary on the Prophecies of Isaiah*. Grand Rapids: Zondervan, 1953.

Allis, Oswald T. *Prophecy and the Church*. Philadelphia: Presbyterian and Reformed, 1945.

_____. *The Unity of Isaiah*. Philadelphia: Presbyterian and Reformed, 1950.

*Ancient Near Eastern Texts*. Edited by James B. Pritchard. Princeton, NJ: Princeton University Press, 1950.

*Ancient Near East in Pictures, The*. Edited by James B. Pritchard. Princeton, NJ: Princeton University Press, 1954.

Anderson, G. W. *The History and Religion of Israel*. London: Oxford University Press, 1966.

Ap-Thomas, D. R. "The Phoenicians." In *Peoples of Old Testament Times*, edited by
     D. J. Wiseman. Oxford: Clarendon Press, 1973.
Archer, Gleason L. *A Survey of Old Testament Introduction*. Chicago: Moody Press,
     1964.
Avi-Yonah, Michael. *The Holy Land*. Grand Rapids: Baker, 1966.
Baab, Otto J. *The Theology of the Old Testament*. New York: Abingdon Press, 1949.
Baillie, John. *The Idea of Revelation in Recent Thought*. New York: Columbia University
     Press, 1945.
Baron, David. *The Visions and Prophecies of Zechariah*. London: Hebrew Christian Tes-
     timony, 1951.
Barton, George. *Archaeology and the Bible*. 7th edition. Philadelphia: American Sunday
     School Union, 1937.
Bickerman, E. J. "The Edict of Cyrus in Ezra One." *Journal of Biblical Literature* 65
     (1946):244–275.
Blenkinsopp, Joseph. "The Prophetic Reproach." *Journal of Biblical Literature* 90
     (1971):267–278.
Bohl, Franz. "Some Notes on Israel in the Light of Babylonian Discoveries." *Journal
     of Biblical Literature* 53 (1934):140–146.
Breasted, J. H. *The Dawn of Conscience*. New York: Charles Scribner's Sons, 1935.
Bright, John. *A History of Israel*. Philadelphia: Westminster Press, 1959.
Bruce, F. F. *Biblical Exegesis in the Qumran Texts*. Grand Rapids: Eerdmans, 1959.
Buber, Martin. *The Prophetic Faith*. Translated by Carlyle Witton-Davies. New York:
     Macmillan, 1949.
Buttenwieser, Moses. *The Prophets of Israel from the Eighth to the Fifth Century*. New
     York: Macmillan, 1914.
Cook, Stanley. *The Old Testament, A Reinterpretation*. New York: Macmillan, 1936.
Cross, Frank M. *The Ancient Library of Qumran and Modern Biblical Studies*. Garden
     City, NY: Doubleday, 1958.
Culver, Robert D. *Daniel and the Latter Days*. Chicago: Moody, 1965.
Davidson, A. B. *Old Testament Prophecy*. Edinburgh: T. & T. Clark, 1903.
_____. "Prophecy and Prophets." In *Dictionary of the Bible*, edited by James Hastings
     et al., vol. IV, pp. 106–127. New York: Charles Scribner's Sons, 1909.
_____. *Theology of the Old Testament*. Edinburgh: T. & T. Clark, 1955.
DeVaux, Roland. *Ancient Israel, Its Life and Institutions*. Translated by J. McHugh.
     New York: McGraw-Hill, 1961.
Dillon, H. *Assyro-Babylonian Liver Divination*. Rome, 1932.
*Documents from Old Testament Times*. Edited by D. Winton Thomas. New York:
     Harper, 1961.
Driver, S. R. *An Introduction to the Literature of the Old Testament*. Edinburgh: T. & T.
     Clark, 1950.
Eichrodt, Walther. *Theology of the Old Testament*. Translated by J. A. Baker. Philadel-
     phia: Westminster Press, 1961.
Eiselen, Frederick C. *Prophecy and the Prophets*. New York: Methodist, 1919.
Eissfeldt, Otto. *The Old Testament, An Introduction*. Translated by P. R. Ackroyd.
     New York: Harper & Row, 1965.

———. "The Prophetic Literature." In *The Old Testament and Modern Study*, edited by H. H. Rowley, pp. 113–161. New York: Charles Scribner's Sons, 1951.

Ellison, H. L. *Men Spake from God*. Grand Rapids: Eerdmans, 1958.

Engnell, Ivan. *Studies in Divine Kingship in the Ancient Near East*. Uppsala: Almquist and Wiksells Boktrycheri, 1943.

Ewald, Heinrich. *Commentary on the Prophets of the Old Testament*. Translated by J. Frederick Smith. London: Williams and Norgate, 1875.

———. *History of Israel*. 8 volumes. London: Longmans, Green, & Co., 1869.

Finegan, Jack. *Light from the Ancient Past*. Princeton, NJ: Princeton University Press, 1954.

Fohrer, Georg. *History of Israelite Religion*. Translated by D. E. Green. New York: Abingdon Press, 1972.

Fosbroke, Hughell. "The Prophetic Literature." In *The Interpreter's Bible*, edited by George A. Buttrick et al., vol. I, pp. 201–211. New York: Abingdon Press, 1952.

Freeman, Hobart E. *An Introduction to the Old Testament Prophets*. Chicago: Moody Press, 1968.

Gaebelein, A. C. *The Prophet Joel*. New York: Our Hope, 1909.

Geoff, Beatrice. "Syncretism in the Religion of Israel." *Journal of Biblical Literature* 58 (1931):151–161.

Girdlestone, Robert B. *The Grammar of Prophecy*. Grand Rapids: Kregel, 1955.

Gottwald, Norman. *A Light to the Nations*. New York: Harper & Bros., 1959.

Graham, W. C. "The Religion of the Hebrews." *Journal of Religion* 11 (1931):242–259.

Gray, George. *Sacrifice in the Old Testament*. Oxford: Clarendon Press, 1925.

Gray, John. *I and II Kings, A Commentary*. Philadelphia: Westminster Press, 1975.

Gressman, Hugo. *Altorientalische Texte und Bilder zum Alten Testament*. Berlin: W. de Gruyter, 1926–27.

Guillaume, A. *Prophecy and Divination Among the Hebrews and Other Semites*. London: Hodder & Stoughton, 1938.

Haldar, Alfred. *Associations of Cult Prophets Among the Ancient Semites*. Uppsala: Almquist and Wiksells Boktrycheri, 1945.

Harrison, R. K. *Introduction to the Old Testament*. Grand Rapids: Eerdmans, 1969.

———. *Old Testament Times*. Grand Rapids: Eerdmans, 1970.

Heschel, Abraham J. *The Prophets*. New York: Harper & Row, 1962.

Hölscher, Gustav. *Hesekiel, der Dichter und das Buch*. Giessen: Alfred Topelmann, 1924.

———. *Die Propheten*. Leipzig: Hinrichs, 1914.

Hooke, S. H. *Babylonian and Assyrian Religion*. Oxford: Blackwell, 1962.

*Interpreter's Bible, The*. Edited by George A. Buttrick et al. 12 volumes. New York: Abingdon Press, 1952.

James, Edwin O. *The Nature and Function of Priesthood*. New York: Barnes and Noble, 1959.

James, Fleming. *Personalities of the Old Testament*. New York: Charles Scribner's Sons, 1954.

Jastrow, Morris. *The Religion of Babylonia and Assyria*. Boston: Ginn & Co., 1898.

———. "*Ro-eh* and *Hozeh* in the Old Testament." *Journal of Biblical Literature* 28 (1909):42–56.

Johnson, Aubrey R. *The Cultic Prophet in Ancient Israel*. Cardiff: University of Wales, 1944.

Kaufmann, Yehezkel. *The Religion of Israel*. Translated by Moshe Greenberg. Chicago: University of Chicago Press, 1960.

Keil, C. F., and Delitzsch, F. *Commentaries on the Old Testament*. 25 volumes. Grand Rapids: Eerdmans, 1952.

Kitchen, Kenneth. *Ancient Orient and Old Testament*. Chicago: Inter-Varsity Press, 1966.

Laetsch, Theodore. *The Minor Prophets*. St. Louis: Concordia, 1956.

Lambert, W. G. "The Babylonians and the Chaldaeans." In *Peoples of Old Testament Times*, edited by D. J. Wiseman. Oxford: Clarendon Press, 1973.

Lange, John P. *A Commentary on the Holy Scriptures*. Translated by Philip Schaff. 14 volumes. New York: Charles Scribner's Sons, 1915.

Leslie, Elmer A. *Isaiah*. New York: Abingdon Press, 1963.

Lindblom, J. *Prophecy in Ancient Israel*. Philadelphia: Fortress, 1963.

Lods, A. "Une tablette inédite de Mari, intéressante pour l'histoire ancienne du prophetisme Sémitique." In *Studies in Old Testament Prophecy*, edited by H. H. Rowley, pp. 103–110. Edinburgh: T. & T. Clark, 1950.

Mace, A. B. "The Influence of Egypt on Hebrew Literature." *Annals of Archaeology and Anthropology* 9 (1922):3–26.

Mattuck, Israel. *The Thought of the Prophets*. New York: Collier Books, 1962.

Meek, Theophile J. *Hebrew Origins*. New York: Harper; 1960.

Mendelsohn, Isaac. "Society and Economic Conditions." In *The World History of the Jewish People*, vol. III, pp. 39–51. Newark: Rutgers University Press, 1971.

Millard, A. R. "The Canaanites." In *Peoples of Old Testament Times*, edited by D. J. Wiseman. Oxford: Clarendon Press, 1973.

Montgomery, James A. *The Book of Daniel*. New York: Charles Scribner's Sons, 1927.

Moscati, S. *Ancient Semitic Civilizations*. London: Elek Books, Ltd., 1957.

Mowinckel, Sigmund. *Psalmenstudien III; Kultprophetie und Prophetische Psalmen*. Kristiania, 1923.

———. "The 'Spirit' and the 'Word' in the Pre-exilic Reforming Prophets." *Journal of Biblical Literature* 53 (1934):199–227.

Noth, Martin. *The History of Israel*. 2nd edition. London: A. & C. Black, 1958.

Oehler, G. F. *Theology of the Old Testament*. Grand Rapids, Zondervan, n.d.

Oesterley, W. O. E., and Robinson, Theodore H. *Hebrew Religion: Its Origin and Development*. 2nd ed., rev. London: Society for Promoting Christian Knowledge, 1944.

Oppenheim, A. Leo. *Ancient Mesopotamia*. Chicago: University of Chicago Press, 1964.

———. *The Interpretation of Dreams in the Ancient Near East*. Philadelphia: American Philosophical Society, 1956.

Payne, J. Barton. *The Theology of the Older Testament*. Grand Rapids: Zondervan, 1962.

Pedersen, Johannes. *Israel: Its Life and Culture*. 2 volumes. London: Oxford University, 1953.

Petrie, Flinders. *Religious Life in Ancient Egypt*. London: Constable, 1924.

Pfeiffer, Charles. *Old Testament History*. Grand Rapids: Baker, 1973.

Pfeiffer, Robert. *Introduction to the Old Testament*. New York: Harper, 1941; rev. ed. 1948.

Porteous, N. W. "Prophecy." In *Record and Revelation*, edited by H. Wheeler Robinson, pp. 216–249. Oxford: Clarendon Press, 1938.

Pusey, E. B. *The Minor Prophets*. Grand Rapids: Baker, 1956.

Robinson, George L. *The Twelve Minor Prophets*. New York: Richard R. Smith, Inc., 1930.

Robinson, H. Wheeler. "The Philosophy of Religion." In *Record and Revelation*, pp. 303–320. Oxford: Clarendon Press, 1938.

_____. *Redemption and Revelation*. London: Nisbet, 1942.

Robinson, Theodore H. *Prophecy and the Prophets in Ancient Israel*. London: Duckworth, 1923.

Rowley, H. H. *The Faith in Israel*. Philadelphia: Westminster Press, 1956.

_____. *Prophecy and Religion in Ancient China and Israel*. New York: Harper, 1956.

_____. *The Rediscovery of the Old Testament*. Philadelphia: Westminster Press, 1946.

_____. *The Servant of the Lord and Other Essays on the Old Testament*. London: Lutterworth, 1952.

_____. *The Unity of the Bible*. Philadelphia: Westminster Press, 1953.

Sauerbrei, C. "The Holy Man in Israel: A Study in the Development of Prophecy." *Journal of Near Eastern Studies* 6 (1947):209–218.

Scott, R. B. Y. *The Relevance of the Prophets*. New York: Macmillan, 1953.

Shanks, Herschel. "Did the Philistines Destroy the Israelite Sanctuary at Shiloh?— The Archaeological Evidence." *The Biblical Archaeology Review* 1 (June, 1975):3–5.

Simons, J. *Handbook for the Study of Egyptian Topographical Lists Relating to Western Asia*. Leiden: E. J. Brill, 1937.

Skinner, John. *Prophecy and Religion*. Cambridge: University Press, 1922.

Smith, J. M. P. "Semitic Prophecy." *The Biblical World* 35 (1910):223–233.

Smith, W. Robertson. *The Old Testament in the Jewish Church*. New York: D. Appleton & Co., 1881.

_____. *The Prophets of Israel*. London: Black, 1907.

Snaith, Norman H. *The Distinctive Ideas of the Old Testament*. London: Epworth, 1962.

Thiele, E. R. *The Mysterious Numbers of the Hebrew Kings*. Rev. ed. Grand Rapids: Eerdmans, 1965.

Thompson, J. A. *The Bible and Archaeology*. Rev. ed. Grand Rapids: Eerdmans, 1972.

Torrey, C. C. *Pseudo-Ezekiel and the Original Prophecy*. New Haven, CT: Yale University Press, 1930.

Unger, Merrill F. *Introductory Guide to the Old Testament*. Grand Rapids: Zondervan, 1951.

_____. *Israel and the Aramaeans of Damascus*. London: James Clarke & Co., 1957.

von Rad, Gerhard. *Old Testament Theology*. Translated by D. M. G. Stalker. New York: Harper, 1962.

Vos, Geerhardus. *Biblical Theology*. Grand Rapids: Eerdmans, 1948.

Walvoord, John F. *Daniel, the Key to Prophetic Revelation*. Chicago: Moody Press, 1971.

Welch, A. C. *Prophet and Priest in Old Israel*. Oxford: Blackwell, 1953.

Whitley, Charles. *The Exilic Age*. Philadelphia: Westminster Press, 1957.

Williams, R. J. "The Egyptians." In *Peoples of Old Testament Times*, edited by D. J. Wiseman. Oxford: Clarendon Press, 1973.

Williams, Walter G. *The Prophets, Pioneers to Christianity*. New York: Abingdon Press, 1956.

Wilson, John. *The Burden of Egypt*. Chicago: University of Chicago Press, 1951.

Wolff, Hans Walter. *Amos the Prophet: The Man and His Background*. Philadelphia: Fortress Press, 1973.

———. *Hosea: A Commentary on the Book of the Prophet*. Philadelphia: Fortress Press, 1974.

Wood, Irving. "Borrowing Between Religions." *Journal of Biblical Literature* 46 (1927):98–105.

Wood, Leon J. *A Commentary on Daniel*. Grand Rapids: Zondervan, 1973.

———. *Distressing Days of the Judges*. Grand Rapids: Zondervan, 1975.

———. *The Holy Spirit in the Old Testament*. Grand Rapids: Zondervan, 1976.

———. *A Survey of Israel's History*. Grand Rapids: Zondervan, 1970.

Wright, C. H. *Zechariah and His Prophecies*. London: Hodder and Stoughton, 1879.

Wright, G. Ernest. *The Old Testament Against Its Environment*. Chicago: Regnery, 1950.

Young, Edward J. *The Book of Isaiah*. 3 volumes. Grand Rapids: Eerdmans, 1965.

———. *An Introduction to the Old Testament*. Grand Rapids: Eerdmans, 1954.

———. *My Servants the Prophets*. Grand Rapids: Eerdmans, 1952.

———. *The Prophecy of Daniel*. Grand Rapids: Eerdmans, 1949.

# Index of Scripture

20:38—231
20:39—231
20:42—231
21:17-24—118
21:17-26—124
21:22—217
21:23—217
22—106
22:1-39—233
22:6—19, 42
22:7—107, 233
22:7-28—103
22:8—107
22:8-28—123, 125
22:10-12—41-42
22:11—42
22:12—42
22:13-28—20
22:14—107
22:16—233
22:17—107, 233, 236
22:19—235
22:20—233
22:24—234
22:25—236
22:26-28—97
22:27, 28—111
22:28—107, 234, 236
22:29-33—195
22:29-40—204
22:39—210
22:42—205
22:43—194 n. 5
22:44—127, 194
22:48, 49—194, 195

**II Kings**

1:1-16—218
1:2—218
1:8—19
2-13—123 n. 14
2:1-5—164
2:3—19
2:3f.—231
2:3-7—164
2:5—19
2:7—19, 123
2:9—86, 255
2:11—210
2:13, 14—246

2:15—19
2:15-18—164
2:19-22—246-247
2:23—19
2:23, 24—247
3—44, 49
3:1—243
3:1-27—247-248
3:2—243
3:4—247, 285
3:4-27—194, 195
3:9-12—98
3:9-14—126
3:13—243
3:15—45, 95
4:1f.—231
4:1-7—248
4:8-37—248, 325
4:9—59
4:18-37—77
4:25—79
4:32-37—221
4:38—164
4:38-41—165, 249
4:42-44—249
4:43—123, 249
5:1-27—249-250
5:5—256
5:16—256
6:1f.—165, 231
6:1, 2—123, 164
6:1-7—250
6:8-12—250
6:13-23—250-251
6:23—251
6:24-7:20—251
6:28, 29—244
8:1, 2—249
8:1-6—251
8:7-13—16, 55, 216
8:7-15—252
8:20-22—262
9:1f.—231
9:1-3—252
9:1-10—126, 216
9:1-12—42-43
9:11—43
9:14-10:11—218
9:14-10:28—252
9:27-29—264

9:30, 33—244
10—108
10:19—79
10:19-28—126, 243
11:1-16—268
11:4-16—227
12:17—290
12:17, 18—227, 267
12:19-21—228
13:7—245
13:14-19—252-253
13:17—70
13:18, 19—70
13:20, 21—253
13:25—245, 290
14:1-6—228
14:1-7—239
14:1-20—228
14:13—228
14:17—228
14:21—284
14:22—285
14:23—289
14:25—123 n. 15, 128, 276, 284, 289, 291
14:28—276
15:1, 6, 8—284
15:8-12—282
15:19, 20—278, 282
15:29—278
16:5-9—298
17:3-6—278
17:4—282
17:7-12—280
18:13-19:37—300, 302
20:20—299 n. 3
21:9—316
21:10—126
21:10-16—323
22:14—127
23:4-14—318
23:15, 16—318
23:16—97
24:1—330
24:2—330, 356
24:6, 8—330 n. 1
24:11-16—130, 331, 355
24:14—332
25:1-21—262
25:12—332

# Index of Subjects